Frommer's®

W9-CFA-427

San Francisco with Kids

3rd Edition

by Noelle Salmi

Here's what the critics say about Frommer's:

"Amazingly easy to use. Very portable, very complete."

—*Booklist*

"Detailed, accurate, and easy-to-read information for all price ranges."
—*Glamour Magazine*

"Hotel information is close to encyclopedic."

—*Des Moines Sunday Register*

"Frommer's Guides have a way of giving you a real feel for a place."
—*Knight Ridder Newspapers*

Wiley Publishing, Inc.

About the Author

Noelle Salmi is a freelance writer who lived and worked in several U.S. cities and many foreign countries before moving to San Francisco in 2001. In addition to her work promoting investment overseas, she worked at a major daily newspaper and later at CNN in Rio de Janeiro, Brazil; Associated Press in Berlin, Germany; and United Press International in New York City. Her articles have appeared in the *Santa Clara Valley Weekly, Jornal do Brasil, The West Side Spirit, Emerging Markets, USA Today,* and *Bay Area Parent.* She is also the author of *Frommer's San Francisco Day by Day.* She lives on Russian Hill with her husband Mika and daughters Annika and Natasha.

Published by:

Wiley Publishing, Inc.

111 River St.
Hoboken, NJ 07030-5774

ISBN: 978-0-470-08017-7
Editors: Michael Kelly and Naomi P. Kraus
Production Editor: M. Faunette Johnston
Cartographer: Elizabeth Puhl
Photo Editor: Richard Fox
Production by Wiley Indianapolis Composition Services

For information on our other products and services or to obtain technical support, please contact our Customer Care Department within the U.S. at 800/762-2974, outside the U.S. at 317/572-3993 or fax 317/572-4002.

Wiley also publishes its books in a variety of electronic formats. Some content that appears in print may not be available in electronic formats.

Manufactured in the United States of America

5 4 3 2 1

Contents

5 Family-Friendly Accommodations   83

6 Family-Friendly Dining   115

7 Exploring San Francisco with Your Kids   168

8 Neighborhood Strolls   204

9 For the Active Family   222

10 Shopping with Your Kids   240

11 Entertainment for the Whole Family   257

12 Side Trips from San Francisco   279

Index   297

List of Maps

For my husband, Mika Salmi, and my daughters, Annika and Natasha.

Acknowledgments

Thank you to so many friends who contributed their thoughts on the best places to play, eat, and shop with children. My sincere appreciation extends to Nina Thompson for her tremendous research help, encyclopedic knowledge of San Francisco, and her ever-upbeat attitude. Thanks to William Veale for his proofreading skills, and to Raili Salmi and Renee Veale for their help at home when it was needed most. I am grateful for the assistance offered by Joan Wernett. Thanks very much to my editor Naomi Kraus for her patience and flexibility. Above all, thanks to my husband Mika for his unending support and encouragement throughout this process, and to my daughters Annika and Natasha for the enthusiasm and energy with which they have helped me to explore San Francisco with kids.

—Noelle Salmi

An Invitation to the Reader

In researching this book, we discovered many wonderful places—hotels, restaurants, shops, and more. We're sure you'll find others. Please tell us about them, so we can share the information with your fellow travelers in upcoming editions. If you were disappointed with a recommendation, we'd love to know that, too. Please write to:

Frommer's San Francisco with Kids, 3rd Edition
Wiley Publishing, Inc. • 111 River St. • Hoboken, NJ 07030-5774

An Additional Note

Please be advised that travel information is subject to change at any time—and this is especially true of prices. We therefore suggest that you write or call ahead for confirmation when making your travel plans. The authors, editors, and publisher cannot be held responsible for the experiences of readers while traveling. Your safety is important to us, however, so we encourage you to stay alert and be aware of your surroundings. Keep a close eye on cameras, purses, and wallets, all favorite targets of thieves and pickpockets.

Other Great Guides for Your Trip:

Frommer's San Francisco
Frommer's San Francisco Day by Day
Frommer's California
San Francisco For Dummies
California For Dummies
Unofficial Guide to California with Kids

Frommer's Star Ratings, Icons & Abbreviations

Every hotel, restaurant, and attraction listing in this guide has been ranked for quality, value, service, amenities, and special features using a **star-rating system.** In country, state, and regional guides, we also rate towns and regions to help you narrow down your choices and budget your time accordingly. Hotels and restaurants are rated on a scale of zero (recommended) to three stars (exceptional). Attractions, shopping, nightlife, towns, and regions are rated according to the following scale: zero stars (recommended), one star (highly recommended), two stars (very highly recommended), and three stars (must-see).

In addition to the star-rating system, we also use **six feature icons** that point you to the great deals, in-the-know advice, and unique experiences that separate travelers from tourists. Throughout the book, look for:

Finds	Special finds—those places only insiders know about
Fun Fact	Fun facts—details that make travelers more informed and their trips more fun
Moments	Special moments—those experiences that memories are made of
Overrated	Places or experiences not worth your time or money
Tips	Insider tips—great ways to save time and money
Value	Great values—where to get the best deals

The following **abbreviations** are used for credit cards:

AE	American Express	DISC	Discover	V	Visa
DC	Diners Club	MC	MasterCard		

Frommers.com

Now that you have this guidebook to help you plan a great trip, visit our website at **www.frommers.com** for additional travel information on more than 3,500 destinations. We update features regularly to give you instant access to the most current trip-planning information available. At Frommers.com, you'll find scoops on the best airfares, lodging rates, and car rental bargains. You can even book your travel online through our reliable travel booking partners. Other popular features include:

- Online updates of our most popular guidebooks
- Vacation sweepstakes and contest giveaways
- Newsletters highlighting the hottest travel trends
- Online travel message boards with featured travel discussions

How to Feel Like a
San Francisco Family

San Francisco has always had a way of calling me back. Although my life has been a whirlwind of travel, it's been punctuated by stays in this glorious part of the world. I was born not far from the city limits, and my parents often brought my brother and me into town. I can't say I remember much from those days because we moved to Puerto Rico before my third birthday and, after that, to Brazil and then Uruguay. But when we returned to the U.S., it was to Southern California, and because my parents retained a fondness for San Francisco, we visited the city regularly.

Perhaps it was inevitable that I would attend college in the Bay Area, so that weekends could be spent exploring San Francisco with roommates and friends. Upon graduating, I was off again: to work at a newspaper in Brazil and write for the Associated Press in Germany before heading to New York for grad school and a job promoting investment overseas. I was mostly on airplanes headed to far corners of the earth, but I fortunately found time to meet my husband, a nomad like myself. Although we moved to Seattle, my international job kept me flying and kept the frequent flier miles multiplying—until the birth of my first daughter, when the travel came to a screeching halt.

Then it happened. San Francisco harkened again. My husband's work brought us here, where our second daughter was born a few months later. Six years out, we are a certified San Francisco family—going to every birthday party venue in town; trekking out to the beach in summer, bundled up in jeans and jackets against the fog; loading up the kids' bikes in the car every week to take them somewhere flat to ride; buying our organic greens at the Farmer's Market; and considering steamed pork buns, shrimp dumplings, and stuffed crab claws (in other words, dim sum) a fine meal for breakfast.

Through all the travel, the Bay Area had always been my spiritual home, if not my real one. Now San Francisco is my family's true residence, one that welcomed us from the moment we arrived. It helps that the city is used to taking in people from all over the globe. Most of the San Franciscans we know seem to have started life somewhere else, although we're always impressed when we meet someone who actually grew up here. The city is so rich with history, culture, and little-known secrets that it's a treat to pick the brains of a lifelong resident. It's been especially exciting to begin writing guidebooks about San Francisco, giving me a terrific excuse to look a little deeper and learn a little more about the wonderful offerings here.

I've made an effort to provide some insights in this book that will make your family's stay in San Francisco more rewarding and memorable. Visits to the city's most famous attractions will certainly be enjoyable, but I hope that you take the time to

The Bay Area

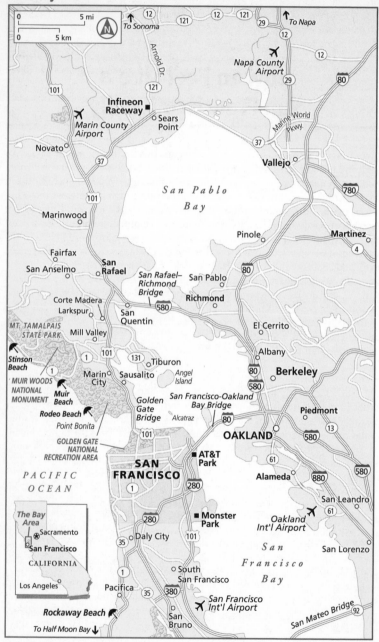

stray off the beaten path—if even just a little. When in Fisherman's Wha. skipping the T-shirt shops and candy vendors of PIER 39 and heading instea. Hyde Street Pier, where you can get a real sense of the city's seafaring past (while kids climb all over antique ships). In Chinatown, go ahead and check out the color- ful tourist stores on Grant Street, but don't miss the exotic and authentic grocers on Stockton Street. And although I know that cashew chicken at the big restaurant in the middle of Chinatown sounds appetizing, consider ordering dim sum out in the Richmond District instead.

One of the terrific things about San Francisco is that a whole lot of the sights and activities that appeal to tourists in general will appeal to families specifically. What kid doesn't enjoy a ride on a cable car? And although everyone loves a stroll along Crissy Field, younger ones will be especially delighted playing on the grassy hills and sandy beaches. Not to mention the ferry ride to Alcatraz Island, which is perfect family fare. Certainly, not every kid will be thrilled by a trip to the San Francisco Museum of Modern Art (SFMOMA), but a terrific children's center is just across the street. For every adult attraction you ante up, I'll see you three that are fabulous with kids. In fact, having little ones is a great excuse to visit the Exploratorium, the California Academy of Sciences, and the San Francisco Zoo—all of which are first-rate.

So get started planning your trip. This chapter is a good place to begin; in it, I sug- gest some of our all-time favorite San Francisco family experiences, in addition to the best hotels and dining spots.

1 Frommer's Favorite San Francisco Experiences

- **Shopping at the Ferry Plaza Farmer's Market:** Perhaps you haven't had a chance lately to stop and smell the roses, admire the toma- toes, or compare the peaches. If that's the case, hop on the F-Market street- car to the Ferry Building and take a stroll around the best outdoor market in the Bay Area. It's a Saturday morn- ing ritual for a great many San Fran- ciscans who come down with their baskets and carefully select the sea- son's finest from organic farmers and local purveyors of fresh sausages, free- range meats, olive oils, honey, and baked goods. The farmers offer tastes of their wares, so your kids may dis- cover what just-picked-at-their-peak fruits taste like—a revelation if they've never had a perfectly ripe pear or apricot. Don't eat breakfast first; along with coffee drinks and a huge array of morning breads, pastries, and sweets from the very nicest bakeries, local restaurants serve specialties that

taste even better eaten with a view of the bay. Beyond Saturday, the market is open Tuesdays, as well as Sundays and Thursdays in spring and fall. See p. 176.

- **Eating Shrimp Dumplings for Breakfast:** If crab claws, pork buns, and steamed dumplings aren't your idea of Sunday brunch, it's time to branch out from omelets and pan- cakes. One of our favorite weekend morning activities is gathering with friends at a large table with a lazy Susan in the middle, while servers bring trays laden with bite-sized Chi- nese delicacies. If you're planning on staying downtown, Yank Sing is the place to go (One Rincon Center, 101 Spear St., at Mission St. © 415/957- 9300). If you're planning a walk at Land's End, consider hopping on the 38-Geary bus and trekking out to Ton Kiang (5821 Geary Blvd., between 22nd and 23rd aves.; © 415/ 387-8273) for a hearty pre-hike

Timeline

...ads the first colonizers to the area and establishes the ... Francisco and Mission Dolores, founding Yerba Buena (San ...

...o declares independence from Spain, and Yerba Buena remains under Mexican rule.

1846 Captain John Montgomery plants the U.S. flag into present-day Portsmouth Square to claim Yerba Buena for the United States. Yerba Buena is renamed San Francisco.

1848 James Marshall discovers gold at Sutter's Mill. Newspaperman Sam Brannan publicizes the discovery, and the Gold Rush begins.

1848 Domingo Ghirardelli sails to San Francisco to join his partner, James Lick, and begin what is to become the city's most famous chocolate factory.

1849 Isadore Boudin, an experienced French baker, introduces the ordinary sourdough yeast used by miners to a French-style loaf of bread and creates San Francisco sourdough bread.

1868 The *Daily Morning Chronicle,* later the *San Francisco Chronicle,* begins publishing.

1873 Andrew Hallidie, inspired by an accident he witnesses when a team of horses slips on a rainy San Francisco hill, invents the cable car.

1887 George Hearst purchases a small daily newspaper, the *San Francisco Examiner,* to promote his race for the U.S. Senate. His son, William Randolph Hearst, turns it into a very successful tabloid.

1892 The "Ellis Island of the West," Angel Island, opens initially as a quarantine station.

1906 On April 18 at 5:12am, a major earthquake rocks San Francisco and starts more than 50 fires, which burn uncontrollably for 3 days. Two-thirds of the city is destroyed, 250,000 people are left homeless, and more than 675 are dead or missing.

brunch. Just get there early, as tables fill up fast. See p. 138.

- **Strolling through Chinatown:** Just steps away from Union Square, you can enter another world—one decorated by bright red, green, and gold banners. The knick-knack shops, traditional herbalists, vendors of ceremonial papers and incense, and grocery stores teeming with live frogs, crabs, and other wriggly seafood are all a visual and cultural treat. A stop by the Golden Gate Fortune Cookie Company just adds to the fun. See chapter 8 for a self-guided walking tour of the neighborhood.

- **Hanging Out at Crissy Field:** What better way to spend the day than to slow down and take in the views of the Golden Gate Bridge and the city from the Bay Area's newest national park? Kids can run around on the hills, check out the gift shop, pile up rocks, or play in the sand. Buy some

1927 Modern-age hockey dawns for the Bay Area with the creation of the California Hockey League.

1934 Alcatraz Island becomes a federal prison.

1936 The San Francisco–Oakland Bay Bridge opens on November 12. It remains one of the largest bridges in the world and carries over 270,000 vehicles each day—more traffic than any other toll bridge.

1937 The Golden Gate Bridge opens to pedestrian traffic on May 26 and to automobile traffic on May 27.

1945 The charter establishing the United Nations is signed in San Francisco's Herbst Theater.

1960 Candlestick Park opens for baseball and football. The last baseball game takes place in 1999.

1965 Jefferson Airplane opens at the Matrix, a club, on Fillmore.

1978 PIER 39 is built. One of San Francisco's most popular attractions, it gets an estimated 10.5 million visitors each year.

1989 On October 17 at 5:04pm, right before the start of the World Series between the Oakland A's and the San Francisco Giants, a 7.1 magnitude earthquake hits the Bay Area. One person dies at Candlestick Park from a heart attack.

2000 Pacific Bell Park (now AT&T Park), the home to the San Francisco Giants, opens.

2004 San Francisco Mayor Gavin Newsom issues more than 4,000 same-sex marriage licenses, which are later annulled by the state's Supreme Court.

2006 Thousands of residents line the streets before dawn on April 18 to mark the 100-year anniversary of "The Great Quake," falling silent at 5:12am. Eleven survivors of the original quake attend the event.

---

nice sandwiches at the Warming Hut and enjoy a picnic at one of the many bayside picnic tables. See p. 173.

- **Riding Bikes down the Embarcadero:** The boulevard is wide and the street is flat, making the Embarcadero an easy family ride. Start at the Bike Hut (see chapter 9) and cruise down the street past the piers, stopping by the Ferry Building to buy picnic food. Walk the bikes down Pier 7 and see if anyone's caught a fish or crab at the end of the pier. Continue toward PIER 39 and Fisherman's Wharf. It may become too crowded to pedal here, but once you reach the Hyde Street Pier, space opens up. Keep going until you get to Aquatic Park, where you can stop to eat your pre-packed lunch.

- **Boating on Stow Lake:** Pile into one of the seriously dilapidated, but safe, electric motorboats (top speed is maybe 5 mph), rowboats, or pedal boats and circle this man-made lake as many times as you can. Bring stale bread for the ducks if you like, and relax as you admire the trees and revel in the laughter of the kids as they attempt to keep the craft from bumping into other boats or landing on the bank. See chapter 9 for more information on this and other outdoor family adventures.

- **Checking Out the Scene at the Maritime National Historical Park:** Young kids will love exploring the antique ships of the Hyde Street Pier (p. 184), running around on the grass at Victorian Park, and gaping at the crazy swimmers in Aquatic Park who brave the Bay's chilly waters. All the while, grownups can marvel at the lovely scenery. Then everyone can grab lunch at the Oakville Grocery (p. 147) in The Cannery, and perhaps listen to some music from a local performer.

- **Hanging Out in Golden Gate Park:** You don't need an agenda to fritter away the hours around San Francisco's most famous park. The antique carousel is a big draw and the old Children's Playground, slated to open as the "Koret Children's Quarter" in May 2007, promises to be a world-class playground. The Japanese Tea Garden is so composed and elegant you'll want to meditate there, but the kids will prefer stepping over the stone walkways and scaling the Drum Bridge. Budding botanists will appreciate the dahlia garden outside the Conservatory of Flowers and will especially enjoy ogling the carnivorous plants inside. The de Young Museum tower affords super city views and the *Three Gems* structure in the sculpture garden is a great place to chill out for a moment. On Sundays, the park is closed to traffic; be sure to look for the skate dancers near 6th Avenue and Fulton Street who put on a fine show. See p. 188.

- **Taking the Ferry to Marin:** Bundle up and catch a Blue and Gold Ferry (p. 198) from Pier 41 to Sausalito or Tiburon. You can take bikes on the boats if you like, but both villages are petite and walkable. The ride is glorious. Remain outside for the full effect of the wind and salt spray. On a clear day, you'll have trouble deciding where to look; the scenery ahead is as thrilling as the view behind you. Sausalito is very touristy, but the stores are fun for window shopping. Tiburon is even more upscale than Sausalito. It won't take long to tour the village; leave someone behind to claim a table at Guaymas, at 5 Main St., where drinks and passable Mexican food on the sunny deck make this trip a little vacation within your vacation.

- **Standing on Market Street Watching the Chinese New Year's Parade:** The crowds are thick and the night can be chilly, but come early to get a good spot for a truly marvelous spectacle. The contestants from the Miss Chinatown USA pageant wave from their float, marching bands travel in from around the Bay Area, and an elaborate dragon winds its away along the route, the traditional finale. It seems like the entire city is either in the parade or watching it. Walk to Portsmouth Square afterward for the night market.

- **Trekking Along the Land's End Trail:** Provided your child won't run off ahead of you, as the trail runs along a steep cliff, there's hardly a more beautiful place to walk in San Francisco. Start at the trailhead on Camino del Mar, parking next to picturesque Lincoln Park, which is dotted with majestic Monterey Cyprus trees. Head west on the trail toward the Cliff House, pausing to admire the view from the "other" side of the Golden Gate Bridge, the sweeping Pacific Ocean, and the Marin Headlands to the north.

- **Sipping a Cappuccino or a Hot Chocolate in a North Beach Cafe:** Preferably this is to be done at an outdoor table, midmorning, on a weekday when everyone else is at work. If the sun's out, all the better.

- **Cheering the Home Team at AT&T Park:** You don't even need to be a baseball fan to derive a lot of pleasure from an afternoon or evening at this gem of a baseball stadium (p. 275).

Bleacher seats go on sale at the park on game days, but if you prefer something fancier, you can usually get good seats online from season ticket holders if nothing's available at Giants Dugout Stores or at the park ticket booth. Kids will have a field day playing at the Coca-Cola Fan Lot playground and chowing down on the notable food concessions. Transportation is a breeze on the N-Judah streetcar; it deposits you at the front gate. American League partisans have the option of taking BART (the local commuter train) across the bay to the Oakland Coliseum.

2 The Best Hotel Bets

- **Best All-Around Family Hotels:** The **Argonaut** (495 Jefferson St.; ℂ 866/415-0704 or 415/563-0800) is my hands-down favorite in this category. It's a charming hotel in a family-friendly neck of the woods. Several kid-friendly attractions are either next door or less than a block away: grassy Victorian Park, the Aquatic Park beach, the Hyde Street Pier, the cable car turnaround, and The Cannery. The whimsical lobby and its adjacent National Maritime Visitors Center will appeal to kids as well. The double queen rooms are well suited to families, and the in-house restaurant serves kids' meals in a beach pail. What more could you want? See p. 104. The warm and friendly **Serrano Hotel** (405 Taylor St.; ℂ 866/289-6561 or 415/885-2500) helps kids entertain themselves by stocking the minibar with toys and making a game library available to guests. See p. 92. The **Handlery Union Square** (351 Geary St.; ℂ 800/843-4343 or 415/781-7800) also gets my vote, mainly for its outdoor, heated pool. See p. 95.

- **Best Amenities for Kids:** The **St. Regis** (125 3rd St.; ℂ 415/284-4000) offers kids their own bathrobes, toys from the SFMOMA gift shop, cookies with their name on them, and special items in the minibar— provided parents call the concierge beforehand. See p. 102. The **Four Seasons** (757 Market St.; ℂ 415/633-3000) supplies cookies and milk on arrival for kids 6 and under and root beer and popcorn for those 7 and up. Kids staying in their own rooms get a specially stocked minibar, and bathrobes are supplied in sizes to fit the whole family. The concierge will also send up other family items—from cribs to board games— on request. See p. 99. The "Family Suite" in the **Hotel Del Sol** (3100 Webster St.; ℂ 877/433-5765 or 415/921-5520) has bunk beds, toys, and board games. Kids also get beach balls and sun visors. See p. 112.

- **Best Suites:** The **Hotel Beresford Arms** (701 Post St.; ℂ 800/533-6533 or 415/673-2600) has 60 Jacuzzi suites, half of which have full kitchens and half of which have kitchenettes. The guest rooms and bathrooms also offer plenty of floor space and all beds are queen beds. See p. 98. Near Union Square, the **Cartwright Hotel** (524 Sutter St.; © **800/919-9779** or 415/421-2865) has a few two-room suites that are beautifully decorated and can be an excellent value. See p. 94. The homey suites at the **Cow Hollow Motor Inn & Suites** (2190 Lombard St.; © **415/921-5800**) contain two bathrooms, two bedrooms, and a kitchen—and must be booked far in advance. For value and space, these offer the sweetest suite deal in town. See p. 112.

- **Best Indoor Pool:** You have to supervise your kids at every hotel pool, but if your kids don't need you to swim with them, you can work out on the poolside cardio equipment at the **Hotel Nikko,** at 222 Mason St. (© **800/248-3308** or 415/394-1111). If you'd prefer to take it easy, the lounge chairs and Japanese hot tub, all under an attractive glass ceiling, are a relaxing alternative. See p. 86. The elegant infinity pool at the **St. Regis** (125 3rd St.; © **415/284-4000**) is so inviting, parents will want to go for a swim even when the kids have had enough. See p. 102. **The San Francisco Marriott** (55 4th St.; © **415/896-1600**) has an indoor pool, which isn't elegant, but is big, clean, and open from 6am to 11pm. See p. 103.

- **Best Outdoor Pool:** As you might have guessed, the competitors for this honor are few. Around Union Square, the award goes to the **Handlery** (351 Geary St.; © **800/843-4343** or 415/781-7800) for a small, heated pool in a pleasant patio. See p. 95. Among Fisherman's Wharf hotels, the **Hyatt at Fisherman's Wharf** (555 N. Point St.; © **800/223-1234** or 415/563-1234) fields far and away the nicest pool. See p. 105. The **Hotel Del Sol** (3100 Webster St.; © **877/433-5765** or 415/921-5520) wins for the best poolside decor, with palm trees and a hammock, but the pool itself is very small. See p. 112.

- **Best Spa:** Yes, this is a family travel guide, but that doesn't mean part of the family can't disappear for an hour or so for a well-deserved facial or massage. Hands-down, the most elegant spa with the latest treatments is found at **The Huntington Hotel** (1075 California St.; © **800/227-4683** or 415/474-5400). See p. 110. That said, the new Remède Spa at the **St. Regis** (125 3rd St.; © **415/284-4000**) may start drawing a following with its specially customized spa treatments. See p. 102.

- **Best In-House Entertainment:** The Top of the Mark at the **Mark Hopkins InterContinental** (Number One Nob Hill; © **800/662-6455** or 415/392-3434) is terrific for drinks, views, or weekend dinner and dancing. If the kids are old enough to leave tucked in bed in a room downstairs, you'll have the pleasure of going out for a nice evening without venturing far from your temporary home. See p. 110. At the **Hotel Bijou** (111 Mason St.; **800/771-1022** or 415/771-1200) a tiny in-house movie theater shows a nightly double billing of filmed-in-San-Francisco movies, so you can round out your day of sightseeing with a low-key evening activity. See p. 96. If you want to do something silly with the kids, take them to the Tonga Room at the **Fairmont Hotel** (950 Mason St.; © **800/441-1414** or 415/772-5000) for appetizers and a mild tropical storm. See p. 109.

- **Best Lobby:** If the kids are into fairy tales, the **Fairmont Hotel** (950 Mason St.; ℭ **800/441-1414** or 415/772-5000) will leave them waiting for Princess Aurora to arrive. See p. 109. For the most stunning lobby in town, the truly opulent, yet tasteful, Art-Deco-inspired **Four Seasons** (757 Market St.; ℭ **415/633-3000**) tops the list. See p. 99.

- **Best If You Have a Car:** For stays around Union Square, the **Galleria Park Hotel** (191 Sutter St.; ℭ **800/792-9639** or 415/781-3060) is built over a parking garage, so it won't take long to retrieve yours. Like all downtown hotels, parking charges are nuts—$30 per day is average—so it's not economical to park here, just convenient. See p. 87. One car per room gets free indoor parking at the **Cow Hollow Motor Inn & Suites** (2190 Lombard St.; ℭ **415/921-5800**). See p. 112. A spot for your car also comes courtesy of the **Hotel Del Sol** (3100 Webster St.; ℭ **877/433-5765** or 415/921-5520; p. 112) or the **Marina Motel** (2576 Lombard St.; ℭ **800/346-6118** or 415/921-9406; p. 113).

- **Best If You Brought the Dog:** The **Hotel Monaco** (501 Geary St.; ℭ **800/214-4220** or 415/292-0100) has packages for pooches that rival anything other hotels have for kids. I don't know if there's an underlying message there. See p. 90. A sister property, the **Serrano Hotel** (405 Taylor St.; ℭ **866/289-6561** or 415/885-2500), will walk your dog by appointment and stocks gourmet pet food, treats, and comfy bedding. See p. 92. The **Hotel Vitale** (8 Mission St.; ℭ **888/890-8688** or 415/278-3700; p. 107) and the **St. Regis** (125 3rd St.; ℭ **415/284-4000;** p. 102) also welcome pets.

- **Best for Walkers:** Steps from Chinatown and the Financial District, and still close to Union Square, the **Hotel Triton** (342 Grant Ave.; ℭ **800/800-1299** or 415/394-0500) is terrific for anyone who wants to get up and explore downtown. See p. 91. If you prefer to stroll along the water, try the **Hotel Vitale** (8 Mission St.; ℭ **888/890-8688** or 415/278-3700; p. 107) or the **Harbor Court Hotel** (165 Steuart St.; ℭ **866/792-8263** or 415/882-1330; p. 108), both of which are across the street from the Embarcadero promenade, one of the best places in the city for a stroll. The **Argonaut Hotel** (495 Jefferson St.; ℭ **866/415-0704** or 415/563-0800) is next to one of the loveliest walking paths in town, which starts at Aquatic Park, runs through woodsy Fort Mason, and takes you along the scenic Marina waterfront. See p. 104.

- **Best for Athletic Families:** Families with older kids might want to try the **Harbor Court Hotel** (165 Steuart St.; ℭ **866/792-8263** or 415/882-1300), next door to the YMCA, which has an Olympic-size pool and is open to hotel guests. The Embarcadero across the street is also a fine place to walk, jog, bike, in-line skate, or skateboard. See p. 108. The **Four Seasons** (757 Market St.; ℭ **415/633-3000**) abuts a massive sports club/L.A. health club. See p. 99.

- **Best Views:** Most of the guest rooms at the **Hotel Vitale** (8 Mission St.; ℭ **888/890-8688** or 415/278-3700) look out onto the bay, while the "Circular" suites offer nearly 180 degrees of windows. See p. 107. Most of the hotels atop Nob Hill offer fine vistas, but the **Mark Hopkins Inter-Continental** (Number One Nob Hill; ℭ **800/662-6455** or 415/392-3434) gets the top honors in this category. See p. 110.

- **Best Hotel Food:** The **Grand Cafe** and **Petit Cafe** in the **Hotel Monaco** (501 Geary St.; ✆ **800/214-4220** or 415/292-0100) provide first-class dining just an elevator ride away. See p. 121. **Cortez** in the **Hotel Adagio** (550 Geary Blvd.; ✆ **800/228-8830** or 415/775-5000) offers excellent cuisine, but while the evening *tapas* menu may be too sophisticated, and pricey, for a family meal, breakfasts are well executed. See p. 95. **Ponzu** in the **Serrano Hotel** (405 Taylor St.; ✆ **866/289-6561** or 415/885-2500) has a great menu of pan-Asian cuisine. See p. 93. The best hotel restaurant for kids has to be **Puccini & Pinetti,** where kids can design their own pizzas. It's next to the **Monticello Inn** (127 Ellis St.; ✆ **866/778-6169** or 415/392-8800). See p. 125. **The Dining Room at the Ritz-Carlton** (600 Stockton St.; ✆ **800/241-3333** or 415/296-7465) is one of the most highly rated restaurants in town.

- **If Price Is No Object:** For extreme luxury and pampering, top honors go to the **St. Regis** (125 3rd St.; ✆ **415/284-4000**). See p. 102. The **Four Seasons** (757 Market St.; ✆ **415/633-3000**) is a close second. See p. 99. If you prefer more traditional opulence, the **Ritz-Carlton** (600 Stockton St.; ✆ **800/241-3333** or 415/296-7465) provides a sumptuous hotel experience. See p. 111.

- **If Price Is the Deal Breaker:** The most charming budget option near Union Square is the **Golden Gate Hotel** (775 Bush St.; ✆ **800/835-1118** or 415/392-3702). Rooms are small but clean and bright, and breakfast is part of the package. See p. 97. If you are planning to stay for a few days, the **Halcyon Hotel** (649 Jones St.; ✆ **800/627-2396** or 415/929-8033) offers safe, comfortable rooms with money-saving kitchenettes. See p. 98. For a family of three willing to share showers and store stuff in lockers, a private room at **Hostelling International San Francisco, Fisherman's Wharf** (Fort Mason, Building 240; ✆ **415/771-7277**) can be had for as little as $60, and comes with a bay view, continental breakfast, use of a kitchen, and free parking. Rates for a family of four start at $80. See p. 107.

- **Best for Peace and Quiet:** Because the **J.W. Marriott Hotel** (500 Post St.; ✆ **800/605-6568** or 415/771-8600) is multistoried and built as a hotel (rather than converted from some other purpose), larger-than-average rooms are far from the street and designed with soundproof windows, so you'll hardly know you're in the city. See p. 87. Even the lobby inside **The Huntington Hotel** (1075 California St.; ✆ **800/227-4683** or 415/474-5400) is quiet. Large rooms high off the street lower the decibel level. See p. 110.

- **Best for Baby:** Call the **Four Seasons** (757 Market St.; ✆ **415/633-3000**) and tell them you're arriving with a baby. They'll set you up with a fully outfitted crib, a diaper storage unit, diapers, wipes, baby shampoo, baby lotion, and so on. See p. 99. **The Laurel Inn** (444 Presidio Ave.; ✆ **800/552-8735** or 415/567-8467) is another top pick for travelers with babies or toddlers, not just for the kitchenettes but also for the neighborhood, which is teeming with families. See p. 113.

- **Best for Toddlers:** When you've got a 2- or 3-year old in tow, nothing comes in handier than a nearby park. You'll find a small one across the street from **The Huntington Hotel** (1075 California St.; ✆ **800/227-4683** or 415/474-5400). Also, if you snag one of the Huntington's rooms with a full kitchen, you'll know what to do when the little tyke wakes up at 5am demanding breakfast. See p. 110. The **Marina Motel** (2576 Lombard St.; ℂ **800/346-6118** or 415/921-9406) is close to two great playgrounds: Moscone and Cow Hollow. Even if you can't snag a unit with a kitchen, all rooms have refrigerators. See p. 113. If you'll be racing back to the hotel for your toddler's nap every afternoon, the **Serrano Hotel** (405 Taylor St.; ℂ **866/289-6561** or 415/885-2500), conveniently located near Union Square, is a good choice. It also keeps complimentary cribs, strollers, and booster seats on hand. See p. 92.

- **Best for Teens:** The **Hotel Triton** (342 Grant Ave.; ℂ **800/800-1299** or 415/394-0500) will wake up the most disaffected teenager with rock 'n' roll in the lobby and a design palette that has "groovy" written all over it. Rooms are small so you won't be sharing, but that's good for the kid who needs some space. See p. 91. The **W Hotel** lobby and bar (181 3rd St.; ℂ **888/625-5140** or 415/777-5300) is a whirlwind of activity that can be fascinating for teens. The clientele considers itself pretty hip. The location, across from Yerba Buena Center, means instant recreation for the kids at the Metreon. See p. 103.

- **Best for Shoppers:** There's no better location for parcel-toting families than the **Westin St. Francis** (335 Powell St.; ℂ **800/WESTIN-1** or 415/397-7000). You can stock up in all those Union Square stores and have your packages back in your room in minutes, ready to reload. See p. 93. If you're in a hurry, confine yourself to the Westfield San Francisco Centre mall at 5th and Mission

streets and hurl your goodies right next door into your room at the **Hotel Milano** (55 5th St.; ℂ **800/398-7555** or 415/543-8555). See p. 104. The **Hyatt Regency San Francisco** (5 Embarcadero Center; ℂ **800/233-1234** or 415/788-1234) is equally well placed for family shopping in the Embarcadero Center. After a long day of shopping, you can feed and entertain the kids as well at the center's cinemas and restaurants. See p. 109.

- **Best for Large Families:** If you wanted to, you could get five kids comfortably situated in a king/king room at the **Monticello Inn** (127 Ellis St.; ℂ **866/778-6169** or 415/392-8800). With room service, it'd be quite a party. See p. 96. The **Hyatt at Fisherman's Wharf** (555 N. Point St.; ℂ **800/223-1234** or 415/563-1234) can set you up in connecting double/doubles and on request will provide a fridge. Even better, coin-op washers and dryers are on every floor, which, if you can get the kids to do a load, will make your return home calmer. See p. 105. The absolute best hotel for big or extended families is **The Laurel Inn** (444 Presidio Ave.; ℂ **800/552-8735** or 415/567-8467), because you can request interconnecting rooms with two double beds and one of the kitchenette units, creating your own custom suite. See p. 113.

- **Best for Long Stays:** Around the Marina, the **Cow Hollow Motor Inn & Suites** (2190 Lombard St.; ℂ **415/921-5800**) provides apartment-style suites with full kitchens and discounts for stays longer than 5 days. See p. 112. The kitchen units at the **Marina Motel** (2576 Lombard St.; ℂ **800/346-6118** or 415/921-9406) are available to those staying 7 nights or more. See p. 113. The **Halcyon**

Fun Fact **San Francisco Firsts**

1847 *The California Star,* a four-page weekly, becomes the first newspaper published in San Francisco.

1848 The first public school in California opens in San Francisco.

1852 The first legal execution in San Francisco takes place on Russian Hill.

1860 The first Pony Express rider begins a trip from Missouri to San Francisco. The 2,000-mile journey takes 10 days.

1880 The world's first motion picture premiers at the San Francisco Art Association Hall.

1888 The poem "Casey at the Bat" by Ernest L. Thayer is published for the first time in the *San Francisco Examiner* newspaper.

1911 The San Francisco Symphony plays its first season.

1912 Women in San Francisco vote for the first time.

1937 Harold Wobber becomes the first person to commit suicide by jumping off the Golden Gate Bridge.

1944 San Francisco Ballet produces the first full-length dance production of *The Nutcracker* in the United States.

1952 The Bay Area Educational Television company is founded, eventually becoming KQED, one of the first public broadcasting companies in America.

1964 The Condor Club in North Beach becomes the country's first topless dance bar.

1965 The band formerly known as "The Warlocks" plays for the first time as "The Grateful Dead" at San Francisco's Fillmore Auditorium.

Hotel (649 Jones St.; ℂ **800/627-2396** or 415/929-8033) also offers bare-boned, but inexpensive, rooms with kitchenettes designed for guests staying for a week at a time. See p. 98.

3 The Best Dining Bets

- **Best Diner:** Film buffs should check out **Mel's Drive-In** (2165 Lombard St.; ℂ **415/921-2867,** and three other locations), which inspired George Lucas's *American Graffiti.* Kids love the meals delivered in paper Cadillacs and the plentiful balloons. See p. 151.
- **Best Burger:** At $7 for a cheeseburger, the burgers at **Burger Joint** (700 Haight St.; ℂ **415/864-3833** and 807 Valencia St.; ℂ **415/824-3494**) don't come cheap. Considering they're made with only the finest ingredients, including naturally raised Niman Ranch beef, they're worth every penny. See p. 156. **Taylor's Refresher** (1 Ferry Bldg.; ℂ **866/328-3663**) comes in a close second, with burgers made from all-natural, local beef, topped with a tasty "secret sauce" and garnished

with lettuce and tomatoes fresh from the Farmer's Market. See p. 140.

- **Best Milkshake:** It's close, but I'm giving this one to **Taylor's Refresher.** Both it and **Burger Joint** (see "Best Burger," above) use San Francisco's luscious Double Rainbow ice cream for their first-rate strawberry, vanilla, and chocolate shakes. But in the summer Taylor's branches out with a to-die-for blueberry shake. See p. 140.

- **Best for Breakfast:** For its inventive omelets, terrific pancakes, and fresh-baked breads, **Ella's** (500 Presidio Ave.; ✆ 415/441-5669) takes the prize in the early meal category. See p. 153. Of course, while in San Francisco, you could always branch out and have dim sum for breakfast (see "Best Dim Sum," below), which I highly recommend.

- **Best Children's Menu:** Kids aren't limited to chicken fingers and fries at friendly **Puccini & Pinetti** (129 Ellis St.; ✆ 415/392-5500). The children's menu includes a salad, fruit, soup, and spaghetti, along with the irresistible make-your-own-pizza option. See p. 125.

- **Best Decor:** Step into **Ana Mandara** (891 Beach St.; ✆ 415/771-6800) and step into Vietnam—complete with tropical foliage, a facade of a Vietnamese home, and Indochinese artifacts. See p. 145.

- **Best Views:** Perched atop a bluff over the open ocean, the **Cliff House Bistro** (1090 Point Lobos Ave.; ✆ 415/386-3330) affords a vista that will take your breath away. See p. 164. If you can't make it out to the Sunset District, try **McCormick & Kuleto's** (900 North Point St.; ✆ 415/929-1730) in Ghirardelli Square for a view of the San Francisco Bay, Alcatraz Island, and the historic ships of the Hyde Street Pier. See p. 145.

- **Best If You Have a Sitter: Gary Danko** (800 North Point St.; ✆ 415/749-2060; p. 144) and **Fleur de Lys** (777 Sutter St.; ✆ 415/673-7779; p. 121) are among the best restaurants in the city, if not the state; better yet, the country.

- **Best for a Nice Dinner with Older Kids: Delfina** (3621 18th St.; ✆ 415/552-4055) is a terrific restaurant with a friendly, hip vibe that older kids will enjoy. The Tuscan/Italian food is also terrific. See p. 158. Another great spot to take older kids is **Café Kati** (1963 Sutter St.; ✆ 415/775-7313). They'll appreciate the intimate, but unpretentious, dining area and the inventive Western-Asian fusion menu. See p. 152.

- **Best for a Nice Dinner with the Grandparents:** Everyone will be delighted with a meal at **Moose's** (1652 Stockton St.; ✆ 415/989-7800), a San Francisco institution. The older generation can enjoy traditional dishes while parents savor inventive California cuisine and kids order off the children's menu. A view of Washington Park and live piano accompaniment will enhance the already terrific dining experience. See p. 141.

- **Best for Big Groups:** If the whole family is in town, head on over to **Kokkari Estiatorio** (200 Jackson St.; ✆ 415/981-0983). The spacious dining room in back can fit even the largest parties, and private dining rooms are also a possibility. The delightful Greek menu includes appetizers that are perfect for sharing and main courses to please every taste. See p. 136.

- **Best Pizza:** For Neapolitan wood-oven fired pizza that tastes good even without cheese, you can't beat **A16** (2355 Chestnut St.; ✆ 415/771-2216). See p. 149. The thin-crust pizzas at **Pizzeria Delfina** (3611 18th St.; ✆ 415/437-6800) include six mouth-watering standards and two tempting daily specials—all worth ordering. See p. 158. For a true-blue slice of American-style cheesy pizza that kids love, **ZA Pizza** (1919 Hyde St.; ✆ 415/771-3100) takes the cake—or, pie, as it were. See p. 155.

- **Best Barbecue:** No whining and no deconstructing the barbecue sauce: you're not in Kansas City, Dorothy. In San Francisco, we think **Memphis Minnie's** (576 Haight St.; ✆ 415/864-7675) does a fine job of smoking brisket and ribs. The slaw is good, too. See p. 158.

- **Best Vegetarian:** You can't beat **Greens** (Building A, Fort Mason; ✆ 415/771-6222) for excellent meatless cuisine—not to mention a lovely, airy dining room and fabulous views. See p. 149. Greens offers vegan dishes as well, but for those wishing to avoid any animal products whatsoever, **Millennium** (580 Geary St.; ✆ 415/345-3900) is the choice. See p. 124.

- **Best Bakery: Tartine** (600 Guerrero St.; ✆ 415/487-2600) actually has to advertise when its bread comes out of the oven (after 4pm, by the way). Otherwise, folks would be hanging around all day to get a loaf of walnut bread, which sells out immediately. See p. 162.

- **Best Cafe:** Not that kids really dig hanging out at cafes, but our kids (and plenty of other customers' kids) love the croissants at **Boulange de Polk** (2310 Polk St.; ✆ 415/345-1107). They munch happily while parents sip cafe au lait and people watch from the sidewalk tables. See p. 154.

- **Best Chinese in Chinatown:** The **R&G Lounge** gets my nod because of its authentic and refreshingly

different menu (631 Kearny St.; ✆ 415/982-7877). See p. 134.

- **Best Chinese Not in Chinatown:** In offering an out-of-Chinatown choice, I'm going to make a plug for **Dragon Well** (2142 Chestnut St.; ✆ 415/474-6888), which offers Chinese food that has been "California-ized," with an emphasis on very fresh, high-quality ingredients and a lot less grease. See p. 167.

- **Best Dim Sum:** San Franciscans seem to be equally divided as to where to get the best dim sum. Many insist it's to be found at **Ton Kiang** in the Richmond District (5821 Geary Blvd.; ✆ 415/387-8273). See p. 167. If you just can't head out that way during your stay, rest assured. On the other hand, I have switched allegiances of late and now give highest kudos to **Yank Sing** (101 Spear St., in the Rincon Center; ✆ 415/957-9300). See p. 138. To help familiarize your kids with dim sum, check out the box "Kids' Guide to Dim Sum," below.

- **Best Thai:** Thai seems to be the new Chinese, with pad Thai overtaking sweet and sour pork as favored takeout fare. For excellent Thai, try **Marnee Thai** in the Sunset (1243 9th Ave.; ✆ 415/731-9999). See p. 166.

- **Best Ethnic Restaurant for Kids:** If the arched ceilings, hand-painted Arabesque plates, and delectable Moroccan menu at **Aziza** (5800 Geary Blvd.; ✆ 415/752-2222) aren't exotic enough, head into the back room, which is full of North African–styled sofas and cushions. Better yet, wait until 7pm on weekends, when the belly dancer arrives. See p. 164.

- **Best Italian:** For a terrific family meal, **Trattoria Contadina** (1800 Mason St.; ✆ 415/982-5728) offers

Kids' Guide to Dim Sum

For some reason, the whole communal aspect of dim sum seems to make my kids more adventurous. Waiters come with plates of food and everyone seated decides whether or not to go for it. When a plate is placed in the middle of the table, you're all in on the fun of trying it together. Of course, it helps that we've figured out what we think our kids will like and have learned to avoid anything that could truly shock them. I'm passing this knowledge on to you with a list of dim sum that most first-timers will definitely enjoy. And if you see fresh-steamed asparagus, snow pea shoots, or any other vegetables being offered, order them as well. They are all excellent.

- *Har gau:* Shrimp dumplings encased in a translucent wrapper and steamed
- *Siu mai:* Rectangles of pork and shrimp in a sheer noodle wrapper
- *Gau choi gau:* Chives, alone or with shrimp or scallops
- *Jun jui kau:* Rice pearl balls with seasoned ground pork and rice
- *Law mai gai:* Sticky rice with bits of meat and mushrooms wrapped in a lotus leaf
- *Char siu bau:* Steamed pork buns—bits of barbecued meat in a doughy roll
- *Guk char siu ban:* Baked pork buns—bits of barbecued meat in a glazed roll
- *Chun guen:* Spring rolls—smaller, less crowded versions of egg rolls
- *Gau ji:* Pot stickers—a thick, crescent-shaped dough filled with ground pork

hearty pastas and a friendly ma-and-pa atmosphere. See p. 143. For truly exceptional Italian cuisine, you can do no better than **Antica Trattoria** (2400 Polk St.; ☎ **415/928-5797**). See p. 154.

- **Best Fish:** At **Great Eastern** (649 Jackson St.; ☎ **415/986-2500**) your dinner gets plucked from the fish tanks in the back of the dining room, so there's no question the fish is fresh. See p. 133. The longtime favorite of city hall movers and shakers, **Hayes Street Grill** (320 Hayes St.; ☎ **415/863-5545**) uses the Bay Area's finest purveyors of fish, meat, and produce and puts out bright, simple plates of recognizable food. See p. 148.

- **Best Mexican: Mamacita** (2317 Chestnut St.; ☎ **415/346-8494**) serves ultra-fresh, flavorful Mexican specialties and makes an excellent guacamole. See p. 150. For inexpensive Mexican food with a view, you could do no better than **Mijita** (One Ferry Building, Number 44; ☎ **415/399-0814;** p. 139), created by one of SF's most renowned chefs. For a humble but terrific burrito, head down to the Mission to **La Corneta Taqueria** (2731 Mission St.; ☎ **415/643-7001**). See p. 161.

- **Best for Aspiring Gourmands:** Take them to **Town Hall** (342 Howard St.; ☎ **415/908-3900**), where the award-winning team of owner-chefs, who are also brothers, whip up American classics that never tasted so good. See p. 130. For something more exotic, the Spanish *tapas* at **Bocadillos** (710 Montgomery St.; ℂ **415/982-2622**) offer plenty of variety and striking new flavors as well. See p. 137.

- **Best Ice Cream:** And the winner is . . . **Mitchell's** (688 San Jose Ave.; ℂ **415/648-2300**) for creamy, luscious ice creams in flavors both exotic (baby coconut, sweet corn) and comforting (Mexican chocolate, vanilla). See p. 162.

- **Best Afternoon Tea:** Treat the kids to a special Prince or Princess Tea at the **Palace Hotel's Garden Court** (2 New Montgomery St., at Market St.; ℂ **415/546-5089**). See p. 127. Closer in tone to an English village teashop is **Lovejoy's Tea Room** (1351 Church St.; ℂ **415/648-5895**), often filled with ladies having a tête-à-tête and little girls practicing to be big girls. See p. 163.

- **Best Outdoor Dining (Daytime):** The very best outdoor dining area belongs to the **Park Chalet** (1000 Great Hwy.; ℂ **415/386-8439**), which opens onto an expansive garden at the western edge of Golden Gate Park. In fact, with glass walls and a glass ceiling, the whole restaurant feels like you're outdoors. See p. 164. A much smaller outdoor dining area next to a pleasant lawn can be found at **Town's End** (2 Townsend St.; ℂ **415/512-0749**). See p. 138.

- **Best Outdoor Dining (Evening):** For a first-class dinner and Oscar-category films under the stars, head to **Foreign Cinema** (2534 Mission St.; ℂ **415/648-7600**). See p. 160.

- **Best Delivery:** For basic Italian at terrific prices delivered to your hotel or home, **Pasta Pomodoro** (1875 Union St. and other locations; ℂ **415/771-7900**) is a very good thing. Their salads and fresh vegetables really round out a meal. See p. 151.

2

Planning Your Trip to San Francisco

Planning a trip is half the fun. It's also critical, especially when you're dealing with a group whose members may all have different interests. Make the kids active participants in your upcoming adventure by talking through the activities you can all enjoy. This chapter provides updated information on those activities, with details on when to go and how to get there.

1 Visitor Information

The San Francisco Convention and Visitors Bureau, 900 Market St. (at Powell St.), Hallidie Plaza, Lower Level, San Francisco, CA 94102 (© **415/391-2000;** www.onlyinsanfrancisco.com), is the best source of specialized information about the city. Even if you don't have a specific question, you might want to request the free Visitors Planning Guide and the San Francisco Visitors Kit. You can also check online for specific information and sign up for the bureau's monthly newsletter, which lists upcoming local events and special travel offers. If you need specific information faxed to you, you can call © **800/220-5747;** follow the prompts to receive information by fax only. The bureau highlights only its members' establishments, so if it doesn't have what you're looking for, that doesn't necessarily mean it doesn't exist.

2 Entry Requirements & Customs

ENTRY REQUIREMENTS
PASSPORTS
For information on how to get a passport, go to "**Passports**" in the "**Fast Facts**" section of chapter 4—the websites listed provide downloadable passport applications as well as the current fees for processing passport applications. International visitors can obtain a visa application at the website of the U.S. State Department at **http://travel.state.gov**.

VISAS
For information on how to get a Visa, go to "**Visas**" in the "**Fast Facts**" section of chapter 4.

The U.S. State Department has a **Visa Waiver Program** allowing citizens of the following countries (at press time) to enter the United States without a visa for stays of up to 90 days: Andorra, Australia, Austria, Belgium, Brunei, Denmark, Finland, France, Germany, Iceland, Ireland, Italy, Japan, Liechtenstein, Luxembourg, Monaco, the Netherlands, New Zealand, Norway, Portugal, San Marino, Singapore, Slovenia, Spain, Sweden, Switzerland, and the United Kingdom. Citizens of these nations need only a valid passport and a round-trip air or cruise ticket upon arrival. If they first enter the United States, they may also visit Mexico,

Canada, Bermuda, and/or the Caribbean islands and return to the United States without a visa. Further information is available from any U.S. embassy or consulate. Canadian citizens may enter the United States without visas; they need only proof of residence.

Citizens of all other countries must have (1) a valid passport that expires at least 6 months later than the scheduled end of their visit to the United States, and (2) a tourist visa, which may be obtained without charge from any U.S. consulate.

MEDICAL REQUIREMENTS

Unless you're arriving from an area known to be suffering from an epidemic (particularly cholera or yellow fever), inoculations or vaccinations are not required for entry into the United States. If you have a medical condition that requires **syringe-administered medications,** carry a valid signed prescription from your physician—the Federal Aviation Administration (FAA) no longer allows airline passengers to pack syringes in their carry-on baggage without documented proof of medical need. If you have a disease that requires treatment with **narcotics,** you should also carry documented proof with you—smuggling narcotics aboard a plane is a serious offense that carries severe penalties in the U.S.

For **HIV-positive visitors,** requirements for entering the United States are somewhat vague and change frequently. For up-to-the-minute information, contact **AIDSinfo** (© 800/448-0440 or 301/519-6616 outside the U.S.; www. aidsinfo.nih.gov) or the **Gay Men's Health Crisis** (© 212/367-1000; www. gmhc.org).

CUSTOMS

WHAT YOU CAN BRING INTO SAN FRANCISCO

Every visitor more than 21 years of age may bring in, free of duty, the following:

(1) 1 liter of wine or hard liquor; (2) 200 cigarettes, 100 cigars (but not from Cuba), or 3 pounds of smoking tobacco; and (3) $100 worth of gifts. These exemptions are offered to travelers who spend at least 72 hours in the United States and who have not claimed them within the preceding 6 months. It is forbidden to bring into the country foodstuffs (particularly fruit, cooked meats, and canned goods) and plants (vegetables, seeds, tropical plants, and the like). Foreign tourists may carry in or out up to $10,000 in U.S. or foreign currency with no formalities; larger sums must be declared to U.S. Customs on entering or leaving, which includes filing form CM 4790. For details regarding U.S. Customs and Border Protection, consult your nearest U.S. embassy or consulate, or **U.S. Customs** (© **202/927-1770;** www. customs.ustreas.gov).

WHAT YOU CAN TAKE HOME FROM SAN FRANCISCO

Canadian Citizens

For a clear summary of Canadian rules, write for the booklet *I Declare,* issued by the **Canada Border Services Agency** (© **800/461-9999** in Canada, or 204/ 983-3500; **www.cbsa-asfc.gc.ca**).

U.K. Citizens

For information, contact **HM Customs & Excise** at © **0845/010-9000** (from outside the U.K., 020/8929-0152), or consult their website at **www.hmce. gov.uk**.

Australian Citizens

A helpful brochure available from Australian consulates or Customs offices is *Know Before You Go.* For more information, call the **Australian Customs Service** at © **1300/363-263,** or log on to **www.customs.gov.au**.

New Zealand Citizens

Most questions are answered in a free pamphlet available at New Zealand consulates and Customs offices: *New*

Zealand Customs Guide for Travellers, Notice no. 4. For more information, contact **New Zealand Customs,** The Customhouse, 17–21 Whitmore St., Box 2218, Wellington (© **04/473-6099** or 0800/428-786; **www.customs.govt.nz**).

3 Money

Like any big city, San Francisco doesn't come cheap. Hotels, food, and admission fees at attractions add up. Fortunately, as I list in chapter 6, you can find plenty of great food at reasonable prices if you know where to look, which is usually not in the most touristy neighborhoods. Likewise, with careful planning, you may be able to score a good deal on a hotel room. Lastly, San Francisco is such a beautiful city that you can do a fair amount of satisfying sightseeing without spending much money at all.

LOWERING THE COST OF FAMILY TRAVEL

Traveling with kids can really add to the cost of a trip. Below are some ways to cut expenses.

• **Share a hotel room with your children.** No, you won't have any privacy, but you will reduce expenses.

A room with two double beds costs the same as a room with one queen, and the majority of hotels won't charge an additional-person fee if that person is related to you and under 18. I've noted the policies in this regard for all the hotel listings in this book. Do be aware that hotels keep track of occupancy and there is a limit—anywhere from two to four or maybe five bodies per guest room, depending on the room size.

• **Reserve a hotel room with a kitchenette.** There aren't a lot in San Francisco, but they do exist, and if you use them to prepare breakfast or even a bag lunch, you will save quite a bit. At a minimum, request a small fridge and coffeemaker, if your room doesn't already have one.

What Things Cost in San Francisco	
Taxi from airport to Union Square (excluding tip)	40.00
One-way adult Muni/bus fare to any city destination	1.50
One-way youth Muni/bus fare to any city destination	.50
A 3-day adult Muni Passport (also good for cable car)	18.00
Regular movie at Metreon for two adults and two kids	34.00
IMAX tickets at Metreon for two adults and two kids	50.00
Alcatraz tickets for two adults and two kids aged 5–11	59.00
San Francisco Zoo tickets for two adults and two kids aged 3–11	32.00
Slice of pizza	2.75
Dim sum brunch for four at Ton Kiang	50.00
Package of 40 Huggies disposable diapers from Walgreen's	12.00
Cone at Mitchell's Ice Cream	2.10
A small fresh orange juice at the Westin St. Francis Hotel	3.20
Four hours of parking in the Union Square Garage	12.00

> ### Value   Free (or Nearly Free) Things to Do with Your Kids in San Francisco
>
> - Take a **City Guides walking tour** (p. 201) in an interesting neighborhood.
> - Check out the **free outdoor concerts** and events at Yerba Buena Gardens Thursdays at noon and weekends between May and October.
> - Take the kids to **Golden Gate Park's Koret Children's Quarter.**
> - Take a free tour of the **Strybing Arboretum and Botanical Gardens** in Golden Gate Park (p. 190).
> - Visit the **de Young Museum.** Take in the impressive architecture, check out the main lobby, savor the view from the museum tower, contemplate Ruth Asawa's ethereal sculptures inside, and stroll through the inspiring sculpture garden outside—all at no cost.
> - Walk across the **Golden Gate Bridge.**
> - Mosey through **Chinatown.** The sights and sounds of this colorful neighborhood are a cultural experience many people would pay to have.
> - Visit the lovely **Hyde Street Pier** at no charge. Adults must pay $5 to board the ships, but kids are free. The nearby **National Maritime Visitors Center** is a hit with adults and kids, and it's free.
> - Hang out at **Crissy Field.** Relish the priceless vista while your kids run around on the grassy hills or play at the beach.
> - Ascend **Nob Hill.** Admire the stained glass at Grace Cathedral, regard the lobby of the Fairmont Hotel, and then take in the panoramic view from the top floor bar of the InterContinental Mark Hopkins Hotel.

- **Be adventurous diners.** The Mission, Chinatown, and the Richmond district have wonderful, inexpensive ethnic restaurants (Mexican, Chinese, Thai, and Middle Eastern, among others) that will expand your horizons without depleting your pocketbook.
- **Purchase a SF Municipal Railway (Muni) Passport** (see chapter 4). And, use buses and streetcars in lieu of renting a car or taking taxis.
- **Minimize the use of a car while in the city.** Parking is prohibitively expensive and frustrating. You'll not only save money, but you may have a more relaxed vacation.
- **Take advantage of what's free.** It may be difficult to schedule your trip around museums' free admission days, which are only once a month,

but there are ways to spend a lovely day without constantly digging into your wallet. (See the box "Free (or Nearly Free) Things to Do with Your Kids in San Francisco," below.)
- **Remember your local memberships.** Zoos, aquariums, and museums offer free or reduced admission prices if you are a member of your local zoo, aquarium, and museum. For example, the San Francisco Zoo, the Aquarium of the Bay, and the California Academy of Sciences all have such reciprocal agreements. So bring your home city's membership cards with you.

ATMS

The easiest and best way to get cash away from home is from an ATM (automated teller machine), sometimes referred to as

- Visit the **California Palace of the Legion of Honor, Asian Art Museum, San Francisco Museum of Modern Art, de Young Museum, Cartoon Art Museum,** or **Contemporary Jewish Museum;** all are free the first Tuesday of each month. The **California Academy of Sciences, Exploratorium,** and **San Francisco Zoo** are free the first Wednesday of each month.
- Ride the Powell/Mason cable car to the **Cable Car Museum** (p. 191) for a close-up look at how the cars work.
- View displays of antique equipment, artifacts from the 1906 earthquake, and local firefighting memorabilia at the **San Francisco Fire Department Museum** (p. 194).
- Head to the **Main Library's children's wing** (p. 277) or bring your wee ones to **story hour** at most public library branches, generally held Tuesday and Thursday mornings. For a schedule, check www.sfpl.org.
- Tour the city on a Muni bus (see "Getting Around," in chapter 4 for suggestions).
- Climb the **Filbert Steps,** the most famous of San Francisco's many staircases, offering lovely views and verdant gardens.
- Spend Saturday morning at the **Ferry Plaza Farmer's Market.** You could almost make a meal of all the fresh fruits, breads, spreads, and other food samples offered by the farmers, breeders, and bakers.
- Walk down the crooked part of **Lombard Street.**

a "cash machine," or "cashpoint." The **Cirrus** (© **800/424-7787;** www.mastercard.com) and **PLUS** (© **800/843-7587;** www.visa.com) networks span the country; you can find them even in remote regions. The back of your bank card shows which network you're on; you can then call or check online for ATM locations in San Francisco. You must know your personal identification number (PIN) and daily withdrawal limit before you depart. *Note:* Remember that many banks impose a fee every time you use a card at another bank's ATM, and that fee can be higher for international transactions (up to $5 or more) than for domestic ones (where they're rarely more than $2). In addition, the bank from which you withdraw cash may charge its own fee. To compare banks' ATM fees within the U.S., use **www.bankrate.com**. For international withdrawal fees, ask your bank.

CREDIT CARDS & DEBIT CARDS

Credit cards are the most widely used form of payment in the United States: **Visa** (Barclaycard in Britain), **MasterCard** (EuroCard in Europe, Access in Britain), **American Express, Diners Club,** and **Discover.** They also provide a convenient record of your expenses and generally offer relatively good exchange rates. You can also withdraw cash advances at banks or ATMs, provided you know your PIN.

Visitors from outside the U.S. should inquire whether their bank assesses a 1–3% fee on charges incurred abroad.

It's highly recommended that you travel with at least one major credit card. You need one to rent a car, and hotels and

Tips **Easy Money**

You'll avoid lines at airport ATMs by exchanging at least some money—just enough to cover airport incidentals and transportation to your hotel—before you leave home.

When you change money, ask for some small bills or loose change. Petty cash will come in handy for tipping and public transportation. Consider keeping the change separate from your larger bills, so that it's readily accessible and you'll be less of a target for theft.

airlines usually require a credit card imprint as a deposit against expenses.

ATM cards with major credit card backing, known as **debit cards,** are now a commonly acceptable form of payment in most stores and restaurants. Debit cards draw money directly from your checking account. Some stores enable you to receive "cash back" on your debit-card purchases as well. The same is true at most U.S. post offices.

TRAVELER'S CHECKS

Traveler's checks are widely accepted in the U.S., but foreign visitors should make sure that they're denominated in U.S. dollars; foreign-currency checks are often difficult to exchange.

You can buy traveler's checks at most banks. Most are offered in denominations of $20, $50, $100, $500, and sometimes $1,000. Generally, you'll pay a service charge ranging from 1% to 4%.

The most popular traveler's checks are offered by **American Express** (① 800/807-6233; ① 800/221-7282 for card holders—this number accepts collect calls, offers service in several foreign languages, and exempts Amex gold and platinum cardholders from the 1% fee.); **Visa** (① 800/732-1322)—AAA members can obtain Visa checks for a $9.95 fee (for checks up to $1,500) at most AAA offices or by calling ① 866/339-3378; and **MasterCard** (① 800/223-9920).

If you do carry traveler's checks, keep a record of their serial numbers separate from your checks in the event that they are stolen or lost. You'll get a refund faster if you know the numbers.

4 When to Go

Because summer is when most kids have vacation, you may be planning to visit San Francisco sometime between **June and August.** Just be warned that the city is at its foggiest at that time. The good news is that most of California is very warm then—so if your trip includes other stops in the state, you may even welcome the city's brisk morning fog.

Expect crowds around Fisherman's Wharf and on the F-Market streetcars. Book Alcatraz Island tickets at least 1 week ahead of time and, after 9am, expect to wait in long lines to board the

Powell Street cable cars. Fortunately, because San Francisco sees fewer conventions in the summer, you may actually get better hotel rates at the business-oriented hotels downtown (although not at Fisherman's Wharf).

The city puts on a show all summer and into fall, with music and dance festivals, street fairs, and special events. Yerba Buena Center, one of the best places for families, offers free world-class concerts in the gardens. It's also prime baseball season; if you're all fans, you'll be delighted to spend the afternoon at AT&T Park.

September and October are usually great months in San Francisco; the fog disappears and the air is warm. Of course, school schedules may be an issue, but perhaps you can fit in a long weekend in the city. Fall brings a huge spike in conventions, but business is normally conducted during the week, leaving hotels to offer weekend packages and discounts.

If you can handle the vagaries of the weather, **winter** is a terrific season to visit. You'll feel like you have the city to yourself during weekdays when everyone else is at work. On the weekends, folks from the surrounding areas make their way into town for shopping and theater. San Francisco is a delight after Thanksgiving, as Union Square puts up a massive Christmas tree and surrounding stores dress themselves up in festive decorations. In November, Chinatown merchants hold a night market fair at Portsmouth Square on Saturdays until 11pm, and shoppers have a field day finishing up their holiday shopping.

In December, some hotels, such as the Ritz-Carlton, hold children's holiday teas, and an outdoor ice skating rink opens at the Embarcadero Center. The San Francisco Ballet dusts off *The Nutcracker* and the American Conservatory Theater gives Scrooge nightmares in its annual performances of *A Christmas Carol.* The air is crisp, the temperatures cool. You won't go home with a tan, but you can have quite a bit of fun.

Spring sees a full calendar of meetings at the Moscone Convention Center, but, as in the fall, hotel rooms become available for leisure travelers on the weekends. San Francisco weather is best in late spring, and Golden Gate Park is particularly beautiful at that time, with trees budding in the Strybing Arboretum and the cherry trees blossoming in the Japanese Tea Garden.

For up-to-the-minute weather reports, log onto www.sfgate.com/weather.

KIDS' FAVORITE SAN FRANCISCO EVENTS

If you have any flexibility in scheduling your trip, some events, such as the Chinese New Year Parade, are so special that it might be worth tweaking your dates to fit them in. It's also fun to discover that an event or performance just happens to be slated during your visit. You can peruse a calendar of events published by the Convention and Visitors Bureau at **www.onlyin sanfrancisco.com/calendar**. In addition, you can subscribe to **www.gocitykids.com**, which offers a weekly e-mail calendar, and also has a calendar you can search by date, with information and phone numbers for all events listed.

Things change, so if your heart is set on participating in any events listed below, phone or check the sponsoring organization's website for dates and times.

January

Anniversary of the Sea Lions' Arrival at PIER 39. Sure, you can watch these pinnipeds loll around, sunbathe, and bark at one another most of the year, but January is the month they arrived at PIER 39. (They came for the herring in 1990.) Toward the middle of the month, PIER 39 honors these

---

Tips **Convention Info**

The San Francisco Convention & Visitors Bureau publishes a summary list of major conventions and trade shows on its website, www.sfvisitor.org/convention. It's wise to check it out before you cement your travel dates, just to find out if you're likely to be competing with your orthodontist or attorney for a hotel room.

San Francisco's Average Temperatures (°F/°C) and Rainfall (in./mm)

	Jan	Feb	Mar	Apr	May	June	July	Aug	Sept	Oct	Nov	Dec
High	56/13	59/15	61/16	64/18	67/19	70/21	71/22	72/22	73/23	70/21	62/17	56/13
Low	43/6	46/8	47/8	48/9	51/11	53/12	55/13	56/13	55/13	52/11	48/9	43/6
Rainfall	4.5/114	4.0/102	3.3/84	1.2/30	0.4/10	0.1/2.5	0.03/0.8	0.1/2.5	0.2/5.1	1.0/25	2.5/64	2.9/74

mammoth mammals with a special party and guests from the Marine Mammal Center. Call ℂ **415/705-5500** or visit www.pier39.com.

February

Chinese New Year Parade and Celebration is a memorable 2-week event culminating in the exciting, loud, and lengthy Chinese New Year's parade down Market Street to Columbus Avenue on the final Saturday evening. Spectators pack the sidewalks, so you'll want to find a good spot early on. Chinatown itself is filled with color and bustles even more than usual, with families buying food for holiday dinners and special red envelopes to fill with New Year's gifts of money for the kids. Call the Chinese Chamber of Commerce at ℂ **415/391-9680** or visit www.chineseparade.com. *Note:* Depending on the Chinese lunar calendar, this event sometimes occurs in early March.

Coinciding with Valentine's Day in mid-February, PIER 39 hosts **Tulipmania,** featuring more than 39,000 tulips throughout the pier. The amazing diversity in size, shape, and color is something to behold. Visitors are welcome to join complimentary landscaping tours each day at 10am. Call ℂ **415/705-5500** or visit www.pier39.com.

March

The **St. Patrick's Day Parade** that runs along Market Street to the Civic Center is always lively. There's a large expatriate Irish community in town, and Ireland's patron saint traditionally gets his due here. Call ℂ **415/675-9885** or visit www.uissf.org.

April

On Easter Sunday, the festive **Union Street Easter Parade & Spring Celebration,** between Gough and Fillmore streets, includes pony rides, a petting zoo, kids' rides and games, a climbing wall, a kids' activities area, costumed characters, and a parade. Phone ℂ **800/310-6563** or visit http://sresproductions.com/union_street_easter.html.

Japantown has held an annual **Cherry Blossom Festival** since 1967. The festival takes place over 2 weekends and offers many events for families, including demonstrations of traditional dance, *taiko* drumming, tea ceremonies, and flower arrangement. There's also a parade, copious food, and, of course, beautiful trees in bloom. Call ℂ **415/563-2313** or visit www.nccbf.org.

May

Cinco de Mayo (5th of May) is a major Mexican festival celebrating the Battle of Puebla against French occupation forces in 1862. A parade down Mission Street is followed by a festival at Civic Center Plaza with music, arts, crafts, low-rider cars, and delicious food that most kids will love. The parade is free; the festival has a small admission charge of around $5 for adults (free for kids under 12). Visit **www.latinbayarea.com**. This fiesta is more family-oriented than **Carnaval** (**www.carnaval.com**) later in the month, which is wilder and very crowded.

The **Youth Arts Festival** is a weeklong exhibition of the visual, performing, and literary arts by middle school and high school students throughout the city. The opening day of the festival, which takes place at Yerba Buena Center, is the most exciting, with activities and an awards presentation. Admission is free. Call ✆ **415/543-1718** or visit www.ybgf.org.

Bay to Breakers started after the 1906 earthquake as a way to boost the city's spirits and remains today the longest consecutively run footrace in the world. Although it attracts top-level international athletes, what will interest your kids are the thousands of participants donned in the wackiest outfits imaginable. Call ✆ **415/359-2800** or visit www.ingbaytobreakers.com.

June

Union Street Art Festival, usually held around the end of May or beginning of June, includes special children's art activities among all the food, wine, and crafts booths and music stages. This is a particularly crowded street fair and parking is next to impossible, so come by public transportation and foot. Call ✆ **800/310-6563** or visit www.unionstreetfestival.com.

The **Haight-Ashbury Street Fair** features tie-dye galore, food, entertainment, and the colorful presence of neighborhood characters. Admission is free. Call ✆ **415/863-3489** or visit www.haightstreetfair.org.

The **Ethnic Dance Festival** is usually held the last 3 weekends in June and takes place at the Palace of Fine Arts behind the Exploratorium. Music and dance groups from all over the world entertain. Tickets are $20 to $30. Call ✆ **415/474-3914** or visit www. ethnicdancefestival.org.

Stern Grove Midsummer Music Festival is one of the great free events of the summer. All sorts of performances—opera, Latin music, jazz—are held Sunday afternoons at 2pm in Sigmund Stern Grove at 19th Avenue and Sloat Boulevard. The venue is easily reached on M-Oceanview or K-Ingleside Muni streetcars or the 27-Monterey bus. Bring a picnic and a blanket. Call ✆ **415/252-6252** or visit www.sterngrove.org.

July

As the largest free jazz festival on the west coast, stretching over 8 blocks, the **Fillmore Street Jazz Festival** draws more than 90,000 visitors over the July 4 weekend. You can listen to music performed on several stages, view art and crafts on display, and taste from all over the world. Call ✆ **800/731-0003** or visit www.fillmorestreetjazzfestival. com.

On the **Fourth of July** itself, the Waterfront Festival takes place around PIER 39 and at Ghirardelli Square and culminates in a fireworks show beginning at 9pm. Call ✆ **415/705-5500** or visit www.pier39.com.

August

Nihonmachi Street Fair, a celebration of the Bay Area's diverse Asian and Pacific American communities, occurs on 1 Saturday and Sunday each August in Japantown, on Post Street between Laguna and Fillmore streets. Asian-American artisans show their creations, and the "Food Fest" features the cooking of Asia and the Pacific Islands. A children's area includes games and the opportunity to learn traditional arts and crafts. Call ✆ **415/771-9861** or visit www.nihonmachistreetfair.org.

September

Ghirardelli Square Chocolate Festival is an annual benefit for Open Hand, a worthy local charity that delivers food to homebound AIDS patients. Chocoholics wander from one tasting to another, provided by local shops and restaurants. Serious eaters can enter the sundae-eating contest. The prize is the winner's weight in chocolate! Call ⓒ **415/775-5500** or visit www. ghirardellisq.com.

San Francisco Blues Festival is a fun weekend at Fort Mason. The festival is complete with food and a few booths with T-shirts and CDs, but the draw is the excellent roster of local and national blues musicians and the setting. For information and tickets call ⓒ **415/979-5588** or visit www.sf blues.com.

Sandcastle Classic, an annual fundraiser for Leap, an artists-in-residence program, turns Ocean Beach into a fantastical canvas for sand castles, pyramids, wild animals, and flights of fancy. It usually takes place at the end of the month, but sometimes occurs in October. Admission is free, but donations are appreciated. Call ⓒ **415/512-1899** or visit www.leap 4kids.org.

October

San Francisco Comedy Day Celebration at Golden Gate Park's Sharon Meadow brings together at least 30 comedians for a Sunday afternoon full of laughter. Visit www.comedyday. com.

Fleet Week, 3the second weekend of October, honors the armed forces and usually brings the Blue Angels to our skies. Plenty of other astonishing aerial acrobatics, the kind that elicit gasps from the crowd, are also on display. PIER 39 presents music and additional fleet week activities. Victoria Park is a prime viewing area, with food stands and a big screen set up for ultra close-up shots. For a detailed listing of events, see **www.fleetweek.us** and **www.airshownetwork.com**.

San Francisco Italian Heritage Parade celebrates Christopher Columbus's contribution to our fair land with a 12:30pm parade beginning at Jefferson and Stockton streets and ending at Washington Square, where the festivities continue. Visit www.sfcolumbus day.org.

Halloween almost seems like an official city holiday in San Francisco. The **Randall Museum Family Halloween Fest** is a daytime event on the Saturday before Halloween for 2- to 12-year-olds. Pumpkin carving, entertainment, and crafts are among the day's offerings at this local treasure. Costumes are most appropriate. Call ⓒ **415/554-9600** or visit www.randallmuseum. org. Down at Yerba Buena Gardens, little ones will be pleased with the **Gardens Halloween Costume Walk,** wherein costumed kiddos collect goodies while it's still daylight. This takes place the Sunday before Halloween. Call ⓒ **415/543-1718** or visit www. ybgf.org.

November

The **Embarcadero Center Lighting Ceremony and Celebration** on the Friday before Thanksgiving is fun if you can get close enough to watch the performances in the ice skating rink. If you can't make it for the building lighting (the four towers gleam during the holiday season), the rink is open for public skating until after the New Year. Skates, for feet of all sizes, may be rented at the ticket booth.

Ritz-Carlton Teddy Bear Teas for children always sell out, especially if you can only attend on a weekend. The holiday teas start after Thanksgiving, but you can make reservations beginning in August; call ⓒ **415/773-6198.**

December

Christmas at Sea, especially suited to children under 10, takes place on board the historic ships docked at the Hyde Street Pier (p. 184), and offers singing, cider, and stories. Call ⓒ **415/ 561-6662** or visit www.maritime.org.

5 Travel Insurance

The cost of travel insurance varies widely, depending on the cost and length of your trip, your age and health, and the type of trip you're taking, but expect to pay between 5% and 8% of the vacation itself. You can get estimates from various providers through **InsureMyTrip.com**. Enter your trip cost and dates, your age, and other information for prices from more than a dozen companies.

TRIP-CANCELLATION INSURANCE

Trip-cancellation insurance will help retrieve your money if you have to back out of a trip or depart early, or if your travel supplier goes bankrupt. Permissible reasons for trip cancellation can range from sickness to natural disasters to the State Department declaring a destination unsafe for travel.

For more information, contact one of the following recommended insurers: **Access America** (© 866/807-3982; www.accessamerica.com); **Travel Guard International** (© 800/826-4919; www.travelguard.com); **Travel Insured International** (© 800/243-3174; www.travelinsured.com); and **Travelex Insurance Services** (© 888/457-4602; www.travelex-insurance.com).

MEDICAL INSURANCE

Although it's not required of travelers, health insurance is highly recommended.

Most health insurance policies cover you if you get sick away from home—but verify that you're covered before you depart, particularly if you're insured by an HMO.

International visitors should note that unlike many other countries, the United States does not usually offer free or low-cost medical care to its citizens or visitors. Doctors and hospitals are expensive, and in most cases will require advance payment or proof of coverage before they render their services. Good policies will cover the costs of an accident, repatriation, or death. Packages such as **Europ Assistance's "Worldwide Healthcare Plan"** are sold by European automobile clubs and travel agencies at attractive rates. **Worldwide Assistance Services, Inc.** (© 800/777-8710; www.worldwideassistance.com) is the agent for Europ Assistance in the United States.

Though lack of health insurance may prevent you from being admitted to a hospital in nonemergencies, don't worry about being left on a street corner to die: The American way is to fix you now and bill the living daylights out of you later.

INSURANCE FOR BRITISH TRAVELERS Most big travel agents offer their own insurance and will probably try to sell you their package when you book a holiday. Think before you sign. **Britain's Consumers' Association** recommends that you insist on seeing the

Travel in the Age of Bankruptcy

Airlines go bankrupt, so protect yourself by **buying your tickets with a credit card.** The Fair Credit Billing Act guarantees that you can get your money back from the credit card company if a travel supplier goes under (and if you request the refund within 60 days of the bankruptcy). **Travel insurance** can also help, but make sure it covers against "carrier default" for your specific travel provider. And be aware that if a U.S. airline goes bust mid-trip, a 2001 federal law requires other carriers to take you to your destination (albeit on a space-available basis) for a fee of no more than $25, provided you rebook within 60 days of the cancellation.

policy and reading the fine print before buying travel insurance. **The Association of British Insurers** (© 020/7600-3333; www.abi.org.uk) gives advice by phone and publishes *Holiday Insurance,* a free guide to policy provisions and prices. You might also shop around for better deals: Try **Columbus Direct** (© 0870/033-9988; www.columbusdirect.net).

INSURANCE FOR CANADIAN TRAVELERS Canadians should check with their provincial health plan offices or call **Health Canada** (© 866/225-0709; www.hc-sc.gc.ca) to find out the extent of their coverage and what documentation and receipts they must take home in case they are treated in the United States.

LOST-LUGGAGE INSURANCE
On flights within the U.S., checked baggage is covered up to $2,500 per ticketed passenger. On flights outside the U.S. (and on U.S. portions of international trips), baggage coverage is limited to approximately $9.07 per pound, up to approximately $635 per checked bag. If you plan to check items more valuable than what's covered by the standard liability, see if your homeowner's policy covers your valuables, get baggage insurance as part of your comprehensive travel-insurance package, or buy Travel Guard's "BagTrak" product.

If your luggage is lost, immediately file a lost-luggage claim at the airport, detailing the luggage contents. Most airlines require that you report delayed, damaged, or lost baggage within 4 hours of arrival. The airlines are required to deliver luggage, once found, directly to your house or destination free of charge.

6 Health & Safety

STAYING HEALTHY
You needn't worry about keeping the kids, and yourselves, healthy in San Francisco. The water is fine to drink, the food is fresh, and no-smoking laws limit your exposure to irritants. The main word of caution is to bring warm clothes, even (or especially) during mid-summer, lest the fog and wind cause a family member to catch a cold. At the same time, don't forget the sunscreen. This is California, after all, and a day of mixed clouds and sunshine can still produce sunburn. Also, don't forget comfortable walking shoes, as there's a good chance you'll be trekking up, and down, a few hills.

Avoiding "Economy Class Syndrome"
Deep vein thrombosis, or as it's known in the world of flying, "economy-class syndrome," is a blood clot that develops in a deep vein. It's a potentially deadly condition that can be caused by sitting in cramped conditions—such as an airplane cabin—for too long. During a flight (especially a long-haul flight), get up, walk around, and stretch your legs every 60 to 90 minutes to keep your blood flowing. Other preventative measures include frequent flexing of the legs while sitting, drinking lots of water, and avoiding alcohol and sleeping pills. If you have a history of deep vein thrombosis, heart disease, or another condition that puts you at high risk, some experts recommend wearing compression stockings or taking anticoagulants when you fly; always ask your physician about the best course for you. Symptoms of deep vein thrombosis include leg pain or swelling, or even shortness of breath.

Healthy Travels to You

The following government websites offer up-to-date health-related travel advice.

- **Australia:** www.dfat.gov.au/travel
- **Canada:** www.hc-sc.gc.ca
- **U.K.:** www.dh.gov.uk/PolicyAndGuidance/HealthAdviceForTravellers/fs/en
- **U.S.:** www.cdc.gov/travel

WHAT TO DO IF SOMEONE IN THE FAMILY GETS SICK AWAY FROM HOME

Consult a pharmacist for minor health matters—your hotel can direct you to the closest drugstore. Walgreen's has three locations with 24-hour pharmacies: 3201 Divisadero St. at Lombard St. in the Marina District (© **415/931-6415**); 498 Castro St. at 18th St. in Noe Valley (© **415/861-6276**); and 1189 Potrero Ave. at 24th St. (© **415/647-0368**). If your child has asthma or any medical condition that requires medication, and there's a chance you'll require extra inhalers, an EpiPen, or whatever, make sure you bring along a prescription from your pediatrician. If your child accidentally swallows something scary, call the State Poison Control hot line, available 24 hours a day, at © **800/876-4766.** Along with important medications, pack an emergency pair of glasses or contact lenses. I list **hospitals** and **emergency numbers** in the "Fast Facts" section of chapter 4.

If you suffer from a chronic illness, consult your doctor before your departure. Pack **prescription medications** in your carry-on luggage, and carry them in their original containers, with pharmacy labels—otherwise they won't make it through airport security. Visitors from outside the U.S. should carry generic names of prescription drugs. For U.S. travelers, most reliable health-care plans provide coverage if you get sick away from home. Foreign visitors may have to pay medical costs upfront and be reimbursed later. See "Medical Insurance," under "Travel Insurance," above.

STAYING SAFE

The general caveats about not walking alone at night, staying in well-lighted areas, and carrying a minimum of cash and jewels on your person are as true in San Francisco as in every major city. Although San Francisco isn't crime-ridden, it is not a 24-hour town like New York, for example, and you could be putting yourself at risk venturing out at 2am. However, since this is a family travel book, let's assume your real worries have to do with keeping your children safe while on vacation.

First, give everyone in your party the hotel's business card upon arrival, and, if you have a cellphone, write that number on the back of the card. Make sure these stay in pockets or backpacks—preferably a front pocket, which is also the safest place for wallets. Never keep valuables in backpacks, as they can be easily and quickly yanked away. Tell your kids that if they turn around and don't see you standing next to them, they shouldn't panic. They may simply have gotten disoriented in the crowd, or you may have turned out of their line of sight. When this happens, they should call out your name—not simply "Mom" or "Dad"—in a clear, loud voice. The last thing you want them to do is wander off trying to find you. If you'll be traveling with teenagers who may want some space, and who don't have their own cellphones, consider short-range walkie-talkies. You most often see these on ski slopes, but they are ideal for families that need to keep in touch.

Discuss with your kids what to do if they get lost: you don't want them walking the streets looking for your hotel. If they don't immediately spot a police officer, they might ask the nearest hotel concierge, store clerk, or restaurant hostess to help—by calling the police or your hotel, for example. Take your child's age and level of common sense into consideration when you think about what he or she could do in the unlikely case that he or she becomes lost. Explain whom to avoid (for example, anyone holding a sign, talking to himself or herself, or begging with dogs and cats as props) and whom to approach for help.

Teenagers, who may be used to some freedom at home, are another matter. If they aren't familiar with busy urban centers and if they haven't already developed some street smarts, I'd think twice before allowing them to wander around alone even during the daytime. There are places where you can give them some space—Metreon (p. 176), the Westfield San Francisco Centre (p. 212), and AT&T Park (p. 56), for example—but it's preferable that they hang out with a companion.

The streets of San Francisco, like most big cities, are filled with drivers who are frustrated and/or talking on their cellphones, so be careful crossing them. This is not the city in which to play chicken with cars. Use the crosswalks, wait for the lights, and check first to make sure some idiot isn't going to run the red light. Be especially careful with buses, particularly those making turns.

Children generally love riding on the streetcars and especially the cable cars. Inside the Muni/BART underground stations, keep yourself and your kids away from the edge of the platform. On cable cars, you are not allowed to hang body parts out the side, despite myriad photos showing people doing just that. It's an excellent way to get hurt the minute a truck or a bus passes by. Jumping on or off a moving cable car is equally dangerous.

Finally, we do have some dodgy neighborhoods you might consider avoiding. The Tenderloin (p. 67) isn't great, although it is home to a huge immigrant population that manages to live side by side with drug addicts, hookers, and vagrants. Evenings are particularly rough; daytime is okay. Parts of Van Ness Avenue, from Civic Center to Broadway Street, are grimy, and some medians are platforms for someone asking for money. Sixth and Seventh streets from Market Street east to Harrison Street are home to an assortment of folks that aren't making a go of it in mainstream society; this is an area to avoid any time day or night.

Like most of the world, San Francisco has long had its problems with residents who have drug and/or alcohol problems, who are mentally unstable, or who live on the edge for other reasons. If you are not panhandled at some point, at the very least your children will ask you what's going on with the crazy guy pushing a shopping cart down the street. You'll have to make your own choices about giving alms or not; but do be prepared for questions from your kids. Consider it a learning experience.

7 Specialized Travel Resources

FAMILY TRAVEL

My husband and I grew up moving from one country and city to another. Our wanderlust did not end when our children were born, and we have taken them with us to places near and far. Here are tips to consider when vacationing with kids:

- Family vacations are about spending time together and having fun. They should not be a marathon to cover as much territory as possible. Pick and choose what you're going to see and do so judiciously, keeping in mind that you won't see and do everything.
- Tired people, no matter their age, are difficult to deal with, so keep the pace slow, plan time to rest, and don't stay up too late at night.
- Hungry people can be worse than tired people, so start the day with a good breakfast, schedule time for lunch, and carry snacks with you.
- You may have arrived together, but you needn't travel in a pack. If it's possible to split up the kids among the adults to give everyone a break, do so—even if just for an hour.
- Be flexible and maintain a sense of humor. If three cable cars packed to the rafters have passed you by, perhaps the fates are telling you to walk. (See "Getting Around" in chapter 4 for more advice.)
- Plan something for everyone in your itinerary. If you want to analyze modern art at the museum, that's okay. Just reward kids for their patience by spending the afternoon rowing boats on Stow Lake or bowling at Yerba Buena Gardens.
- Ask your children what they would like to do during the trip. Give them options, make a calendar, and follow through on some of their suggestions. This doesn't mean they are in charge. It means they get to participate in a bit of decision-making.
- Give them a camera. Either buy an inexpensive digital camera for your kids, or let them use yours (carefully) once in a while. It's empowering and cheap—since you can just delete all the pictures with people's heads cut

off—and provides a new way for your kids to think about sightseeing.
- Have them keep a journal. Even before they could write, we gave our girls notebooks so they could draw pictures of things they saw on each trip. Now, on vacations, they enjoy spending the few minutes before dinner arrives writing about their day.

Recommended family travel websites include **Family Travel Forum** (www.familytravelforum.com), a comprehensive site that offers customized trip planning; **Family Travel Network** (www.familytravelnetwork.com), an award-winning site that offers travel features, deals, and tips; **Traveling Internationally with Your Kids** (www.travelwithyourkids.com), a comprehensive site offering sound advice for long-distance and international travel with children; and **Family Travel Files** (www.thefamilytravelfiles.com), which offers an online magazine and a directory of off-the-beaten-path tours and tour operators for families.

ADVICE FOR SINGLE PARENTS

Parents traveling without partners will appreciate San Francisco's low-key, friendly disposition. Chances are hotel staff, restaurant employees, and people on the street will be happy to assist you in a pinch. It's good to keep a relaxed attitude when traveling with kids, but it's especially important when you're the one corralling the offspring. Go slowly and don't try to do too much; savor the break from the routine and the opportunity to be in a new setting together.

Online, the **Single Parent Travel Network** (www.singleparenttravel.net) offers excellent advice, travel specials, a bulletin board, and a free electronic newsletter. The **Family Travel Forum** (www.familytravelforum.com) also hosts a single parent travel bulletin board for tips from fellow travelers.

ADVICE FOR GRANDPARENTS

Mention the fact that you're a senior citizen when you make your travel reservations. Check with your airline (especially America West, Continental, and American) to see if they offer senior discounts; many hotels also offer discounts for seniors. In most cities, people over the age of 60 qualify for reduced admission to theaters, museums, and other attractions, as well as discounted fares on public transportation.

One reliable agency that targets traveling grandparents is **Elderhostel** (© 877/426-8056; www.elderhostel.org), which arranges study programs for those aged 55 and over in the U.S. and in more than 80 countries around the world. Of particular interest are the "Intergenerational" programs. Most courses last 5 to 7 days in the U.S. (2–4 weeks abroad), and many include airfare, accommodations in university dormitories or modest inns, meals, and tuition.

Members of **AARP** (formerly known as the American Association of Retired Persons), 601 E St. NW, Washington, DC 20049 (© **888/687-2277;** www. aarp.org), get discounts on hotels, airfares, and car rentals. AARP offers members a wide range of benefits, including *AARP: The Magazine* and a monthly newsletter. Anyone over 50 can join.

The **U.S. National Park Service** offers a **Golden Age Passport** that gives seniors 62 years or older lifetime entrance to all properties administered by the National Park Service—national parks, monuments, historic sites, recreation areas, and national wildlife refuges—for a one-time processing fee of $10, which must be purchased in person at any NPS facility that charges an entrance fee. Besides free entry, a Golden Age Passport also offers a 50% discount on federal-use fees charged for such facilities as camping, swimming, parking, boat launching, and tours. For more information, go to www.nps.gov/fees_passes.htm or call © **888/467-2757.**

Recommended publications offering travel resources and discounts for seniors include: the quarterly magazine *Travel 50 & Beyond* (www.travel50andbeyond. com); *Travel Unlimited: Uncommon Adventures for the Mature Traveler* (Avalon); *101 Tips for Mature Travelers,* available from Grand Circle Travel (© 800/221-2610 or 617/350-7500; www.gct.com); and *Unbelievably Good Deals and Great Adventures That You Absolutely Can't Get Unless You're Over 50* (McGraw-Hill), by Joan Rattner Heilman.

TRAVELERS WITH DISABILITIES

Most disabilities shouldn't stop anyone from traveling in the U.S. There are more options and resources out there than ever before.

Most of San Francisco's major museums and tourist attractions have wheelchair ramps. Many hotels offer special accommodations and services for wheelchair users and other visitors with disabilities. Check with the San Francisco Convention and Visitors Bureau (p. 17) for the most up-to-date accessibility information.

The **Golden Access Passport** gives visually impaired or permanently disabled persons (regardless of age) free lifetime entrance to all properties administered by the National Park Service, the U.S. Fish and Wildlife Service, the U.S. Forest Service, the U.S. Army Corps of Engineers, the Bureau of Land Management, and the Tennessee Valley Authority. This may include national parks, monuments, historic sites, recreation areas, and national wildlife refuges. You may pick up a Golden Access Passport at any NPS entrance fee area by showing proof of medically determined disability and eligibility for benefits under federal law. Besides free entry, the

Golden Access Passport also offers a 50% discount on federal-use fees charged for such facilities as camping, swimming, parking, boat launching, and tours. For more information, go to www.nps.gov/fees_passes.htm or call © **888/467-2757.**

Many travel agencies offer customized tours and itineraries for travelers with disabilities. Among them are **Flying Wheels Travel** (© 507/451-5005; www.flyingwheelstravel.com); **Access-Able Travel Source** (© 303/232-2979; www.access-able.com); and **Accessible Journeys** (© 800/846-4537 or 610/521-0339; www.disabilitytravel.com). **Avis Rent a Car** has an "Avis Access" program that offers such services as a dedicated 24-hour toll-free number (© **888/879-4273**) for customers with special travel needs; special car features such as swivel seats, spinner knobs, and hand controls; and accessible bus service.

Organizations that offer assistance to disabled travelers include **MossRehab** (www.mossresourcenet.org); the **American Foundation for the Blind (AFB)** (© **800/232-5463;** www.afb.org); and **SATH (Society for Accessible Travel & Hospitality)** (© 212/447-7284; www.sath.org). **AirAmbulanceCard.com** is now partnered with SATH and allows you to preselect top-notch hospitals in case of an emergency.

The community website **iCan** (www.icanonline.net/channels/travel) has destination guides and several regular columns on accessible travel. Also check out the quarterly magazine *Emerging Horizons* (www.emerginghorizons.com.); and *Open World* magazine, published by SATH.

FOR GAY & LESBIAN PARENTS

San Francisco is well known as a bastion of gay and lesbian households, many of which include kids. If you hope to connect with any, start by contacting **Our Family Coalition** (© 415/981-1960; www.ourfamily.org), a grass-roots organization for families with gay/lesbian/bisexual/transgender members. Check their website for a calendar of social and educational events. You might also want to visit the **San Francisco Lesbian, Gay, Bisexual, and Transgender Community Center** at 1800 Market St., San Francisco, CA 94102 (© **415/865-5555**). It's easily reached on the F-Market and J-Church streetcars. Other sites to check out include www.familypride.org, www.gayparentingpage.com, and www.rfamilyvacations.com.

The **International Gay and Lesbian Travel Association (IGLTA)** (© **800/448-8550** or 954/776-2626; www.travel iglta.com) is the trade association for the gay and lesbian travel industry, and offers an online directory of gay- and lesbian-friendly travel businesses.

Many agencies offer tours and travel itineraries specifically for gay and lesbian travelers. Among them are **Above and Beyond Tours** (© 800/397-2681; www.abovebeyondtours.com); **Now, Voyager** (© 800/255-6951; www.nowvoyager.com); and Olivia **Cruises & Resorts** (© 800/631-6277; www.olivia.com).

Gay.com Travel (© 800/929-2268 or 415/644-8044; www.gay.com/travel or www.outandabout.com) is an excellent online successor to the popular *Out & About* print magazine. It provides regularly updated information about gay-owned, gay-oriented, and gay-friendly lodging, dining, sightseeing, nightlife, and shopping establishments in every important destination worldwide.

The following travel guides are available at many bookstores, or you can order them from any online bookseller: *Spartacus International Gay Guide* (Bruno Gmünder Verlag; www.spartacusworld.com/gayguide) and *Odysseus: The International Gay Travel Planner* (Odysseus Enterprises Ltd.); and the *Damron* guides (www.damron.com), with separate, annual books for gay men and lesbians.

TRAVELING WITH PETS

Fortunately, many San Francisco hotels accept pets, although in some cases these are limited to one cat or dog (and in, at least a few hotels, just dogs). With beautiful open spaces like Crissy Field and Golden Gate Park, you'll find plenty of places to take Fido. Just beware of San Francisco's leash laws: at some parks, you may notice all the dogs off-leash. Depending where you are, that may be technically illegal and the moment you take off your dog's leash, an irate parent may let you know just where to put that leash.

8 Planning Your Trip Online

SURFING FOR AIRFARE

The most popular online travel agencies are **Travelocity** (**www.travelocity.com**, www.travelocity.ca, or www.travelocity.co.uk), **Expedia** (**www.expedia.com**, www.expedia.ca, or www.expedia.co.uk), and **Orbitz** (www.orbitz.com).

In addition, most airlines now offer online-only fares that even their phone agents know nothing about. The "Getting There" section below, lists websites of airlines that fly to and from the Bay Area.

Other helpful websites for booking airline tickets online include:

- www.biddingfortravel.com
- www.cheapflights.com
- www.hotwire.com
- www.kayak.com
- www.lastminutetravel.com
- www.opodo.co.uk
- www.priceline.com
- www.sidestep.com
- www.site59.com
- www.smartertravel.com

SURFING FOR HOTELS

In addition to **Travelocity, Expedia,** and **Orbitz** (see above), the following websites will help you with booking hotel rooms online:

- www.hotels.com
- www.quickbook.com
- www.travelaxe.net
- www.travelweb.com
- www.tripadvisor.com

Frommers.com: The Complete Travel Resource

For an excellent travel-planning resource, we highly recommend **Frommers.com** (www.frommers.com), voted Best Travel Site by *PC Magazine*. We're a little biased, of course, but we guarantee that you'll find the travel tips, reviews, monthly vacation giveaways, bookstore, and online-booking capabilities to be thoroughly indispensable. Special features include our popular **Destinations** section, where you can access expert travel tips, hotel and dining recommendations, and advice on the sights to see in more than 3,500 destinations around the globe; the **Frommers.com Newsletter,** with the latest deals, travel trends, and money-saving secrets; and our **Travel Talk** area featuring **Message Boards,** where Frommer's readers post queries and share advice, and where our authors sometimes show up to answer questions. Once you finish your research, the **Book a Trip** area can lead you to Frommer's preferred online partners' websites, where you can book your vacation at affordable prices.

It's a good idea to **get a confirmation number** and **make a printout** of any online booking transaction.

SURFING FOR RENTAL CARS

For booking rental cars online, the best deals are usually found at rental-car company websites, although all the major online travel agencies also offer rental-car reservations services. For most travelers the difference between Hertz, Avis, and Budget is negligible.

TRAVEL BLOGS & TRAVELOGUES

To read a few blogs about San Francisco, try sf.metblogs.com or the *San Francisco Chronicle* blogs on its website at www.sfgate.com/community/blogs. More general travel blogs include:

- www.gridskipper.com
- www.salon.com/wanderlust
- www.travelblog.com
- www.travelblog.org
- www.worldhum.com
- www.writtenroad.com

9 The 21st-Century Traveler

INTERNET ACCESS AWAY FROM HOME
WITHOUT YOUR OWN COMPUTER

To find cybercafes in your destination check **www.cybercaptive.com** and **www.cybercafe.com**. San Francisco doesn't have many cybercafes, but most of its **public libraries** offer free Internet access. In addition, **FedEx Kinko's** and similar businesses offer Internet access for a fee. Avoid **hotel business centers** and **Internet kiosks,** such as in most major airports, unless you're willing to pay exorbitant rates.

WITH YOUR OWN COMPUTER

More and more hotels, cafes, and retailers are signing on as Wi-Fi (wireless fidelity) "hotspots." Being the high-tech hub that it is, just a stone's throw from Silicon Valley, San Francisco has plenty of hotspots and an increasing number of hotels are offering Wi-Fi, often for free. Mac owners have their own networking technology, Apple AirPort. **T-Mobile Hotspot** (www.t-mobile.com/hotspot) serves up wireless connections at more than 1,000 Starbucks coffee shops nationwide. **Boingo** (www.boingo.com) and **Wayport** (www.wayport.com) have set up networks in airports and high-class hotel lobbies. IPass providers (see below) give you access to a few hundred wireless hotel lobby setups. To locate other **free wireless hotspots** in cities around the world, go to **www.personaltelco.net/index.cgi/WirelessCommunities**.

For dial-up access, most business-class hotels in the U.S. offer dataports for laptop modems, and a few thousand hotels in the U.S. and Europe now offer free high-speed Internet access. In addition, major Internet Service Providers (ISPs) have **local access numbers** around the world, allowing you to go online by placing a local call. The **iPass** network also has dial-up numbers around the world. You'll have to sign up with an iPass provider, who will then tell you how to set up your computer for your destination(s). For a list of iPass providers, go to **www.ipass.com** and click on "Individuals Buy Now." One solid provider is **i2roam** (www.i2roam.com; ✆ **866/811-6209** or 920/235-0475).

Wherever you go, bring a **connection kit** of the right power and phone adapters, a spare phone cord, and a spare Ethernet network cable—or find out whether your hotel supplies them to guests. For information on electrical currency conversions, see "Electricity," in the "Fast Facts" section of chapter 4.

Online Traveler's Toolbox

Veteran travelers usually carry some essential items to make their trips easier. Following is a selection of handy online tools to bookmark and use.

- **Restaurant reviews** (sanfrancisco.citysearch.com and www.yelp.com)
- **Events tickets** (www.theatrebayarea.org/tix, www.ticketweb.com, and www.cityboxoffice.com)
- **San Francisco Chronicle** (www.sfgate.com)
- **Airplane food** (www.airlinemeals.net)
- **Airplane seating** (www.seatguru.com and www.airlinequality.com)
- **Maps** (www.mapquest.com)
- **Subway Navigator** (www.subwaynavigator.com)
- **Time and date** (www.timeanddate.com)
- **Universal currency converter** (www.xe.com/ucc)
- **Visa ATM locator** (www.visa.com), **MasterCard ATM locator** (www.mastercard.com)
- **Weather** (www.intellicast.com, www.sfgate.com/weather, and www.weather.com)

CELLPHONE USE IN THE U.S.

Just because your cellphone works at home doesn't mean it'll work everywhere in the U.S. (thanks to our nation's fragmented cellphone system). It's a good bet that your phone will work in major cities, but take a look at your wireless company's coverage map on its website before heading out; T-Mobile, Sprint, and Nextel are particularly weak in rural areas. If you need to stay in touch at a destination where you know your phone won't work, **rent** a phone that does from **InTouch USA** (© **800/872-7626;** www.intouchglobal.com) or a rental car location, but beware that you'll pay $1 a minute or more for airtime.

If you're venturing deep into national parks, you may want to consider renting a **satellite phone ("satphones").** It's different from a cellphone in that it connects to satellites rather than ground-based towers. Unfortunately, you'll pay at least $2 per minute to use the phone, and it only works where you can see the horizon (i.e., usually not indoors). In North America, you can rent Iridium satellite phones from **RoadPost** (www.roadpost.com; © **888/290-1606** or 905/272-5665). InTouch USA (see above) offers a wider range of satphones but at higher rates.

If you're not from the U.S., you'll be appalled at the poor reach of our **GSM (Global System for Mobiles) wireless network,** which is used by much of the rest of the world. Your phone will probably work in most major U.S. cities; it definitely won't work in many rural areas. (To see where GSM phones work in the U.S., check out www.t-mobile.com/coverage/national_popup.asp.) And you may or may not be able to send SMS (text messaging) home.

In downtown San Francisco, **Triptel Mobile Rental Phones,** 1525 Van Ness Ave., between California and Pine streets (© **415/474-3330;** www.triptel.com), rents cellphones at $3 per day, or $15 per week. Airtime rates are 95¢ per minute for domestic calls, with an additional $1.25 per minute for international calls. Triptel also sells SIM cards for travelers bringing their own phones.

10 Getting There

BY PLANE

The two major airports closest to San Francisco are **San Francisco International (SFO),** which is 14 miles south of downtown, and **Oakland International Airport (OAK),** across the Bay Bridge off Interstate 880. SFO is closer and more airlines fly into this major hub. Oakland is smaller and easier to navigate, but fares for cabs and shuttle buses into the city are about 50% higher.

It's worth checking your options flying into either airport, as you'll sometimes find a cheaper or more convenient flight arriving in Oakland. The Oakland airport also often enjoys better weather than San Francisco, where flights can be delayed due to foggy conditions or be relegated to circling the skies while waiting for an available runway. The great news at SFO is the beautiful new International Terminal and the BART extension.

Airlines that fly into the Bay Area include **Air Canada** (© 888/247-2262; www.aircanada.ca), **Alaska** (© 800/252-7522; www.alaskaair.com), **American** (© 800/433-7300; www.aa.com), **British Airways** (© 800/247-9297; www.ba.com), **Continental** (© 800/525-0280; www.continental.com), **Delta** (© 800/221-1212; www.delta.com), **Jet-Blue** (© 800/538-2583; www.jetblue.com), **Northwest** (© 800/225-2525; www.nwa.com), **Southwest** (© 800/435-9792; www.southwest.com), **United** (© 800/241-6522; www.ual.com), and **US Airways** (© 800/428-4322; www.usairways.com).

IMMIGRATION & CUSTOMS CLEARANCE   Foreign visitors arriving by air, no matter what the port of entry, should cultivate patience and resignation before setting foot on U.S. soil. Clearing immigration control can take as long as 2 hours. This is especially true in the aftermath of the September 11, 2001, terrorist attacks, when U.S. airports considerably beefed up security clearances. People traveling by air from Canada, Bermuda, and certain Caribbean countries can sometimes clear Customs and Immigration at the point of departure, which is much faster.

GETTING INTO TOWN FROM THE AIRPORT
San Francisco International Airport (SFO)

SFO (www.flysfo.com) consists of four main terminals: North (Terminal 3), South (Terminal 1), Central (Terminal 2), and International. The baggage level of each terminal also houses an information booth. Bank of America operates a branch on the mezzanine level of the

---

Tips Kids with Colds

It's even more difficult for kids to make their ears pop during takeoff and landing than it is for adults. The eustachian tube is especially narrow in children, and the passage is even tighter when mucous membranes are swollen. This can make ascent and descent especially painful—even dangerous—for a child with congested sinuses. If your little one is suffering from a cold or the flu, it's best to keep him grounded until he recuperates, if that's an option. If you simply must travel with your child as scheduled, give him an oral child's decongestant an hour before ascent and descent or administer a spray decongestant before and during takeoff and landing.

> **Tips Prepare to Be Fingerprinted**
>
> As of January 2004, many international visitors traveling on visas to the United States will be photographed and fingerprinted at Customs in a new program created by the Department of Homeland Security called **US-VISIT**. Non-U.S. citizens arriving at airports and on cruise ships must undergo an instant background check as part of the government's efforts to deter terrorism by verifying the identity of incoming and outgoing visitors. Exempt from the extra scrutiny are visitors entering by land or those (mostly in Europe; see p. 17) that don't require a visa for short-term visits. For more information, go to the Homeland Security website at **www.dhs.gov**.

North terminal, and you can locate ATMs on the upper level of all terminals. The number for **general information** is © **650/821-8211;** for **transit information** call © **650/817-1717.** The traveler's information desk in each terminal can also give you information on how to get where you're going.

To access the Rental Car Center from the Airport terminals, take the AirTrain Blue Line, which operates daily 24 hours a day. AirTrain stations are located in all terminals, parking garages, the Rental Car Center, and SFO's BART station. If you need a car seat (required for children who weigh less than 60 lb.), inquire when you make your rental reservations. Once you have loaded up the vehicle, follow the airport signs to Highway 101 North to drive into San Francisco. Stay toward the left so that you don't end up on Interstate 280. If your destination is Union Square, Nob Hill, or SoMa, exit at 4th Street. Traffic is manageable until rush hour, from 3 to 7pm.

If you aren't driving, you can reach your destination by taxi, shuttle, and BART. **Taxis** pick up passengers at the center island outside the baggage claim level of the airport. The 14-mile drive to Union Square takes 20 to 30 minutes depending on the time of day and should cost around $35 plus tip.

Shuttle vans offer door-to-door service from the airport, but the driver may make up to three stops before reaching your hotel. Shuttles pick up passengers from the upper-level center islands; a uniformed guide will direct you to the appropriate van. Be prepared to wait from 10 to 20 minutes for the one heading in your direction. Look for exact shuttle fares posted throughout the airport—most are now charging around $13 per person, which may make a cab a better deal. **SuperShuttle** (© **800/258-3826;** www.supershuttle.com) is my favorite of the services and you don't need advance reservations from the airport. (You do need reservations for a shuttle *to* the airport, however.)

After years of wrangling and millions of dollars in construction, the **Bay Area Rapid Transit** (BART; © **510/464-6000;** www.bart.gov) extension to SFO is now operational. The airport's BART station is located in the International Terminal. The AirTrain connects passengers to all terminals, the BART rail station, and the Rental Car Center. The BART train, which departs from the international terminal, takes about 30 minutes to reach downtown San Francisco and costs $4.95, making it by far the most inexpensive way to reach the city. I'm a huge fan of mass transit and would encourage you to use BART, but I have one caveat: If you're traveling with lots of luggage and not enough hands to manage it, take a cab. Otherwise, you may end up at the

Powell Street BART station facing a 10-minute walk to your hotel. (San Francisco doesn't have huge numbers of taxis on its streets like London or New York, so don't count on catching a cab.) If you're also dealing with tired children, the journey from BART to your lodgings isn't going to make a wonderful start to the vacation.

Oakland International Airport (OAK)

Oakland International (✆ **510/563-3300;** www.flyoakland.com) consists of two terminals, one of which (Terminal 2) is pretty much devoted to Southwest Airlines. Both terminals have ATMs and information booths. All the major **rental car companies** have counters inside the terminals as well. If you are driving into San Francisco, exit the airport on Hegenberger Road. Follow it north to Interstate 880 toward San Francisco. From there, follow the signs to Interstate 80 to San Francisco. When you reach the Bay Bridge, you'll stop at a toll booth and pay $3 to cross. On the other side, take the 5th Street exit to get to Union Square.

All ground transportation at the airport is on one level. **Bayporter Express** (✆ **877/467-1800;** www.bayporter.com) is the best choice for a shuttle. It picks up passengers from Terminal 1 at the center island and from Terminal 2 around the corner from baggage claim. The fare to San Francisco is $26 for one person, $38 for two in the same party, and $7 for kids under 12. You need to make reservations for the 45- to 90-minute drive. Cabs will run $40 or more depending on traffic and take 30 to 40 minutes.

BART is another option. You can catch the **AirBART shuttle** (✆ **510/465-2278**), which runs every 15 minutes in front of either terminal. The fare is $2 (adult) and 50¢ (children) for the 15-minute ride to the Oakland Coliseum BART station. From there, you'll transfer to a BART train into San Francisco; the

---

Tips **Getting Through the Airport**

- Arrive at the airport 1 hour before a domestic flight and 2 hours before an international flight; if you show up late, tell an airline employee and he or she will probably whisk you to the front of the line.
- Beat the ticket-counter lines by using airport electronic kiosks or even online check-in from your home computers, from where you can print out boarding passes in advance. Curbside check-in is also a good way to avoid lines.
- Bring a current, government-issued photo ID such as a driver's license or passport. Children under 18 do not need government-issued photo IDs for flights within the U.S., but they do for international flights to most countries.
- Speed up security by removing your jacket and shoes before you're screened. In addition, remove metal objects such as big belt buckles. If you've got metallic body parts, a note from your doctor can prevent a long chat with the security screeners.
- Use a TSA-approved lock for your checked luggage. Look for Travel Sentry certified locks at luggage or travel shops and Brookstone stores (or online at **www.brookstone.com**).

fare is $3.15. Purchase your tickets from well-marked kiosks inside the airport or at the BART station. If you're staying around Union Street, you'll probably want to get off at the Powell Street stop.

FLYING FOR LESS: TIPS FOR GETTING THE BEST AIRFARE

- Passengers who can book their ticket either **long in advance or at the last minute,** or who **fly midweek** or **at less-trafficked hours** may pay a fraction of the full fare. If your schedule is flexible, say so, and ask if you can secure a cheaper fare by changing your flight plans.

- Search **the Internet** for cheap fares (see "Planning Your Trip Online," earlier in this chapter).

- Keep an eye on local newspapers for **promotional specials** or **fare wars,** when airlines lower prices on their most popular routes. You rarely see fare wars offered for peak travel times, but if you can travel in the off-months, you may snag a bargain.

- Try to book a ticket **in its country of origin.** If you're planning a one-way flight from Johannesburg to New York, a South Africa–based travel agent will probably have the lowest fares. For foreign travelers on multi-leg trips, book in the country of the first leg; for example, book New York–Chicago–Montréal–New York in the U.S.

- **Consolidators,** also known as bucket shops, are great sources for international tickets, although they usually can't beat Internet fares within North America. Start by looking in Sunday newspaper travel sections; U.S. travelers should focus on the *New York Times, Los Angeles Times,* and *Miami Herald.* U.K. travelers should search in the *Independent, The Guardian, or The Observer.* **Beware:** Bucket shop tickets are usually nonrefundable or

rigged with stiff cancellation penalties, often as high as 50% to 75% of the ticket price, and some put you on charter airlines, which may leave at inconvenient times and experience delays. Several reliable consolidators are worldwide and available online. **STA Travel** has been the world's lead consolidator for students since purchasing Council Travel, but their fares are competitive for travelers of all ages. **Flights.com** (© 800/TRAV-800; www.flights.com) has excellent fares worldwide, particularly to Europe. They also have "local" websites in 12 countries. **FlyCheap** (© 800/FLY-CHEAP; www.1800fly cheap.com) has especially good fares to sunny destinations. **Air Tickets Direct** (© 800/778-3447; www.air ticketsdirect.com) is based in Montreal and leverages the currently weaker Canadian dollar for low fares; they also book trips to places that U.S. travel agents won't touch, such as Cuba.

- Join **frequent-flier clubs.** Frequent-flier membership doesn't cost a cent, but it does entitle you to better seats, faster response to phone inquiries, and prompter service if your luggage is stolen or your flight is canceled or delayed, or if you want to change your seat. And you don't have to fly to earn points; **frequent-flier credit cards** can earn you thousands of miles for doing your everyday shopping. With more than 70 mileage awards programs on the market, consumers have never had more options. Investigate the program details before you sink points into any one. Consider which airlines have hubs in the airport nearest you, and, of those carriers, which have the most advantageous alliances, given your most common routes. To play the frequent-flier game to best advantage,

Tips **Don't Stow It—Ship It**

Though pricey, it's sometimes worthwhile to travel luggage-free. Specialists in door-to-door luggage delivery include **Virtual Bellhop** (www.virtualbellhop. com), **SkyCap International** (wwww.skycapinternational.com), **Luggage Express** (www.usxpluggageexpress.com), and **Sports Express** (www.sports express.com).

consult Randy Petersen's **Inside Flyer** (**www.insideflyer.com**). Petersen and friends review all programs in detail and post regular updates on changes in policies and trends.

LONG-HAUL FLIGHTS: HOW TO STAY COMFORTABLE

• Your choice of airline and airplane will definitely affect your leg room. Find more details about U.S. airlines at **www.seatguru.com**. For international airlines, the research firm Skytrax has posted a list of average seat pitches at **www.airlinequality.com**.

• Emergency exit seats and bulkhead seats typically have the most legroom. Emergency exit seats are usually left unassigned until the day of a flight, (to ensure that someone able-bodied fills the seats); it's worth getting to the ticket counter early to snag one of these spots for a long flight. Many passengers find that bulkhead seating (the row facing the wall at the front of the cabin) offers more legroom, but keep in mind that bulkheads are where airlines often put baby bassinets, so you may be sitting next to an infant.

• To have two seats for yourself in a three-seat row, try for an aisle seat in a center section toward the back of coach. If you're traveling with a companion, book an aisle and a window seat. Middle seats are usually booked last, so chances are good you'll end up with three seats to yourselves. And in the event that a third passenger is

assigned the middle seat, he or she will probably be more than happy to trade for a window or an aisle.

• Ask about entertainment options. Many airlines offer seatback video systems where you get to choose your movies or play video games—but only on some of their planes. (Boeing 777s are your best bet.)

• To sleep, avoid the last row of any section or the row in front of an emergency exit, as these seats are the least likely to recline. Avoid seats near highly trafficked toilet areas. Avoid seats in the back of many jets—these can be narrower than those in the rest of coach. You also may want to reserve a window seat so you can rest your head and avoid being bumped in the aisle.

• Get up, walk around, and stretch every 60 to 90 minutes to keep your blood flowing. This helps you avoid **deep vein thrombosis**, or "economy-class syndrome." See the box "Avoiding 'Economy Class Syndrome,'" under "Health & Safety," p. 28.

• Drink water before, during, and after your flight to combat the lack of humidity in airplane cabins. Avoid alcohol, which will dehydrate you.

FLYING WITH KIDS

If you plan carefully, you can make it fun to fly with your kids.

• You'll save yourself a good bit of aggravation by **reserving a seat in the bulkhead row.** You'll have more

Tips Coping with Jet Lag

Jetlag is a pitfall of traveling across time zones. If you're flying north–south and you feel sluggish when you touch down, your symptoms will be the result of dehydration and the general stress of air travel. When you travel east–west or vice-versa, however, your body becomes thoroughly confused about what time it is, and everything from your digestive system to your brain is knocked for a loop. While very young children may have a hard time adjusting to time changes, it often seems that older kids have more flexible body clocks than their parents.

Traveling east, say from Hawaii to Atlanta, is more difficult on your internal clock than traveling west, say from Boston to San Francisco, because most peoples' bodies are more inclined to stay up late than fall asleep early.

Here are some tips for combating jet lag:

- **Reset your watch** to your destination time before you board the plane.
- **Drink lots of water** before, during, and after your flight. Avoid alcohol.
- **Exercise and sleep well** for a few days before your trip.
- If you have trouble sleeping on planes, **fly eastward on morning flights**.
- **Daylight** is the key to resetting your body clock. At the website for **Outside In** (www.bodyclock.com), you can get a customized plan of when to seek and avoid light.

legroom, your children will be able to spread out and play on the floor underfoot, and the airline might provide bassinets (ask in advance). You're also more likely to find sympathetic company in the bulkhead area, as other families with children tend to be seated there. The only drawback is that in the bulkhead row you can't always lift the armrest for little ones to rest their head on your lap.

- Be sure to **pack items for your kids in your carry-on luggage,** such as toys, books, pacifiers, and chewing gum, to help them relieve ear pressure buildup during ascent and descent.
- **Have a long talk with your children** before you depart for your trip. If they've never flown before, explain to them what to expect. If they're old enough, you may even want to describe how flight works and how air travel is even safer than riding in a

car. Explain to your kids the importance of good behavior in the air—how their own safety can depend upon their being quiet and staying in their seats during the trip.

- **Pay extra careful attention to the safety instructions** before takeoff. Consult the safety chart behind the seat in front of you and show it to your children. Be sure you know how to operate the oxygen masks, as you will be expected to secure yours first and then help your children with theirs. Be especially mindful of the location of emergency exits. Before takeoff, plot out an evacuation strategy for you and your children.
- Ask the flight attendant **if the plane has any special safety equipment for children.** Make a member of the crew aware of any medical problems your children have that could manifest during flight.

- **Be sure you've slept sufficiently** for your trip. If you fall asleep in the air and your child manages to break away, there are all sorts of sharp objects that could cause injury. Especially during mealtimes, it's dangerous for a child to be crawling or walking around the cabin unaccompanied by an adult.

- **Be sure your child's seatbelt remains fastened properly** and try to reserve the seat closest to the aisle for yourself. This will make it harder for your children to wander off—in case, for instance, you're taking the redeye or a long flight and you do happen to nod off. You will also protect your child from jostling passersby and falling objects—in the rare but entirely possible instance that an overhead bin pops open.

  In the event of an accident, unrestrained children often don't make it—even when the parent does. Experience has shown that it's impossible for a parent to hold onto a child in the event of a crash, and children often die of impact injuries.

  For the same reason, sudden turbulence is also a danger to a child who is not buckled into his own seat belt or seat restraint. According to *Consumer Reports Travel Letter,* the most common flying injuries result when unanticipated turbulence strikes and hurtles passengers from their seats.

- **Try to sit near the lavatory,** though not so close that your children are jostled by the crowds that tend to gather there. Consolidate trips there as much as possible.

- Try to **accompany children to the lavatory.** They can be easily bumped and possibly injured as they make their way down tight aisles. It's especially dangerous for children to wander while flight attendants are blocking passage with their service carts. On crowded flights, the flight crew may need as much as an hour to serve dinner. It's wise to encourage your kids to use the rest room as you see the attendants preparing to serve.

- Be sure to **bring clean, self-containing compact toys.** Leave electronic games at home. They can interfere with the aircraft navigational system, and their noisiness, however lulling to children's ears, will surely not win the favor of your adult neighbors. Magnetic checker sets, on the other hand, are a perfect distraction, and small coloring books and crayons also work well, as do card games like Go Fish.

- Some airlines **serve children's meals first.** When you board, ask a flight attendant if this is possible, especially if your children are very young or seated toward the back of the plane. After all, if your kids have a happy flight experience, everyone else in the cabin is more likely to as well.

- You'll certainly be grateful to yourself for packing **tidy snacks** like rolled dried fruit, which are much less sticky and wet, and more compact and packable, than actual fruit. Healthy granola bars are also a good alternative to crumbly cookies. Ginger snaps, crisp and not as crumbly as softer cookies, will also help curb mild cases of motion sickness. And don't forget to stash a few resealable plastic bags in your purse. They'll prove invaluable for storing everything from half-eaten crackers and fruit to checker pieces and matchbox cars.

CHILD SEATS: THEY'RE A MUST

According to *Consumer Reports Travel Letter,* the National Transportation Safety

Board says that, since 1991, the deaths of and injury of some children could have been prevented had the children been sitting in restraint systems during their flights. Even in the event of moderate turbulence, children sitting on a parent's lap can be thrust forward and injured. When you consider that a commercial aircraft hits a significant amount of turbulence at least once a day on average, you'd do well to think about investing a few hundred dollars for a safety seat.

The FAA recommends that children under 20 pounds ride in a rear-facing child-restraint system, and says children that weigh 20 to 40 pounds should sit in a forward-facing child-restraint system. Children over 40 pounds should sit in a regular seat and wear a seat belt.

All child seats manufactured after 1985 are certified for airline use, but make sure your chair will fit in an airline seat—it must be less than 16 inches wide. You may not use booster seats or seatless vests or harness systems. Safety seats must be placed in window seats—except in exit rows, where they are prohibited, so as not to block the passage of other travelers in the case of an emergency.

GETTING TO SAN FRANCISCO BY CAR

You can get to San Francisco along three major highways. Interstate 5 runs through the center of the state and intersects with Interstate 580, which leads to Interstate 80 to the Bay Bridge. The drive from Los Angeles to San Francisco on I-5 is about 6 hours and there aren't many places to stop for food, so plan accordingly. Highway 101 is the other major roadway from Southern California and it's the route to use for reaching Marin County, Napa, and Sonoma, and other points north. The drive from Los Angeles to San Francisco on 101 takes 7 hours if you don't stop along the way. If you are taking a leisurely drive through California, Highway 1,

which runs along the coast, is the most scenic route and takes you by Santa Cruz and Monterey, both fun cities for kids. The trip takes at least 8 hours.

Approach the city with patience if you have decided to motor here. The freeways seem to become more crowded every day and afternoon rush hour on the Bay Bridge is a misnomer: no one rushes anywhere. Traffic on the Golden Gate Bridge on the weekends is also pretty dreadful. Make sure the kids have plenty of things to do in the car—portable cassette or CD players with books on tape and music are nearly as important as a spare tire.

Drivers arriving from the east will cross the Bay Bridge ($3 toll) and head toward downtown on 5th Street or toward North Beach and Fisherman's Wharf on Fremont Street. Cars coming from the south on Highway 101 will see the city skyline on their left a few miles past Monster Park (the former Candlestick Park). Downtown exits here are either 7th or 4th streets. If you're driving from the coast heading south, you'll enter San Francisco by the Golden Gate Bridge. Once you pass the tollbooth ($5 toll unless three or more of you drive through on a weekday between 4 and 6pm; at that time it's free for carpoolers), exit along the bay to Van Ness Avenue.

GETTING TO SAN FRANCISCO BY TRAIN

Amtrak (© 800/872-7245 or 800/USA-RAIL; www.amtrak.com) doesn't stop in San Francisco proper but lands in Emeryville or Oakland (depending on the point of origin), both in the East Bay. From Emeryville, an Amtrak bus takes passengers into downtown San Francisco, stopping at the Ferry Building, Fisherman's Wharf, Union Square, and the Caltrain station. From Oakland, the Amtrak bus takes passengers to the Financial District.

11 Packages for the Independent Traveler

Package tours are simply a way to buy the airfare, accommodations, and other elements of your trip (such as car rentals, airport transfers, and sometimes even activities) at the same time and often at discounted prices.

One good source of package deals is the airlines themselves. Most major airlines offer air/land packages, including **American Airlines Vacations** (© 800/321-2121; www.aavacations.com), **Delta Vacations** (© 800/221-6666; www.delta vacations.com), **Continental Airlines Vacations** (© 800/301-3800; www.co

vacations.com), and **United Vacations** (© 888/854-3899; www.unitedvacations. com). Several big **online travel agencies**—Expedia, Travelocity, Orbitz, Site59, and Lastminute.com—also do a brisk business in packages.

Travel packages are also listed in the travel section of your local Sunday newspaper. Or check ads in the national travel magazines such as *Arthur Frommer's Budget Travel Magazine, Travel & Leisure, National Geographic Traveler*, and *Condé Nast Traveler*.

12 Recommended Books, Films & Music

As one of the most beautiful places on the planet, San Francisco has been a favorite of movie studios since the birth of film. In fact, the first public motion picture was presented in San Francisco—silhouettes of a horse, a dog, and a human gymnast were shown to viewers using a primitive projector made from a box with light, a lens, and a reflector. The following list of films and books will pique the interest of the most recalcitrant traveler in

the jewel of the left coast, although you probably won't find much resistance to begin with for this trip.

For younger children, rent the 1998 version of *The Parent Trap*. This remake, no longer starring Hayley Mills, darn it, has a fabulous scene at the famous Fairmont Hotel atop Nob Hill. Or screen Disney's modern Cinderella story, *The Princess Diaries*. Its heroine, Mia, an awkward young girl who lives with her

---

(Tips Ask Before You Go

Before you invest in a package deal or an escorted tour:

- Always ask about the **cancellation policy.** Can you get your money back? Is there a deposit required?
- Ask about the **accommodations choices and prices** for each. Then look up the hotels' reviews in a Frommer's guide and check their rates online for your specific dates of travel. Also find out what types of rooms are offered.
- Request a complete **schedule** (escorted tours only).
- Ask about the **size** and demographics of the group (escorted tours only).
- Discuss what is included in the **price** (transportation, meals, tips, airport transfers, etc.) (escorted tours only).
- Finally, look for **hidden expenses.** Ask whether airport departure fees and taxes, for example, are included in the total cost—they rarely are.

widowed mom, discovers that she is an actual princess when her enchanting grandmother comes to visit. Another classic is *Mrs. Doubtfire* starring the city's own Robin Williams, who passes himself off as a British nanny in order to spend time with his children after separating from their mother, played by Sally Field. The family lives on Steiner Street and there are several great shots of the city in the film. For older kids, there is an endless supply of great material, from *Star Trek IV: The Voyage Home,* where the Enterprise and its crew set down in San Francisco to seek "nuclear wessels" across San Francisco Bay to *X-Men III: The Last Stand,* which includes a scene featuring Yerba Buena Gardens and Metreon. Reese Witherspoon's apartment in *Just Like Heaven* had San Francisco views, and Jennifer Lopez plays a San Francisco local in *The Wedding Planner.*

The zany Barbra Streisand and Ryan O'Neill screwball comedy *What's Up, Doc?* takes viewers down Lombard Street, through the Chinese New Year Parade, and down the Alta Plaza steps in Pacific Heights to the Bay. Another must-see film is *Foul Play* with Chevy Chase and Goldie Hawn racing frantically up and down just about every hill in the city in a quest to save the pope from being murdered at the Opera House. And who can resist the Dirty Harry movies, starring Clint Eastwood as the hard-boiled detective? Alfred Hitchcock also loved San Francisco and set three of his films here, including *Vertigo.*

Books are also useful to raise awareness of the city. For younger readers there are some great picture and storybooks available about San Francisco. Herb Caen, the city's famous columnist until his death in 1997, brought together some of its most famous characteristics—fog, cable cars, and Chinese New Year—in an enchanting

tale, *The Cable Car and the Dragon* (Chronicle Books, 1986). *Humphrey, the Lost Whale: A True Story* (Heian, 1986), by Wendy Tokuda and Richard Hall, is a beautiful book available in English and Japanese. It tells the tale of a group of local people who band together to save a humpback whale that swims into San Francisco Bay by mistake. *The City by the Bay: A Magical Journey Around San Francisco* (Chronicle Books, 1993), by Tricia Brown and the Junior League of San Francisco, is a wonderful picture book that turns famous neighborhoods and landmarks into whimsical illustrations. This is perfect for introducing kids 4 to 8 years old to the culture and sights of the city. Another terrific book is a reprint of a 1962 classic by Miroslav Sasek, *This is San Francisco* (Universe Publishing, 2003). Even older kids will love the drawings of fishtailed Cadillacs and drive-in restaurants in this detail-rich picture book.

Older children might enjoy a travel guide geared to their age group. *Kidding Around San Francisco* (Avalon Travel Publishing, 1996), by Bobi Martin, offers tips on the neighborhoods, historical facts, and provides readers with a great resource for their trip. Included are activities and trivia to keep kids busy while in the city and a scrapbook at the back encourages them to create memories of their visit. A novel set in the city can also act as a catalyst to interest older children. In *Peppermints in the Parlor* (Atheneum, 1980), by Barbara Brooks Wallace, recently orphaned Emily Luccock finds herself embroiled in a murder mystery in Golden Gate Park when she moves to San Francisco to live with her aunt and uncle. In Sid Fleischman's *By the Great Horn Spoon!* (Little Brown & Co., 1963), a 12-year-old boy strikes it rich in San Francisco during the gold rush after stowing away on a journey from Boston.

3

Suggested Itineraries

When you've got kids in tow, sometimes just getting out of your hotel in the morning can feel like a major accomplishment. Deciding where to go after that can seem more daunting still.

The itineraries in this chapter will help take the guesswork out of how to spend your time in San Francisco. I've included the major sights that will interest both adults and kids, and arranged them in a manner that takes advantage of San Francisco's relatively compact size, leading you from one nearby attraction to another.

If you have only 1 day to spend in San Francisco, the "Best in One Day" tour introduces you to the city's most enduringly popular highlights and gives you a chance to take in its beloved views as well. Should you have more time, take the "Best in Two Days" and "Best in Three Days" tours on days 2 and 3.

1 The Best of San Francisco in 1 Day

If you have just 1 day in San Francisco, this itinerary introduces you to many of the city's most famous attractions without leaving your kids, or you, in a heap. You'll visit Union Square, ride a scenic cable car route, tour Fisherman's Wharf, take a break in North Beach, and gape at the sights, sounds, and smells of Chinatown. While it seems like a lot, it's quite manageable—all attractions are located within 2 square miles. I've avoided overly ambitious suggestions in order to factor in slower walkers, emergency potty breaks, and the tough time you may have tearing the kids away from PIER 39. This itinerary will keep your family moving from one colorful place to the next, giving your child(ren) little time to complain of boredom. Indeed, with the "crookedest street in the world," antique ships, and noisy sea lions, chances are your kids will want to keep going even when you're tuckered out. Just in case, I've noted plenty of playgrounds and grassy areas where everyone can take a break.

Powell-Hyde cable car turnaround at Powell and Market streets.

❶ Union Square/Market Street/ Powell-Hyde Cable Car Line ✸

If you're staying in a hotel, there's a good chance you'll be near the Powell-Hyde cable car line. (That said, if you're staying in Fisherman's Wharf, you may prefer to start this tour at stop no. 3 below and then fit in time for Union Square after visiting Chinatown.) Your first stop, the cable car "turnaround" at the corner of Market and Powell streets, is the heart of San Francisco's shopping scene. Given the ever-present queue for the cable car, you'll want to get there early, which may mean you'll be out before the stores open. Even so, you'll enjoy people-watching, from local worker bees starting their day to other early-rising tourists to street performers getting ready to perform to the occasional odd bird carrying a sign lamenting the coming doomsday. It's certainly a lively spot to start your excursion. See p. 173.

② San Francisco Cable Cars (& Cable Car Museum) ★★

A cable car ride is an attraction in itself. Created in 1973 as an alternative to horse-drawn carriages, which proved difficult and at times even dangerous on the city's steep hills, cable cars actually have no engines. Instead, cables running underground on the cable car lines move at a constant speed of 9½ mph. The car's conductor, called a "gripper," controls a lever that opens and closes a vise-like grip on the cable to either move or stop. The Powell-Hyde line runs up some of San Francisco's steepest streets, giving you a good sense of the city's photogenic, hilly topography. You'll pass right by the Cable Car Museum (p. 191). If it's past 10am, take a moment to check it out. It's free and quite interesting. If it's closed, perhaps you can take a detour there later when you are in Chinatown.

③ Lombard Street ★

After passing the Cable Car Museum, the cable car continues climbing Nob Hill and then turns north onto Russian Hill's tree-lined Hyde Street. At the top of Hyde Street, get off at the intersection with Lombard Street, the so-called "crookedest street in the world." Snap some photos of Alcatraz Island, the San Francisco Bay, Coit Tower, and Telegraph Hill—just try not to do so from the middle of the street, as some over-enthusiastic sightseers are wont to do. Then stroll down, and back up, the Lombard Street steps; in spring and early summer, the street is lined with colorful blossoms. See p. 176.

④ Victoria Park, Ghirardelli Square & Aquatic Park ★★

Now you can either walk the three extremely steep blocks down Hyde Street toward Fisherman's Wharf, or hop back on the cable car. Either way, you'll end up at Victoria Park, a lovely expanse of grass at the edge of the San Francisco Bay. Walk left 1 block to Ghirardelli Square, an old-time chocolate factory now housing shops and restaurants. Since it'll be too early for ice cream, you'll have an excuse not to wait in line at the Ghirardelli Soda Fountain and Chocolate Shop (p. 147). Instead, take in the view of the bay and Alcatraz Island and walk down through Victoria Park to the water's edge. At any time of day, you're likely to find hardy (or perhaps just crazy) souls swimming in the frigid 50-something degree waters, often without wetsuits. Many are part of the Dolphin Club, founded by German immigrants in 1877, whose clubhouse now sits on the Hyde Street pier.

⑤ Hyde Street Pier ★★★

Walk over to the Hyde Street pier (p. 184) and purchase tickets to board the antique ships. Enjoy stunning views of the bay and the Golden Gate Bridge while your children explore an elegant 19th-century square-rigger, an 1890 ferryboat chock-full of antique cars, and a 100-year-old tugboat. After checking out engine rooms, captain's quarters, and even a replicated turn-of-the-20th-century concession stand, cross the street to the Maritime National Historical Park Visitor Center for a look at intricate model boats and more info on the city's seafaring past. The visitor center is in The Cannery, a 1907 structure that was once the world's largest peach-canning facility and now houses a collection of stores, including the enchanting Lark in the Morning music shop, and eateries. Stop by The Cannery courtyard to see if any musicians are playing.

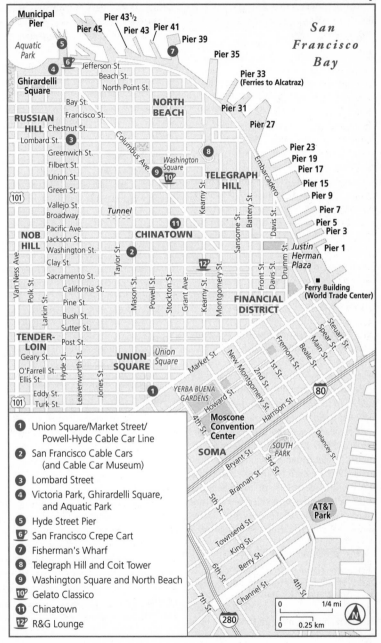

Municipal Pier
Pier 43½
Pier 45   Pier 43   Pier 41
Pier 39
Aquatic Park
Pier 35
Jefferson St.
Pier 33 (Ferries to Alcatraz)
Ghirardelli Square
Beach St.
North Point St.
Bay St.
NORTH BEACH
Pier 31
RUSSIAN HILL
Francisco St.
Pier 27
Chestnut St.
Lombard St.
Pier 23
Greenwich St.
Pier 19
Washington Square
Pier 17
Filbert St.
TELEGRAPH HILL
Pier 15
Union St.
Green St.
Pier 9
Vallejo St.
Pier 7
Broadway
Tunnel
Pier 5
Pacific Ave.
Pier 3
NOB HILL
Jackson St.
CHINATOWN
Justin Herman Plaza
Pier 1
Washington St.
Clay St.
Ferry Building (World Trade Center)
Sacramento St.
California St.
Pine St.
FINANCIAL DISTRICT
Bush St.
Sutter St.
TENDER-LOIN
Post St.
Geary St.
UNION SQUARE
Union Square
O'Farrell St.
Ellis St.
Eddy St.
Turk St.
YERBA BUENA GARDENS
Market St.
Howard St.
Moscone Convention Center
SOMA
SOUTH PARK
Bryant St.
Brannan St.
AT&T Park
Townsend St.
King St.
Berry St.
Channel St.

San Francisco Bay

1 Union Square/Market Street/ Powell-Hyde Cable Car Line
2 San Francisco Cable Cars (and Cable Car Museum)
3 Lombard Street
4 Victoria Park, Ghirardelli Square, and Aquatic Park
5 Hyde Street Pier
6 San Francisco Crepe Cart
7 Fisherman's Wharf
8 Telegraph Hill and Coit Tower
9 Washington Square and North Beach
10 Gelato Classico
11 Chinatown
12 R&G Lounge

0   1/4 mi
0   0.25 km

⑥ SAN FRANCISCO CREPE CART ✲
This quaint cart offers savory and sweet crepes, with fillings like ham and cheese or bananas and chocolate, to be enjoyed in the lovely courtyard at The Cannery, sometimes to the accompaniment of live music from folksy local performers. See p. 148.

⑦ Fisherman's Wharf ✲

Head east toward the heart of Fisherman's Wharf (p. 182). At Pier 45, step into the Musée Mécanique (p. 185), a fun antique arcade. If your kids like big boats and battles, splurge on tours of the SS *Jeremiah O'Brien*, a WWII "Liberty Ship," and the WWII submarine USS *Pampanito* (p. 187). My girls are staunch pacifists, but they still loved the tours. As you continue east, steer clear of the cheesy tourist shops—you'll find plenty of souvenirs later on in Chinatown—and brace yourselves for the crowds at PIER 39 (p. 186). PIER 39 is my least favorite place on the wharf, but my opinion clearly counts for little, since it's actually the third most visited U.S. tourist destination, behind Disneyworld and Disneyland. If you can get past the candy, cookie, and fudge shops, what does it actually have going for it? Three things: an enjoyable, albeit pricey, aquarium; an antique carousel; and the city's infamous, smelly sea lions. Between those three things, a plethora of toy stores, and the aforementioned sweet shops, good luck tearing the kids away.

⑧ Telegraph Hill & Coit Tower ✲

After the bustle of Fisherman's Wharf, you'll enjoy the serene city views from atop Telegraph Hill, named for a semaphore installed there in 1850 to alert residents of ships' arrivals, and crowned by a strange obelisk called Coit Tower. The trek may be too much for little legs. Fortunately, the no. 39-Coit bus takes you from the corner of Stockton and Beach streets right up to Coit Tower. Check out the murals by students of Diego Rivera inside Coit Tower and splurge on an elevator ride to the top. Afterwards, walk or bus back down to Washington Park. See p. 197.

⑨ Washington Park & North Beach ✲

Now relax in Washington Square, one of the city's oldest parks, dating to 1847. Let the children play in the small playground while you take in the scene in this historic neighborhood. In the 1870s, Genoese and Sicilian immigrants set up countless Italian restaurants, cafes, and bakeries in the neighborhood, and they worshiped at the lovely Saints Peter & Paul Church overlooking the park. (Today, the church offers services in English, Italian, and Chinese.)

 ⑩ GELATO CLASSICO ✲
After your trek, it's time to reward yourselves with some lovely Italian ice cream at Gelato Classico, located steps away from Washington Park. See p. 143.

⑪ Chinatown ✲✲✲

Wander south on Stockton Street, and the sights and sounds of Chinatown come into focus. Stockton Street is the "real" Chinatown, where the area's residents come to buy groceries and medicines and to socialize. Check out the fascinating, seemingly chaotic grocery stores, before turning left toward Grant Street, which runs parallel to Stockton Street. Grant

Street is the tourists' Chinatown, festooned with colorful banners and offering a dizzying array of knick-knacks to buy for the friends back home. Don't miss Waverly Place, with its painted balconies, and the Golden Gate Fortune Cookie Co. on Ross Alley. See p. 179.

12′ R&G LOUNGE ★★
This is one of the better places to eat in Chinatown, but you've got to know how to order. Pass on the Westernized menu and ask what fresh fish is available. Order it prepared simply with garlic or salt and pepper, and be ready for a delicious feast. See p. 134.

2 The Best of San Francisco in 2 Days

This second day in San Francisco is likely to be your kids' favorite. I've listed quite a few attractions specifically designed for the younger set, which adults will certainly enjoy as well. You'll also stroll through a residential area and walk through world-class parks that are regular stomping grounds for local families, giving you a taste of life in the city. In addition to the bay views you enjoyed on Day 1, you'll get a chance to espy San Francisco's other coast, the one that looks out onto the wild Pacific Ocean.

From the corner of Stockton and Sutter streets, take the no. 30-Stockton bus to Chestnut and Fillmore streets; if going straight to the second stop on the tour, take the no. 30 bus to Broderick and Beach streets. (The no. 30X-Marina express also stops at Chestnut and Fillmore sts. and then at Scott & Beach sts.)

❶ Chestnut Street/The Marina District ★

If the kids have awakened early and are ready to go, head to this popular residential street lined with restaurants, shops, and cafes for a taste of San Francisco city life. There's a good chance you'll see other moms or dads out and about pushing strollers and buying the morning paper, or local urbanites popping into Peet's Coffee & Tea for a double latte before hopping on the bus downtown. If you have the time, head to **The Grove** (p. 151), grab a cup of joe and maybe some oatmeal for the kids, and enjoy the local scene. If you got a late start, or if the family lingered over breakfast at your hotel, skip this stop and head straight to no. 2.

❷ Exploratorium ★★★

Considered by some reputable sources as the best science museum in America, your kids may well list the Exploratorium as their favorite place in San Francisco. This hands-on museum offers so many exhibits that you really should arrive right when it opens at 10am to have at least an hour and a half to enjoy just a fraction of them. If your kids are young, they'll find easy-to-understand exhibits at the light and optics area at the rear, while the biology displays on the mezzanine level will fascinate older kids. If a toddler amongst you is overwhelmed by all the activity, have a parent take him or her to the back play area for a break, but don't linger there too long, as there is simply so much to see. (*Note:* If your kids aren't big walkers, consider having light lunch at the Exploratorium Cafe; if they like to walk, then head for lunch at the Crissy Field Center, as noted below.) See p. 173.

❸ The Palace of Fine Arts & the Wave Organ ★

When you step out of the darkened Exploratorium Hall into the light of day, take a moment to appreciate the lovely scenery at the Palace of Fine Arts (p. 175) abutting the Exploratorium. Have your kids look at the ducks and run on the grass before heading north on Baker Street, crossing Marina Boulevard and continuing to the water's edge. Walk onto the breakwater, where you'll see the bizarre Wave Organ (p. 216), created by scientists from the Exploratorium.

❹ Crissy Field ★★★
Head west to view this re-created wetlands area, which less than a decade ago was an unsightly abandoned military airstrip. You'll see joggers, dog walkers, bike riders of all ages, stroller-pushers, and plenty of other locals enjoying what is the youngest national park in the Bay Area, located next to the Golden Gate Bridge. Crissy Field is best at this time of day, when the morning fog has worn off but the afternoon winds, which attract expert wind- and kite-surfers from throughout the Bay Area, have not yet picked up.

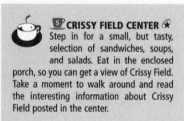

❺ CRISSY FIELD CENTER ★
Step in for a small, but tasty, selection of sandwiches, soups, and salads. Eat in the enclosed porch, so you can get a view of Crissy Field. Take a moment to walk around and read the interesting information about Crissy Field posted in the center.

❻ de Young Museum ★★★
After lunch, walk or take the Presidio-Go shuttle to Richardson Avenue and Francisco Street. There, transfer to the no. 28-19th Avenue bus. Take it to the corner of Fulton Street and 19th Avenue; then walk east to the de Young Museum (p. 193). Reopened in October 2005, the de Young has established itself as San Franciscan's favorite new gallery. Many areas of the museum, including the main lobby, tower, and sculpture garden, are free to visitors, but it's well worth paying the entrance fee (free to all kids under 12)

to see the museum's spectacular collection of indigenous art from Africa, Oceania, and the Americas. Head up to the Tower, which affords great views of northwest San Francisco and the Pacific Ocean, vistas you won't have seen from Coit Tower. The sculpture garden is also sure to entertain the kids, especially as they can actually touch the sculptures and even walk inside one of them.

❼ Golden Gate Park ★★★
Enjoy the rest of the afternoon in Golden Gate Park (p. 188), one of the greatest urban parks in America. From the de Young Museum, you'll be just steps away from the Rose Garden and only a short walk from the Conservatory of Flowers (p. 188), with exotic flora from all over the world, including carnivorous and aquatic plants. The lovely building itself and the remarkable flower garden laid out before are sure to delight little girls. South of the Conservatory across JFK Drive you'll find the Carousel and the Koret Children's Quarter, a refurbished playground set to open in May 2007. Just behind the de Young in the opposite direction from the Rose Garden is the lovely Japanese Tea Garden and, across the street from that, the Botanical Gardens. West of the Botanical Gardens is Stowe Lake, where you can rent paddle or row boats.

❽ Ocean Beach ★
When you take the no. 5-Fulton bus (board at Fulton St. and 8th Ave.) out to Ocean Beach, you'll see a San Francisco vista too many tourists miss out on. For while one part of the city's shoreline opens out onto the Bay, the western shore of the San Francisco peninsula meets the Pacific Ocean. The water here is not safe for swimming, although expert surfers can't stay away from its powerful waves. You can always walk onto the beach, although the sand is far from pearly white. If you time it right, you may be in time to enjoy the sunset.

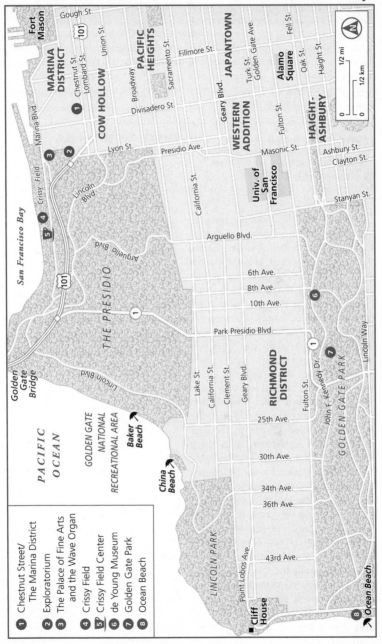

San Francisco in 2 Days

San Francisco Bay

PACIFIC OCEAN

Fort Mason

Gough St.
Union St.
Chestnut St.
Lombard St.
Marina Blvd.

MARINA DISTRICT

COW HOLLOW

Broadway
Divisadero St.

PACIFIC HEIGHTS

Fillmore St.
Sacramento St.

Lyon St.
Presidio Ave.

Geary Blvd.

WESTERN ADDITION

JAPANTOWN

Turk St.
Golden Gate Ave.

Fell St.

Fulton St.

Alamo Square

Oak St.
Haight St.

HAIGHT-ASHBURY

Masonic St.
Ashbury St.
Clayton St.

Crissy Field

Lincoln Blvd.

California St.

Univ. of San Francisco

Stanyan St.

Arguello Blvd.

Arguello Blvd.

THE PRESIDIO

6th Ave.
8th Ave.
10th Ave.

Park Presidio Blvd.

Lake St.
California St.
Clement St.
Geary Blvd.

RICHMOND DISTRICT

Fulton St.

John F. Kennedy Dr.

GOLDEN GATE PARK

Lincoln Way

25th Ave.
30th Ave.
34th Ave.
36th Ave.

Golden Gate Bridge

Lincoln Blvd.

GOLDEN GATE NATIONAL RECREATIONAL AREA

Baker Beach

China Beach

LINCOLN PARK

43rd Ave.

Point Lobos Ave.

Cliff House

Ocean Beach

1/2 mi
1/2 km
0
0

1. Chestnut Street/ The Marina District
2. Exploratorium
3. The Palace of Fine Arts and the Wave Organ
4. Crissy Field
5. Crissy Field Center
6. de Young Museum
7. Golden Gate Park
8. Ocean Beach

3 The Best of San Francisco in 3 Days

If you're lucky enough to have a third day in San Francisco, then start it by heading back to Fisherman's Wharf so that you can take that Alcatraz tour you didn't have time for on Day 1. You'll also explore some of the most altered neighborhoods in the city, former industrial areas that now house a growing share of the city's cultural, visual, and culinary highlights. Along the way, you'll find plenty of time for the kids to stretch their legs and run around.

F-Market streetcar to Pier 33 or no. 10-Townsend bus from Sansome and Sacramento streets to the Embarcadero and Bay Street.

❶ Alcatraz Island ★★★

What could be so special about an old prison? Plenty. To begin with, the ferry ride over to Alcatraz Island gives you the chance to get out onto the bay and see how lovely San Francisco looks from the water. Of course, most kids enjoy a fun boat ride as well. The prison audio tour, updated in late 2006, is better than ever, giving you the eerie sense of what it was like for prisoners, guards, and even the guards' families to live on a windswept rock in the middle of the Bay. You'll hear about some of the nation's most famous criminals and death-defying escape attempts sure to enthrall kids and adults alike. Order tickets well ahead of time; online is best, as you can print them out at home and head straight to the ferry line-up at Pier 33. I recommend taking the first ferry of the day, at 9:30am, as the prison will be less crowded when you arrive. Bring sweaters, comfortable shoes, and something to eat (or choose from the paltry snacks on the ferry), as there's no concession stand on the island. See p. 169. (*Note:* If you were unable to reserve Alcatraz tickets in time, take a 1-hour bay cruise on the Blue & Gold fleet. In addition to lovely vistas of the city and an up-close look at the Golden Gate Bridge, an audio track imparts plenty of history and local city lore. See p. 198.)

❷ F-Market Streetcar & the Embarcadero Promenade

After Alcatraz, hop on the F-Market streetcar headed toward Market Street. The F-Market line uses refurbished streetcars from around the world, so you might find yourself on a turn-of-the-century trolley from Kansas City or an antique streetcar from Milan. The picturesque streetcars are part of the overall upgrade to this section of town, which was fueled by the 1989 earthquake that destroyed the unattractive elevated freeway that once obscured the water's edge. The new promenade now bordering the waterfront all the way from Fisherman's Wharf to AT&T Park is a delightful place to stroll or cycle, with 13-foot-tall metal pylons and bronze plaques embedded in the promenade sidewalk and imprinted with photographs, drawings, poetry, and historical facts about the waterfront.

❸ Ferry Building ★★★

You'll arrive at the Ferry Building, at once a reminder of San Francisco's maritime history and a symbol of the city's position as an important culinary center. Before the construction of the bay's bridges and the underwater BART tunnel, the Ferry Building oversaw one of the most complex ferry systems in the country. After a multi-million-dollar renovation completed in 2003, the Ferry Building is now home to a number of upscale shops offering gourmet, organic, and/or sustainably raised meats, vegetables, breads, chocolates, and even mushrooms. Two to four

San Francisco in 3 Days

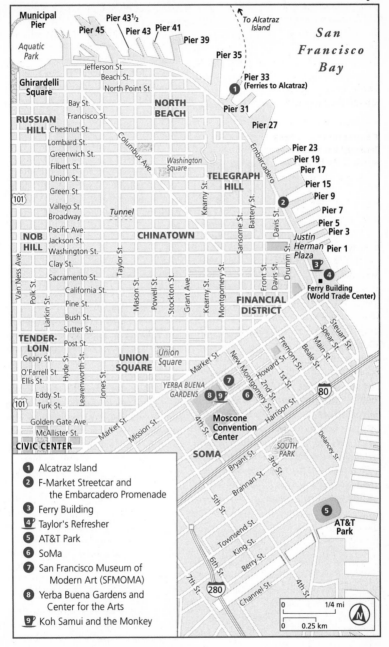

Municipal Pier
Aquatic Park
Ghirardelli Square
Pier 45
Pier 43½
Pier 43
Pier 41
Pier 39
Pier 35
Pier 33 (Ferries to Alcatraz)
Pier 31
Pier 27
Pier 23
Pier 19
Pier 17
Pier 15
Pier 9
Pier 7
Pier 5
Pier 3
Pier 1

To Alcatraz Island

San Francisco Bay

Jefferson St.
Beach St.
North Point St.
Bay St.
Francisco St.
Chestnut St.
Lombard St.
Greenwich St.
Filbert St.
Union St.
Green St.
Vallejo St.
Broadway
Pacific Ave.
Jackson St.
Washington St.
Clay St.
Sacramento St.
California St.
Pine St.
Bush St.
Sutter St.
Post St.
Geary St.
O'Farrell St.
Ellis St.
Eddy St.
Turk St.
Golden Gate Ave.
McAllister St.

RUSSIAN HILL
NORTH BEACH
TELEGRAPH HILL
NOB HILL
CHINATOWN
TENDER-LOIN
UNION SQUARE
FINANCIAL DISTRICT
CIVIC CENTER
SOMA
SOUTH PARK

Columbus Ave.
Washington Square
Tunnel
Van Ness Ave.
Polk St.
Larkin St.
Hyde St.
Leavenworth St.
Jones St.
Taylor St.
Mason St.
Powell St.
Stockton St.
Grant Ave.
Kearny St.
Montgomery St.
Sansome St.
Battery St.
Front St.
Davis St.
Drumm St.
Embarcadero

Justin Herman Plaza
Ferry Building (World Trade Center)

Union Square
Market St.
Mission St.
New Montgomery St.
2nd St.
Howard St.
Fremont St.
1st St.
Beale St.
Main St.
Spear St.
Steuart St.
Harrison St.
3rd St.
4th St.
Bryant St.
Brannan St.
5th St.
6th St.
7th St.
Townsend St.
King St.
Berry St.
Channel St.
Delancey St.

YERBA BUENA GARDENS
Moscone Convention Center
AT&T Park

101
80
280

1 Alcatraz Island
2 F-Market Streetcar and the Embarcadero Promenade
3 Ferry Building
4 Taylor's Refresher
5 AT&T Park
6 SoMa
7 San Francisco Museum of Modern Art (SFMOMA)
8 Yerba Buena Gardens and Center for the Arts
9 Koh Samui and the Monkey

0   1/4 mi
0   0.25 km

times a week, depending on the season, the Ferry Building holds a world-class Farmer's Market, attracting San Franciscans of all stripes who are passionate about good food and quality ingredients. Take a moment to walk out back and check out the ferries, which now primarily service commuters who live in Marin County, come and go. See p. 176.

 TAYLOR'S REFRESHER ★
To San Franciscans, high-quality, sustainably produced food needn't always be expensive or complicated. It can, and should, be available in the everyday comfort foods we all enjoy. Step inside and order a juicy burger made with locally raised meat and topped with tomatoes and lettuce fresh from the Farmer's Market. Your taste buds will notice the difference between this and an ordinary diner, but your wallet won't. See p. 140.

❺ AT&T Park ★

This is an optional stop if you're not sports fans, but you'll have less time for the attractions in SoMa. If you do go, public transportation will prove more efficient than feet, so take the N-Judah streetcar headed toward AT&T Park. Get off at the 2nd & King Station. On non-game days, the ballpark has a playground just for kids. After the kids have had a chance to play, take the no. 15-3rd St. bus to 3rd and Mission streets.

❻ SoMa ★★★

Like the revamped Embarcadero, this section of town has undergone its own transformation since the early 1990s. Once an industrial wasteland, SoMa is now home to many top museums and galleries. The recently opened Museum of the African Diaspora (p. 194) will soon be joined by the Contemporary Jewish Museum and the Mexican Museum. Moreover, the Yerba Buena Center, with its waterfalls,

lawn, and playgrounds, provides a pleasant respite.

❼ San Francisco Museum of Modern Art (SFMOMA) ★★★

If you only have time to check out one museum in SoMa, this should be it. The SFMOMA boasts one of the more extensive collections of 20th- and 21st-century art in the country, and is housed in an impressive building designed by the Swiss architect Mario Botta. If the kids are tired—or not big museum-goers—head straight to the permanent collection on the second floor. The wacky Warhols, colorful Lichtensteins, and magical Matisses are sure to perk them up. You'll also see some impressive sculpture and a Calder mobile or two. See p. 194.

❽ Yerba Buena Gardens & Center for the Arts ★★★

In addition to a 775-seat theater, art galleries, and a 5-acre garden, you'll also find a children's playground, an antique carousel, and other family-friendly attractions here. If you have time, pop into Zeum, where the kids can make their own claymation-style film clips or create their own cartoon character. If you want some downtime, have the kids play at the playground or enjoy the fountain dedicated to Martin Luther King, Jr., while you savor the interesting architectural vantage points offered in this urban oasis.

 KOH SAMUI & THE MONKEY
Just behind the Yerba Buena Center on Brannan Street, you'll find this low-key Thai restaurant serving both familiar and more inventive Thai fare (p. 132). If the family wants more options, then head for the Metreon food court, where family members can choose from Asian noodles, sushi, pizzas, or well-made burritos (p. 131).

4

Getting to Know San Francisco

San Francisco has a lot going for it. For its geographic setting, it ranks as one of the loveliest cities on earth. The tolerant, open-minded population includes a dynamic mix of cultures from around the globe. The city produces some of the most innovative cuisine in the country and is home to a plethora of cultural institutions as well. Finally, from this little nook in Northern California, one can readily visit some of the most dramatic mountains, beautiful beaches, and stunning national parks in the world.

San Francisco occupies the northernmost tip of a 32-mile-long peninsula. Its western coast is battered by a chilly and unrelentingly forceful piece of the Pacific Ocean, while its eastern side looks out onto the calm waters of San Francisco Bay, the Bay Bridge, and the towns and mountains beyond. To the north, the photogenic Golden Gate Bridge spans the tiny opening to the bay, less than 2 miles in length, and connects San Francisco to the picturesque hills of Marin County. San Francisco has its own share of hills, and as such offers visitors one fabulous view after another.

The city's 790,000-plus residents include ethnic groups from every corner of the globe. Enclaves of African-American, Chinese, El Salvadoran, Brazilian, Irish, Italian, Japanese, Mexican, Middle Eastern, Russian, and Vietnamese residents, among others, make it possible for locals and visitors alike to experience a world of cultures within 47 square miles. San Francisco's cosmopolitan roots can be traced to the gold rush. Before then the sleepy town of Yerba Buena—settled by the Spanish in 1776, claimed by Mexico in 1822, and declared part of the U.S. in 1848 (and renamed San Francisco)—was little more than a military outpost, a port, and some ranchland. That all changed when newspaper publisher Sam Brannan took it upon himself in 1849 to publicize the discovery of gold in the American River, 130 miles east.

The gold rush attracted a rash of fortune hunters, adventurers, savvy business folk, and opportunists from across America, as well as immigrants from as far away as China. The vast majority made no money digging for gold; their luck came from ending up in San Francisco. Newcomers quickly created havens within the city to support and sustain their cultures. Neighborhoods emerged with predominant characteristics and, whether by foresight or fate, over the decades they have managed to maintain their individuality despite the forces of popular culture. San Franciscans, although there's no single accurate description of that species, believe in the virtues of diversity and self-expression. And that's another reason why, along with those hills and that view, you just have to love it here.

1 Orientation

VISITOR INFORMATION

The San Francisco Convention and Visitors Bureau operates the **Visitor Information Center** on the lower level of Hallidie Plaza on Powell and Market streets (© **415/391-2000;** www.onlyinsanfrancisco.com). The staff is multilingual and genuinely helpful. Visit the information center for books; maps; Municipal Railway passes for buses, streetcars, and cable cars; souvenirs; and tons of brochures to guide you further. It's open Monday through Friday 9am to 5pm and weekends 9am to 3pm.

Warning: Around Fisherman's Wharf and elsewhere, you may see manned booths with signs proclaiming themselves tourist information centers. These booths are operated by organizations such as the Fisherman's Wharf Merchants' Association or by tour companies, boat lines, or other attractions, and, as such, are not the best source of unbiased advice. For that, you should phone or visit the Visitor Information Center.

THE LAY OF THE LAND

The city is divided up into neighborhoods as diverse and interesting as their inhabitants. Streets, for the most part, are laid out in a traditional grid pattern, with two major exceptions: Market Street and Columbus Avenue. Market Street cuts through town from the Embarcadero up toward Twin Peaks in the Sunset District. Columbus Avenue runs at an angle through North Beach starting at the Transamerica Pyramid and ending near the Hyde Street Pier. Another important thoroughfare, Geary Boulevard, runs all the way from Market Street through town to Ocean Beach.

Even the traditionally laid out roads are confusing when a hill gets in the way and the street ends abruptly only to emerge on the other side, which is particularly annoying if you're driving. Travel with a map; I like the *San Francisco Transit Rider Map and Guide* (see "Maps" in the "Fast Facts" section at the end of this chapter for details on finding one). Numbered *streets,* by the way, are downtown, south of Market Street. Numbered *avenues* (notice the subtle difference) are found in the Richmond and Sunset districts southwest of downtown.

NEIGHBORHOODS IN BRIEF

Union Square Named for the historic plaza it encompasses, Union Square is the cultural and commercial heart of San Francisco. This is where tourists, and plenty of residents, come to shop. The roughly 22 square blocks bordered by Market, Mason, Bush, and Kearny streets house San Francisco's greatest concentration of hotels in every rate category, clothing stores, galleries, and theaters. Equally plentiful in Union Square are restaurants, although they cater mainly to tourists and businesspeople. (With a few exceptions, San Francisco's better dining options, at any price range, are located in other neighborhoods.)

You'll find no shortage of noise and congestion here, but green space is another matter. The actual Union Square plaza, located within Stockton, Powell, Geary, and Post streets, once provided the greenery that is otherwise absent in the city center, but a 2002 redesign of the plaza did away with a lot of it. In an effort to make the plaza less welcoming to the homeless residents who dozed there, the city replaced its lawns with a 245-foot-long floor of granite and scattered plants. At least the new design is better suited to hosting the square's frequent art exhibits and cultural events. Also on the plaza is the **TIX Bay Area half-price ticket booth** (see chapter 11 for more information on the TIX booth).

Despite Union Square's urban feel—with not a playground to speak of—families may want to consider lodging in this area because it offers the most options for hotels. Moreover, it's close to many other city attractions, with readily available public transportation. Finally, if your children are actually old enough to enjoy shopping as much as you do, this could be the neighborhood for you.

South of Market SoMa, as the blocks encompassed by Market, 10th, Steuart, and King streets (including South Beach and AT&T Park) are familiarly known, exemplifies the best and worst of urban life. Here you will find some of the city's top cultural institutions, such as the **San Francisco Museum of Modern Art** and the **Yerba Buena Center for the Arts.** With its lovely gardens, galleries, and performance space, and numerous attractions for children of all ages, the Yerba Buena Center is a testament to successful urban planning.

With the expansion of the **Westfield San Francisco Centre** mall and recent opening of a massive Bloomingdale's, whose doors open south to SoMa, the neighborhood has now integrated more fully into the Union Square shopping scene. In SoMa you'll also find the continuously expanding **Moscone Convention Center; Metreon,** with its own collection of kid-friendly attractions; and the temporary home of the **California Academy of Sciences.** Delightful bay views and **AT&T Park** are around the corner in nearby South Beach. Brand new restaurants seem to pop up daily in this former industrial neighborhood, the **Museum of the African Diaspora** has recently arrived, and both the Jewish Museum and the Mexican Museum are slated to move into new homes here soon.

But the ongoing development has not yet reached all of SoMa, and just 1 block west of the toniest shopping mall in town is the heart of skid row: 6th and 7th streets below Market Street. Market Street itself is also home to a share of the city's homeless residents. So although SoMa has some of the city's greatest cultural attractions and even a few of its best hotels, families with young children may prefer lodging in a less gritty part of town.

Chinatown It's with good reason that Chinatown is the second most visited destination in San Francisco, behind Fisherman's Wharf. The densely populated area between Broadway, Taylor, Bush, and Montgomery streets is every bit as colorful, crowded, and atmospheric as advertised. The much-photographed Dragon Gate entrance on Grant Street leads to one tourist shop after another, all visually enhanced by colorful banners in red, gold, and green.

If you're in the market for a rhinestone tiara or sets of chopsticks, this is nirvana. Kids love all the little knickknacks: you could lose many hours poking around the stores, snacking on freshly baked fortune cookies, and wandering the alleyways. Stockton Street, with its exotic grocery stores and traditional herb shops, is equally alluring. Overall, Chinatown is great for shopping and eating, and several of its restaurants are listed in chapter 6. Given the noise and crowds, however, it's not a great area for hotels, and I've listed only one in chapter 5.

San Francisco Neighborhoods

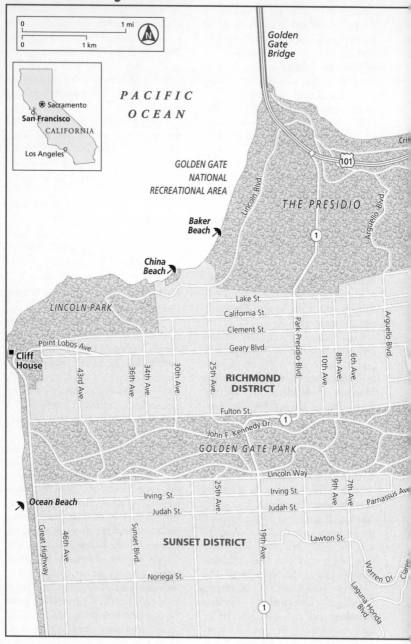

San Francisco Bay

Fisherman's Wharf

Pier 41

Pier 39

Pier 33 (Ferries to Alcatraz)

Aquatic Park

Jefferson St.

Beach St.

North Point St.

Bay St.

Fort Mason

Ghirardelli Square

NORTH BEACH

Coit Tower

Marina Blvd.

MARINA DISTRICT

RUSSIAN HILL

Columbus Ave.

TELEGRAPH HILL

Chestnut St.

Lombard St.

"Crookedest Street"

101

The Embarcadero

COW HOLLOW

Union St.

Van Ness Ave.

Polk St.

Hyde St.

Taylor St.

CHINATOWN

Battery St.

Broadway

Franklin St.

Gough St.

Jackson St.

Washington St.

Powell St.

Stockton St.

Grant Ave.

Kearny St.

FINANCIAL DISTRICT

Lyon St.

PACIFIC HEIGHTS

NOB HILL

Transbay Transit Terminal

Presidio Ave.

Divisadero St.

Sacramento St.

California St.

TENDER-LOIN

Sutter St.

UNION SQUARE

Yerba Buena Gardens

1st St.

California St.

Fillmore St.

Post St.

Geary St.

Moscone Convention Center

Geary Blvd.

JAPANTOWN

101

Market St.

Mission St.

Howard St.

Folsom St.

3rd St.

WESTERN ADDITION

Turk St.

Golden Gate Ave.

CIVIC CENTER

SOMA

80

4th St.

5th St.

Univ. of San Francisco

Fulton St.

Alamo Square

Fell St.

8th St.

9th St.

Bryant St.

Harrison St.

6th St.

7th St.

Masonic St.

Oak St.

HAIGHT-ASHBURY

Haight St.

Central Skyway

101

10th St.

Ashbury St.

Clayton St.

BUENA VISTA PARK

Duboce Ave.

14th St.

Castro St.

Market St.

101

280

16th St.

South

17th St.

POTRERO HILL

17th St.

THE CASTRO

Church St.

Dolores St.

MISSION DISTRICT

Guerrero St.

Mission St.

Van Ness Ave.

Harrison St.

Bryant St.

Potrero Ave.

Rhode Island St.

101

TWIN PEAKS

Castro St.

Market St.

24th St.

Clipper St.

Cesar Chavez St. (Army St.)

Fisherman's Wharf   This is one of the country's most popular tourist attractions, just behind Disneyworld and Disneyland. Depending where you are in Fisherman's Wharf, it can feel a lot like Disneyland as well. Stretching from Van Ness Avenue to Kearny Street, and from the piers to Bay Street, the wharf is home to **PIER 39,** a conglomeration of tacky tourist shops and overpriced restaurants. The pier certainly has a lot for kids to love, including an aquarium; a carousel; playful stores like Puppets on the Pier; an endless array of chocolate, ice cream, and cookie shops; and the noisy, smelly, but irresistible sea lions. Steps away from the pier, the cheesy attractions continue, with places like **Rainforest Cafe** offering lackluster food in a gimmicky environment.

Now that I've dampened your expectations, let me say that the western side of Fisherman's Wharf, opposite from PIER 39, is actually quite nice, getting better every year, and worth a visit. Glimpses of the area's maritime past are visible in the wonderful antique boats of the **Hyde Street Pier.** Here you'll also find an upscale shopping mall at **Ghirardelli Square,** a pleasant stretch of lawn for kids to run around, a tiny beach, The Cannery courtyard, and the Municipal Pier, with its sweeping views of the Bay and the Golden Gate Bridge.

With all the tourists, it's no surprise most of the national chains have hotels here, many with pools. Although most of the lodging here is not very inspiring, it is certainly family-friendly.

North Beach   Landfill came between the waves and North Beach more than 100 years ago, just one of many changes this historic neighborhood has experienced. Situated roughly from Broadway to Lombard and Grant to Taylor streets, it rubs shoulders with Telegraph Hill to the east and Russian Hill to the west. Columbus Avenue, the main artery, cuts through at an angle, brushing up against Washington Square Park, the village square. Once populated by the Italian immigrants from Genoa and Sicily who founded the area's fishing industry, North Beach is slowly giving way to Chinatown—at least on its southern edge, as Chinese shops creep up Stockton Street past Broadway.

There's still plenty of Mediterranean warmth, lots of pasta, and cafes galore. Although no good family accommodations exist in North Beach, it's a delightful spot to come to stroll, shop, and dine.

The Embarcadero   If one can use the term "idyllic" to describe an urban amble, then a walk along the Embarcadero anywhere between Beach Street and AT&T Park certainly qualifies. Although the 1989 Loma Prieta earthquake wreaked havoc on homes and lives throughout the Bay Area, one positive outcome was the release of the waterfront from the ugly shadow of the Embarcadero Freeway, which was damaged and subsequently demolished. The area's renewal has been astonishing and has added immeasurably to the beauty of the city. In the past few years, an extension to the Municipal Railway lines has brought streetcar service to the entire Embarcadero as far as Fisherman's Wharf.

Most recently, the 1896 **Ferry Building** at the foot of Market Street was completely rehabilitated. The attractive building now contains an array of gourmet food stores and excellent restaurants. Outside, you can browse the Ferry Plaza Farmer's Market two to four times a week (depending on time of year), and excursions to the Saturday market have become a regular part of many a San Franciscan's schedule. Not far from the Ferry Building, the **Embarcadero Center,** a set of five multi-use towers along Drumm Street beginning at Market Street, houses upscale chain stores, restaurants, a movieplex, and a seasonal outdoor ice skating rink.

The few hotels that grace the area are priced in the high-moderate to luxury range, but dining options run the gamut from very inexpensive to big-night-out. Just slightly off the beaten tourist path, this would be a fun, convenient area in which to stay with kids of any age.

Nob Hill   Along California Street from Leavenworth to Stockton streets, Nob Hill is one of the oldest and most fashionable neighborhoods in town. It was once the exclusive turf of the railroad barons Leland Stanford, Mark Hopkins, Charles Crocker, and Collis P. Huntington—collectively known as the "Big Four." The properties where their mansions once stood now support fancy hotels, a private club, expensive apartment buildings, and the striking Grace Cathedral. This is a wonderful place for families to stay: Huntington Park and the largely residential feel provide a nice respite from the congestion of the city center, yet it's just a 5-minute walk from Union Square. Also, the California cable car line runs right by most of the hotels. The downside for those on foot is a steep uphill walk from Union Square to get back to the hotel. There's also cost: most of the hotels here are lovely, but also quite pricey.

Financial District   Encompassing prime real estate roughly between Montgomery Street and the Embarcadero on the west side of Market Street, the Financial District is the business center of San Francisco. The once-controversial Transamerica Pyramid at Montgomery and Clay streets is a skyline landmark, worth a closer look

for the miniature forest of redwood trees planted next to the building on the east side. Eating lunch around here is easy: Belden Place, an alley between Kearny, Bush, and Pine streets, offers outdoor dining in good weather and European ambience all year round, and the Crocker Galleria between Post, Sutter, and Montgomery streets offers good fast food, in addition to upscale shopping opportunities. You'll also find a growing collection of informal, organic, and healthy lunch spots geared to the working crowd.

Despite these perks, this wouldn't be my first choice of a neighborhood to stay in. The streets are practically deserted at night, except for homeless people. But on the upside, it's really quiet.

Civic Center and Hayes Valley   With the opening of the Asian Art Museum in its brilliant new building on Larkin Street, Civic Center is even more of a must-stop for visitors. Bound by Golden Gate Avenue and Franklin, Hyde, and Market streets, this is home to City Hall; the opera, ballet, and symphony stages; the new main library; and the Civic Center Plaza. However, as a meeting ground for much of the city's homeless population, the neighborhood is less than ideal after dark. It's busy during the performing arts season, but even then, take a cab at night. The area has some hotels, but families should think twice before lodging around here.

Hayes Valley, west of Civic Center and tucked between Franklin, Webster, Grove, and Page streets, is dotted with hip boutiques featuring local designers, gift shops, and restaurants that leave you feeling like you've discovered something cool. As a transitional neighborhood, this isn't the safest place to stay, but it might be worth a trip during the day for some shopping.

The Marina and Cow Hollow
Trendy single urbanites and young families call these picturesque neighborhoods home. The commercial blocks of the Marina and Cow Hollow, Chestnut Street, and Union Street, are delightfully crammed with cafes, boutiques, and gift shops. Restaurants abound, some of them inexpensive, and most of them family-friendly.

In addition to the prime shopping, you'll find several choice attractions here, including the **Exploratorium** and the **Palace of Fine Arts,** the **Marina Green,** and **Fort Mason,** all of which have major kid appeal. It's also in close proximity to the **Golden Gate Bridge** and the **Presidio.** A fair number of travelers end up staying in the Marina, especially those attached to automobiles, because the parking is either free or at least reasonable. Most accommodations are in the motel range and line ever-busy Lombard Street, but there are some better-than-average places to sleep. Know where you're going if you venture out for the evening; sections of Lombard are dicey late at night.

The Presidio Founded in 1776 as a Spanish garrison, this northwest corner of San Francisco remained a military installation for over 200 years. The U.S. took over in 1846 and later planted several pine and eucalyptus trees, eventually changing the sandy, barren hills into a delightful wooded area with over 400,000 trees. In 1994, the army handed over control of all 1,500 acres to the National Park Service, to become part of the **Golden Gate National Recreation Area.** Today families come here to hike, play golf, sunbathe at Baker Beach, visit the beautiful Palace of the Legion of Honor, and even play a few frames at a little bowling alley. The old officer's club has a well-stocked visitor's center,

and the old military PX market is now "Sports Basement," the cheapest place in town to buy sporting equipment.

My all-time favorite part of the Presidio is **Crissy Field,** which was reopened in 2002 as the Bay Area's newest national park. An easy walk along Crissy Walk takes you all the way to Fort Point, at the foot of the Golden Gate Bridge. The Presidio has no tourist accommodations, just plenty of things to do.

Japantown and the Western Addition Once upon a time, this neighborhood off Geary Boulevard, between Webster and Laguna streets, housed one of the largest concentrations of Japanese outside Japan. During World War II, when the city's Japanese residents were interred in camps, the area became home to other settlers, some of them African Americans who were recruited to California to work in the shipyards. Today, Japantown houses less than 4% of San Francisco's Japanese population. South of Geary Boulevard, which cut the neighborhood in two when it was widened in the '60s, the area is predominately African American and residential.

At first glance, Japantown appears to consist of a large pagoda and an unattractive indoor shopping center. Hidden inside these cement blocks, however, are good, inexpensive Japanese restaurants and some interesting shops. The **Kabuki Cinema** anchors one corner and the Kabuki Springs & Spa is located next door. The Peace Plaza, with its flat, cement waterfall, is also a good place for kids to stretch their legs. Japantown sponsors two festivals every year, the Cherry Blossom Festival in April and the Nihonmachi Street Fair in August (see chapter 2 for details on each).

Alamo Square (between Hayes, Fulton, Steiner, and Scott sts.) fronts

---

Tips Getting to Golden Gate Park

When you study a map of the city, it appears as if it's an easy walk along Hayes, Oak, Fell, Page, or Haight streets from the Civic Center to Golden Gate Park. Appearances are deceiving. You'll encounter a number of hills along this route, which takes you through areas that are somewhat blighted, noisy with traffic, rough in spots, and unattractive. Save your legs for the park and get there on a bus or streetcar.

---

the group of restored Victorian homes known as "postcard row." The houses are so picture-perfect, they have become as much a symbol of San Francisco as the Golden Gate Bridge and the cable cars.

Pacific Heights   The most expensive neighborhood in San Francisco is bordered by Broadway, Pine, Divisadero, and Franklin streets. Even the private schools here are housed in mansions. If you have an interest in architecture, you'll enjoy visiting the Haas-Lilienthal House, an 1886 Queen Anne Victorian decorated with period furniture at 2007 Franklin St. at Washington Street. Get the children to come along by promising a peek at Mrs. Doubtfire's fictional digs on 2640 Steiner Street at Broadway. Portions of *The Princess Diaries* were filmed at The Hamlin School, a private K–8 girls' school occupying a mansion on Broadway at Buchanan Street. Danielle Steel, the romance writer, lives in the 1913, 55-room Spreckles Mansion, which takes up all the space between Washington, Jackson, Gough, and Octavia streets, if you can imagine that. Directly in front of Ms. Steel's house is Lafayette Park, which has a small playground. An even better park is Alta Plaza at Steiner and Clay streets, with tennis courts and a newly refurbished playground that afford great city views.

Neighborhood residents do much of their shopping along Fillmore Street from California to Jackson streets, and there are some excellent restaurants here, too. It's a wonderful neighborhood in which to spend some time— too bad the cozy inns here are all geared towards couples.

Russian Hill   Circled by Broadway, Polk, Chestnut, and Taylor streets, this hill was named for the Russian fur traders rumored to be buried here in the 1820s. The Polk Street section of the neighborhood has become Frenchified of late and sports some *très* chic antiques shops, cafes, and a brasserie. Hyde Street provides upside access to the wiggly part of Lombard Street (the Powell-Hyde cable car takes you right there), and Macondry Lane, immortalized in Armistead Maupin's *Tales of the City,* is tucked between Leavenworth and Taylor just north of Green Street. Your kids may be excited to know that the ice cream shop at the corner of Hyde and Union streets is the original Swensen's Creamery. It's a very residential area, with no real accommodations options.

Haight-Ashbury   Bordered on the west by Golden Gate Park, on the north by Fulton Street, on the east by Divisadero Street, and by Waller Street to the south, gritty Haight-Ashbury has never fully put the 1960s behind it. This isn't a complete bummer, by any means; the main drag, Haight Street, is filled with vintage clothes—much of it on hangers and for sale—as well as independently-owned stores that you won't see in your local indoor mall.

The street is also action-packed, albeit with people looking for handouts, but it's historic, man. I wouldn't recommend families overnight at any of the local bed-and-breakfasts. As I recall from my own visits to San Francisco in bygone years, teens feel a magnetic pull to this place. If you have some with you, definitely have lunch here on your way to or from Golden Gate Park.

Laurel Heights and Presidio Heights
In this small, upscale residential neighborhood centered around California Street between Presidio and Arguello streets, one could get the impression that a baby stroller is the price of admission. There are lots of them here, all filled with actual babies, and there are lots of stores catering to young families in the Laurel Village Shopping Center and on Sacramento Street just 1 block to the north. Come here to check out the delightful children's clothing stores, to do some grown-up shopping for home furnishings and fancy shoes, or to gawk at the large homes in Presidio Heights. Technically in the Presidio, but bordering Presidio Heights, is the Julius Kahn Park, with a fabulous playground and grassy fields. The one worthwhile family hotel here, the **Laurel Inn,** is great for families who want to stay in a "real" neighborhood.

The Mission District Stretching from 16th Street to Cesar Chavez Street, between Dolores Street and Potrero Avenue, the predominately Hispanic Mission District is lively, congested, and earthy. For tourists, Mission Dolores at 16th Street and lovely palm tree–lined Dolores Street are worth a visit if you're interested in historic San Francisco. **Dolores Park,** 2 blocks south, is a fine spot for views and a little Frisbee—but beware the unleashed dogs. The 24th Street corridor is a terrific market street for Latino

food lovers, and Valencia and Guerrero streets between 16th and 23rd streets are brimming with hip little dining and drinking venues. The Mission has been redefining itself over the past 2 decades. It's the heart of the Latino community, a little bit funky, a little bit hipper than thou—and it's frankly unsafe on certain blocks. Don't linger around the BART stations on 16th or 24th streets and don't hang around late at night unless you're with people who know the area. Do come for dinner, but make sure to take a cab back to your hotel. (Parking is nearly impossible here, so driving isn't recommended anyway.) The **Precita Eyes Mural Art Center** offers guided tours of Mission District murals and high points—a great way to gain some insight into the community.

The Castro A huge rainbow flag, the symbol of gay activism, reigns over the center of this historic community where Market Street meets Castro Street. There aren't many family-friendly hotels here, but you'll find many fun, well-priced restaurants in the area. The Castro Theater is handsome to look at and fun to attend, particularly if you can catch one of the legendary sing-along screenings of the *Sound of Music.* Otherwise, there's not much for children around here.

Noe Valley In the late '80s, families began moving in droves into this hilly neighborhood south of the Castro, transforming petite Victorians into stylishly remodeled homes. You'll find a number of shops and cafes on 24th Street between Diamond and Church streets. The playground at Douglass and 27th streets, and the Walter Haas playground at Diamond Heights Boulevard and Addison Streets, are both delightful. The neighborhood is otherwise pretty quiet.

The Richmond District   The largely residential Richmond District reaches from Arguello to the Pacific on the northern edge of Golden Gate Park. It's a bit out of the way to base yourself here, but there are some attractions that will appeal to visitors. The main drag, Geary Boulevard, boasts all kinds of Asian, Russian, and Middle Eastern restaurants and groceries. Clement Street is the other Chinatown, less dense but still filled with imports, small bakeries, and delicatessens. The **California Palace of the Legion of Honor** museum in Lincoln Park, the **Cliff House,** and **Land's End** all have Richmond District zip codes.

The Sunset District   This is the city's other large residential area, on the southern side of Golden Gate Park. It borders Ocean Beach, which can be splendid on the few fogless days of summer. (It's more likely to be sunny in the spring or early fall). Just be wary of ocean currents, which are dangerous at all times of year, and especially so in fall and winter. The **San Francisco Zoo** is the Sunset's main visitor attraction, followed by Stern Grove's summer Sunday concerts or a hike at **Fort Funston.** If you happen to take the N-Judah streetcar to Golden Gate Park, you might want to browse the stores and restaurants along Irving Street and 9th Avenue. Like the Richmond, this isn't an area most people would choose to stay in because it's too far from downtown.

The Tenderloin   The blocks enclosed by Sutter and Taylor streets and Van Ness and Golden Gate avenues, directly west of Union Square, are known as the Tenderloin. This is home to recent immigrants who are living alongside massage parlors, flophouses, bars, and individuals in various stages of deterioration doing what they can to hold on. It's rough. This is no place to roam in the evening, with or without children, so I don't recommend choosing a hotel in this neighborhood. The one haven very worth dropping by is **Glide Memorial Church** on O'Farrell and Jones streets. Sunday services are eye-opening—old-fashioned sermonizing, rousing music, and a cross-section of residents.

2 Getting Around

BY PUBLIC TRANSPORTATION

San Francisco's Municipal Railway, known simply as "Muni" (📞 **415/673-6864**), operates the city's buses, streetcars, and cable cars. For detailed route information, call Muni or visit its website at **www.sfmuni.com**. Another helpful website is **http://transit.511.org**, which also lists schedules and route maps.

CITY BUSES & STREETCARS

Muni streetcars run underground exclusively from Van Ness Avenue to the Embarcadero and mostly aboveground in the outlying neighborhoods, from 6am until 1am. Five lines (J, K, L, M, and N) make identical stops below Market Street, including Van Ness Avenue, Civic Center, Powell and Montgomery streets, and the Embarcadero. Past Van Ness Avenue the routes veer in different directions. The N-Judah services the Haight-Ashbury area and parallels Golden Gate Park on its way down Judah Street to the ocean. At the Embarcadero, this line also travels to AT&T Park by way of King Street near the Cal Train station. The J-Church line passes near Mission Dolores and the Castro on its way to Noe Valley and points south. The L-Taraval travels through the Sunset District within walking distance of the San Francisco Zoo.

San Francisco Mass Transit

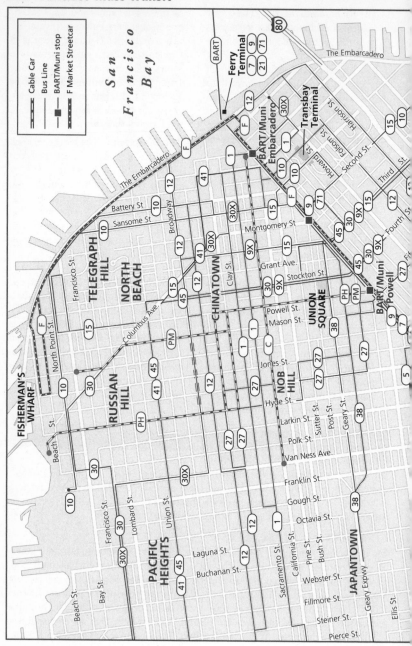

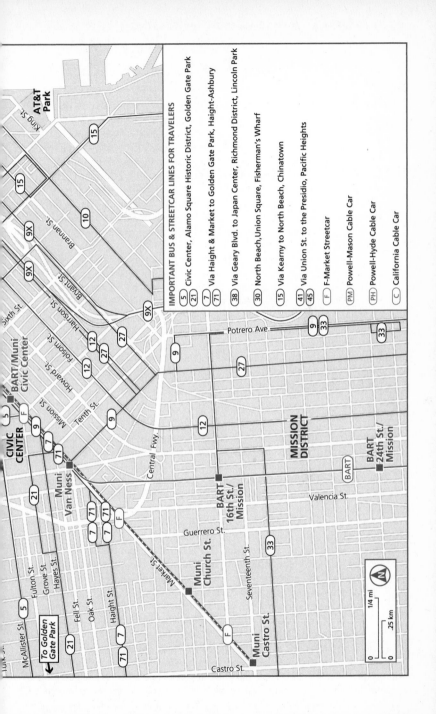

IMPORTANT BUS & STREETCAR LINES FOR TRAVELERS

- (5) Civic Center, Alamo Square Historic District, Golden Gate Park
- (21) Via Haight & Market to Golden Gate Park, Haight-Ashbury
- (7) Via Geary Blvd. to Japan Center, Richmond District, Lincoln Park
- (71)
- (38) North Beach, Union Square, Fisherman's Wharf
- (30) Via Kearny to North Beach, Chinatown
- (15) Via Union St. to the Presidio, Pacific Heights
- (41)
- (45)
- (F) F-Market Streetcar
- (PM) Powell-Mason Cable Car
- (PH) Powell-Hyde Cable Car
- (C) California Cable Car

AT&T Park

CIVIC CENTER

BART/Muni Civic Center

MISSION DISTRICT

BART 16th St./Mission

BART 24th St./Mission

Muni Van Ness

Muni Church St.

Muni Castro St.

To Golden Gate Park

Potrero Ave.

Valencia St.

Castro St.

Seventeenth St.

Guerrero St.

Market St.

Central Fwy.

Tenth St.

Howard St.

Folsom St.

Harrison St.

Bryant St.

Brannan St.

Sixth St.

King St.

McAllister St.

Fulton St.

Grove St.

Hayes St.

Fell St.

Oak St.

Haight St.

1/4 mi

25 km

Value   Easy Riding: Ways to Save on Public Transportation

Muni passports can be a bargain for visitors who plan to take buses, streetcars, or cable cars often. A 1-day passport is $11; a 3-day passport is $18; and a 7-day passport is $24. Kid and senior passports don't exist, but Muni sells monthly youth/discount passes for $10. Passports and $3 Muni maps (a necessary item) can be purchased at the Visitor Information Center on Hallidie Plaza; at Tix Bay Area on Union Square; at the baggage level information booths at SFO; at the cable car ticket booths at Powell and Market sts., Hyde and Beach sts., and Bay and Taylor sts.; and at several drug stores throughout the city. Passes and passports can be found at the cable car ticket booths at Powell and Market or Beach and Hyde streets. Single-day passports are available on board the cable cars as well. For other outlets, check Muni's website at **www.sfmuni.com**.

Dedicated tourists should consider investing in **Citypass,** a booklet of discounted tickets to six major attractions, including the Museum of Modern Art; the Palace of the Legion of Honor and de Young Museum; the Exploratorium; a Blue & Gold Bay Cruise; the Aquarium by the Bay; and your choice between the California Academy of Sciences and the Asian Art Museum. Citypass also contains a 7-day Muni Passport, making this an attractive package if you can manage to visit all of the above. Citypass is $49 for adults and $39 for kids age 5 to 17. They can be purchased at the participating attractions, at the Visitor Information Center at Halladie Plaza, or online at **www.citypass.com**.

The F-Market line was started up in 2000 and equipped with a collection of carefully restored vintage streetcars from around the United States and Europe. These charming old-timers run from the Castro all the way along Market Street to the Embarcadero and Fisherman's Wharf. A popular method to reach the Ferry building and the piers, these cars are packed during summer and on weekends.

Muni buses, many of which are connected to an overhead electrical system, run from 6am until midnight. Bus stops are indicated by street corner signs and yellow bands painted on utility poles and curbs. Muni has 80 lines, so you can probably get to where you'd like to go . . . eventually. This isn't exactly rapid transit.

Fares on buses and streetcars are $1.50 for adults and 50¢ for children 5 to 17, seniors 65 and over, and disabled individuals. Kids under 5 ride free. Exact change is required. When you enter the front door and drop your fare into the fare box, the driver will hand you a paper transfer, valid for up to 2 hours of rides in any direction. Turnstiles inside the underground Muni stations accept only coins; change machines are located on the walls next to the BART ticket dispensers.

There is no simple way to handle strollers on either buses or streetcars, although, with the exception of the F-Market cars, streetcars are more spacious. If you are traveling with a baby, an easy-to-fold umbrella stroller will be the most practical piece of equipment. If you can manage with a baby front pack or backpack, you'll be even better off. Toddlers are another issue. Since you really will need a stroller at some point during a walk, you'll have to practice releasing the closure and folding the stroller while holding the child at the same time. This is even more fun if you have more than one small child to deal with.

CABLE CARS

No visit to San Francisco would be complete without a ride on one of the cable cars. Three cable car routes traverse the downtown area. The most scenic is the Powell-Hyde line, starting off at Powell and Market and ending at the turnaround by Ghirardelli Square. Next is the Powell-Mason line, which also begins at Powell and Market and then meanders through North Beach, ending on the east side of Fisherman's Wharf. The third is the California Street line that leaves from Market and California, crests at Nob Hill, and ends abruptly at Van Ness Avenue. The queues to board the Powell Street cars at the turnarounds, at either end, can be daunting; but if you don't board there, you may not get on. Tickets are $5 one-way (free for kids under 5 and only $1 before 7am and after 9pm), making those Muni passes look even better.

Cable cars run from 6am to 1:30am. To avoid standing in line, plan on traveling during off-peak hours. A great idea is to wake the family early and ride the cable car to a breakfast spot. Or take the cable car back to your hotel after dinner. Alternatively, you could head for the California Street cars, which are less popular because the route isn't as exciting, although the hill is quite steep. For more about the cable cars, see chapter 7.

BART

Please note: **Bay Area Rapid Transit** (BART; ℂ **415/989-2278**) is not Muni. Both systems share the same underground stations downtown, but the similarities end there. BART tickets are not valid on Muni and vice versa. The sleek silver-and-blue BART trains travel along the Market Street corridor, then make stops on Mission Street (16th and 24th sts.), in Glen Park, and south in Colma and the San Francisco International Airport. Other lines head to Berkeley, Oakland and other East Bay cities. Purchase BART tickets from machines inside the stations. Fares to and from any point within San Francisco are $1.40; outside the city they range up to $5. For schedules and route information, call the number above or log on to the website **www. bart.gov**.

BY CAR

Driving in San Francisco can be frustrating, to say the least. If you are unfamiliar with the territory and your copilot has issues reading maps, your vacation could turn chilly (or very, very loud) from the moment you exit the motorway. Along with aggressive local drivers, one-way streets, no right/left turns when you really need one, and dead ends, there's a decided lack of parking and too many overanxious meter maids ready

---

Tips Feeding the Meters

Most city parking meters take nickels, dimes, and quarters, and have time limits of anywhere from 15 minutes to 4 hours. Meters that are green on top usually have 15- to 30-minute time limits. Even if you come back and put more quarters in the meter, overstaying the time limit can still be cause for a ticket. Check your tires to make sure a meter maid has not swiped them with chalk (usually in bright orange or blue).

to pounce. Fortunately, it isn't necessary to drive to many of the places you'll want to go. When driving is imperative, you can easily rent a car for the day. For those of you who are arriving in the city by car, park at your hotel and do your best to use public transportation or walk.

RENTAL CARS

There's no reason to rent a car at the airport only to park it in San Francisco while you tour on foot or by Muni. With a reservation, you can pick up a rental car in the city on the day you'll be using it. Most rental car companies will be delighted to pick you up and drop you off right at your hotel if necessary, but many have offices near Union Square.

Companies that have offices downtown include **Avis,** 675 Post St. (© **415/885-5011;** www.avis.com); **Budget,** 321 Mason St. (© **415/292-8981;** www.budget.com); **Enterprise,** 222 Mason St. (© **415/837-1700;** www.enterprise.com); **Hertz,** 433 Mason St. (© **415/771-2200;** www.hertz.com); and **Thrifty,** 350 O'Farrell St. (© **415/788-8111;** www.thrifty.com).

DRIVING RULES

California law requires that both drivers and passengers wear seat belts. Children up to age 6 or who weigh less than 60 pounds must use a car seat or booster seat. Cars may turn right on a red light (unless otherwise indicated) after making a complete stop and yielding to traffic and pedestrians. Also, make a complete stop at stop signs, not a rolling stop; our local traffic police love to write tickets for that seemingly innocuous offense. Cable cars and streetcars always have the right-of-way, as do pedestrians, whether or not they use intersections and crosswalks—although if they don't,

---

Great Garages

When you approach a garage, read the signs carefully. You may see a sign offering a cheap all-day rate. In fact, that rate may apply only to cars that arrive early in the morning. After that, rates can be as high as $3 every 15 minutes! The garage by PIER 39 advertises a $6 flat rate in bold letters; impossibly small writing underneath explains that validation from one of PIER 39's overpriced restaurants is required. The best rates are at city-owned garages, many of which are listed here:

Union Square Garage, 333 Post St.; $2.50/first hour, $12/4 hours.

Sutter-Stockton Garage, 444 Stockton St. (Union Sq.); $2/first hour, $9/4 hours.

Ellis-O'Farrell Garage, 123 O'Farrell St. (Union Sq.); $2.50/first hour, $9/4 hours.

Fifth and Mission Garage, 833 Mission St. (SoMa); $2.50/first hour, $10/4 hours.

Portsmouth Square Garage, 733 Kearny St. at Clay (Chinatown); $2.50/first hour, $9/4 hours.

North Beach Garage, 735 Vallejo St. near Powell; $2.50/first hour, $9/4 hours.

Tips San Francisco Parking Secrets

- Purchase a roll of quarters for the meters and keep them in the glove compartment so that you can take advantage of any street spaces you're lucky enough to encounter.

- Between 4 and 6pm, parking is prohibited on major crosstown roads and pretty much anywhere downtown. Start cruising the Financial District, Union Square, Nob Hill, or SoMa about 10 minutes before 6pm and get ready to pounce on the space of your choice.

- Take the first parking spot that's within walking distance of your destination. (And by walking distance I don't mean two doors down; I mean more like 4 blocks.)

- Street parking spaces are usually spoken for before they are actually available. Watch for people walking toward cars with keys in hand and for brake lights turning on. Wait for the space to open up and take it.

- Pay close attention to street signs. In some neighborhoods, parking for non-residents (those without a city-issued sticker on their bumper) is limited to 1 or 2 hours.

- If parking places suddenly seem widely available, check the signs. It may be street sweeping time. Meter maids parade along the street writing $40 tickets just before the sweepers show up. Once the machines have rumbled by, you can safely park.

- Curb your car's wheels when parking on a hill: turn them toward the curb when facing downhill and away from the curb when parking uphill. Although this won't actually contribute to your finding a parking place, it will help you retain any that you have found. It will also keep you from getting a ticket.

- Be grateful for parking garages and use them. City-owned garages are cheaper than privately owned ones.

- Sometimes, the old parking karma just isn't working. If valet parking is available, take it. It's worth it to avoid a headache.

they're at risk for a jaywalking ticket or worse. On Market Street, one lane is exclusively for buses. Avoid driving on Market Street anyway, because the way the lights are timed is infuriating, and you can't make a left turn anywhere. Pull over when using a cellphone.

PARKING

Park in a city-owned garage. They seem expensive, but not compared to the ticket you're going to get if you attempt to park on the street for any length of time. Legal street parking spaces do exist; they are next to unpainted curbs and usually are accompanied by meters. Yellow, white, green, and red curbs are all off limits; the exceptions are commercial zones (the yellow curbs), which are open to cars after delivery hours. Pay attention to the signs liberally posted on the streets. Be very aware of tow-away zones. You cannot park on most streets downtown between 4 and 6pm without running the risk of having your vehicle towed. And never park in front of a driveway. Otherwise, AutoReturn, an independent contractor for the City's towing services, may take your vehicle to its storage lot at 415 7th Street, between Harrison & Folsom streets. If you return to your parking space but your car isn't there, check with AutoReturn online at www.autoreturn.com or call 𝒞 **415/553-1239** to see if it's been towed or merely stolen. It's likely been towed, and that means you get to visit City Tow to pay the fine and the storage charges. Such a misadventure will run you a minimum of $188 (most forms of payment accepted).

BY TAXI

Hailing a cab on most city streets is a hit-or-miss proposition, but spotting a taxi downtown is easier, especially in front of hotels. When moving around with kids, it's probably best to phone (or have your hotel phone) a cab company because that's the only way to guarantee that you'll be retrieved. The major cab companies are **Desoto Cab** (𝒞 415/970-1300), **Luxor Cabs** (𝒞 415/282-4141), **Metro Cab** (𝒞 415/920-0715), **Veteran's Cab** (𝒞 415/552-1300), and **Yellow Cab** (𝒞 415/626-2345).

Rates are around $2.85 for the first mile and 45¢ for each one-fifth of a mile as well as for each minute of waiting or traffic delay. If you take a cab from the airport to downtown, a $2 San Francisco Airport exit fee is added to the fare. The approximate fare from the airport is $29 to $44, depending on where you're staying. According to one of the companies I contacted, taxis are not required to provide infant or child car seats. If you hire a town car (for example, to bring you and your kids from the airport), they should be able to provide one, but be sure to ask when you make your reservation.

3 Planning Your Outings

Successful touring with kids requires preplanning or an extremely mellow attitude, and preferably both. (In fact, an extremely mellow attitude is as important as a warm jacket.) Deciding beforehand, even the night before, what you'd like to do each day is much preferable to winging it. Otherwise, you're going to waste time debating whether to go to Fisherman's Wharf or the zoo or Chinatown and not be prepared for any of them. In chapter 3, I listed some suggested itineraries that should help you plan your time in San Francisco.

Before you arrive in San Francisco, spend some time with the kids talking about the activities and attractions the city has to offer and make a list that includes both adult-oriented and kid-oriented sites. Make a family calendar, but don't overschedule; one outing in the morning and one in the afternoon is enough, because playing tourist can be exhausting. Once you've all had some input into deciding where to go and what to do, give everyone old enough to carry a backpack a copy of the itinerary. That way, if someone starts to whine about going to their chosen attraction, you can point to the calendar and remind them that their time will come. This advice is good no matter what ages your kids are, assuming that they are old enough to state an opinion.

Getting around the city with your children should be hassle free, for the most part. The one exception is if it's necessary to cart around baby paraphernalia such as strollers and diaper bags because it's difficult to get on and off buses when your hands are full and the bus is crowded. In this case, you'll want to plan your itinerary to decrease your dependence on public transportation and walk as much as possible, or take advantage of the wider entrances and exits on Muni streetcars. Again, for families with kids of any age, always factor in extra time to get around—even if you are driving, since there's a good chance you'll either get lost or spend 20 minutes looking for parking. San Francisco buses are slow; in addition to the scheduled stops, there's traffic to deal with and the occasional breakdown. The streetcars are a little better time-wise, but can be crowded. Remember, in a new destination, part of the pleasure really is in the journey itself. That's certainly the case in San Francisco.

TOP NEIGHBORHOODS FOR FAMILY OUTINGS
UNION SQUARE

Although few obvious children's attractions exist in what is first and foremost a shopping paradise, Union Square is the psychological heart of the city and should be considered as a launching pad for other excursions. Kids may find the crowds, clanging cable cars, and big buildings exciting. Moreover, Union Square itself now hosts entertainment, both ad hoc and planned. In the winter months, the plaza's enormous Christmas tree and Macy's holiday decorations are especially festive. Specifically, kid-friendly activities here include riding the glass elevator at the Westin St. Francis Hotel, greeting the beefeater-clad doorman at the Sir Francis Drake, and visiting the Disney Store. Teens may enjoy checking out the Levi's and Diesel stores, among other shops.

When Nature Calls: The ladies lounge at Neiman Marcus has one of the better bathrooms in town and is the best indoor place to nurse your baby. Macy's also has several restrooms. The big hotels are also great for bathroom breaks.

SOUTH OF MARKET (SOMA)

The walk from Union Square east to the SoMa neighborhood takes maybe 5 minutes and brings you into an amazing cultural zone. The Yerba Buena Gardens, Metreon, the Cartoon Art Museum, SFMOMA (the San Francisco Museum of Modern Art), and the California Academy of Sciences can all be reached on foot and can certainly make up a full day's program. Families with determined teens may want to tour the Westfield San Francisco Centre mall at 5th and Market streets as well.

When Nature Calls: The Westfield mall has a children's area tailor-made for changing diapers and nursing. The children's section downstairs in Bloomingdale's has spacious restrooms and an area for nursing moms. Metreon is also well equipped with toilets.

CHINATOWN

North of Union Square, a short walk up Grant Street, is the entrance to Chinatown. The draw here for you and yours is the sights and sounds of a community that is steeped in local history but which preserves its unique foreign culture. Possible stops include the playgrounds at St. Mary's Square or Portsmouth Square, the Chinese Cultural Center, the Canton Bazaar, the Golden Gate Fortune Cookie Company, and lunch.

When Nature Calls: Local merchants probably will not let you to use their bathrooms (few shopkeepers will in any neighborhood), so in an emergency make your way to the Chinatown Holiday Inn across from Portsmouth Square on Kearny Street. Remind everyone to use the toilet after lunch if you are eating at a restaurant. Nursing moms can feel free to feed their babies on a park bench here or anywhere in town, really. Just throw a blanket over your shoulder and chest for a little privacy.

Tips Enjoying Fisherman's Wharf

Fisherman's Wharf is on the water, of course. That often means fog, or at least a cool breeze. So bring sweaters. If you plan to take the ferry to Alcatraz, bring jackets as well. Schedule rest/play periods to help avoid meltdowns and consider packing snacks—the food in this area can be crummy and expensive.

FISHERMAN'S WHARF

Children could easily be entertained here for an entire day. For a more tranquil visit, hang out on the Ghirardelli side, where kids can climb aboard the Hyde Street Pier boats, frolic at the Aquatic Park beach, and listen to music in the courtyard of The Cannery. For a healthy dose of over-stimulation, walk east to see PIER 39's sea lions, the Aquarium of the Bay, and Musée Mécanique, and to catch the ferries for a bay cruise. Two scenic public transportation options from Union Square are the Powell-Hyde cable car or the F-Market streetcar.

When Nature Calls: The best public restroom here is on the Hyde Street Pier. Public bathrooms are also located on the second floor of The Cannery, at Ghirardelli, and on PIER 39. Nursing moms will have to grab a blanket and a bench. Try the courtyard at The Cannery or the east side of PIER 39.

GOLDEN GATE PARK

The 1,000-plus acres making up this urban oasis are filled with activities that will excite both children and their parents. Kids will love the Koret Children's Quarter (to reopen May 2007), the antique carousel, Japanese Tea Garden, and Stow Lake, and adults can admire Strybing Arboretum and the picturesque Conservatory of Flowers. It's easy to get to the park using public transportation, but kids may tire of the walk to reach the various attractions within it. A rest stop at one of the cafes or restaurants on 9th Avenue may help. The de Young Museum is a highlight of the park.

When Nature Calls: Public restrooms are available inside the de Young Museum, as well as near the Children's Playground, Stow Lake, and the Conservatory of Flowers. Nursing moms can find any comfortable spot or head for the Strybing Arboretum.

FAST FACTS: San Francisco

American Automobile Association (AAA) The office at 150 Van Ness Ave. provides maps and other information for members. Call ✆ **800/AAA-HELP** (800/222-4357) for emergency roadside service or ✆ 415/565-2012 for general information. You'll also find an AAA office on 160 Sutter St. at Kearny St. (✆ **415/433-2722**; www.csaa.com).

American Express For traveler's checks, travel information, and member services visit the office at 455 Market St., at 1st Street (✆ **415/536-2600**). Open Monday through Friday from 9am to 5:30pm, Saturday from 10am to 2pm.

Area Codes Local area codes are 415 for San Francisco, 650 for San Mateo County, and 510 for Oakland and Berkeley.

ATM Networks You'll practically trip over ATMs in the Financial District and on Market Street. Try to avoid using them after dark.

Babysitters Most hotel concierge will simply provide referrals to a babysitting service, which guests must then call on their own. Three recommended local companies supply short-term sitters: **American ChildCare Service** (© 415/285-2300; http://americanchildcare.com), **The Core Group** (© 415/206-9046; www.thecoregroup.org), and **Town & Country Resources** (© 800/398-8810 or 415/567-0956; www.tandcr.com). All advertise that their nannies are thoroughly screened and trained, and all have 4-hour minimums. Hourly fees range from $14 to $25. For $100 per child, you can give them a memorable night out through the **Explorer's Club** (© 415/902-7014; www.eckidsclub.com), a tour company catering to kids (see p. 201 for a full review).

Business Hours Most retail stores open at 10am and close at 6pm or 7pm. Many have extended hours on Thursday and Friday nights. Department stores are also open on Sundays from noon until 5pm.

Camera Repair **Discount Camera** at 33 Kearny St. near Union Square (© 415/392-1100) is a terrific resource for equipment and repairs. **San Francisco Camera & Repair Co.** at 1066 Market St. at 6th St. (© 415/431-4461) offers friendly customer service.

Car Rentals See "Getting Around," earlier in this chapter.

Climate See "When to Go," in chapter 2.

Currency The most common bills are the $1 (a "buck"), $5, $10, and $20 denominations. There are also $2 bills (seldom encountered), $50 bills, and $100 bills (the last two are usually not welcome as payment for small purchases).

  Coins come in seven denominations: 1¢ (1 cent, or a penny); 5¢ (5 cents, or a nickel); 10¢ (10 cents, or a dime); 25¢ (25 cents, or a quarter); 50¢ (50 cents, or a half dollar); the gold-colored Sacagawea coin, worth $1; and the rare silver dollar.

  For additional information see "Money," p. 19.

Dentists Call the **San Francisco Dental Society** for 24-hour referrals (© 415/421-1435; www.sfds.org). The **San Francisco Dental Office**, 131 Steuart St. (© 415/777-5115), offers emergency service and comprehensive dental care Monday, Tuesday, and Friday from 8am to 4:30pm, Wednesday and Thursday from 10:30am to 6:30pm.

Doctors **St. Francis Memorial Hospital,** 900 Hyde St., between Bush and Pine streets (© 415/353-6000), offers 24-hour emergency care. The hospital's physician-referral service number is © 800/333-1355. Your hotel can also contact on-call doctors who make house calls.

Drinking Laws No one under 21 can drink or purchase alcohol legally in California. All clubs, bars, supermarkets, and liquor stores check the identification of anyone who appears younger than 30. Alcohol is sold 7 days a week at supermarkets, corner stores, and wine shops between the hours of 6am and 2am. Bars do not serve liquor past 2am.

Driving Rules See "Getting Around," earlier in this chapter.

Earthquakes California gets them, but you most likely won't experience the real thing firsthand. Just in case, you should know a few basic precautionary measures. When you're inside a building, seek cover; do not run outside. Stand under a doorway or against a wall, or get under a sturdy table, and stay away from windows. When you exit a building after a substantial quake, use stair-wells, not elevators. If you are in a car, pull over to the shoulder and stop—but not until you are away from bridges, overpasses, telephone poles, and power lines. Stay in your car. If you are outside walking, stay away from trees, power lines, and the sides of buildings. If you are in an area with tall buildings, find a doorway in which to stand. Above all, do not panic and frighten your children. Earthquakes end quickly.

Electricity Like Canada, the United States uses 110 to 120 volts AC (60 cycles), compared to 220 to 240 volts AC (50 cycles) in most of Europe, Australia, and New Zealand. Downward converters that change 220–240 volts to 110–120 volts are difficult to find in the United States, so bring one with you.

Embassies & Consulates All embassies are located in the nation's capital, Washington, D.C. Some consulates are located in major U.S. cities, and most nations have a mission to the United Nations in New York City. If your country isn't listed below, call for directory information in Washington, D.C. (© **202/ 555-1212**) or log on to **www.embassy.org/embassies**.

The embassy of **Australia** is at 1601 Massachusetts Ave. NW, Washington, DC 20036 (© **202/797-3000;** www.austemb.org). There are consulates in Atlanta, Chicago, Honolulu, Los Angeles, New York, and San Francisco. In San Francisco, the consulate is at 575 Market St., Suite 1800 (© **415/536-1970**).

The embassy of **Canada** is at 501 Pennsylvania Ave. NW, Washington, DC 20001 (© **202/682-1740;** www.canadianembassy.org). There are 13 Canadian consulates in the U.S., including locations in Buffalo (New York), Detroit, Los Angeles, New York, and Seattle. In San Francisco, the consulate is at 580 California St., 14th floor (© **415/834-3180**).

The embassy of **Ireland** is at 2234 Massachusetts Ave. NW, Washington, DC 20008 (© **202/462-3939;** www.irelandemb.org). Irish consulates are in Boston, Chicago, New York, and San Francisco. In San Francisco, the consulate is at 100 Pine St., 33rd floor (© **415/392-4214**).

The embassy of **New Zealand** is at 37 Observatory Circle NW, Washington, DC 20008 (© **202/328-4800;** www.nzemb.org). New Zealand consulates are in Los Angeles and New York.

The embassy of the **United Kingdom** is at 3100 Massachusetts Ave. NW, Washington, DC 20008 (© **202/588-7800;** www.britainusa.com). Other British consulates are in Atlanta, Boston, Chicago, Houston, Los Angeles, New York, San Francisco, and Seattle. In San Francisco, the consulate is at 1 Sansome St., Suite 850 (© **415/617-1300**).

Emergencies Dial **911** for police, fire, or medical emergencies.

Holidays Banks, government offices, post offices, and many stores, restaurants, and museums are closed on the following legal national holidays: January 1 (New Year's Day), the third Monday in January (Martin Luther King, Jr., Day), the third Monday in February (Presidents' Day), the last Monday in May (Memorial Day), July 4 (Independence Day), the first Monday in September (Labor Day), the second Monday in October (Columbus Day), November 11 (Veterans' Day/Armistice Day), the fourth Thursday in November (Thanksgiving Day), and December 25 (Christmas). The Tuesday after the first Monday in November is Election Day, a federal government holiday in presidential-election years (held every 4 years, and next in 2008).

Hospitals **San Francisco General Hospital,** 1001 Potrero Ave. (© **415/206-8000**), accepts uninsured emergency patients, but the wait can be brutally long and uncomfortable. If you have insurance, head to **California Pacific Medical Center** at 2333 Buchanan St. at Sacramento Street (© **415/600-3600**).

Hotlines The following hotlines are available in San Francisco: **Poison Control Center** (© 800/876-4766), **Rape Crisis Center** (© 415/647-7273), and **Family Service Agency** (© 415/474-7310).

Information The **San Francisco Visitor Information Center** is in the lower level of Hallidie Plaza, 900 Market St., at Powell Street (© **415/391-2000;** www.onlyinsanfrancisco.com).

Internet Access Perhaps because everyone already has a computer here, San Francisco has few Internet cafes. The closest one to Union Square is **Cafe.com,** 120 Mason St. near Eddy Street (© **415/433-4001**), open daily. Other options, without the ambience, include **Copy Central,** 110 Sutter St. at Montgomery Street (© **415/392-6470**), and **FedEx Kinko's,** 1967 Market St., near Gough (© **415-252-0864**). If you are staying in the Marina, the closest FedEx Kinko's is on 3225 Fillmore St. near Lombard Street (© **415/441-2995**). The **Main Library,** 100 Larkin St. at McAllister Street (© **415/557-4400**), also has a number of terminals you can use for free. If you have your own computer, several places offer wireless Internet access, including some hotel lobbies and cafes like the **Grove,** with locations on Chestnut Street and Fillmore Street (see chapter 6).

Legal Aid If you are "pulled over" for a minor infraction (such as speeding), never attempt to pay the fine directly to a police officer; this could be construed as attempted bribery, a much more serious crime. Pay fines by mail, or directly into the hands of the clerk of the court. If accused of a more serious offense, say and do nothing before consulting a lawyer. Here the burden is on the state to prove a person's guilt beyond a reasonable doubt, and everyone has the right to remain silent, whether he or she is suspected of a crime or actually arrested. Once arrested, a person can make one telephone call to a party of his or her choice. International visitors should call your embassy or consulate.

Lost & Found Be sure to tell all of your credit card companies the minute you discover your wallet has been lost or stolen and file a report at the nearest police precinct. Your credit card company or insurer may require a police report number or record of the loss. Most credit card companies have an emergency toll-free number to call if your card is lost or stolen; they may be able to wire you a cash advance immediately or deliver an emergency credit card in a day or two. Visa's U.S. emergency number is © **800/847-2911** or 410/581-9994.

American Express cardholders and traveler's check holders should call © **800/ 221-7282.** MasterCard holders should call © **800/307-7309** or 636/722-7111. For other credit cards, call the toll-free number directory at © **800/555-1212.**

If you need emergency cash over the weekend when all banks and American Express offices are closed, you can have money wired to you via **Western Union** (© **800/325-6000;** www.westernunion.com).

Mail At press time, domestic postage rates were 24¢ for a postcard and 39¢ for a letter. For international mail, a first-class letter of up to 1 ounce costs 84¢ (63¢ to Canada and Mexico); a first-class postcard costs 75¢ (55¢ to Canada and Mexico); and a preprinted postal aerogramme costs 75¢. For more information go to **www.usps.com** and click on "Calculate Postage."

Maps The best city map I've seen and used is the **San Francisco Transit Rider Map and Guide,** published by Great Pacific Recreation and Travel Maps (www.greatpacificmaps.com). Order a copy from the company's website or buy one at the Visitors Information Center. You can also find it for $6 at many Walgreen's stores. AAA is an excellent source of maps, free to members.

Measurements See the chart on the inside front cover of this book for details on converting metric measurements to U.S. equivalents.

Newspapers & Magazines The major papers are the morning *San Francisco Chronicle* and the afternoon *San Francisco Examiner.* They are distributed from sidewalk kiosks and boxes. The free weekly *San Francisco Bay Guardian* is the best source of events listings. Find a copy in cafes and in sidewalk newspaper boxes around the city. *San Francisco* and *7×7* magazines are the monthly city glossies at newsstands everywhere.

Passports **For Residents of Australia:** You can pick up an application from your local post office or any branch of Passports Australia, but you must schedule an interview at the passport office to present your application materials. Call the **Australian Passport Information Service** at © **131-232,** or visit the government website at www.passports.gov.au.

For Residents of Canada: Passport applications are available at travel agencies throughout Canada or from the central **Passport Office,** Department of Foreign Affairs and International Trade, Ottawa, ON K1A 0G3 (© **800/567- 6868;** www.ppt.gc.ca). *Note:* Canadian children who travel must have their own passport. However, if you hold a valid Canadian passport issued before December 11, 2001, that bears the name of your child, the passport remains valid for you and your child until it expires.

For Residents of Ireland: You can apply for a 10-year passport at the **Passport Office,** Setanta Centre, Molesworth Street, Dublin 2 (© **01/671-1633;** www. irlgov.ie/iveagh). Those under age 18 and over 65 must apply for a €12 3-year passport. You can also apply at 1A South Mall, Cork (© **021/272-525**) or at most main post offices.

For Residents of New Zealand: You can pick up a passport application at any New Zealand Passports Office or download it from their website. Contact the **Passports Office** at © **0800/225-050** in New Zealand or 04/474-8100, or log on to **www.passports.govt.nz.**

For Residents of the United Kingdom: To pick up an application for a standard 10-year passport (5-yr. passport for children under 16), visit your nearest passport office, major post office, or travel agency, or contact the **United Kingdom Passport Service** at © 0870/521-0410 or search its website at **www.ukpa.gov.uk**.

Pets All the hotels in the Kimpton chain (such as the Monaco, Serrano, and Argonaut) accept dogs and cats, as do some upscale properties like the St. Regis. Other hotels, such as the Nikko, limit pets to dogs. Dogs must be leashed in most city parks, and you must pick up after them.

Pharmacies **Walgreens,** the Starbucks of drugstores, has stores just about everywhere. Phone © 800/WALGREEN (www.walgreens.com) for the address and phone number of the nearest store. Around Union Square, Walgreen's is at 135 Powell St. (© 415/391-4433), open Monday through Saturday from 8am to midnight and Sunday from 9am to 9pm, but the pharmacy has more limited hours. Branches at Divisadero Street (at Lombard Street), Castro Street (at 18th Street), and Potrero Ave. (at 24th Street) have 24-hour pharmacies.

Police The emergency number is © 911. Call from any phone (no coins are needed from pay phones). The non-emergency number is © 415/553-0123.

Radio Stations Find our National Public Radio affiliate, KQED, at 88.5 FM. News and sports may be found at KCBS 710 AM.

Reservation Services For hotel reservations, consult **SF Reservations** (© 800/677-1500 or 510/628-4450; www.hotelres.com).

Restrooms Dark green public lavatories are located by Union Square on Geary Street, on the waterfront at PIER 39, on Market Street near the cable car turnaround, on Powell Street, and at the Civic Center, among other locations. They cost 25¢ and are clean and safe. Also try hotels, museums, department stores, and service stations. Most restaurants reserve their facilities for patrons only.

Safety See "Health & Safety," in chapter 2.

Smoking California law prohibits smoking in public buildings, restaurants, and bars. Many hotels are completely nonsmoking, and others have limited floors for smokers. Inquire when you phone for reservations.

Taxes Sales tax of 8.5% is added to all purchases. The hotel tax is 14%.

Taxis See "Getting Around," earlier in this chapter.

Telephones For directory assistance, dial © 411. Pay phones (which are getting difficult to find) cost 35¢ to 50¢ for local calls.

Generally, hotel surcharges on long-distance and local calls are astronomical, so you're better off using your **cellphone** or a **public pay telephone.** Many convenience groceries and packaging services sell **prepaid calling cards** in denominations up to $50; for international visitors these can be the least expensive way to call home. Many public phones at airports now accept American Express, MasterCard, and Visa credit cards. **Local calls** made from public pay phones in most locales cost either 25¢ or 35¢. Pay phones do not accept pennies, and few will take anything larger than a quarter.

Most long-distance and international calls can be dialed directly from any phone. **For calls within the United States and to Canada,** dial 1 followed by the area code and the seven-digit number. **For other international calls,** dial 011 followed by the country code, city code, and the number you are calling.

Calls to area codes **800, 888, 877,** and **866** are toll-free. However, calls to area codes **700** and **900** (chat lines, bulletin boards, "dating" services, and so on) can be very expensive—usually a charge of 95¢ to $3 or more per minute, and they sometimes have minimum charges that can run as high as $15 or more.

For **reversed-charge or collect calls,** and for person-to-person calls, dial the number 0 then the area code and number; an operator will come on the line, and you should specify whether you are calling collect, person-to-person, or both. If your operator-assisted call is international, ask for the overseas operator.

For **local directory assistance** ("information"), dial 411; for long-distance information, dial 1, then the appropriate area code and 555-1212.

Telegraph and telex services are provided primarily by Western Union. You can telegraph money, or have it telegraphed to you, very quickly over the Western Union system, but this service can cost as much as 15 to 20 percent of the amount sent.

Most hotels have **fax machines** available for guest use (be sure to ask about the charge to use it). Many hotel rooms are even wired for guests' fax machines. A less expensive way to send and receive faxes may be at stores such as **The UPS Store** (formerly Mail Boxes Etc.), with convenient locations within the city, including 588 Sutter St. (② **415/834-1555**).

Time Zone California is on Pacific Standard Time, 3 hours behind New York and 8 hours behind London.

Useful Telephone Numbers For **transit information,** phone ② **415/817-1717.**

Visas For information about U.S. visas go to **http://travel.state.gov** and click on "Visas." Or go to one of the following websites:

Australian citizens can obtain up-to-date visa information from the **U.S. Embassy Canberra,** Moonah Place, Yarralumla, ACT 2600 (② **02/6214-5600**); or by checking the U.S. Diplomatic Mission's website at **http://usembassy-australia.state.gov/consular.**

British subjects can obtain up-to-date visa information by calling the **U.S. Embassy Visa Information Line** (② **0891/200-290**) or by visiting the "Visas to the U.S." section of the American Embassy London's website at **www.us embassy.org.uk.**

Irish citizens can obtain up-to-date visa information through the **Embassy of the USA Dublin,** 42 Elgin Rd., Dublin 4, Ireland (② **353/1-668-8777**); or by checking the "Consular Services" section of the website at **http://dublin.us embassy.gov.**

Citizens of **New Zealand** can obtain up-to-date visa information by contacting the **U.S. Embassy New Zealand,** 29 Fitzherbert Terrace, Thorndon, Wellington (② **644/472-2068**); or get the information directly from the "For New Zealanders" section of the website at **http://usembassy.org.nz.**

5

Family-Friendly Accommodations

Families seeking a place to hang their hats will find plenty of options in San Francisco. In addition to several internationally recognized hotel chains, the city boasts an outstanding collection of smaller hotels in every price category. Companies like Kimpton Hotels and Joie de Vivre Hospitality have transformed a number of historic buildings (and even some lowly motels) into luxurious boutique inns, delightful mid-priced hotels, and inexpensive, but festive, family accommodations.

Although downtown hotels rely mainly on convention and business travelers to fill rooms, they are becoming increasingly kid-friendly—especially as it becomes more popular to take the family along on work trips. Many higher-end hotels offer kids' gift packs at check-in, and concierges provide information on child-oriented activities in town. Several hotel restaurants also feature kids' menus. Moreover, nearly all city hotels allow children to stay free in parents' rooms and provide cribs at no charge.

Because many hotels in the city center are housed in older buildings, guest rooms are often small and interconnecting rooms not an option. This also means that it's hard to find truly budget options downtown, since rooms aren't big enough for a family of four—meaning you'd have to spring for a suite or two rooms. In the moderate range, though, you'll find a bigger selection of Union Square hotels with rooms to fit a family of four, and the number is increasing every year. Even with expanded bathroom counter space and other upgrades made to better accommodate families, you should be prepared for cozy quarters nonetheless in the less expensive accommodations.

The most family-oriented hotels are in Fisherman's Wharf and the Marina, and because they're housed in more modern buildings, many have rooms that will accommodate more than just a couple and a crib. You'll find the best rates in the Marina, but in any case most of the hotels in these neighborhoods lack the charm of the downtown hotels. There are a few notable exceptions, which I've listed in this chapter.

Do consider some of the more unique hotels San Francisco has to offer. The

---

Tips **Rubber Ducky Not Included**

Most hotel bathrooms have combination shower/bathtubs, but lower priced accommodations may have only showers. If your kids are still in the tub-only phase, ask about bathtubs when making your reservation.

Tips **Reservation Tips**

Many hotels provide you with a booking reference number. Upon request, hotels send you written confirmation of your reservation by fax, e-mail, or snail mail. Keep this paperwork handy, as it will be helpful if you decide to modify your plans. If you do cancel a reservation, request a cancellation number. This is very important, especially if you made your reservation with a credit card.

selection of boutique hotels is quite inspiring. For those who prefer the known comforts of bigger hotel chains, not to worry: I've included a considerable selection of those as well.

When choosing a part of town in which to stay, think about family members' special needs or interests. Perhaps a little one takes a midday nap, so a central location would be best. If you have active young children, you may appreciate the playgrounds within walking distance of Marina or Nob Hill hotels. Teens may prefer Union Square or SoMa for proximity to shopping and the Metreon. If your family's main interests are classic attractions such as Alcatraz and Ghirardelli Square, Fisherman's Wharf could be the place (although the heavy concentration of tourists has its drawbacks, such as overpriced, mediocre food). For more information about the lodging merits of each neighborhood, refer to the "Neighborhoods in Brief" section of chapter 4.

To get the most bang for your buck at any price point, timing helps. If your dates are flexible, you may benefit from reduced hotel rates. Downtown hotels are cheapest on weekends, whereas the opposite is often true in the Marina and Fisherman's Wharf. During conventions, Union Square and SoMa hotel rates jump, but you could luck out if a hotel hasn't managed to sell all of its rooms. It may be willing to offer steep discounts.

Whereas downtown hotel prices don't vary much with the seasons, Marina and Fisherman's Wharf rates climb in the summer. Given the summertime fog, the price increase has less to do with the best time to visit San Francisco than with when most families take their vacations. If you buck the trend and come in the late winter, you'll save money.

The cheapest rooming option is usually one room with two queen beds. With little ones, that could mean lights out well before mom and dad are ready to pack it in. If that's the case, or if you have older kids who need their space, the next best option is a suite, which tends to run cheaper than two interconnecting rooms. Just be alert: some hotels throw a pullout sofa into an extra-big room and call it a suite. If you want separate rooms, make sure that's what you're getting.

RESERVATION SERVICES San Francisco Reservations (© 800/677-1570 or 510/628-4450; www.hotelres.com) is a Bay Area company with a local call center. This no-fee service has access to hundreds of Bay Area hotels, a well designed website, and accurate descriptions. Online resources for good rates include www.placestostay.com and www.hotels.com. For bed-and-breakfast reservations, try **Bed & Breakfast Inns Online** (© 615/868-1946; www.bbonline.com).

If you plan a longer visit, consider bucking the hotel options altogether and lodge in a house or apartment. Agencies offer furnished apartments for stays as brief as 4 nights, and some Internet sites offer home exchanges with families in other cities and countries. I've listed some of these agencies and sites below.

American Marketing Systems (www. amsires.com) and **Executive Suites** (www.executivesuites-sf.com) offer furnished apartment rentals for stays of a few days or more, although rates can be high. To research house exchanges, check out **Homelink International** (www. homelink.org), **Home Base Holidays** (www.homebase-hols.com), and **International Home Exchange Network** (www. homexchange.com).

A NOTE ON PRICES   I have listed "rack rates"—a hotel's highest room price—in categorizing my hotel picks. You will probably get a much better quote when you call. Occupancy rates were about 78% in 2006, a solid year-over-year increase since a slump in 2001. Nonetheless, weekend discounts, family packages, and other promotions are still possible. In this chapter, I've classified hotels based on cost for a family of four staying in one room, unless a specific hotel has space constraints that require staying in a suite or two connecting rooms. Prices do not include the 14% hotel tax, nor does it include parking, which can run from free to $50 a night.

GETTING THE BEST RATE   Despite the slow rise in average hotel room prices since the 2001 slump, every moderate and high-end hotel I visited insisted that guests can almost certainly book rooms at rates well below the published rack rates—unless several business conventions are in town at the same time. The first step to doing so is checking multiple sources. Surf the Internet first and then call both the central reservations number, if there is one, and in-house reservations. Find which source has the best deal. Many hotels not only match a rate you have found on the Internet but also, in some cases, beat it.

It's important that you check with in-house reservations. I've had three different websites indicate a hotel was booked only to call the hotel directly and find that it had one room left (a suite, which didn't fit into the Internet's standard room category) that could be had for a steal. Moreover, folks in-house can provide the most detailed information about the hotel and the specific room type you may be interested in. You can also tell the hotel agent that you are traveling with children and inquire about special offers they may have.

As your arrival date nears, inquire again about any special deals. At check-in, don't hesitate to ask if you can upgrade to a bigger room or a higher floor. If the hotel has no hope of selling these better rooms for the next few nights, they may be willing to upgrade you at no additional charge.

KITCHENETTES   Kitchenettes are a rarity in San Francisco, and I've noted nearly all that are available. Reserve for them well in advance.

POOLS   Some kids will be happy anywhere you take them as long as there's a pool. But given San Francisco real estate

---

☂ Tips   Meals on a Budget

Having breakfast in your hotel room cuts back on restaurant bills. Also, some kids wake up at the crack of dawn when in new surroundings or time zones, well before any cafes are open. If you can't get a kitchenette, a fridge (and a coffeemaker for mom and dad) will do. If they're not already in your room, many hotels will provide these at no charge. Buy some disposable dishware, plastic cutlery, and some milk and cereal (or bread and butter, if that's what you're used to at home) and you're all set.

(Tips **The Corner Room**

Don't forget to ask if the hotel has a corner room. In some instances, the corner room has more light (windows on two walls) and more space than a standard room, but costs the same.

---

prices, few hotels devote precious space to swimming facilities, and most pools that do exist are petite. Almost all the San Francisco hotels with pools are listed in this chapter.

ACCESSIBILITY The Americans with Disabilities Act requires that hotels built within the past 20 years accommodate the need of disabled travelers. However, San Francisco hotels are often located in older buildings that are exempt from this rule. If you or anyone in your family requires appropriately designed hotel rooms, look for a property that's been remodeled recently or built after 1985. Discuss your needs with the reservations clerk.

1 Union Square/Financial District

This is the heart of the city, the focal point for shopping and entertainment. It's exciting, urban, and uniquely San Franciscan—and it's where you'll find the greatest range of accommodations. The downside for some families is the congestion and lack of greenery.

VERY EXPENSIVE

Hotel Nikko ⚐   Although this Eastern-influenced hotel caters largely to corporate travelers, it holds one of the few, and one of the most spacious, indoor swimming pools in the city. The pool is connected to the Nikko's health club, but the staff insists that guests tend to exercise in the early morning and evening, which means the rest of the day children can splash around freely. The pool is located in an expansive glass-roofed atrium, which also houses exercise equipment and Japanese hot tubs, so you can work out or enjoy a soak while you keep on eye on the kids.

Decor is tastefully understated, and rooms get a lot of natural sunlight. With a pull-out sofa and "guest washroom," the Nikko's junior suites are quite family-friendly. Even standard double/double rooms are large and have entryways that give the impression of more space. Views start above the 10th floor. Rooms on the three executive-level "Nikko Floors" also have vanities and more spacious bathrooms, and the Nikko Lounge offers board games and Internet access, so your teenagers can still IM their pals at home. The Nikko welcomes all pets. (Just be sure to inform the hotel if you plan to leave a Great Dane in your room for the day, so they can alert the housekeeping staff!) The white marble lobby is stark, but kids will enjoy the indoor fountain, which has become a multi-currency wishing well. The hotel also houses Anzu restaurant, specializing in sushi and steak, but offering a children's menu as well.

222 Mason St. (between Ellis and O'Farrell sts.), San Francisco 94102. ⟨ **800/248-3308** or 415/394-1111. Fax 415/394-1106. www.hotelnikkosf.com. 533 units, including 22 suites. $189–$359 double; $795–$2,900 suite. Kids under 18 stay free in parent's room. Rollaways $30, cribs free. AE, DC, DISC, MC, V. Valet parking $40; oversized vehicles $45. Pets welcome. **Amenities:** Restaurant; pool; health club; concierge; business center; salon; gift shop; 24-hr. room service; massage; babysitting; laundry service; dry cleaning; executive level rooms. *In room:* A/C, plasma TV, CD player, fax, high-speed Internet access, minibar, fridge (on request), coffeemaker, hair dryer, iron, safe.

JW Marriott Hotel San Francisco   The Marriott chain acquired this hotel from the Pan-Pacific Hotel chain in 2006. Despite a decor in lovely earth tones that was completely redone in 2005, the Marriott chain plans a complete "soft" renovation (changes in fabrics, carpets, and wallpaper, but no structural changes) beginning in June 2007. Let's hope Marriott keeps the style in the rooms as lovely as it was. Despite not knowing how the hotel will soon look, I can attest to comfortably large rooms. While rollaways are not permitted in the standard rooms, a family of four will fit comfortably into the 400-square-foot, deluxe rooms with two double beds. Those rooms also have two sinks, and all the bathrooms have deep-soaking tubs, separate showers, gleaming marble floors, and even TVs (that's in addition to the LCD televisions in the bedrooms). Rollaways are permitted in the suites, which also interconnect to double/double rooms, accommodating large families. Rooms above the 17th floor have the best views. As for the lobby, located on the third floor, it is imposing: it's housed in a massive atrium, with glass-fronted elevators whizzing guests to their rooms on high.

500 Post St. (at Mason St.), San Francisco, CA 94102. © **800/605-6568** or 415/771-8600. Fax 415/398-0267. www. jwmarriottunionsquare.com. 337 units, including 8 suites, all non-smoking. $360–$420 double; from $670 suite. Kids under 12 stay free in parent's room. Rollaways at varying prices, cribs free. AE, DC, DISC, MC, V. Valet parking $42; oversized vehicles $48. **Amenities:** Restaurant; fitness center; concierge; business center; 24-hr. room service; babysitting; laundry service; dry cleaning. *In room:* A/C, TV, high-speed Internet access, minibar, coffeemaker, hair dryer, iron, safe.

EXPENSIVE

Galleria Park Hotel ⚡   Closer to the financial district than other hotels in the Union Square vicinity, this small, luxury property (built in 1911) is quieter at night than many other downtown hotels. Setting it apart from its competitors are a unique rooftop jogging track/garden that offers an out-of-the-way spot to let off some steam and an easy-access parking garage underneath the hotel. If you have a car and need it quickly, the valet won't have to hike a few blocks to fetch it. Also appealing is the hotel's proximity to the Galleria Shopping Center, with its very respectable food court.

Rooms and bathrooms are small to moderate in size. They have been renovated in the past few years and are comfortable, conservatively decorated, and pleasing. Double/doubles are going to be cozy, but weekend and winter rates are low enough that you could aim for two connecting rooms. Suites are certainly another option. The king-bedded one-bedroom suites have separate living rooms with a pullout sofa. It's not large enough to add a crib or rollaway, however. The lobby area retains an old-fashioned charm and the staff, especially the concierge, is well trained and friendly. Enjoy free coffee and tea in the morning and a wine reception in the evening.

191 Sutter St. (at Kearny St.), San Francisco, CA 94104. © **800/792-9639** or 415/781-3060. Fax 415/433-4409. www.galleriapark.com. 177 units, including 7 suites. $139–$259 double; $199–$599 suite. Kids under 12 stay free in parent's room. Rollaways $20, cribs free. AE, DC, DISC, MC, V. Valet parking $40; oversized vehicles $45. **Amenities:**

Taking the Night Off

See "Fast Facts," in chapter 4, for information on hiring babysitters. When a hotel says it provides babysitting, it really means it has a list of recommended agencies that provide bonded, screened caregivers. It's up to you to make the arrangements, which ideally should be done in advance.

Accommodations Near Union Square & the Financial District

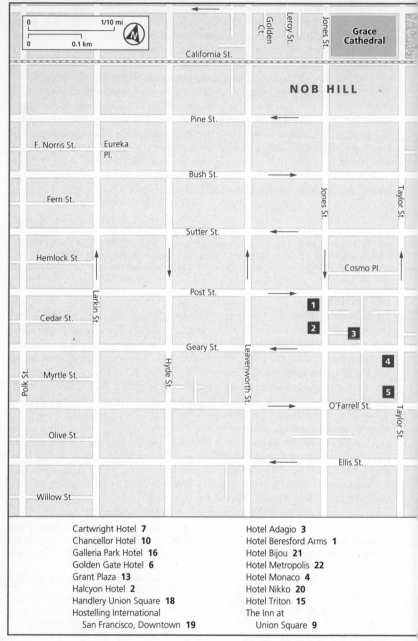

Cartwright Hotel **7**
Chancellor Hotel **10**
Galleria Park Hotel **16**
Golden Gate Hotel **6**
Grant Plaza **13**
Halcyon Hotel **2**
Handlery Union Square **18**
Hostelling International
    San Francisco, Downtown **19**

Hotel Adagio **3**
Hotel Beresford Arms **1**
Hotel Bijou **21**
Hotel Metropolis **22**
Hotel Monaco **4**
Hotel Nikko **20**
Hotel Triton **15**
The Inn at
    Union Square **9**

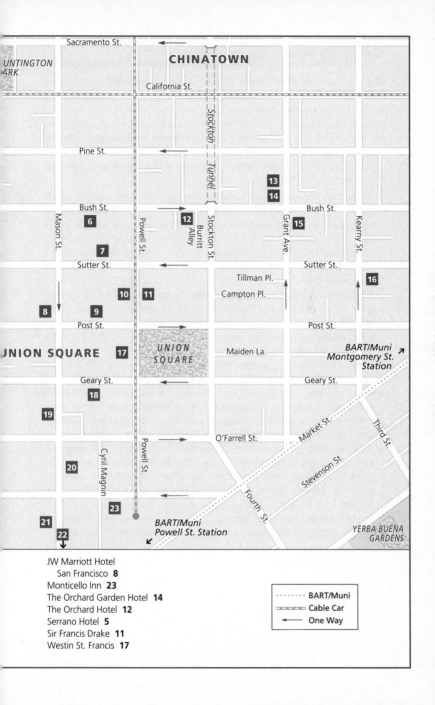

JW Marriott Hotel
San Francisco **8**
Monticello Inn **23**
The Orchard Garden Hotel **14**
The Orchard Hotel **12**
Serrano Hotel **5**
Sir Francis Drake **11**
Westin St. Francis **17**

Making the Most of the Concierge

Nearly all upscale hotels have concierges, and many smaller inns offer concierge services from the front desk. Too often, these people go under-utilized by guests who don't know the full range of services concierges can provide. Beyond merely giving directions to Fisherman's Wharf, concierges are there to act as guests' problem solvers. The best ones take real pleasure in helping, and the more challenging the request, the better. When you're on vacation, why not truly relax, and let the concierge be your personal assistant during your stay?

- **House cars:** Upper-end hotels often have house cars available to drop off guests in the Financial District or elsewhere within 2 to 5 miles of the hotel. Businesspeople use the service most, but any guest can enjoy this perk. If you want to take the kids to AT&T Park to watch some baseball, or you need a ride to a restaurant, request a house car through the concierge desk. There's usually no charge, but you may tip the driver at your discretion.

- **Restaurants:** Every concierge will make dinner reservations for guests, and I recommend having the concierge phone ahead no matter where you are dining. If a restaurant is booked, the concierge may have more pull squeezing you in than you would on your own. But don't ask the concierge for any old restaurant recommendation. (I've been to some unremarkable, touristy places that way.) It's more effective to name two or three options and have the concierge tell you more about each one.

- **Other services:** You needn't limit requests to restaurant reservations. Concierges can also book Alcatraz or other cruises, car rentals, or even spa treatments—whatever requires a phone call. They can buy tickets to a sporting or entertainment venue or amend airline reservations.

- **Solutions:** Did a child get sick? Head right to the concierge, who will make it a personal mission to ensure a doctor sees your kid as soon as possible. Concierges will also oblige less urgent requests, like reserving doggy day care or finding a last-minute gift. You don't even have to be checked into the hotel. You can fax and e-mail the concierge with your arrival date and particular request. If he or she does go beyond the call of duty, gratuities are always appreciated—although never expected.

Restaurant; exercise room; concierge; room service (5–9pm); babysitting; laundry service; dry cleaning. *In room:* A/C, TV, CD player, free wireless high-speed Internet access, minibar, fridge, hair dryer, iron.

Hotel Monaco 🐾🐾 A star in the Kimpton hotel chain, this refurbished 1910 landmark is a refreshing change from other high-end hotels. The Art Deco decor in the impressive lobby is vibrant and festive, and sure to please any child who sees it. Kids will also love the freshly baked cookies at the front desk and the pet goldfish that keeps them company in their hotel room (on request). This property is so pet-friendly it offers special packages for pooches, and guests actually check in with dogs more regularly than with children. Parents will like the complimentary wine and cheese reception in the lobby daily at 5pm. Dining options are the Grand Cafe (p. 121), inside a beautifully restored turn-of-the-20th-century ballroom, and the Petit Cafe, with simpler fare more suited for kids. Adults can take turns pretending they're at a resort at the newly renovated spa and health club on the bottom floor. If you're flying, check to see if the house car is available to take you to the airport; the cost is about the same as a taxi.

The vividly designed rooms and bathrooms are larger than those at the Serrano down the block; the doubles here are just spacious enough for a crib. Suites come with a very large bathroom, sofa bed in the living room, a VCR, and two televisions.

501 Geary St. (at Taylor St.), San Francisco, CA 94102. ℭ **800/214-4220** or 415/292-0100. Fax 415/292-0111. www.monaco-sf.com. 201 units, including 35 suites. $229–$399 double; $379–$649 suite. Kids under 17 stay free in parent's room. No rollaways; cribs free. AE, DC, DISC, MC, V. Valet parking $39; oversized vehicles $45. Pets welcome. **Amenities:** 2 restaurants; bar; health club/spa/exercise room; concierge; courtesy car; 24-hr. room service; massage; babysitting; laundry service; dry cleaning. *In room:* A/C, TV with movies, DVD, CD player, video games, free wireless high-speed Internet access, minibar, fridge, coffeemaker, hair dryer, iron, safe.

Hotel Triton 𝒢𝒢 You'll score big points with your pre-teens or teenagers at this rock 'n' roll–themed boutique hotel. Staffed by creative types wearing studded leather belts or hipster outfits, this may be the zaniest property in the colorful Kimpton chain. The fantastical lobby decor is rivaled only by the groovy tunes spun by the hotel staff, and suites have been designed by the likes of Carlos Santana, Jerry Garcia, and Woody Harrelson. The eco-friendly hotel uses biodegradable cleaning products, recycles as much paper as possible, and even serves organic coffee. That coffee is served with biscotti lobby-side in the morning, while in the evenings a DJ often provides music to accompany the daily free wine and beer hour.

Of course there's a catch: the whimsical rooms and bathrooms are teensy. Because interconnecting rooms are not available, families have the choice of occupying two separate rooms, squeezing into a double/double, or reserving a suite. Although kids may love to stay in the Red Hot Chili Peppers suite, be aware that most suites are actually one-room studios with a king bed and a queen-size sleeper sofa. Of course, the diminutive size may be worth it if your child is fortunate enough to share an elevator ride with one of the many bands that often stay at the hotel.

342 Grant Ave. (at Bush St.), San Francisco, CA 94108. ℭ **800/800-1299** or 415/394-0500. Fax 415/394-0555. www. hoteltriton.com. 140 units, including 7 suites. $169–$269 double; suites from $269. Kids under 12 stay free in parent's room. Rollaways in suites only, cribs free. AE, DC, DISC, MC, V. Valet parking $37. Pets welcome. **Amenities:** Exercise room; concierge; business center; room service (limited hours); laundry service; dry cleaning. *In room:* A/C, TV with movies and games, iPod available, CD player, free high-speed Internet access, minibar, coffeemaker, hair dryer, iron.

The Inn at Union Square This diminutive hotel primarily serves business travelers but is worth considering for its competitive rates and location just 1 block from Union Square. The bright and airy rooms come mainly with king and queen beds, although there is one room with two double beds. There are no adjoining rooms, but the more spacious rooms can comfortably fit a rollaway, and suites with pullout sofa beds are also available. Every floor (except the second) has a separate clubroom featuring complimentary breakfast in the mornings, wine and appetizers in the evenings, and hot tea and cookies after 8pm. The clubrooms also have fridges for guests' use. Gym passes are also available. Concierge services are available from the front desk. In all, the hotel's small size makes for an intimate feel and personalized service, which must be why satisfied guests return again and again.

440 Post St. (between Mason and Powell sts.), San Francisco, CA 94102. © 800/288-4346 or 415/397-3510. Fax 415/989-0529. www.unionsquare.com. 30 units. $239–$249 double; $269–$329 suite. Kids under 14 stay free in parent's room. Cribs free. AE, DC, DISC, MC, V. Valet parking $36; oversized vehicles $41; self-parking $25. **Amenities:** Laundry service; dry cleaning. *In room:* TV w/movies, CD player, high-speed Internet access, hair dryer, iron, safe.

The Orchard Hotel ★★ This is one of the few downtown boutique hotels constructed as an entirely new building (in 2000). That means you get spacious rooms compared to other nearby hotels in this price category, large bathrooms with separate showers and tubs, and nicely soundproofed walls. Since each floor has few rooms, and therefore less foot traffic, the hotel says the only noise you're likely to hear is the occasional ring of the cable car bell. The still-new decor has an Art Deco touch with plenty of wood and muted colors. Only the waterfall-type fountain in the lobby seems out of place. Funky fountains aside, pluses at the Orchard include complete entertainment centers in every room, free DVDs, complimentary "Euro-continental" breakfast (the "Euro" part means cheeses and cold cuts are served alongside the freshly baked pastries), and Aveda products. Should you find the platform beds too firm, you can request a pillow-top mattress cover. Finally, the hotel is one of a handful of San Francisco hotels that have earned a "Green Seal of Approval" for environmental design, use of biodegradable cleaning products, and other eco-friendly touches. The major drawback is that the Orchard was originally envisioned as a business hotel, so rooms are designed for two people. If your party includes more than parents and an infant, you'll have to get interconnecting rooms or spring for one of the two-room suites, which have entertainment centers in both rooms and can be had for just $100 more than the lowest-available rate on the standard room.

665 Bush St. (at Stockton St.), San Francisco, CA 94108. © 888/717-2881 or 415/362-8878. Fax 415/362-8088. www.theorchardhotel.com. 104 units, including 9 suites. $149–$299 double; $249–$399 suite. Rollaways in suites only; cribs $25. AE, DC, DISC, MC, V. Valet parking $34. **Amenities:** Restaurant; bar; exercise room; concierge; courtesy car; room service (limited hours); laundry service; dry cleaning. *In room:* A/C, TV with movies and games, CD player, free high-speed Internet access, fridge, minibar, coffeemaker, hair dryer, iron.

Serrano Hotel ★★ The Serrano is one of the most family-friendly options in the neighborhood. The richly-colored Spanish Revival lobby isn't overwhelmingly large, and cozy seating under a beamed ceiling is arranged in small groups. During the complimentary evening wine reception, a tarot card reader drops by to entertain and a chair masseuse is on hand—just what your shoulders need, if you've been carrying your tired kids around town. As at most Kimpton hotels, one TV channel is dedicated to yoga, and a complimentary yoga basket is available. Guests can borrow games from an extensive game library to play in the lobby or in their rooms. In keeping with the

---

A Growing Orchard

While not open at press time, **The Orchard Garden Hotel** (© 888/717-2881 or 415/399-9807; Fax 415/393-9917; www.theorchardgardenhotel.com) has the same ownership as the impressive Orchard Hotel. The Orchard Garden will supposedly have more rooms suitable for large families, albeit at about $20 more per room, and is also notable as the first California hotel to receive LEED-NC certification (Leadership in Energy & Environmental Design for New Construction) from the U.S. Green Building Council. The hotel is located at 466 Bush St. (at Grant Ave.), just a couple of blocks east of its sister property.

whimsical theme, you'll find yo-yos, mini Etch A Sketches, and cards, all for a fee, in the minibars. Another unique perk for young families are complimentary strollers and booster seats. Check the website for family and pet packages.

The building dates from the 1920s, although it was entirely renovated in 1999. Rooms are lushly designed with warm colors and patterns, double-paned windows, and small, well-stocked bathrooms. Double/doubles are too small for a family of four. Instead, consider a queen deluxe with a connecting double/double (best for large families); an executive king with a bed, sofa bed, and large marble bathroom; or a suite. The suites have a king bed and king sofa bed, each in its own room. Corner rooms have views and are a bit more spacious. The hotel's Ponzu restaurant serves breakfast and tasty Asian-inspired dinner dishes.

405 Taylor St. (at O'Farrell St.), San Francisco, CA 94102. ⓒ 866/289-6561 or 415/885-2500. Fax 415/474-4879. www.serranohotel.com. 236 units, including 129 suites. $159–$299 double; $279–$499 suite. Kids under 18 stay free in parent's room. Cribs free. AE, DC, DISC, MC, V. Valet parking $39; oversized vehicles $49. Small pets welcome. **Amenities:** Restaurant; exercise room and sauna; business center; room service (limited hours); babysitting; laundry service; dry cleaning. In room: A/C, TV w/movies and games, free high-speed Internet access, minibar/fridge, hair dryer, iron, laptop-size safe.

Sir Francis Drake   If you can snag a great deal at this historic hotel, it's an option worth considering. But if you can't find a room rate well below the advertised rack rates, I wouldn't recommend it. Certainly, the 1928 hotel is in a premier location by Union Square and on the cable car line. The Harry Denton Starlight Lounge on the top floor is legendary, only slightly less famous than the hotel's beefeater-clad doormen. (Tom Sweeney, who has been opening doors to guests for over a quarter-century, is a verifiable San Francisco icon.) And the grandiose, chandelier-lit lobby, complete with a sweeping marble staircase, offers a majestic taste of the Old World.

Unfortunately, many of the colorfully decorated rooms are small, and the bathrooms even tinier, with hardly any counter space. But if you don't mind forgoing queen beds, the executive double/double rooms are relatively spacious and have a bonus second bathroom. They can be had for $199, if you search the Kimpton website for specials. There are some interconnecting rooms as well. Unlike at other Kimpton properties, you will find neither complimentary morning coffee nor afternoon wine in the lobby, but the hotel does have two good restaurants on site: Caffe Espresso and Scala's Bistro. The view is better and the street noise less audible on the upper floors.

450 Powell St. (at Sutter St.), San Francisco, CA 94102. ⓒ 800/795-7129 or 415/392-7755. Fax 415/391-8719. www.sirfrancisdrake.com. 417 units, including 4 parlor suites and 1 presidential suite. $239–$319 double. Suites from $599. Kids 18 and under stay free in parent's room. Rollaways $20, cribs free. AE, DC, DISC, MC, V. Valet parking $40; oversized vehicles $45. Pets welcome. **Amenities:** 2 restaurants; lounge; exercise room; concierge; business center; room service (limited hours); babysitting; laundry service; same-day dry cleaning. In room: A/C, TV w/movies and games, wireless high-speed Internet access, minibar/fridge, hair dryer, iron.

Westin St. Francis (Overrated   The historic St. Francis Hotel, a survivor of the 1906 earthquake, is a veritable hubbub of activity. With its location just across from Union Square and steps away from serious shopping, downtown theaters, and the cable cars, the hotel's expansive lobby has always been a convenient meeting place for tourists, walking tours, friends taking tea, and the occasional elementary school group on a field trip to ride the glass elevators to the 27th floor. Travelers under 12 receive Westin Kids Club backpacks with age-appropriate promotional items like light socket covers and sippy cups. Rooms are outfitted with comfortable "Heavenly Bed" and "Heavenly Bath" and good linens.

Despite its size, perpetually crowded lobby, and, quite frankly, impersonal feel, the hotel's prime location on Union Square seems to make it very popular. If high energy, location, and the historical aspects intrigue you, here's some advice: phone in-house reservations and be as specific as possible about your needs. Prices can fluctuate wildly due to the many room configurations, some less desirable than others. Standard queen rooms are barely large enough for two. Traditional queen rooms have more space, and can accommodate a crib or rollaway. The deluxe double/doubles are very spacious with renovated bathrooms, and the Grandview rooms have smarter decor. Ask for a view or a corner room if you want natural light and avoid rooms by the ever-busy elevators. Hallways go on forever. If your child has forgotten his sweatshirt, you'll have to go back to the room with him unless he's outfitted with a compass and a map.

335 Powell St. (at Geary St.), San Francisco, CA 94102. © 800/WESTIN-1 or 415/397-7000. Fax 415/774-0124. www.westin.com. 1,195 units. $149–$569 double; $250–$5,000 suite. Kids under 18 stay free in parent's room. Roll-aways and cribs free. AE, DC, DISC, MC, V. Valet parking $45; oversized vehicles $52. Small dogs welcome. **Amenities:** Restaurant/bar; health club; concierge; business center; shopping arcade; 24-hr. room service; massage; babysitting; laundry service; dry cleaning. *In room:* A/C, TV, high-speed Internet access, minibar, hair dryer, iron, safe.

MODERATE

Cartwright Hotel *★ (Value*   Guest rooms in this low-key, old-fashioned hotel are on the small side, so you really can't share with the kids. Although it was renovated in 2004 with brand-new furniture, the bathrooms are also petite. That said, the two-bedroom suites are a real find because you can snag one for around $250 in the off-season. They're comfortable and cozy, with softly colored walls, and a few are furnished with antiques. The hotel's complimentary deluxe breakfast includes a station where the kids can make their own waffles. Early evenings, the staff hosts a wine reception to help you unwind from a busy day of sightseeing. A library off the lobby, equipped with comfy sofas, a large-screen television, and free wireless Internet access (bring your own laptop), is another plus.

Location-wise, the hotel receives extra points. It's just north of Union Square, 3 blocks from the Chinatown Gate. All the cable car lines are nearby without being so close that you hear their every bell and whirr. The staff also provides concierge services, such as making dinner reservations. If you like a truly European ambience, where you drop your keys off at the reception desk and see the same faces each morning and afternoon, you'll be pleased. For independent vacationers who require comfort and value, but not hand-holding, the Cartwright delivers.

524 Sutter St. (near Powell St.), San Francisco, CA 94102. © 800/919-9779 or 415/421-2865. Fax 415/398-6345. www.cartwrighthotel.com. 114 units, including 5 suites. $109–$259 double; $199–$369 suite. Kids under 18 stay free in parent's room. Rollaways $20 but only in suites, cribs free. AE, DC, DISC, MC, V. Valet parking $35; self-parking $25. Pets welcome. *In room:* A/C (not all rooms), CD player, free wireless Internet access, coffeemakers, hair dryer (on request), iron (on request).

Chancellor Hotel   Across the street from Saks Fifth Avenue and less than a block from Union Square, the Chancellor, built in 1914, is a typical old-time San Francisco hotel. Its prime location makes up for unimaginative decor, as do nice touches such as coffee, apples, and cookies at the reception desk; a pleasant staff; free local calls; and a pillow menu with selections such as firm, soft, hypoallergenic, down, and even snore-reducing (useful when sharing rooms). Rooms come with one queen bed or two twin beds, and interconnecting rooms are available. The hotel has two suites, each with a double bed and pullout sofa. From higher-floor, street-side bedrooms ending in 00 through 05, you'll have views of the cable cars and Union Square. Bathrooms are moderately sized, and each tub comes with its own rubber ducky.

The in-house restaurant, Luques, serves breakfast, lunch, and dinner. Older kids will appreciate the free high-speed Internet access available in the lobby. Check the website or call the hotel about special package rates, which can be much lower than published rates.

433 Powell St. (between Post and Sutter sts.), San Francisco, CA 94102. ℂ 800/428-4748 or 415/362-2004. Fax 415/362-1403. www.chancellorhotel.com. 137 units, including 2 suites. $175 double; $230–$300 suite. Rollaways $15, cribs free. AE, DC, DISC, MC, V. Valet parking $30; oversized vehicles $41; self-parking $22. **Amenities:** Restaurant; concierge; room service (7am–10pm); laundry service; dry cleaning. *In room:* TV w/movies, high-speed Internet access, fridge (on request), hair dryer, iron, safe.

Handlery Union Square ⚜ *Value*   A family-owned and -operated hotel for more than 50 years, the Handlery is notable for being the only downtown hotel with an outdoor, heated pool. Although the lobby feels like a throwback to an '80s nightclub, the staff is excellent and the hotel is a good deal in a central location. Older kids will be happy with the wireless high-speed Internet access (for a fee) all over the hotel, including in guest rooms. The room decor is nice enough, but guest rooms and bathrooms in the historic Geary Street side of the hotel are small—the king-bedded standards have just enough room for a crib. The Club Rooms on the O'Farrell Street side are quite spacious, with a dressing area, robes, and extra amenities. Because the tiled pool deck gets occasional sun, the best rooms in the house are poolside Club Rooms, which aren't much more expensive than those in the historic section. Connecting rooms are available, as are rooms with two queen beds, and Club Rooms also have sleeper sofas for added value. You'll probably want to go out to eat—the Daily Grill, the hotel's on-site restaurant, is lackluster.

351 Geary St. (between Powell and Mason sts.), San Francisco, CA 94102. ℂ 800/843-4343 or 415/781-7800. Fax 415/781-0216. www.handlery.com. 377 units. $189–$289 double; $325–$750 suite. Kids under 15 stay free in parent's room. Rollaways $10, cribs free. AE, DC, DISC, MC, V. Valet parking $41; oversized vehicles $50. **Amenities:** Restaurant; pool; sauna; concierge; barbershop; gift shop; room service (limited hours); babysitting; laundry service; dry cleaning; executive-level rooms. *In room:* A/C, TV w/movies and video games, high-speed Internet access, fridge, coffeemaker, hair dryer, iron, safe.

Hotel Adagio ⚜⚜ *Value*   Hospitality company Joie de Vivre took over this property (formerly the Shannon Court Hotel), poured in $13 million, changed the name, and completely transformed the interior. Reopened in 2003, the Hotel Adagio emerged as one of the best values in Union Square. Inspired by the color scheme of the original 1929 Spanish Revivalist decor, the new modern furnishings come in pleasing shades of burnt sienna, orange, and brown. Guest rooms are more spacious than in most historic buildings, and the bathroom fixtures have been completely updated as well. Although bathroom counter space is limited, it is more generous than at other downtown hotels in this price range. Moreover, guest rooms come equipped with two phone lines (one cordless), flat-screen TVs, and spacious closets.

If you go for two interconnecting rooms (rooms ending in 04 and 05—a double/double and a king room), this hotel ends up in the expensive category for a family of four. But the rooms with two queen beds, of which there are 25 in the hotel, are quite spacious and can comfortably fit four people, with plenty of floor space left over for luggage. In addition, the "junior suites," which are really one big room, combine a king bed and a queen pullout sofa bed. Some of the junior suites also have bigger bathrooms with even more counter space.

The front desk provides concierge services and, if they know your kids are coming, will welcome them to the hotel with a small toy. The exercise room is spacious and well-equipped, and the business center has free high-speed wireless Internet access, as do all the guest rooms. The lobby serves complimentary coffee in the morning and lemonade and cookies in the afternoon. Although the on-site restaurant, Cortez, is excellent, it's not ideal for a family meal.

550 Geary St. (between Taylor and Jones sts.), San Francisco, CA 94102. ✆ **800/228-8830** or 415/775-5000. Fax 415/775-9388. www.thehoteladagio.com. 171 units, including 2 penthouse suites. From $149 double; from $309 suite. Kids under 18 stay free in parent's room. Rollaways $20; cribs free. AE, DC, DISC, MC, V. Valet parking $33; oversized vehicles up to $75. **Amenities:** Restaurant; exercise room; courtesy car; business center; room service (limited hours); massage (in-room); babysitting; laundry service; same-day dry cleaning; executive-level rooms. *In room:* Portable A/C, TV w/movies and video games, CD player, free high-speed Internet access, minibar/fridge, coffeemaker, hair dryer, iron, safe.

Hotel Bijou   Movie-loving families can check out the 10-seat screening room, "Le Petit Theatre Bijou," off the hotel lobby. A double bill of films shot in San Francisco plays every evening at 7 and 9:30pm. The hotel will also feature kids' movies on request at other times of the day. There's even a candy counter at the front desk.

The Joie de Vivre hotel group livened up this 1911 building with plenty of vibrant paint: think burgundy, yellow, and purple. But the guest rooms, named after locally made films, remain tiny, and the bathrooms are especially small. Given its location on a less savory section of Mason Street, the Bijou is best left to experienced travelers with savvy kids who want an inexpensive, but fun, hotel.

111 Mason St. (at Eddy St.), San Francisco, CA 94102. ✆ **800/771-1022** or 415/771-1200. Fax 415/346-3196. www.hotelbijou.com. 65 units. $129–$179 double. Kids 12 and under stay free in parent's room. Rollaways $15; cribs free. AE, DC, DISC, MC, V. Valet parking $27; oversized vehicles $37. **Amenities:** Continental breakfast; concierge; laundry service; dry cleaning. *In room:* TV, dataport, hair dryer, iron.

Hotel Metropolis   The Metropolis is the only hotel in San Francisco that boasts a suite just for kids. Designed by the hotel's president, who is also a mother, the kids' room of the suite has a bunk bed, a child-size desk, a huge chalkboard, and loads of toys. A bedroom for parents is connected to this miniature play land, as is a living room that can accommodate the nanny or more siblings. The suite is frequently booked and the hotel is considering adding another. If you can't get the suite, ask if any of the interconnecting doubles are available; more adventurous kids may prefer staying in a guest room that actually feels like a hotel, rather than another IKEA-furnished kid's room. All rooms are compact and the bathrooms tiny, but the decor is light and fresh.

Unfortunately, the hotel is located at the south end of Mason Street, on one of the grittier blocks around Union Square, and I might feel uncomfortable returning late in the evening (although a security guard is on duty overnight and the reception desk is staffed 24 hrs.). Even 1 block north is an improvement, so just use caution and consider taking a cab if you're out late.

25 Mason St. (between Eddy and Turk sts.), San Francisco, CA 94102. ✆ **800/553-1900** or 415/775-4600. Fax 415/775-4606. www.hotelmetropolis.com. 105 units. $99–$200 double; from $250 suite. Kids under 17 stay free in parent's room. Rollaways $10; cribs free. AE, DC, DISC, MC, V. Valet parking $29. **Amenities:** Exercise room; meditation room; business center; laundry service; dry cleaning. *In room:* TV w/movies and video games, fax, free wireless Internet access, coffeemaker, hair dryer, iron.

Monticello Inn ★★   As one might surmise from the name, this charming hotel has a decidedly Jeffersonian bent, buttressed by its Federal-period lobby and literary theme. In addition to an evening wine hour, the hotel hosts weekly book readings in the "library" on Wednesday evenings, and keeps a selection of classics in the suites for guests' use. The tastefully decorated lobby and recently redecorated rooms, hued in royal blue and white, are appealing. Although none of this may sound specifically family-oriented, the central location, friendly staff, and great rates make this an option worth considering. Check for special family deals that include parking and attraction coupons, or other deals such as the "literary rate" package. Room configurations include one-bedroom suites with a sofa bed in the parlor and robes in the closets, compact double/doubles, and spacious king/king rooms in which the beds face each other. (This last configuration seems made for a slumber party.) A restaurant connected to the building, Puccini & Panetti, has a special children's menu, coloring books, and enough pizza and pasta dishes to calm any hunger pangs. Along with lunch, dinner, and take-out, the restaurant also provides room service from 11:30am to 10pm.

127 Ellis St. (between Powell and Mason sts.), San Francisco, CA 94102. © **866/778-6169** or 415/392-8800. Fax 415/398-2650. www.monticelloinn.com. 91 units, including 20 suites. $119–$259 double; $189–$309 suite. Kids under 18 stay free in parent's room. Rollaways $15; cribs free. AE, DC, DISC, MC, V. Valet parking $33; oversized vehicles $48. **Amenities:** Restaurant; concierge; room service (limited hours); laundry service; dry cleaning. *In room:* A/C, TV w/movies and video games, CD player, minibar, coffeemaker (on request), hair dryer, iron.

INEXPENSIVE

Golden Gate Hotel *(Value* This charming 1913 Edwardian bed-and-breakfast sits on a relatively quiet block, close to the cable car lines and within walking distance of Nob Hill, Union Square, and Chinatown. The cozy rooms, decorated with white wicker furniture, antique bureaus, and floral prints, have either two twin beds or one queen and space for little else. At most, you could squeeze a crib into the queen room. Families often choose from one of the two downstairs rooms, which share a common bathroom. One room has two double beds, and the other has a double and a twin. Families of four stay for $125 in summer and less in the off-season. Another off-season bargain is a room with a queen bed that connects to a tiny room with two twin beds—all for as little as $180. (In summer, the rate is much higher.) The queen room has a bath, and there are additional shared tubs and toilets in the hall.

Innkeepers John and Renate Kenaste, and daughter Gabriele, are polite hosts who maintain some nice touches in their family-run inn such as vintage clawfoot tubs, an antique bird-cage elevator, and complimentary afternoon tea with homemade cookies. The continental breakfast included in the room rate features coffee, tea, croissants, and muffins. There's also Humphrey, a friendly golden retriever. *Note:* During peak months in summer, rates push the Golden Gate into the moderate price category.

775 Bush St. (between Powell and Mason sts.), San Francisco, CA 94108. © **800/835-1118** or 415/392-3702. Fax 415/392-6202. www.goldengatehotel.com. 25 units, some w/shared bathrooms. Rooms w/shared bath $95 double, rooms w/private bath $150 double. Rates include continental breakfast. Futon $15; cribs free. AE, DC, MC, V. Self-parking $15. *In room:* TV, free wireless Internet access, hair dryer (on request), iron (on request).

Grant Plaza This no-frills spot sits in the heart of bustling Chinatown, 1 block from the Chinatown gate and 3 blocks from Union Square. The bare-bones rooms are compact and most of the tiny bathrooms have showers only, not tubs, but it is one of the few places downtown where you'll find a room for under $100 (rooms with two double beds start at $89). That said, I recommend staying only on the top floor, where the rooms are newer and farther from the street noise. A handful of double/double rooms have bathrooms with tubs and connect to a walk-in-closet-sized sitting room with a pullout sofa bed. You could almost call it a suite, and it's just $20 extra. The hotel has no kitchen, but cafes and restaurants are just steps away from the hotel lobby.

465 Grant Ave. (at Pine St.), San Francisco, CA 94108. © 800/472-6899 or 415/434-3883. Fax 415/434-3886. www.grantplaza.com. 72 units. $69–$89 double; $109 suite. Rollaways and cribs $10. AE, DC, DISC, MC, V. Self-parking $20. *In room:* TV, high-speed Internet access, hairdryer, iron (on request).

Halcyon Hotel *Value*   Penny pinchers will appreciate this clean, low-key option only a few blocks from Union Square. Here you'll find rock-bottom rates; kitchenettes in every room equipped with a toaster, microwave, coffeemaker with complimentary coffee, and a small fridge; coin-operated laundry facilities with free detergent and bleach; and a friendly general manager by the name of Dennis Hale who truly wants to ensure your stay in San Francisco is a good one. The carpets in the tiny guest rooms were recently replaced with pleasant laminated flooring in a pale pine style and the hallway floors were also due to be replaced by early 2007. The guest room walls were also slated for painting when this book went to press, something they sorely needed. The mattresses, bedspreads, and furniture could also use replacing, but for these low rates near Union Square, perhaps that's too much to ask. Room configurations vary; one family option is a twin bed bunked over a double bed. The hotel says that, technically, it permits no more than three guests in a room, but does offer a complimentary floor futon "for emergencies." If anyone in your group has physical limitations, you may want to think twice before booking here, as the hotel is located uphill from Union Square, and once inside, you'll have to take the stairs. If you have cats or dogs, they are welcome to stay for an additional $5 per day.

649 Jones St. (between Geary and Post sts.), San Francisco, CA 94102. © 800/627-2396 or 415/929-8033. Fax 415/441-8033. www.halcyonsf.com. 25 units. $79–$129 double; $510–$590 weekly. Minimum length of stay Oct–Apr is 7 days. Kids under 18 stay free in parent's room. No rollaways; free cribs. AE, DC, DISC, MC, V. Self-parking $14–$16. **Amenities:** Access to nearby health club; concierge; tour desk; laundry facilities; free fax in lobby. *In room:* TV, kitchen, fridge, coffeemaker, hair dryer, iron, safe.

Hostelling International San Francisco–Downtown   For less than $30 per person, your family can experience dorm life in an old San Francisco–style building right in the heart of Union Square. Occupying five sparsely decorated floors, rooms here are simple and clean. Each has two or three bunk beds with linens, a sink, a closet, and lockers (bring your own locks or buy some at the front desk). Although most private rooms share hallway bathrooms, a few have private facilities. Prices are per person in the dorm rooms and per double bed in the private room. Since kids under 12 are an additional $14 per night, the hostel option becomes less of a deal when you add more than one child. Among several common rooms is a large kitchen-style room with refrigerator space, toasters, and a microwave, but no stoves or ranges.

312 Mason St. (between Geary and O'Farrell sts.), San Francisco, CA 94102. © 888/GOHIUSA or 415/788-5604. Fax 415/788-3023. www.sfhostels.com. 105 units (39 private, 241 dorm beds). Hostelling members $23–$25 per person in dorm; nonmembers $26–$28 per person in dorm; $60–$70 in private room w/shared bath; $67–$85 in private room w/private bath. Children under 12 $14 when accompanied by a parent. Rates include continental breakfast. AE, DC, DISC, MC, V. **Amenities:** TV lounge; limited kitchen; Internet access at kiosk for small fee; free wireless Internet access; laundry facilities. *In room:* Lockers, no phone.

Hotel Beresford Arms   This old-fashioned lodging is a true value proposition for families of four and up. A family-owned hotel with heavy burgundy lobby decor and slightly scuffed guest room furniture, the Beresford Arms is not going to win any awards for style. But spacious room configurations, most with kitchens or kitchenettes, and low rates do keep some customers coming back. All rooms have queen beds, so here a double/double room actually has two queen beds, meaning four of you can share a room pretty comfortably. Moreover, rooms are big enough to fit your luggage and still leave you space to walk. Finally, the bathrooms may have outdated decor, but they are large enough to accommodate a few people trying to get their teeth brushed and hair combed at the same time. The 60 "Jacuzzi" suites all feature Jacuzzi tubs and half have full kitchens, while the other half have kitchenettes with no stove. All have refrigerators, which come stocked with minibar items. There's also a small grocery store across the street for other items you may need. At breakfast time, you'll find coffee, pastries, and fresh fruit in the lobby, where you can also enjoy free WiFi Internet access (which the hotel hopes to expand to the entire hotel in 2007). Cats and dogs are welcome, but usually only in the smoking rooms.

701 Post St. (at Jones St.), San Francisco, CA 94109. ℂ 800/533-6533 or 415/673-2600. Fax 415/929-1535. www. beresford.com/arms. 95 units. $119–$129 double; $140–$159 Jacuzzi suite. Kids under 12 stay free in parent's room. Rollaways $10. AE, DC, DISC, MC, V. Valet parking $20. **Amenities:** Access to nearby health club ($10/day); laundry services; free Internet access in lobby. *In room:* TV/VCR, dataport, minibar, hair dryer (upon request), iron.

2 South of Market (SoMa)

Hotels here are close to shopping, museums, and great family entertainment, including the Yerba Buena Center. As an up-and-coming part of town, SoMa enjoys some of the city's newest restaurants and attractions. The downside to the newness is constant construction. Also, some sections of the neighborhood have not yet emerged, and the unsavory 6th and 7th streets should definitely be avoided.

VERY EXPENSIVE

Four Seasons 🎖🎖🎖   The lobby of this über-luxurious hotel is a sleek, spacious, multi-roomed tribute to Art Deco elegance. The extremely professional concierges will stop at nothing to ensure that every family member's needs are met. Milk and cookies greet kids 6 and under; those 7 and up get root beer and popcorn. Children staying in their own room receive a personal minibar key, entitling them to such goodies as milk, Oreos, and granola bars (and unlike the room rates, these snacks—at a dollar or two apiece—are deliberately inexpensive to keep parents happy). The hotel even supplies bathrobes to fit every member of the family. Parents of infants get a fully outfitted crib, diaper genie, wipes, baby shampoo, and so on.

Each of the tastefully opulent and sizable rooms is outfitted with a Sony PlayStation and CD player. The concierge can also send up a VCR, DVD player, or board games on request. Several interconnecting rooms, such as a king room and a double queen, are available. The junior suites feature a king room and living room with a foldout sofa bed. All of the spacious marble bathrooms have separate tubs and showers. Four Seasons guests have access to the adjacent Sports Club/LA, which has a pool. For kids planning to splash around, the concierge will supply passes to the San Francisco Marriott hotel pool, which is accessible via the hotel's back entrance.

757 Market St. (at 3rd St.), San Francisco, CA 94103. ℂ 415/633-3000. Fax 415-633-3001. www.fourseasons. com/sanfrancisco. 277 units. $430–$530 double; from $845 suite. $30 for 3rd adult in room; kids under 18 stay free in parent's room. No rollaways; cribs free. AE, DC, DISC, MC, V. Valet parking $44. Small pets welcome (1 per room). **Amenities:** Restaurant; bar; health club; concierge; courtesy car; business center; room service; massage; babysitting; laundry service; dry cleaning. *In room:* A/C, TV w/movies, games, high-speed Internet access, minibar, coffeemaker (on request), hair dryer, iron, safe.

Accommodations Around Town

The Argonaut **7**

Cow Hollow Motor Inn & Suites **3**

Fairmont Hotel **14**

Four Seasons **19**

Harbor Court Hotel **25**

Holiday Inn Fisherman's Wharf **8**

Hostelling International San Francisco,
  Fisherman's Wharf **6**

Hotel Del Sol **4**

Hotel Milano **17**

Hotel Vitale **24**

The Huntington Hotel **13**

Hyatt at Fisherman's Wharf **9**

Hyatt Regency San Francisco **23**

The Laurel Inn **1**

The Marina Inn **5**

Marina Motel **2**

Mark Hopkins InterContinental **15**

Palace Hotel **20**

Radisson Hotel Fisherman's Wharf **11**

Ritz-Carlton **16**

San Francisco Marriott **18**

San Remo Hotel **12**

St. Regis Hotel **22**

Tuscan Inn **10**

W Hotel **21**

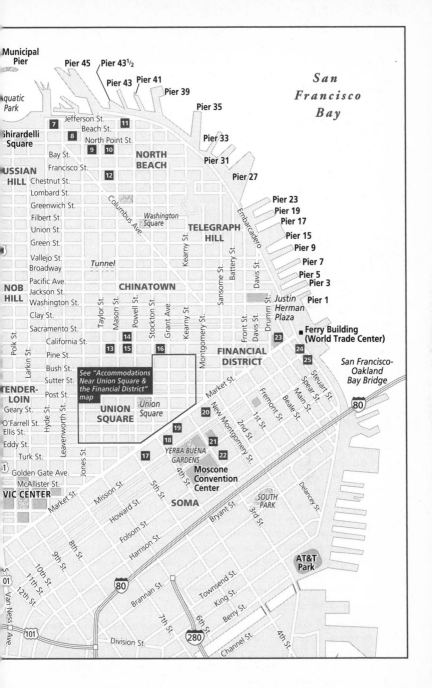

Municipal
Pier

Aquatic
Park

Ghirardelli
Square

RUSSIAN
HILL

NOB
HILL

Polk St.
Larkin St.

TENDER-
LOIN

VIC CENTER

Pier 45   Pier 43½
     Pier 43   Pier 41
              Pier 39
                    Pier 35

Jefferson St.
Beach St.
North Point St.

Bay St.
Francisco St.
Chestnut St.
Lombard St.
Greenwich St.
Filbert St.
Union St.
Green St.
Vallejo St.
Broadway
Pacific Ave.
Jackson St.
Washington St.
Clay St.
Sacramento St.
California St.
Pine St.
Bush St.
Sutter St.
Post St.
Geary St.
O'Farrell St.
Ellis St.
Eddy St.
Turk St.
Golden Gate Ave.
McAllister St.

7   **11**
8
9 **10**
12

NORTH
BEACH

Columbus Ave.

Washington
Square

Tunnel

CHINATOWN

Taylor St.
Mason St.
Powell St.
Stockton St.
Grant Ave.
Kearny St.

TELEGRAPH
HILL

Kearny St.

Montgomery St.
Sansome St.
Battery St.
Front St.
Davis St.

Embarcadero

Pier 33
Pier 31
Pier 27
Pier 23
Pier 19
Pier 17
Pier 15
Pier 9
Pier 7
Pier 5
Pier 3
Pier 1

*San
Francisco
Bay*

Justin
Herman
Plaza

● Ferry Building
(World Trade Center)

San Francisco-
Oakland
Bay Bridge

14
13 **15**   **16**

See "Accommodations
Near Union Square &
the Financial District"
map

UNION
SQUARE

Union
Square

19
18
17

YERBA BUENA
GARDENS

Moscone
Convention
Center

SOMA

FINANCIAL
DISTRICT

Market St.

New Montgomery St.
Fremont St.
Beale St.
Main St.
Spear St.
Steuart St.

20
21
22

2nd St.
1st St.

4th St.
5th St.
Mission St.
Howard St.
Folsom St.
Harrison St.

3rd St.
Bryant St.

SOUTH
PARK

Delancey St.

23
24
25

80

Hyde St.
Leavenworth St.
Jones St.

8th St.
9th St.
10th St.
11th St.
12th St.

Van Ness Ave.

101

280

80

Brannan St.
7th St.
6th St.

Townsend St.
King St.
Berry St.

AT&T
Park

Channel St.
4th St.

Division St.

Market St.

Palace Hotel ★★   This landmark hotel—built in 1875, rebuilt after the 1906 fire, restored in 1991, renovated again in 2003, and still honored by the National Trust for Historic Preservation—is aptly named. The over-the-top decor, complete with burgundy carpeting, massive chandeliers, marble columns, and the spectacular glass-roofed Garden Court restaurant (made with 80,000 panes of glass), will make kids think they've entered into an actual royal residence. Bedrooms, though not nearly as ornate, are sizable, and even the standard doubles are large enough to accommodate a crib. Marble bathrooms and 14-foot ceilings add to the grandeur; in-room refrigerators, 24-hour room service, and three restaurants, including the excellent Kyo-ya (Japanese/sushi), add convenience. The Palace Spa contains an attractive indoor lap pool with a glass ceiling (children must be supervised by someone 16 or over).

The hotel is close to several SoMa attractions, including the SFMOMA and Yerba Buena Center, and the Montgomery Street Muni/BART station and F-Market streetcar stops are on the corner. At check-in, kids receive gift bags with cups and caps, as well as a list of kid-friendly sights and activities. Weekend specials can include rates well below the published rack rates.

2 New Montgomery St. (at Market St.), San Francisco, CA 94105. ℂ **800/325-3589** or 415/512-1111. Fax 415/243-8062. www.sfpalace.com. 552 units, including 34 suites. $529–$589 double; from $775 suite. Kids under 17 stay free in parent's room. Rollaways $50; cribs free. AE, DC, DISC, MC, V. Valet parking $48. **Amenities:** 3 restaurants (2 w/kids' menus); bar; pool; spa/exercise room; concierge; courtesy car; business center; room service; massage; babysitting; laundry service; dry cleaning. *In room:* A/C, TV, high-speed Internet access, fridge, hair dryer, iron, safe.

St. Regis Hotel ★★★   For hotels in the upper price echelons, it can be hard to rank one luxurious alternative over the other. While I prefer the Four Seasons for the size of its guest rooms, I give the prize for top luxury family hotel to the St. Regis for its marvelous pool, a feature most kids highly prize. At the Four Seasons, you have to head out the back door to the Marriott for use of an uninspiring pool in an antiseptic, tiled room—not quite the same as popping down the elevator in your swimsuit and plush hotel bathrobe to arrive at a soothing light-filled space housing a glorious, 50-foot-long infinity pool. Kids at the St. Regis are also plenty well pampered. If you talk to the concierge in advance, the hotel will invite the kids to "check in" and sign their names on arrival. Kids will find personalized notes for them in the guest room, as well as a cookie with their own name on it—not to mention kid-sized bathrobes, a toy from the SFMOMA Museum store, and a children's room service menu.

The newest addition to San Francisco's collection of luxury hotels, the St. Regis is decidedly sleek and modern, although the liberal use of rich exotic woods—such as arrestingly beautiful slabs of Mozambican hardwood for the guest room doors and exquisite Polynesian-inspired artwork using Australian lacewood in each guest room—keep the place feeling warm and welcoming. The hotel also boasts $3.5 million worth of art pieces, which could be like a free museum tour for your kids

---

⟨ **Fun Fact**   **Stump the Tour Guide**

Everyone knows that Enrico Caruso, the world-famous opera star, was staying at the Palace Hotel when the great earthquake of 1906 struck. He is remembered, too, for running out of the hotel and vowing never to return to San Francisco. *Question:* What was he wearing when he made his escape? *Answer:* A towel. I don't know if he returned it.

throughout the hotel's common area. The limestone and marble bathrooms with deep-soaking tubs and separate showers featuring dual shower heads are divine, and many rooms have lovely views of Yerba Buena Gardens. For families, a good configuration could be the king room with an interconnecting double/double room. As an extra luxury, the St. Regis's Remède spa, sure to become a destination in itself, customizes each treatment to the client in question.

125 3rd St. (at Mission St.), San Francisco, CA 94103. ☎ **415/284-4000.** Fax 415-284-4100. www.stregis.com/san francisco. 260 units. $339–$689 double; from $650 suite. Kids under 12 stay free in parent's room. Rollaways and cribs free. AE, DC, DISC, MC, V. Valet parking $45. Pets welcome. **Amenities:** 2 restaurants; bar; health club; concierge; courtesy car; business center; room service; massage; babysitting; laundry service; dry cleaning. *In room:* A/C, TV w/DVD, CD, high-speed Internet access, minibar, hair dryer, iron (on request), safe.

EXPENSIVE

San Francisco Marriott   I first checked out this hotel because it has a pool, and as I stated at the beginning of this chapter, I intend to list as many hotels with pools as possible—provided they're worth listing. When I walked into the lobby, I started to wonder. Serving guests in a whopping 1,498 rooms (!), the lobby of this conference-oriented hotel is predictably frenetic and crowded at most times of the day. The escalator ride up from the lobby takes you to the mezzanine level, inside an ambitious four-story atrium decorated with palm trees, fountains, and enough flora and fauna to shame even Walt Disney himself. If you can figure out the complicated elevator options, including low-rise, mid-rise, and high-rise, all detailed in a lengthy menu posted next to the lifts themselves, then you will eventually find yourself in an endless hallway carpeted in garish colors.

Despite all that, it turns out some families keep coming back. Why? First, the indoor pool, which is plenty big and is open from 6am to 11pm. Second, if you can get the right guest room, it can be fairly spacious, and the decor is mercifully more subdued than that found in the hotels' public spaces. Beds are also reportedly quite comfortable, although the double/doubles really are like enlarged twin beds (not queens). If you can get a room in the high tower, you'll get a great view. With two restaurants and two delis on the premises, you'll always find something to feed empty tummies fast. Lastly, while it might be too much for adult sensibilities, the kids will probably love the atrium's over-the-top pseudo tropical decor.

55 4th St. (between Market and Mission sts.), San Francisco, CA 94103. ☎ **415/896-1600.** Fax 415/486-8101. www. marriott.com. 1,498 units, including 134 suites. $199–$349 double; $499–$3,250 suite. Kids under 18 stay free in parent's room. Free rollaways and cribs. AE, DC, DISC, MC, V. Valet parking $49. **Amenities:** 2 restaurants; 2 bars; indoor pool; health club; tour desk; car rental; business center; laundry service; dry cleaning. *In room:* A/C, TV w/movies, dataport, high-speed Internet access, hair dryer, iron, safe.

W Hotel 🎯   This ultra-hip hotel seems better suited to families with older children. Teens will feel quite sophisticated hanging around the lobby or cafe at this trendy hotel, playing the chess or backgammon games that sit on small tables, or taking notes on the hip young things who work and play here. Right across the street from Yerba Buena Center and 1 block from the Metreon, it's a perfect location for young adults, who could easily entertain themselves for hours at the Metreon alone.

The ultra-cool attitude continues in the guest rooms, which are sleek, modern, and subtly accented—rather than overcome—by color. Wall units house entertainment centers, and shutters replace curtains on the windows. (The clean lines are handsome, but they don't block light completely.) Sharing a double/double could cut housing rates back to the moderate range. Connecting king and double/double rooms work well for larger families. Rollaway beds are only allowed in Cool Corner king rooms. Fantastic Suites, starting at $1,000, connect a Cool Corner room with a sitting room that has a Murphy bed. Other child-pleasing features include an indoor lap pool and room service. Adults will appreciate the views and the 24-hour concierge services.

181 3rd St. (at Howard St.), San Francisco, CA 94103. (*C*) **888/625-5140** or 415/777-5300. Fax 415/817-7823. www. whotels.com. 423 units. $199–$329 double; $1,000–$1,800 suite. Kids under 18 stay free in parent's room. Rollaways $30, cribs free. AE, DC, DISC, MC, V. Valet parking $45. Dogs and cats welcome ($25 per day). **Amenities:** Restaurant (no kids' menus); bar; pool; exercise room; concierge; business center; room service; babysitting; laundry service; dry cleaning. *In room:* A/C, TV, DVD, CD player, high-speed Internet access, minibar, coffeemaker, hair dryer, iron, safe.

MODERATE

Hotel Milano   Designed to resemble an Italian villa, this small, modern hotel is one of the better SoMa hotels in this price category. The convenient location is steps away from several entertainment venues, the Westfield San Francisco Centre shopping mall, the Metreon, and Yerba Buena Gardens. You can also reach the Muni and the F-Market streetcars in moments. Room sizes vary, but the larger rooms are certainly more spacious than typical downtown hotels in this price range. Bathrooms use lots of black marble; bedrooms are masculine in feel with black-trimmed woods and upholstery— but the hotel is overdue for some fresh fabrics on windows and beds. The double/doubles are really dual queens and big enough to share with the kids and still have space for your luggage. There are no connecting rooms or suites suitable for a crowd, but the staff does its best to provide families with the largest rooms available.

55 5th St. (between Mission and Market sts.), San Francisco, CA 94103. (*C*) **800/398-7555** or 415/543-8555. Fax 415/543-5885. www.hotelmilanosf.com. 108 units. $109–$299 double. Kids under 12 stay free in parent's room. Additional person $20. Rollaways $20, cribs free. AE, DC, DISC, MC, V. Valet parking $30; oversized vehicles $35. **Amenities:** Restaurant; bar; fitness center; concierge; room service (6am–1am); babysitting; laundry service; dry cleaning; executive level rooms. *In room:* A/C, TV, high-speed Internet access, minibar, fridge, hair dryer, iron, safe.

3 Fisherman's Wharf

As the most visited tourist destination in San Francisco, Fisherman's Wharf has plenty of family activities, and a few of its hotels have outdoor pools. But the lopsided ratio of tourists to locals makes for a slew of tacky T-shirt shops and lousy restaurants. At least it's next to the bay, and the area's western edge, towards Ghirardelli, is quite scenic.

EXPENSIVE

The Argonaut 👧👧   I've long wondered why anyone would want to stay in Fisherman's Wharf. Upon seeing the Argonaut, which opened its doors in August 2003, I not only stopped wondering, I wanted to check in immediately. It helps that the hotel is located on the wharf's more picturesque western end. The hotel building, originally built in 1907 and now property of the National Park Service, is part of The Cannery, a historic structure that once housed the world's largest peach canning facility. The $40 million restoration to create this attractive new hotel left the red brick walls, Douglas fir beams, and wood-plank floors beautifully intact.

The overall decor, which pokes fun at traditional nautical themes, is fresh and appealing. It extends to the sizable guest rooms and bathrooms, which are hued in bright blue, white, and silver. Room configurations include two queens or one king, and a few king rooms also have a pullout sofa. Bay views are an option, as are interconnecting rooms and suites. Rooms have DVD and CD players, and if you pop down to the lobby for the complimentary wine hour, your teens or tweens can take advantage of the two computers with free high-speed wireless Internet access there.

Too bad the Argonaut doesn't have a pool. Then again, if it did, the other wharf hotels might go out of business. When you call, ask whether the Neptune's Adventure package is still available. At last check, it granted a family of four a double queen room, passes to PIER 39 attractions and the Hyde Street Pier, clever kids' gifts, tickets for the cable car a mere block away, and a full breakfast at the hotel's Blue Mermaid Chowder House (p. 146), one of the few good family restaurants in the area.

495 Jefferson St. (at Hyde St.), San Francisco, CA 94109. ℭ **866/415-0704** or 415/563-0800. Fax 415/563-2800. www.argonauthotel.com. 252 units. $199–$249 double. Suites $599–$1,000. Kids under 17 stay free in parent's room. Rollaways $20, cribs free. AE, DC, DISC, MC, V. Valet parking $36; oversized vehicles $51. Pets welcome. **Amenities:** Restaurant; concierge; courtesy car; room service (6am–2am); babysitting; laundry service; dry cleaning; executive-level rooms. *In room:* A/C, TV w/games and movies, DVD player, free high-speed Internet access, minibar/fridge, coffeemaker, hair dryer, iron.

MODERATE

Holiday Inn Fisherman's Wharf   This is one of the few hotels in town with an outdoor pool and patio, fun to have when the weather cooperates. It's the best part of the property, which sits off busy North Point Street and Columbus Avenue. The entrance is welcoming, but the guest rooms, off a poorly lit hallway, are unimpressive, and some are rather bleak. Bathrooms are better; while on the small side, they include some useful amenities such as magnifying mirrors. The in-house restaurants are mediocre, although they do adhere to the "Kids Eat Free" corporate promotion for guests under 12 dining with their parents. For the price, you can do better.

1300 Columbus Ave. (at N. Point St.), San Francisco, CA 94133. ℭ **415/771-9000.** Fax 415/771-7006. www.holiday inn.com. 585 units. $199–$244 double; from $350 suite. Kids under 18 stay free in parent's room. Rollaways $5, cribs free. AE, DC, DISC, MC, V. Self-parking $28. **Amenities:** 2 restaurants; coffee shop; heated outdoor pool; exercise room; concierge; business center; gift shop; room service (limited hours); babysitting; laundry service; dry cleaning; laundromat on site; executive-level rooms. *In room:* A/C, TV, high-speed wireless Internet access, coffeemaker, hair dryer, iron, safe.

Hyat at Fisherman's Wharf ℛ   If you must stay in Fisherman's Wharf and your kids really want a pool, the Hyatt is the best choice; it ranks a good notch above the other big hotel chains in the neighborhood. Its outdoor pool sits in a protected courtyard away from the street with an inviting spa, attractive chaises and tables, and a nearby indoor shower. The guest rooms and bathrooms, already designed with families in mind, were fully renovated in 2006. The new color combination of rich, chocolate brown set against bright white and ice blue is nicely understated. Connecting rooms and double/doubles are available, and complimentary rollaways are available upon request. In-room coffeemakers are available, but the most practical amenities may be the coin-operated washer/dryers on every floor.

The hotel's restaurant serves all day in a sports-bar-like atmosphere surrounded by a total of 28 TVs, one of them measuring a whopping 126 inches. Older kids will enjoy the game room, complete with two pool tables, shuffleboard, and arcade machines. The staff is friendly and helpful, especially the concierge, who will provide you with discount coupons for wharf attractions. Look for room deals on the Hyatt website, but don't expect attractive weekend rates. Weekends here see high occupancy.

555 N. Point St. (between Jones and Taylor sts.), San Francisco, CA 94133. ℭ **800/233-1234** or 415/563-1234. Fax 415/486-4444. www.fishermanswharf.hyatt.com. 313 units. $168–$268 double. $400–$1,200 suites. Kids 18 and

under stay free in parent's room. Rollaways and cribs free. AE, DC, DISC, MC, V. Valet parking $38. **Amenities:** Restaurant; heated outdoor pool; exercise room; Jacuzzi; sauna; concierge; courtesy car; room service (limited hours); babysitting; laundry service; dry cleaning; executive-level rooms. *In room:* A/C, TV, high-speed wireless Internet access, fridge (on request, $10 per day), coffeemaker (on request), hair dryer, iron, safe.

Radisson Hotel Fisherman's Wharf   If you want a waterfront view and an outdoor pool without breaking the bank, you'll find them here. The Radisson holds the distinction of being the only big chain hotel in Fisherman's Wharf actually on the waterfront. Jefferson Street runs in front of the hotel, but beyond that is just the bay itself. Also, it's sandwiched between the most popular piers on the Wharf, PIER 39 to the east and Piers 41 and 43, from where the Bay Cruises and the Alcatraz ferries depart, to the west. And it has an outdoor heated pool.

Otherwise, there isn't much charm to the place. One wonders what the architects who built structures like this in the 1960s were thinking, and the dreary color scheme desperately needs a touch-up. The concrete complex covers an entire city block, and shares retail space with other big chains such as the Gap, Subway, Ben & Jerry's, and the International House of Pancakes (which is the closest breakfast spot, unless you buy a cup of java from the coffee cart inelegantly occupying the lobby). At least the guest rooms and bathrooms are a decent size and, of course, you've got the bay vistas to remind you that you are, in fact, in San Francisco.

250 Beach St. (between Mason and Powell sts.), San Francisco, CA 94133. (C) **866/327-5199** or 415/392-6700. Fax 415/986-7853. www.radissonsanfrancisco.com. 355 units. $149–$259 double. Kids under 17 stay free in parent's room. Rollaways $10, cribs free. AE, DC, DISC, MC, V. Self-parking $28. **Amenities:** Restaurant; heated outdoor pool; exercise room; concierge; business center; babysitting; laundry service; dry cleaning; executive-level rooms. *In room:* A/C, TV w/pay-per-view, free wireless high-speed Internet access, fridge (on request), coffeemaker, hair dryer, iron, safe.

Tuscan Inn 👁👁   For years, the Tuscan Inn could proudly call itself the best hotel in Fisherman's Wharf. Now that title will have to be passed on to the Argonaut. (Both hotels are part of the Kimpton hotel group.) Tuscan Inn rates are lower than the Argonaut's, but the inn is located on the less picturesque end of Fisherman's Wharf and doesn't have bay views. One thing both hotels lack is a pool, so if you're dead-set on one in this neighborhood, you'll have to go with one of the national chains.

What the Tuscan Inn does have are spacious guest rooms and bathrooms handsomely furnished in warm, inviting colors. Rooms are filled with amenities, including a combination honor bar/fridge, and you can bring Fido with you too. The comfortable lobby puts out hot chocolate and biscotti in the mornings, not just coffee and tea, and hosts a complimentary wine hour in the evenings. More important, the concierge here is friendly and intelligent, setting the tone for the rest of the staff.

Room configurations include double/doubles, but if you are coming to the city between November and April, ask about off-season rates for king premieres (a king bed and a sofa bed) or suites, which are sometimes available at excellent rates. The hotel's Cafe Pescatore (p. 146), specializing in reasonably-priced Italian fare, opens onto a pleasant outdoor dining area on the sidewalk.

425 N. Point St. (between Mason and Taylor sts.), San Francisco, CA 94133. (C) **800/648-4626** or 415/561-1100. Fax 415/561-1199. www.tuscaninn.com. 221 units. $159–$209 double; $249–$299 suite. Kids under 18 stay free in parent's room. Rollaways $20, cribs free. AE, DC, DISC, MC, V. Valet parking $32; oversized vehicles $42. Pets welcome ($25 per room). **Amenities:** Restaurant; concierge; courtesy car; room service (limited hours); babysitting; laundry service; dry cleaning; executive-level rooms; free local calls. *In room:* A/C, TV, free wireless Internet access, minibar/fridge, coffeemaker, hair dryer, iron.

INEXPENSIVE

Hostelling International San Francisco, Fisherman's Wharf   This option is best for small, adventurous families. Beds here are bunked dorm-style, and bathrooms are down the hall. What sets this place apart from other hostels is its location in the middle of a national park at Fort Mason. Through the windows of this converted army barrack, trees frame a view of Alcatraz and the San Francisco Bay. Although most rooms hold 8 to 12 beds, a few rooms have only 3 or 4 beds. These smaller rooms have the best vistas and can be reserved for families. You'll find small lockers in lieu of closets, so bring locks. All guests have access to a full kitchen, complimentary continental breakfast, and a common area with a cozy fireplace. An on-site cafe serves lunch and dinner, and the friendly volunteers at the information desk can book tours. The caveat is that rates are per person, which is why this option may be best for families of three. Although it's a great atmosphere, with interesting types of people from around the world, and you get free parking, the plastic-covered mattresses, shared showers, and absence of closets may not be worth the cost for four (or more) people.

Fort Mason, Building 240, San Francisco, CA 94123. © 415/771-7277. Fax 415/771-1468. www.sfhostels.com. 164 beds. Singles $20–$28. Rates include continental breakfast. AE, DISC, MC, V. Free parking. **Amenities:** Cafe; kitchen; Internet access at kiosk for small fee; laundry facilities. *In room:* Free wireless Internet access, lockers, no phone.

San Remo Hotel   Built in 1906 by Bank of Italy (later Bank of America) founder A. P. Giannini, this charming Italianate Victorian originally housed Italian immigrants, among others, made homeless after the earthquake and fire. These days, European travelers and vacationing families on a budget are happy to find the San Remo. An unabashedly old-fashioned pension, the period furnishings, beveled glass, and Victorian detailing take you back to a bona fide slice of San Francisco that's all but disappeared. The bedrooms, which look like they were decorated by someone's grandmother, are small and quaint. Reminiscent of European boarding houses, rooms have no phones, televisions, or en suite bathrooms. Guests share one of many polished and tidy restrooms down the hall.

Families of three can stay in a room with one queen and one twin for $90 or less. Larger families will be relegated to twin-bedded rooms for the kids and queen rooms for the adults—the rooms don't connect, so this hotel isn't ideal for families with younger kids. The location is within walking distance to North Beach, Fisherman's Wharf, and public transportation, but this is a tough neighborhood in which to park. Bottom line: the San Remo isn't for everybody. If you expect a high level of service and comfort on your vacation, you'll be better off at a mainstream hotel.

2237 Mason St. (near Chestnut St.), San Francisco, CA 94133. © 800/352-7366 or 415/776-8688. Fax 415/776-2811. www.sanremohotel.com. 62 units. $60–$90 double. No rollaways or cribs. AE, DC, MC, V. Self-parking $14. **Amenities:** Laundry facilities. *In room:* No phone.

4 The Embarcadero

Following the 1989 earthquake and the 1990s building boom, this forgotten part of town saw the construction of new condominiums and commercial space. Although hotels remain scarce, the proximity to downtown, the Ferry Building, and plentiful public transportation make this waterfront neighborhood an ideal place to stay.

VERY EXPENSIVE

Hotel Vitale 🐸🐸   Opened in 2005, the Vitale bills itself as the "only luxury waterfront hotel" in San Francisco, offering "luxury naturally." What this means for you and yours is fabulous views from many of the guest rooms, decor in soothing earth tones, playful photographs of nature, and other "natural" touches such as hallway lighting fixtures that evoke sunlight streaming through a forest canopy. Also, to be clear on the meaning of "waterfront," the Vitale does have a largely unobstructed, and very lovely, view of the San Francisco Bay, but it's actually across the street from the water's edge. Also, I would note that while the Vitale has plenty of opulent touches such as sandstone bathroom floors and some deep-soaking tubs (not all rooms have bathtubs), not all the details add up to the same exclusive experience one might find at more established luxury chains such as the Ritz-Carlton or St. Regis. The spa consists of just three treatment rooms; the fitness center is quite petite; and while guests may use the YMCA pool for free, it is 1 block down the street.

That's not to suggest you shouldn't choose the Hotel Vitale if you can get a good deal. For families, a good option could be one of the six Family Studio suites, which feature a larger room with a king bed and a pull-out sofa, as well as a small dining table. A few of these suites have a curtain that parents can pull across the room to separate the sleeping little ones while the adults watch a movie in bed. Unfortunately, these suites don't offer views of the water. A possibility that does feature the Vitale's signature views is one of the seven interconnecting room configurations, pairing a king bed room with a spa shower, but no tub, with a room that has two twin beds as well as a bathtub. One word of caution: the Vitale is also home to the indoor-outdoor Americano Bar, which is packed with 20-somethings most nights of the week. The upshot of all is that I've listed the Vitale because it's in a very desirable location, offers fabulous views, and boasts very new, well-decorated rooms. But because the family suites don't have the views and the Americano Bar is not quite a kid-friendly scene, I'd try to get a good deal on room prices before booking.

8 Mission St. (at Steuart St.), San Francisco, CA 94105. © **888/890-8688** or 415/278-3700. Fax 415/278-3750. www.hotelvitale.com. 199 units. $329–$399 double; $379–$699 suite. $30 for 3rd adult in room; kids under 18 stay free in parent's room. No rollaways; cribs free. AE, DC, DISC, MC, V. Valet parking $42. Dogs welcome, $35 fee. **Amenities:** Restaurant; bar; fitness center; concierge; courtesy car; business center; room service; massage; babysitting; laundry service; dry cleaning. *In room:* A/C, TV w/movies, free high-speed Internet access, minibar, coffeemaker (on request), hair dryer, iron, safe.

EXPENSIVE

Harbor Court Hotel   This hotel is in one of the best locations in town, offering lovely views of the San Francisco Bay and the Bay Bridge. You'll be steps away from the Ferry Building and its gourmet offerings and you'll have immediate access to the Embarcadero promenade for lovely waterside strolls or bike rides. Moreover, you'll be within walking distance of the SoMa attractions, and public transportation options—from buses to streetcars to the BART—abound. Compared with the newer Hotel Vitale just down the street, the Harbor Court is simply a better value. The lobby is a great indicator of the Harbor Court's overall feel: it's chic, trendy, and intimate without being too cool for us regular folk. One of the better restaurants in town is off the lobby as well: Ozumo serves sushi, Japanese grill dishes, and a range of sakes. As delicious as some of the dishes are, however, I wouldn't call that hip restaurant a family-friendly destination. In fact, and herein lies the rub, the hotel itself was really designed more for couples and business travelers, as it has no double/double rooms. You can reserve a twin-bedded room for the kiddies, but you'll be sleeping elsewhere because the maximum occupancy here is two, unless you splurge on the two-bedroom suite.

That basically makes it suitable for couples toting a baby or families with kids old enough to sleep in their own non-interconnected guest room.

But with the great location, excellent rates, awesome views, and full use of the YMCA next door (including its Olympic-sized pool, fitness center, and even a babysitting facility), the Harbor Court is definitely worth looking into. Check the website for packages and weekend specials.

165 Steuart St. (between Mission and Howard sts.), San Francisco, CA 94105. (C) **866/792-6283** or 415/882-1300. Fax 415/882-1313. www.harborcourthotel.com. 131 units. $139–$239 double; $499 suite. No rollaways; cribs free. AE, DC, DISC, MC, V. Valet parking $38. **Amenities:** Restaurant; complimentary evening beer and wine reception; pool; health club; concierge; courtesy car; laundry service; dry cleaning. *In room:* A/C, TV, CD player, fax, free wireless Internet access, minibar, complimentary morning coffee and tea, hairdryer, iron.

Hyatt Regency San Francisco   Although it's a huge corporate hotel where your children are likely to get lost if they head to your room without a detailed map, the Hyatt Regency's terrific location at the foot of Market Street makes up for every failing. Guests can enjoy the delightful Ferry Building across the street, and several shops, restaurants, and cinemas are at hand throughout the Embarcadero Center. Rooms are well equipped and very spacious, and many have bay views. Given the size of the rooms, the Hyatt Regency is the cost-efficient choice for families wanting to stay in the neighborhood. In addition, you'll find two restaurants, sundries, and an on-site fitness center. I remember staying here when I was a kid, and being enthralled with the indoor glass elevators that travel up the massive, 17-story indoor atrium, which were featured in the Mel Brooks film *High Anxiety.* Kids today still find those elevators an entertainment center in and of themselves.

5 Embarcadero Center (at Market St.), San Francisco, CA 94111. (C) **800/233-1234** or 415/788-1234. Fax 415/398-2567. www.sanfranciscoregency.hyatt.com. 803 units, including 39 suites. $159–$350 double, $25 3rd adult in room. Rollaways and cribs free. Kids under 18 stay free in parent's room. AE, DC, DISC, MC, V. Valet parking $43. **Amenities:** 2 restaurants; bar; exercise room; concierge; business center; gift shop; room service (6am–midnight); babysitting; laundry service; dry cleaning; executive-level rooms. *In room:* A/C, TV, high-speed Internet access, minibar, fridge (on request), coffeemaker, hair dryer, iron.

5 Nob Hill

The hillcrest where San Francisco's early millionaires built their mansions is home to some of the city's most elegant hotels. Views from guest rooms here are among the best in town, and the area feels residential even though it's just a few blocks from the city center. Kids will enjoy the nearby park and playground. The downside for little ones is the steep walk uphill from Union Square, but you can always catch the California cable car line, which runs close by. Room rates here are very high, but if your timing is right you may get a good deal.

VERY EXPENSIVE

Fairmont Hotel   Children of any age will be impressed arriving at this landmark 1907 hotel, which adorns one side of Nob Hill with its imposing facade and colorful flags. Inside, the expansive lobby's high ceilings, marble columns, and chandeliers will leave little girls expecting Cinderella to turn up. Despite the splendor, the overall feeling is relaxed and friendly. Guest rooms in the historic building are spacious by any standard, and the closets are so large that many will comfortably fit a crib or even a rollaway! If you prefer separate showers and tubs—and a stellar view—select a room in the tower building. Numerous combinations of suites and rooms, with king beds, queens, or double/doubles, are available.

Be sure to mention that you're traveling with kids when you call in-house reservations. The hotel has age-appropriate amenities such as milk and cookies at check-in, knapsacks, and maps, plus 8- to 11-year-olds qualify to act as "doorman for a day." Now, don't get excited: no one's putting your kids to work while you take off for Saks. But kids get to wear a hat, blow a whistle, and have a photo taken with the doorman—all at no charge. The gorgeous Laurel Court dining room serves afternoon tea with a choice of menus, including one for children. The kitschy Tonga Room provides a tropical rainstorm during happy hour (with inexpensive hors d'oeuvres). If your kids are *Eloise* fans, or just have excellent taste, they'll love this hotel.

950 Mason St. (at California St.), San Francisco, CA 94108. (C) **800/441-1414** or 415/772-5000. Fax. 415/772-5013. www.fairmont.com/sanfrancisco. 591 units. $199–$499 double; from $500 suite. Kids under 17 stay free in parent's room. Rollaways $30; cribs free. AE, DC, DISC, MC, V. Valet parking $45. **Amenities:** 2 restaurants; outdoor terrace; bar; concierge; business center; salon; 24-hr. room service; babysitting; laundry service; dry cleaning; complimentary morning coffee and tea in lobby. *In room:* A/C, TV w/movies and games, fax, high-speed Internet access, dataport, minibar, hair dryer, iron, safe.

The Huntington Hotel ★★

Owned and operated for more than 80 years by a local family, the Huntington Hotel keeps a lower profile than the neighboring Nob Hill hotels, but is equally upscale. For those traveling with young children, there are a few reasons to consider this hotel. The location is great: Huntington Park across the street has a nice playground for under-8s, which may offer a well-deserved break for a kid who has followed parents around the sights all day. Grace Cathedral, kitty-corner to the hotel, is also a serene place to walk and stretch your legs, and the cable car stop is next door. Moreover, the building was originally conceived as an apartment bloc, so many of the rooms are very spacious and can easily fit a crib.

The hotel's most family-friendly feature may be the seven suites that have kitchenettes, a rarity in upscale hotels. In addition to the suites, connecting king and a double/double rooms are also an option. Although elegant, the decor is a bit heavy and in need of updating. The Luxury and Huntington rooms on the upper floors have great views, but the Deluxe and Superior rooms on the lower floors are larger. The hotel's exquisitely beautiful spa, which unfortunately is not open to guests under 16, is one of the nicest in San Francisco and offers divine treatments of every sort. The Big Four restaurant, dark and clubby, exudes more than a hint of old San Francisco.

1075 California St. (at Taylor St.), San Francisco, CA 94108. (C) **800/227-4683** or 415/474-5400. Fax 415/474-6227. www.huntingtonhotel.com. 135 units. From $380 double; from $540 suite. Kids 5 and under stay free in parent's room. Rollaways and cribs free. AE, DC, DISC, MC, V. Valet parking $29. **Amenities:** Restaurant; bar; pool (16 and over only); spa/exercise room; concierge; courtesy car; room service (6am–11:30pm); massage; babysitting; laundry service; dry cleaning. *In room:* A/C, TV w/movies, fax, high-speed Internet access, kitchenettes available, hair dryer, safe.

Mark Hopkins InterContinental ★★

The Mark Hopkins, named after the founder of the Central Pacific Railroad, opened in 1926 and remains a San Francisco landmark. The hotel is very family-friendly, providing a teddy bear and a backpack of kids' amenities for 2- to 11-year-olds, as well as kids' menus in all the restaurants. (Ask about the "Kids in Tow" program when you make a reservation.) With advance notice, the hotel will rent strollers or other baby paraphernalia for you.

Guest rooms are classy and plush, with fine fabrics and maple furnishings. Views from the upper floors are unsurpassed. The big news for families is the recent opening of the hotel's Club InterContinental, located on the lobby floor. For an additional $60 a day per room (no additional charge if you're staying in a suite at the standard rate), families have access to an entertainment and food lounge that will be a big hit with older children. Kids can choose from more than 50 DVDs at "TV Central," peruse a collection of teen magazines, listen to XM satellite radio on wireless headsets, or play board games. The plethora of food—including baked goods and fruits for breakfast, lunch snacks at noon, high tea with minisandwiches in the afternoon, and a "sweet dreams" offering of milk and cookies in the evening—means you'll take care of at least one daily meal for the family, making the club's daily access charge well worth it.

The 19th-floor Top of the Mark restaurant/bar offers a Sunday brunch and keeps coloring books on hand for small guests who like to keep busy. It's been a landmark since 1939, and many non-guests make their way up to gawk at the view from the panoramic windows. With a *prix-fixe* gourmet dinner and dancing on weekend evenings to a live orchestra, you needn't stray far from the kiddies to enjoy a lively night out on the town.

Number One Nob Hill (at California and Mason sts.), San Francisco, CA 94108. ℂ **800/662-6455** or 415/392-3434. Fax 415/421-3302. www.markhopkins.net. 380 units, including 39 suites. $399–$499 double; $650–$4,250 suite. Kids under 18 stay free in parent's room. Rollaways $30; cribs free. AE, DC, DISC, MC, V. Valet parking $45. **Amenities:** Restaurant; bar; exercise room; concierge; business center; 24-hr. room service; massage (also in-room); babysitting; laundry service; dry cleaning; concierge-level rooms; town car (first-come, first-served); doctor upon request. *In room:* A/C, TV, high-speed Internet access, minibar, coffeemaker, hair dryer, iron, safe.

Ritz-Carlton 𝄞𝄞𝄞 As if it wasn't already elegant enough, the Ritz just underwent a $12.5 million renovation—adding a touch of modern sophistication to its traditional, yet ever so posh, decor. The secret for getting the most out of this hotel is to communicate your every wish to reservations, letting them know whether you're traveling with the nanny, celebrating a special occasion, or accompanied by a child who just brought home a perfect report card. These folks are looking for a reason to spoil you. If your little boy is into action figures, let the concierges know and they'll gladly oblige with a super-hero welcome gift. Pets under 10 pounds are welcome and also entitled to customized amenities, such as doggie beds and bowls.

Rooms range from deluxe doubles to executive suites, which are larger than most one-bedroom apartments in San Francisco. A deluxe with two double beds will still have plenty of room for a crib or rollaway, but if you're sharing with your kids, ask for one of the Stockton Street rooms, which are a bit larger. A handful of connecting rooms are also available. An extra $100 per night will grant you access to the Club Lounge, which comes with a dedicated concierge and a constant parade of food, from an ample breakfast to evening hors d'oeuvres with fruit, snacks, and drinks. Although more expensive than the Mark Hopkins lounge, it may still be a worthwhile investment. Visits during the holidays are especially fun for kids—the Ritz organizes a kids' Halloween tea in October, a teddy bear tea in December, and other annual events. During non-holiday times of year, kids can participate in a scavenger hunt throughout the hotel, with prizes awarded at the front desk.

600 Stockton St. (at California St.), San Francisco, CA 94108. ℂ **800/241-3333** or 415/296-7465. Fax 415/291-0288. www.ritzcarlton.com/hotels/san_francisco. 336 units. From $475 double; from $600 suite. Additional person $30. Rollaways and cribs free. AE, DC, DISC, MC, V. Valet parking $59. Pets under 10 lbs welcome. **Amenities:** 2 restaurants; bar; indoor pool; health club; concierge; courtesy car; business center; 24-hr. room service; massage; laundry service; dry cleaning; executive-level rooms. *In room:* A/C, TV w/games and movies, DVD, high-speed Internet access, minibar, fridge, coffeemaker, hair dryer, iron, safe.

6 Marina/Cow Hollow

These largely residential neighborhoods are teeming with restaurants, cafes, and boutique shops. The high concentration of families makes for great local playgrounds, and the lovely Marina Green, with its view of the Golden Gate Bridge, is an attraction on its own. The downside is that most hotels here are on Lombard Street, a busy thoroughfare lined with chain restaurants and gas stations.

MODERATE

Cow Hollow Motor Inn & Suites ★ *Finds*   The motel side of this popular, nonsmoking establishment has spacious guest rooms in mostly king bed and double/double combinations. (There are three double/queen rooms). All have good-sized bathrooms with plenty of counter space. The decor is plain, but clean and new—it was redecorated in 2003. With free indoor parking to boot, it's a great deal. Just make sure your room doesn't overlook Lombard Street, as even the double-paned windows don't block out the noise. Just in case, the front desk provides free earplugs.

The real treasures are the 12 suites located in the adjacent building on Chestnut Street. These are brightly decorated one- or two-bedroom apartments that are true homes-away-from-home, with living rooms, fully equipped kitchens, and dining rooms with wood flooring. The two-bedroom suites have two bathrooms, and one of the one-bedroom rentals contains two double beds. Coin-operated washers and dryers are on every floor. The trick is to reserve far in advance—up to a year for visits over holidays. The Inn also discounts the suites an extra $25 per day for stays longer than 5 days.

2190 Lombard St. (at Steiner St.), San Francisco, CA 94123. © 415/921-5800. Fax 415/922-8515. www.cowhollow motorinn.com. 129 units. $86–$135 double; $225–$275 suite. Kids under 12 stay free in parent's room. Additional person $10. Rollaways $10; cribs free. AE, DC, MC, V. Free parking (1 car per room). *In room:* A/C, TV, free high-speed Internet access, fridge (on request, $5 extra), coffeemaker, hair dryer, iron (on request).

Hotel Del Sol   Once upon a time, the Del Sol was a modest motel with the good fortune to be located in Cow Hollow, away from noisy Lombard Street. Then the clever hospitality company, Joie de Vivre, came along. Many gallons of bright yellow, green, and blue paint later, a star was born. She's even got the swimming pool, hammocks, and palm trees to prove it. Most of the all-nonsmoking guest rooms and suites surround a tiled, color-washed interior courtyard that triples as a parking complex, pool area, and complimentary breakfast bar.

Double/doubles are fine for small families, but if you can, take advantage of the one-bedroom suites with pullout sofas in the living rooms, or the sole "Family Suite" complete with bunk beds, small-scale furniture, toys, and board games. The three so-called kitchenette units are actually bedrooms with a galley containing a counter, sink, fridge, and microwave (no stove). This was once an inexpensive 1960s motel, and the square footage hasn't changed along with the new paint. Rooms are smallish, bathrooms miniscule, ceilings low, and walls thin. If you like the free parking, swimming pool, and Marina location, this place is for you. If you want lots of space, think again.

3100 Webster St. (at Greenwich St.), San Francisco, CA 94123. © 877/433-5765 or 415/921-5520. Fax 415/931-4137. www.thehoteldelsol.com. 57 units. $129–$189 double; $189–$249 suite. Rates include continental breakfast. Kids under 12 stay free in parent's room. Futon, rollaway, or crib $10. AE, DC, DISC, MC, V. Free parking. **Amenities:** Heated outdoor pool; passes to nearby health club ($15); laundry service; dry cleaning. *In room:* A/C, TV, DVD, CD player, free wireless Internet access, fridge (on request, $10), coffeemaker (on request), hairdryer, iron, safe.

INEXPENSIVE

The Marina Inn ★ *Value*   This inexpensive but tidy inn is most suitable for small families with one or possibly two young children. All guest rooms have queen beds, and a few have an additional twin bed. Depending on floor space, the very accommodating

staff can provide a rollaway, crib, or foam mattress. Larger families would require taking multiple rooms, but you'll still spend very little for comfortable accommodations that include a continental breakfast of coffee, juice, pastries, and toasted bagels in a pleasant breakfast nook. The pine beds, armoires, and tables in every guest room are simple and lovely. Inside rooms obtain natural light from light wells but are very quiet; the bright outside rooms pick up noise from ever-busy Lombard Street. Moscone Playground, a popular destination for young families, is just 2 blocks away. Also close by are Chestnut Street, a great walking street with some of my favorite family-friendly restaurants, and the famously crooked part of Lombard Street. Compared to the generic motels along Lombard, the Marina Inn is a Victorian oasis in a safer section of the neighborhood.

3110 Octavia St. (at Lombard St.), San Francisco, CA 94123. ℂ 800/274-1420 or 415/928-1000. Fax 415/928-5909. www.marinainn.com. 40 units. $65–$135 double. Rates include continental breakfast. Kids under 5 stay free in parent's room, Additional guests $10. Rollaways and cribs $10. AE, DC, DISC, MC, V. Self-parking from $16 in public lots 3 blocks away. **Amenities:** Concierge; business center. *In room:* TV, free wireless Internet access, hair dryer (on request), iron (on request).

Marina Motel ☆   The flower-bedecked Marina Motel blends into the surrounding stucco and concrete structures, so be on the lookout for the courtyard entrance between Broderick and Divisadero streets. This is a good option if you have a car, because the parking is off street in little garages and it's free. The guest rooms, all of which face the courtyard, are easily the most charming in the neighborhood. They've recently been redecorated with pine furniture, Italian tiles in the bathrooms, and attractive quilts, and every room has a refrigerator and coffeemaker. In addition to double/doubles and family suites (two bedrooms with a shared bathroom), there are two units with fully stocked kitchens. Management's preference is to rent the kitchen units by the week, so discuss your options with the reservations desk if you'll be staying for a shorter period.

Chestnut Street shopping and dining is a short walk away. The Presidio's Lombard Gate entrance is also within walking distance, and you can take advantage of the free Presidio shuttle buses to get around inside. The 30-Stockton Muni bus from Chestnut Street brings Marina visitors through North Beach, Chinatown, and Union Square. You may spend more time traveling to other neighborhoods, but at the Marina Motel you'll spend a lot less on accommodations.

2576 Lombard St. (between Broderick and Divisadero sts.), San Francisco, CA 94123. ℂ 800/346-6118 or 415/921-9406. Fax 415/921-0364. www.marinamotel.com. 39 units. $75–$135 double; $109–$189 suite. Kitchens available for stays of 5 nights or more ($10 extra). Additional person $20. Rollaways and cribs $10. AE, DISC, MC, V. Free parking. Dogs welcome ($10 per night). *In room:* TV, free wireless Internet access, fridge, coffeemaker, hair dryer, iron.

7 Laurel Heights

This solidly residential neighborhood is a good choice for young families or anyone who wants respite from the urban jungle. Sacramento Street shopping has something for everyone, kids included, and Laurel Village, almost an old-fashioned strip mall, draws crowds of locals.

MODERATE

The Laurel Inn ☆☆ *Value*   One of the few hotels in the neighborhood, the Laurel Inn is terrific and a good value. It's ideal for large families—18 units have kitchenettes. Don't be dismayed by the motor lodge exterior. Inside, it's polished and sleek. Configured with either two double beds or a king and a sofa bed, many of the warm and inviting guest rooms interconnect as well. All the rooms are spacious enough to accommodate a crib and some have panoramic city views. For $10 per day, you can make use of the Jewish Community Center's health club across the street; you'll find a state-of-the-art fitness facility, large indoor pools, and plush locker rooms.

The hotel caters to kids with cookies and lemonade in the afternoons, and a complimentary continental breakfast with fresh juices and an array of muffins and pastries helps jump-start the mornings. Moreover, the neighborhood is safe and quiet. Despite the location away from the tourist zone, convenient bus lines are just outside the front door, including the 3-Jackson to Union Square and the 1-California to Chinatown and the financial district.

444 Presidio Ave. (at California St.), San Francisco, CA 94115. 𝄐 **800/552-8735** or 415/567-8467. Fax 415/928-1866. www.thelaurelinn.com. 49 units. $189–$219 double. Rates include continental breakfast. Kids under 12 stay free in parent's room. Additional guests $10. Rollaways $10; cribs free. AE, DC, DISC, MC, V. Free parking. Pets welcome w/some restrictions; call for details. **Amenities:** Nearby health club access ($10); laundry service; dry cleaning; CD and video lending library. *In room:* TV/VCR, CD player, wireless Internet access, hair dryer, iron.

6

Family-Friendly Dining

San Francisco is a food-lover's city. Even before renowned local chef Alice Waters gave birth to California cuisine, San Francisco took advantage of its access to fresh seafood, local produce, and ethnic influences to foster a thriving dining scene. To the north, east, and south are dozens of small family farms, many organic, which supply city restaurants. In addition, the melting pot of immigrants has added serious depth to the epicurean offerings. Great Mexican food abounds in the Mission, and you'll find Chinese, Japanese, Vietnamese, and Thai restaurants everywhere. Although North Beach has its share of Italian restaurants, you can also find Spanish, Indian, and Greek cuisine very close by.

With so many tantalizing options, it would be a shame to stick to pizza simply because you have the kids in tow—although San Francisco does have some excellent pizzerias, which are listed in this chapter. Experiencing the city's fabulous food needn't deplete your wallet; ethnic restaurants are often inexpensive, and many moderately priced restaurants are home to capable, aspiring young chefs. Likewise, many of the city's best chefs have opened casual eateries, sometimes next door to their original restaurants, where they can showcase their talent at more affordable prices.

Although trying San Francisco's varied cuisine may mean you'll be taking young kids out of their culinary comfort zone, and that you'll be eating in restaurants not populated exclusively by families,

you'll soon discover that San Franciscans are a friendly bunch and that most chefs will be happy to accommodate tiny palates should the need arise. My husband and I have dragged our kids to any number of local restaurants and found that, by following the guidelines I list below (see the "Dining Out in Peace" box), we've been able to enjoy many wonderful dinners and, at the same time, introduce our girls to new and interesting foods.

With that spirit of discovery in mind, I've listed several dining options in this chapter that are not specifically designed for families but to which kids will certainly feel welcome. I have, however, passed over those restaurants that are simply not suitable for kids under 12. The exceptions are two restaurants I suggest if you have a babysitter.

Note that I've listed several restaurants outside the main tourist zones of Union Square, Fisherman's Wharf, and North Beach. In most cases, the best food at the best prices is served in places like the Mission, Noe Valley, or Russian Hill—residential neighborhoods where restaurants may have a more welcoming attitude and where local residents are more likely to bring their kids.

But keeping in mind tight schedules and the need to eat when hunger strikes, I've included plenty of options near the top tourist sights as well. Moreover, while I've tried to include varied cuisine, sometimes everyone just needs to take a break from the sightseeing frenzy, sit, and find

Tips Dining Out in Peace

- **Set the ground rules.** Before entering a restaurant, remind kids that you are going to a special place and that a few key rules apply, such as inside voices and good manners.
- **Bring entertainment.** Crayons, markers, paper, stickers, and so on, will give your children something to do while awaiting their food. If the kids are old enough, bring postcards for them to write.
- **Try word games.** "I Spy" is a good one. Another word game involves one person naming something in a category, such as food. The next person names a word in the same category that starts with the last letter of the previous word (for example, orange, eggplant, tomato, onion . . .).
- **Remember the value of conversation.** Talk with your kids about what you did during the day or what you have planned for the next one. That will help pass the time and encourage restaurant-appropriate behavior.
- **Decide who's "on duty."** Decide ahead of time which adult will have to interrupt his or her meal, should a child act up. Take turns at each meal.
- **Use time-outs.** If your normally polite child acts up, immediately and quietly take him or her outside. This will avoid embarrassment, and will be a lesson to the child. You shouldn't have to do this more than a few times before your child gets the message.

something on the menu the kids will like. For those moments, I've included plenty of restaurants that are tailor-made for big, messy, family meals.

A NOTE ABOUT PRICES The restaurants in the reviews that follow are categorized as Very Expensive, Expensive, Moderate, and Inexpensive, based on an approximation of what a family of four would spend for nonalcoholic drinks and four main courses. If this family would have to pay $150 or more for a meal, I consider that restaurant **Very Expensive;** from $85 to $150 **Expensive;** between $50 and $85, **Moderate;** under $50, **Inexpensive.** I've included cafes, pizzerias, and casual, order-at-the-counter places under the Inexpensive header, and restaurants that have positioned themselves as combining high-quality ingredients and value in the Moderate column.

The Expensive category includes afternoon tea in hotels, usually costly, but delightful if you like that sort of thing. Very Expensive restaurants are for the evenings you've hired a babysitter, unless you're rearing a future Julia Child or Jacques Pepin and wish to inspire her or him. Tax in San Francisco is 8.5%. Tip 15% for good service; more for exemplary service; and at your discretion for poor service.

CHAINS & FAST FOOD You don't find a lot of national chains or even fast-food restaurants in any but the most touristed neighborhoods, such as Union Square and Fisherman's Wharf. For the most part you'll find San Franciscans, with or without kids, prefer chef-driven restaurants with unique identities. As for fast food, you can't do much better than a burrito, but I do understand that kids

- **Make exceptions.** Your child may normally drink milk with dinner. Permit him or her to have a Shirley Temple (7Up and grenadine with a cherry). This will make dinner out seem special.
- **Use rewards and bribery.** Tell kids that if they behave well and eat their dinner, they'll get a bowl of vanilla ice cream for dessert.
- **Be flexible.** If the kids are tired, skip the appetizers or order food that is quick to prepare. If they've reached their limit, have one parent take them outside to stretch their legs or look for a dessert spot while the other parent pays the bill.
- **Slow down.** Before dinner, take them back to the hotel for a nap to rest up or to a playground to let loose some pent-up energy.
- **Eat early.** If you plan to eat at a more elegant restaurant or if it's the weekend, arrive early, before the restaurant gets full. (Plan a post-dinner walk or activity, such as seeing the sea lions at Fisherman's Wharf in summer or the Union Square Christmas tree in winter.)
- **Do lunch.** Some of the city's finer restaurants are open for lunch. Why not make lunch your special meal of the day? The ambience may be more kid-friendly, the prices lower, and your children better behaved. Then you can all have pizza for dinner, and you won't feel you've missed out.
- **Relax.** San Franciscans are very friendly, and most restaurants are delighted to have children come dine with them.

crave pizzas or burgers once in a while. Instead of pointing you to the nearest McDonald's, however, I have done my best to offer alternatives including locally owned diners and regional chains of Italian restaurants, noodle bars, and pizza parlors.

1 Restaurants by Cuisine

AFTERNOON TEA
Laurel Court (Nob Hill, $$$, p. 133)
Lovejoy's Tea Room (The Castro/
  Noe Valley, $$, p. 163)
Palace Hotel ⭐ (SoMa, $$$, p. 127)

AMERICAN
Blue Front Cafe (The Haight, $,
  p. 156)
Blue Mermaid Chowder House
  (Fisherman's Wharf, $$, p. 146)
Chow ⭐ (The Castro/Noe Valley, $,
  p. 163)

Cliff House Bistro (The Richmond/
  Sunset, $$$, p. 164)
Dolores Park Cafe ⭐ (Mission, $,
  p. 161)
Dottie's True Blue Cafe (Union
  Square/Financial District, $,
  p. 126)
Ella's ⭐ (Japantown/Pacific Heights/
  Presidio Heights, $, p. 153)
Firefly ⭐⭐ (The Castro/Noe Valley,
  $$, p. 163)
Fog City Diner (The Embarcadero/
  South Beach, $$, p. 137)

Key to Abbreviations: $$$$ = Very Expensive $$$ = Expensive $$ = Moderate $ = Inexpensive

Franciscan (Fisherman's Wharf, $$$, p. 145)

The Grove ✦ (Marina/Cow Hollow, Japantown/Pacific Heights/ Presidio Heights, $, p. 151)

McCormick & Kuleto's ✦ (Fisherman's Wharf, $$$, p. 145)

Park Chalet ✦ (The Richmond/ Sunset, $$, p. 164)

Park Chow ✦ (The Richmond/ Sunset, $, p. 166)

Polker's Gourmet Burgers (Russian Hill, $, p. 155)

Rainforest Cafe (Fisherman's Wharf, $$$, p. 146)

Tadich Grill (Union Square/ Financial District, $$, p. 126)

Taylor's Refresher ✦ (Embarcadero/ South Beach, $, p. 140)

Town Hall ✦✦✦ (SoMa, $$$, p. 130)

ASIAN

Betelnut ✦ (Marina/Cow Hollow, $$, p. 150)

The Citrus Club (The Haight, $, p. 158)

Long Life Noodle Company & Jook Joint (Embarcadero/ South Beach, $, p. 139)

Zao Noodle Bar (Japantown/Pacific Heights/Presidio Heights, $, p. 154)

ASIAN-FUSION

Café Kati ✦✦ (Japantown/Pacific Heights/Presidio Heights, $$$, p. 152)

BAKERY

Beard Papa's ✦ (SoMa, $, p. 132)

Boulange de Polk ✦ (Russian Hill, $, p. 154)

Citizen Cake ✦ (Civic Center/ Hayes Valley, $$, p. 148)

Tartine ✦ (Mission, $, p. 162)

BARBECUE

Memphis Minnie's ✦ (The Haight, $, p. 158)

BELGIAN FRIES

Frjtz (Civic Center/Hayes Valley, Fisherman's Wharf, $, p. 149)

BREAKFAST/BRUNCH

Blue Front Cafe (The Haight, $, p. 156)

The Canvas Cafe/Gallery (The Richmond/Sunset, $, p. 165)

Crossroads Café ✦ (The Embar- cadero/South Beach, $, p. 139)

Dolores Park Cafe ✦ (Mission, $, p. 161)

Dottie's True Blue Cafe (Union Square/Financial District, $, p. 126)

Ella's ✦ (Japantown/Pacific Heights/ Presidio Heights, $, p. 153)

The Grove ✦ (Marina/Cow Hollow, Japantown/Pacific Heights/ Presidio Heights, $, p. 151)

Polker's Gourmet Burgers (Russian Hill, $, p. 155)

Town's End ✦ (Embarcadero/ South Beach, $$, p. 138)

CALIFORNIA

Citizen Cake ✦ (Civic Center/ Hayes Valley, $$, p. 148)

Crossroads Café ✦ (The Embarcadero/South Beach, $, p. 139)

de Young Cafe ✦ (The Richmond/ Sunset, $, p. 166)

Foreign Cinema ✦✦ (The Mission, $$$, p. 160)

Gary Danko ✦✦✦ (Fisherman's Wharf, $$$$, p. 144)

Hayes Street Grill ✦ (Civic Center/ Hayes Valley, $$$, p. 148)

Moose's ✦✦ (North Beach, $$$, p. 141)

Myth Café ✦ (Embarcadero/ South Beach, $, p. 140)

Oakville Grocery ✿ (Fisherman's
Wharf, $, p. 147)

Restaurant LuLu ✿ (SoMa, $$$,
p. 127)

Sellers Markets ✿ (Union Square/
Financial District, $, p. 127)

Town's End ✿ (Embarcadero/South
Beach, $$, p. 138)

Zuni Cafe ✿ (Civic Center/
Hayes Valley, $$$, p. 148)

CHICKEN

Il Pollaio ✿ (North Beach, $, p. 144)

CHINESE

Dragon Well ✿ (Marina/Cow Hollow,
$, p. 151)

Great Eastern Restaurant (Chinatown,
$$, p. 133)

Hunan Home's Restaurant
(Chinatown, $, p. 134)

Lichee Garden (Chinatown, $,
p. 134)

R&G Lounge ✿ (Chinatown, $,
p. 134)

CHINESE/DIM SUM

Ton Kiang ✿ (The Richmond/Sunset,
$, p. 167)

Yank Sing ✿✿ (Embarcadero/
South Beach, $$, p. 138)

CREPES

Crepe Express (The Haight, $,
p. 158)

Frjtz (Civic Center/Hayes Valley,
Fisherman's Wharf, $, p. 149)

San Francisco Crepe Cart ✿
(Fisherman's Wharf, $, p. 148)

Ti Couz ✿ (The Mission, $, p. 162)

ECLECTIC

The Canvas Cafe/Gallery (The
Richmond/Sunset, $, p. 165)

FRENCH

Fleur de Lys ✿✿✿ (Union Square/
Financial District, $$$$, p. 121)

Grand Cafe (Union Square/Financial
District, $$$, p. 121)

GREEK

Kokkari Estiatorio ✿✿✿
(Embarcadero/South Beach $$$,
p. 136)

HAMBURGERS

Burger Joint ✿ (The Haight,
The Mission, $, p. 156)

In-N-Out Burger (Fisherman's Wharf,
$, p. 147)

Polker's Gourmet Burgers
(Russian Hill, $, p. 155)

Mel's Drive-in (Marina/Cow Hollow,
SoMa, The Richmond/Sunset, $,
p. 151)

Taylor's Refresher ✿ (Embarcadero/
South Beach, $, p. 140)

ICE CREAM

Ben & Jerry's (The Haight, $, p. 156)

Gelato Classico ✿ (North Beach, $,
p. 143)

Ghirardelli Ice Cream and Chocolate
Shop (Fisherman's Wharf, $,
p. 147)

Mitchell's Ice Cream ✿ (The Mission,
$, p. 162)

Norman's Ice Cream & Freezes ✿
(Fisherman's Wharf, $, p. 147)

Swensen's Creamery (Russian Hill, $,
p. 155)

Tango Gelato ✿ (Pacific Heights, $,
p. 153)

Toy Boat Dessert Cafe ✿ (The
Richmond/Sunset, $, p. 167)

INDIAN/PAKISTANI

Indian Oven ✿ (The Haight, $$,
p. 155)

Naan-N-Curry (North Beach, $,
p. 144)

ITALIAN

A16 ✿✿✿ (Marina/Cow Hollow, $$,
p. 149)

Antica Trattoria ✿✿✿ (Russian Hill,
$$$, p. 154)

Cafe Pescatore (Fisherman's Wharf,
$$, p. 146)

Delfina ✸✸✸ (The Mission, $$$, p. 158)

Joe DiMaggio's Italian Chophouse ✸ (North Beach, $$$, p. 141)

L'Osteria del Forno ✸✸ (North Beach, $$, p. 142)

Mario's Bohemian Cigar Store (North Beach, $, p. 144)

Pasta Pomodoro (Marina/Cow Hollow, North Beach, Japantown/Pacific Heights/Presidio Heights, The Castro/Noe Valley, The Richmond/Sunset, $, p. 151)

Pazzia (SoMa, $$, p. 131)

Puccini & Pinetti (Union Square/Financial District, $$, p. 125)

Rose Pistola (North Beach, $$$, p. 141)

Trattoria Contadina ✸ (North Beach, $$, p. 143)

JAPANESE

Isobune (Japantown/Pacific Heights/Presidio Heights, $$, p. 152)

Juban Yakiniku House (Japantown/Pacific Heights/Presidio Heights, $$, p. 152)

Sanraku ✸ (Union Square/Financial District, $$, p. 126)

MEDITERRANEAN

Blue Front Cafe (The Haight, $, p. 156)

Foreign Cinema ✸✸ (The Mission, $$$, p. 160)

Zuni Cafe ✸ (Civic Center/Hayes Valley, $$$, p. 148)

MEXICAN

La Corneta Taqueria ✸ (The Mission, $, p. 161)

La Rondalla (The Mission, $, p. 161)

Mamacita ✸ (Marina/Cow Hollow, $$, p. 150)

Mijita ✸ (Embarcadero/South Beach, $, p. 139)

Pancho Villa Taqueria ✸ (The Mission, $, p. 162)

MOROCCAN

Aziza ✸✸ (The Richmond/Sunset, $$, p. 164)

PIZZA

Amici's East Coast Pizzeria (Embarcadero/South Beach, Marina/Cow Hollow, $, p. 139)

A16 ✸✸✸ (Marina/Cow Hollow, $$, p. 149)

Blondie's Pizza (Union Square/Financial District, $, p. 126)

Giorgio's Pizzeria ✸ (The Richmond/Sunset, $, p. 166)

Pizzeria Delfina ✸✸ (The Mission, $$, p. 160)

Pizzetta 211 ✸ (The Richmond/Sunset, $$, p. 165)

ZA Pizza ✸ (Russian Hill, $, p. 155)

SANDWICHES

'wichcraft ✸ (SoMa, $, p. 132)

SEAFOOD

Blue Mermaid Chowder House (Fisherman's Wharf, $$, p. 146)

Franciscan (Fisherman's Wharf, $$$, p. 145)

Hayes Street Grill ✸ (Civic Center/Hayes Valley, $$$, p. 148)

McCormick & Kuleto's ✸ (Fisherman's Wharf, $$$, p. 145)

Tadich Grill (Union Square/Financial District, $$, p. 126)

SPANISH/TAPAS

Bocadillos ✸ (Embarcadero/South Beach, $$, p. 137)

SUSHI

Isobune (Japantown/Pacific Heights/Presidio Heights, $$, p. 152)

Sanraku ✸ (Union Square/Financial District, $$, p. 126)

THAI

Koh Samui & The Monkey (SoMa, $, p. 132)

Marnee Thai ✮ (The Richmond/ Sunset, $, p. 166)

2001 Thai Stick ✮ (Japantown/ Pacific Heights/Presidio Heights, $, p. 153)

VEGETARIAN

Greens ✮✮✮ (Marina/Cow Hollow, $$$, p. 149)

Millennium (Union Square/ Financial District, $$$, p. 124)

VIETNAMESE

Ana Mandara ✮ (Fisherman's Wharf, $$$, p. 145)

Slanted Door ✮✮✮ (The Embarcadero/South Beach, $$$, p. 137)

2 Union Square/Financial District

VERY EXPENSIVE

Fleur de Lys ✮✮✮ FRENCH   Ironically, the first entry in a chapter called "Family-Friendly Dining" doesn't really fit that description. It is one of two exceptions I've listed for a night when you have a babysitter and want an incredible evening. It's clear from the moment you walk in the door and see the regal, intimate dining room, tented in 900 yards of richly-patterned red and gold fabric, that Fleur de Lys is the epitome of ultra-luxurious dining. In keeping with the warm, inviting decor, the impeccable service is comfortably unpretentious.

As for the awe-inspiring food, the man behind the mastery is award-winning chef Hubert Keller, a native of the Alsace region of France who is now among the best chefs in the world. Keller's kitchen is firmly rooted in classic French cooking, but includes some playful touches inspired by his new country, such as truffle-infused popcorn and an amazing mini foie gras hamburger. Choose from a menu of three, four, or five courses and expect to be blown away by such offerings as seared Moroccan spiced sea scallops with pomegranate *jus,* cauliflower flan, and Osetra caviar or veal *tournedos* scented with foamy lobster bisque and veal essence. A vegetarian tasting menu, with options such as truffled white bean soup with green garlic fondue and wild mushrooms, is also available. The desserts and cheese selection are obscenely delicious, and the wine list includes several hundred selections. (Although I've noted this isn't a place for kids, I did once spot two pre-teen boys dining with their parents; they were well behaved and seemed to enjoy the experience.)

777 Sutter St. (between Jones and Taylor sts.). ✆ **415/673-7779**. www.fleurdelyssf.com. Reservations essential. 3-course menu $70, 4-course $79, 5-course $92. Mon–Thurs 6–9:30pm; Fri 5:30–10:30pm; Sat 5–10:30pm. Closed Sun. AE, DC, DISC, MC, V. Muni: No. 2-Clement, no. 3-Jackson, no. 4-Sutter, or no. 27-Bryant to Jones St.

EXPENSIVE

Grand Cafe FRENCH   The restaurant certainly lives up to its name in terms of decor and style: from the soaring ceilings, massive columns, and wall-sized murals that depict turn-of-the-20th-century Paris to the fine food, this brasserie is abuzz with energy and activity. Located next to the Hotel Monaco and close to the theaters around Union Square, tourists and locals gravitate to the stunning dining room for California-inspired French dishes prepared in an open kitchen with a theatrical flair. Typically French appetizers include foie gras or escargot, while entrees may include herb-encrusted striped bass or bacon-wrapped pork tenderloin. The Grand Cafe's coveted banana cream pie continues to grace the menu, even as chefs come and go.

Dining in Union Square & the Financial District

Belden Place **9**
Blondie's Pizza **8**
The Cellar at Macy's **6**
Crocker Galleria **12**
Delta Tower **15**

Dottie's True Blue Cafe **4**
Fleur de Lys **2**
Grand Cafe **5**
Lee's Deli **13**
Millennium **3**

Puccini & Pinetti **7**
Sanraku **1**
Sellers Markets **11**
Specialty's Café
  and Bakery **14**
Tadich Grill **10**

0 ─── 1/10 mile
0 ─── 100 meters

···· **M** · BART/Muni
═══ Cable Car
←── One Way

Belden Place—A Slice of Europe in San Francisco

If you want to eat downtown without slumming it at a diner or breaking the bank at a posh, pricey restaurant, come to Belden Place. This alley in the Financial District, bordered by Kearny, Montgomery, Pine, and Bush streets, is lined with moderately priced restaurants cooking up French, Italian, Catalan, and other Mediterranean fare. The lane is patronized by plenty of business people, but the outdoor tables and colorful banners lend an informal feeling, so don't hesitate to bring the kids. Stroll on over and take your pick from the following:

Starting at the Pine Street side of Belden Place is **Brindisi Cucina di Mare** (88 Belden Place; ℰ **415/593-8000**), specializing in Italian seafood. From stuffed calamari and seafood risotto to plenty of kid-friendly pasta, most main courses are under $20. **Belden Taverna** (52 Belden Place; ℰ **415/986-8887**) is the newest addition to the alley, serving California-inspired Mediterranean food such as braised short ribs, herb-crusted chicken breast, and grilled rib eye, all of which may appeal to young meat eaters. Entrees range from $14 to $25.

Named for its address, **B44** (44 Belden Place; ℰ **415/986-6287**) is a Catalan-style bistro, serving nine kinds of paella, including meat, seafood, and vegetarian at $17 to $21 each. Salads, small plates, and dishes such as roasted salt cod or roasted rabbit are also on the menu. The tasty food could

While the food is tasty, it's not always as majestic as the room that houses it. For a taste of grandeur without the grand prices, check out the adjacent, more casual Petit Cafe for grilled dishes such as hangar steak or salmon, pizzas from a wood-fired oven, salads, sandwiches, and desserts. Even in the main room, children may order off the Petit Cafe menu.

501 Geary St. (at Taylor St.). ℰ 415/292-0101. www.grandcafe-sf.com. Highchairs, boosters. Reservations recommended. Main courses $12–$22 lunch, $19–$29 dinner; Petit Cafe $8–$17. AE, DC, DISC, MC, V. Breakfast Mon–Fri 7–10:30am, Sat brunch 8am–2:30pm, Sun brunch 9am–2:30pm; lunch Mon–Sat 11:30am–2:30pm; dinner Sun–Thurs 5:30–10pm, Fri–Sat 5:30–11pm. Petit Cafe, Sun–Thurs 11:30am–11pm; Fri–Sat 11:30am–midnight. Muni: Powell-Hyde or Powell-Mason cable car to Union Sq., and then walk 2 blocks west.

Millennium VEGETARIAN/VEGAN   Admittedly, Millennium is not for everyone. Some vegetarian eateries are so good even the most avowed carnivores will find something to love. One such place is Greens in the Marina (p. 149). But Millennium is not just vegetarian. It's vegan, meaning you won't find any animal products on the premises. Even honey is a no-no (although I'm told there's a bottle of the stuff hidden in the back). Without eggs or dairy, concocting a meal meat-eaters can sink their teeth into becomes more challenging.

But I list this place precisely because so many young adults are opting out on meat these days, and at least here teens won't be groaning at the menu and then ordering little more than plain lettuce leaves. They can choose instead from various meatless concoctions that are rich in flavors and protein. One note of advice: Stick to dishes that don't try to mimic ones traditionally made with animal products. If you find fried green tomatoes or Indian samosa pastries with roasted eggplant and zucchini on the be too challenging for less adventurous kids. Just next door, **Plouf** (40 Belden Place; ✆ **415/986-6491**) offers mussels prepared seven different ways, as well as French-accented salads, sandwiches, fish, and meats. All lunch items are under $20, but there are few kid-friendly choices on the menu other than fish and chips.

A better choice for families is at 28 Belden Place: **Café Tiramisu** (✆ **415/ 421-7044**; www.cafetiramisu.com). Kids will appreciate the Italian fare, including pasta dishes from $14 to $18 that those with smaller appetites can easily share. Main courses such as *cioppino,* Italian seafood stew, or veal scaloppini range from $17 to $23 (up to $34 at dinner). The most moderately priced pick of the bunch is Parisian-Bistro inspired **Café Bastille** (22 Belden Place; ✆ **415/986-5673**). While parents savor French onion soup, quiche, or grilled steak and fries, kids can share a French hot dog on a baguette with cheese and fries. Most lunch choices are $9 to $18, and dinner is just a tad more.

But perhaps you want something more traditional, and you've reached the end of the alley. You're in luck. On the corner at 374 Bush Street you'll find **Sam's Grill** (✆ **415/421-0594**), one of the oldest restaurants in San Francisco. Grab a cozy wooden booth and order charcoal-broiled fish, roasted chicken, or a simple pasta dish. Entrees range from $10 to $29.

seasonally changing menu, you won't be disappointed. But the warm spinach salad with tofu tempura left me wishing for real goat cheese, and the truffled vegetable gratin with garlic chive polenta cried out for real cream. One plus is that the restaurant can accommodate any food aversion or allergy. Call ahead and let them know your kid is allergic to eggs, dairy, soy, wheat, and nuts, and they'll happily put something together.

580 Geary St. (at Jones St.). ✆ 415/345-3900. www.millenniumrestaurant.com. Highchairs, boosters. Reservations recommended. Main courses $20–$22. AE, DC, DISC, MC, V. Sun–Thurs 5:30–9:30pm; Fri–Sat 5:30–10:30pm. Muni: No. 27-Bryant or no. 38-Geary to Jones St., or Powell-Hyde or Powell-Mason cable car to Union Sq., and then walk 2 blocks west.

MODERATE

Puccini & Pinetti ITALIAN   This is one Union Square restaurant the kids will definitely enjoy. Children are awfully pleased with the restaurant's activity pack, which includes crayons, and the make-your-own pizza option, where servers bring the pizza dough and fixings to the table so that young chefs can create exactly what they want. For adults, the menu offers plenty of hearty pasta dishes and well-known Italian favorites such as eggplant parmigiana and veal piccata. Service is considerate, and the colorful decor welcoming. You can treat Puccini & Pinetti as a casual dinner stop or make an evening of it.

129 Ellis St. (at Cyril Magnin St.). ✆ 415/392-5500. www.pucciniandpinetti.com. Kids' menu, highchairs, boosters. Reservations accepted. Main courses $13–$21 lunch, $14–$25 dinner; kid's menu $4–$8. AE, DC, DISC, MC, V. Mon–Sat 11:30am–4pm; Mon–Thurs 4–10pm; Fri–Sat 4–11pm; Sun 5–10pm. Muni: Powell-Hyde or Powell-Mason cable car to Union Sq., and then walk 2 blocks south on Powell to Ellis and turn right.

Sanraku *(★ finds)* JAPANESE/SUSHI   Every neighborhood in San Francisco has a smattering of restaurants boasting "artistic," "exciting," or just plain cheap sushi. That is all well and good, but raw fish is raw fish. It should be fresh and prepared by sushi chefs who know what they're doing. Although it's tough to mess up a California roll, it's equally hard to serve a truly delicious slice of *maguro* (tuna) sashimi, but Sanraku succeeds in doing just that. The simple decor and casual atmosphere belie the truly fresh and well-prepared sushi. Some people may wonder what a sushi joint is doing in a family guide, but at least in these parts kids are well acquainted with sushi. My family and I are regulars here. While Dad and I sip sake, the girls enjoy steamed *edamame* (soybeans), avocado and California rolls, and cooked shrimp sushi. Sanraku is moderately priced, but ordering a la carte could edge the bill into the expensive category. For more dollar-conscious options, consider the combination dinners, such as sushi and sashimi, sushi and tempura, or sushi and teriyaki beef, which come with steamed rice, a house salad, and fresh fruit.

704 Sutter St. (at Taylor St.). (✆ **415/771-0803**. www.sanraku.com. Highchairs, boosters. Reservations accepted. Main courses $9–$25. AE, DC, DISC, MC, V. Mon–Sat 11am–10pm; Sun 4–10pm. Muni: No. 2-Clement, no. 3-Jackson, no. 4-Sutter, or no. 27-Bryant to Taylor St.

Tadich Grill AMERICAN/SEAFOOD   People come to the Tadich Grill as much for the history as for the food. Businesspeople and tourists alike appreciate the clubby, traditional feel of San Francisco's oldest restaurant, which started life in a different location more than 150 years ago. The long bar, dark wood interior, and gruff waiters may seem intimidating to little ones, so settle the family into one of the many cozy booths to better enjoy the old-time feel. Stick to uncomplicated and traditional dishes, such as shrimp louie, grilled fish of the day, clam chowder, or creamed spinach, and you will eat well. The Tadich doesn't take reservations, so be prepared to stand in line.

240 California St. (between Front and Battery sts.). (✆ **415/391-1849**. Boosters. Reservations not accepted. Main courses $15–$34. MC, V. Mon–Fri 11am–9:30pm; Sat 11:30am–9:30pm. Muni: F-Market streetcar to Front St. or no. 1-California or no. 41-Union bus to California St.

INEXPENSIVE

Blondie's Pizza PIZZA   The staff here cuts and sells huge wedges of thick-crusted pizzas slathered with tomato sauce, cheese, and various toppings at a constant pace. At $2.75 a slice, you can feed an army and still have change left over for a cable car ticket. You can order pepperoni, but if you ask for carrots and broccoli, you've even got yourself a healthy meal. You won't find tables here, but the benches at Union Square are just 2 blocks away.

63 Powell St. (between Ellis and Market sts.). (✆ **415/982-6168**. Pizza $2.75–$3 per slice. No credit cards for regular orders. (AE, MC, V accepted on orders over $30.) Mon–Sat 10am–10pm; Sun 10am–9:30pm. Muni: Powell-Hyde or Powell-Mason cable car to Ellis St.

Dottie's True Blue Cafe AMERICAN/BREAKFAST   The best meal to have here is breakfast (some locals and tourists claim it's the best in town), but the place is so small that you'll have to wait—unless you have a family of early risers. The big portions of house-made breads, cornmeal pancakes, French toast, eggs, gourmet sausages, fresh orange juice, and cheery trim make the wait well worth it. The lunch menu features hearty salads, sandwiches, and burgers.

522 Jones St. (between Geary and O'Farrell sts.). (✆ **415/885-2767**. Highchairs. Reservations not accepted. Main courses $6–$11. DISC, MC, V. Wed–Sun 7:30am–3pm. Muni: Powell-Hyde or Powell-Mason cable car to Union Sq., and then walk 3 blocks west on Geary to Jones and turn left.

Sellers Markets ★ *Finds* CALIFORNIA   When I've got to run an errand down-town on a weekday, I try to do it around lunchtime so that I can swing by Sellers Markets. At first glance, it's a sleek lunch spot for the Financial District worker bees. Then you notice that everyone there is young and healthy looking. After that you realize these are no ordinary sandwiches and salads. In fact, all the meats, cheeses, and breads at Sellers Markets come from "artisans," as Jim and Deb Sellers like to call the local ranchers, farmers, and bakers who provide the ingredients for such mouth-watering possibilities as the BBQ chicken sandwich made with free-range pulled rotisserie chicken and melted smoked mozzarella. You'll also find a generous selection of salads, from a Cobb salad with naturally raised pancetta to a sushi-grade ahi tuna salad. For the kids, try one of the thin-crust pizzas or the ham and cheese baguette. Sellers Markets also serves breakfast, so if you're up and about early stop in for a breakfast pizza or an egg "a" muffin, a fried egg on an "artisan" English muffin with additional toppings like Niman Ranch bacon or locally made goat cheese and spinach. *Note:* Sellers Markets will have opened a new location at 595 Market St., at 2nd St., by the time you read this. It'll be open Monday to Thursday 7:30am to 7:30pm and Fridays until 3pm, so if the family is hungry for an early dinner, check it out.

388 Market St. (at Pine and Front sts.) ✆ 415/956-3825. www.sellersmarkets.com. No reservations. Breakfast main courses $4.25–$5.95. Lunch main courses $6.75–$9.95. Mon–Fri 7:30am–3pm. AE, DISC, MC, V. Muni: Any streetcar to Front St.

3 South of Market (SoMa)

EXPENSIVE

Palace Hotel ★ AFTERNOON TEA   Tea under the stained-glass dome of the Garden Court at the Palace Hotel, which is every bit as grand as the poshest hotels in London, is a celebratory affair. Linen and silver grace the elegant tables, and the menu consists of the customary dainty sandwiches, scones, and sweets, served with tea of your choice. The Palace cleverly offers a special "Princess" and "Prince" tea for children 12 and under. Along with the sandwiches and pastries, children receive a crown and scepter, and are treated royally as well.

2 New Montgomery St. (at Market St.). ✆ 415/546-5089. www.gardencourt-restaurant.com. Kids' menu, high-chairs, boosters. Reservations recommended. Tea service $34–$46; children's tea $28. AE, DC, MC, V. Sat 1–3pm. Muni: Any streetcar to Montgomery St. station.

Restaurant LuLu ★ CALIFORNIA   Seasonally changing dishes at this enduringly popular SoMa restaurant might include leek, goat cheese, and bacon tart; stuffed pumpkin blossoms; and grilled prawn risotto. Served on large plates, they are meant to be shared. Rotisserie specials alternate during the week—Wednesday may be leg of

---

Fun Fact High Tea

The British tradition of high tea is quite different from afternoon tea. High tea was a hearty meal eaten by the working class around the kitchen table, which often featured high-back chairs—hence the name. Afternoon tea is a more delicate affair with guests perched on the end of cushioned chairs and settees, with the lady of the house playing "Mother," a term of endearment bestowed on the person in charge of pouring the tea.

Dining Around Town

A16 **2**
A G Ferrari Foods **53**
Amici's East Coast Pizzeria **6, 57**
Ana Mandara **27**
Antica Trattoria **37**
Beard Papa's **52**
Betelnut **10**
Blue Mermaid Chowder House **29**
Bocadillos **45**
Boulange de Polk **38**
Café Kati **15**
Cafe Pescatore **36**
Chow **23**
Citizen Cake **19**
Crossroads Café **59**
Dragon Well **4**
Ella's **1**
Ferry Building **63**
Fog City Diner **42**
Franciscan **34**
Frjtz **18, 25**
Gary Danko **28**
Ghirardelli Ice Cream and Chocolate Shop **24**
Greens/Greens to Go **9**
The Grove **3, 14**
Hayes Street Grill **20**
In-N-Out Burger **33**
Isobune **17**
Juban Yakiniku House **16**
Koh Samui & The Monkey **56**
Kokkari Estiatorio **43**
Laurel Court **46**
Long Life Noodle Company & Jook Joint **62**
Mamacita **2**
Mastrelli's Delicatessen **66**
McCormick & Kuleto's **26**
Mel's Drive-in **8, 48**
Metreon **50**
Mijita **67**
Myth Café **44**
Norman's Ice Cream & Freezes **31**
Oakville Grocery **30**
Palace Hotel **54**
Pasta Pomodoro **22**
Pazzia **55**
Polker's Gourmet Burgers **39**
Rainforest Cafe **35**
Restaurant LuLu **49**
Rincon Center **60**
San Francisco Crepe Cart **32**
Santa Barbara Ice Creamery **5**
Slanted Door **64**
Swensen's Creamery **40**
Tango Gelato **12**
Taylor's Refresher **65**
Tonga Room at the Fairmont Hotel **46**
Town Hall **58**
Town's End **58**
2001 Thai Stick **13**
Westfield San Francisco Centre **47**
'wichcraft **47**
Yank Sing **61**
Yerba Buena Gardens **51**
ZA Pizza **41**
Zao Noodle Bar **7, 11**
Zuni Cafe **21**

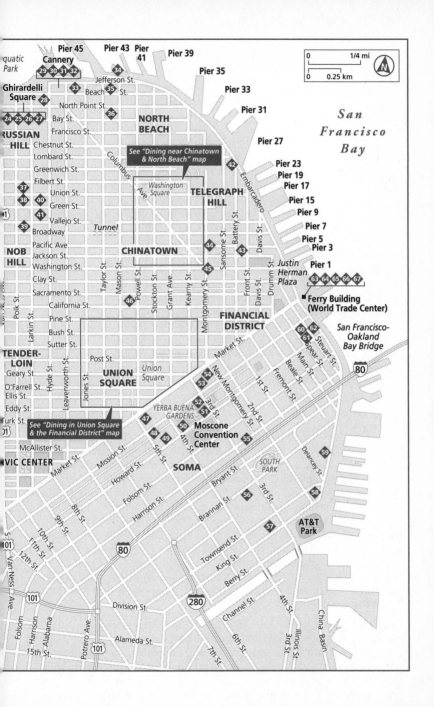

Aquatic Park

Pier 45 Pier 43 Pier 41 Pier 39

Pier 35

Pier 33

Cannery

29 30 31 32

Ghirardelli Square **28**

24 25 26 27

Jefferson St.
34
Beach St. **35**

North Point St. **36**

Bay St.

Francisco St.

NORTH BEACH

Pier 31

Pier 27

RUSSIAN HILL

Chestnut St.

Lombard St.

Greenwich St.

Filbert St.

37
38 40
41
39

Union St.

Green St.

Vallejo St.

Broadway

Pacific Ave.

Jackson St.

Washington St.

Clay St.

Sacramento St.

California St.

Pine St.

Bush St.

Sutter St.

Columbus Ave.

Washington Square

See "Dining near Chinatown & North Beach" map

TELEGRAPH HILL

42

San Francisco Bay

Pier 23
Pier 19
Pier 17
Pier 15
Pier 9
Pier 7
Pier 5
Pier 3

Tunnel

CHINATOWN

44
45

43

Justin Herman Plaza

Pier 1

63 64 65 66 67

NOB HILL

Taylor St.
Mason St.
Powell St.
Stockton St.
Grant Ave.
Kearny St.
Montgomery St.
Sansome St.
Battery St.
Front St.
Davis St.
Drumm St.

46

FINANCIAL DISTRICT

Ferry Building (World Trade Center)

Polk St.
Larkin St.

TENDER-LOIN

Hyde St.
Leavenworth St.
Jones St.

Post St.

Geary St.

O'Farrell St.

Ellis St.

Eddy St.

Turk St.

McAllister St.

CIVIC CENTER

Market St.

San Francisco–Oakland Bay Bridge

60 62
61

Steuart St.
Spear St.
Main St.
Beale St.
Fremont St.
1st St.
2nd St.

80

Union Square

UNION SQUARE

54
53

New Montgomery St.
3rd St.

See "Dining in Union Square & the Financial District" map

YERBA BUENA GARDENS

47
48 49

52
51
50

Moscone Convention Center

55

SOMA

59

Mission St.

Howard St.

Folsom St.

Harrison St.

Bryant St.

Brannan St.

SOUTH PARK

Delancey St.

56
58

57

AT&T Park

8th St.
9th St.
10th St.
11th St.
12th St.

80

Townsend St.

King St.

Berry St.

Channel St.

4th St.
3rd St.
Illinois St.
China Basin

101

Van Ness Ave.

Folsom
Harrison
Alabama

15th St.

Potrero Ave.

Division St.

Alameda St.

7th St.

6th St.

280

101

0   1/4 mi

0   0.25 km

N

129

Food Courts

What could be more democratic than a food court? Having a wide variety of options reduces strife for families with different tastes, which is just about every family I know. Also, kids have fun waiting in the line of their choice and exercising a bit of independence. In the Union Square area, the **Crocker Galleria** at 50 Post St., at Montgomery Street, has a terrific food court on the third level, open Monday through Friday until 6pm and Saturdays until 5pm. It's always packed at lunch with office workers seeking a quick, inexpensive bite. At the Fountain Café you'll find breakfast bagels, eggs, and baked goods in the morning and sandwiches and burgers at lunch. Get a chili fix at Chili Up; the different versions come with tortillas or corn bread. You'll also find counters for Leila Mediterranean Cuisine, 360 Degree Gourmet Burritos, New Asia Restaurant, and Niji Japanese Grill, among other international options. To avoid the rush, arrive before 11:30am or after 1pm and grab a table in the light-filled atrium.

The Cellar in Macy's on Geary and Stockton streets, is not technically a food court, but it does have a Jamba Juice, a Wolfgang Puck Express Café, a Boudin Bakery, a Ben & Jerry's, and a cookie counter. If you're in SoMa, the food court in the new portion of the **Westfield San Francisco Centre** at 5th and Mission streets is a vast improvement over the low-end eateries that once were the only options. Now you can choose from Andale Mexican cuisine, Askew Grill, Bistro Burger, and, what may become the food court's most coveted destination, Out the Door, part of famed chef Charles Phan's collection of restaurants (see Slanted Door on p. 137). In addition to these

lamb day, while Saturday is reserved for roast duck—but the mouth-watering rosemary-scented chicken is a staple. (Just make sure you're not seated too close to the rotisserie, lest you come out smelling like smoked meat.) With its upscale clientele and sophisticated menu, Lulu's feels quite grown-up, but the recently added children's menu, offering linguini, cheese pizza, or a grilled cheese sandwich, means kids will find something they can enjoy as well. Moreover, the large, multi-room space and constant buzz of diners means you won't have to worry about noisy children making a scene; no one will hear them. In its price category, Lulu's is one of the more family-friendly options in the neighborhood.

816 Folsom St. (between 4th and 5th sts.). ✆ 415/495-5775. www.restaurantlulu.com. Highchairs, boosters. Reservations accepted. Main courses $15–$30. AE, DC, MC, V. Sun–Thurs 11:30am–10pm; Fri–Sat 11:30am–11pm. Muni: No. 30-Stockton or no. 45-Union-Stockton bus to Folsom St.

Town Hall 𝕬𝕬𝕬 AMERICAN   This outstanding tribute to New American cuisine opened to great fanfare in early 2004, and the hype is well deserved. The co-owning brothers Mitchell and Steven Rosenthal earned their fame as chefs at one of San Francisco's more upscale, glitzy restaurants, Postrio, but the mood at Town Hall is much more low-key. Housed in a 100-year-old former electric warehouse, Town Hall's decor evokes early American architecture and sensibilities, with exposed brick walls, crisp white ribbed wainscoting, and Craftsman-style tables and chairs. The food echoes the and other choices, a gourmet grocery opens to the food court, which has seating for up to 800 customers.

And therein lies the rub. The choices may be enticing, but hanging out with 799 other customers in a basement food court is not my idea of fun (although my elder daughter thought it seemed like a grand idea; you never know what'll please the kids). If your family is set on a food court, consider the more manageably sized food court at **Metreon** at 4th and Mission streets. There, the Firewood Cafe provides pizzas and tasty salads, and Luna Azul makes generously sized burritos. You'll also find yummy Asian specialties and first-class Japanese fare at these branches of the Long Life Noodle Co. and Sanraku, which are described on p. 139 and 126, respectively.

The most attractive food court is **Rincon Center,** at 101 Spear St., between Mission and Howard streets. The 1930s Moderne/Art Deco building is on the National Register of Historic Places and contains an 85-foot waterfall inside the dramatic atrium and murals in the former post office lobby. For a truly cosmopolitan experience, you can send emissaries to Arabi for top-notch Middle Eastern salads, to Sorabol for Korean grilled meats and soup, to Thai to Go for pad Thai, to Wazwan for Indian dishes and naan bread, and to Taqueria Pepe's for burritos. Burgers, pizzas, sandwiches, and soups are also to be had. Yank Sing, the preeminent dim sum restaurant, has a lovely dining room here, which I highly recommend if you have time for a more leisurely lunch (p. 138). With the exception of Yank Sing, which is open daily, the restaurants in Rincon Center are open weekdays from 11am to 3pm.

American feel, drawing on traditions from around the country, with a special nod to New Orleans. Starters may include cornmeal-fried oysters on baby spinach with creamy bacon dressing or warm biscuits with local ham and pepper jam. Two stellar dishes we've enjoyed include wild king salmon with corn and shrimp hash, cherry tomatoes, and hush puppies and a naturally raised pork chop with smashed potatoes, English peas, and fava beans in garlic parsley butter. For dessert, don't miss the butterscotch and chocolate *pot de crème.* I've spotted pre-teens here at dinnertime, but you may prefer bringing the kids here for lunch. Dinner is still quite a scene.

342 Howard St. (at Fremont St.). ✆ 415/908-3900. www.townhallsf.com. Highchairs, boosters. Reservations recommended. Main courses $10–$17 lunch, $19–$26 dinner. AE, DC, MC, V. Mon–Fri lunch 11:30am–2:30pm; Sun–Thurs 5:30–10pm; Fri–Sat 5:30–11pm. Muni: Any streetcar on Market to Fremont St., and then walk 2 blocks south.

MODERATE

Pazzia ITALIAN   This restaurant, a quick walk from the Yerba Buena Center and the Museum of Modern Art, serves simple and satisfying dishes like excellent pizza, delicious pasta, and roasted meats and chicken. The uncomplicated menu is a delightful California twist on traditional Italian fare. The staff is warm and friendly to kids, and it's definitely a family-oriented little place. If you're in the area and want a real, sit-down meal, there's no better pick for the price.

337 3rd St. (between Folsom and Harrison sts.). © **415/512-1693.** Highchairs. Reservations recommended. Main courses $8–$25. AE, DISC, MC, V. Mon–Fri lunch 11:30am–2:30pm; Mon–Thurs dinner 6–10pm, Fri–Sat dinner 6–10:30pm. Muni: Any streetcar to Montgomery St. station; no. 15-3rd, no. 30-Stockton, or no. 45-Union to Folsom St.

INEXPENSIVE

In addition to the options below, you can find a branch of Mel's Drive-in in this neighborhood (p. 151).

Beard Papa's ✿ BAKERY When this Japanese chain of cream puffs hit the U.S., it became an overnight sensation. Outside of Japan, Beard Papa's can be enjoyed in Hawaii, New York, L.A., and now San Francisco. What's the secret to these luscious cream puffs? Beard Papa's claims it could be their special 2-hour process mixing custard cream, real whipped cream, and Madagascar vanilla beans to produce the filling, a process that's repeated several times a day. Or maybe it's the ultra fresh crust. Or the interesting way the cream puffs are just a little less sweet than you'd expect them to be. Well, you'll just have to come find out for yourselves. You can get the traditional cream puffs served plain or dipped in chocolate on any day, but unusual fillings like strawberry, green tea, or pumpkin are strictly seasonal.

99 Yerba Buena Lane (at Mission St., between 3rd and 4th sts.). © **415/978-9972.** Westfield San Francisco Centre, 865 Market St. (at 5th St.) © **415/978-9972.** www.beardpapasf.com. Cream puffs $1.75 each or $20/dozen. AE, MC, V. Mon–Sat 10am–8pm; Sun 10am–6:30pm. Muni: No. 30-Stockton or no. 45-Union-Stockton bus to Mission St.

Koh Samui & The Monkey THAI Thai seems to be the new Chinese, with spring rolls and pad Thai having taken the place of broccoli beef and cashew chicken as favored take-out fare. But if you want a break from the "typical" Thai food you find most places these days, come to Koh Samui. Combinations sure to whet your appetite include crushed sesame scallops in yellow curry sauce or pumpkin curry chicken. Certainly, you'll find plenty of familiar menu items, from green papaya salad to green curry chicken. For the kids, order the wok-tossed noodles with peanut sauce or even some of the satays. As long as you steer clear of anything marked with an asterisk (for spicy), the kids will be fine. Be sure to order the fried bananas for dessert. "The Monkey" part of the name refers to the attractive shop next door, selling Thai antiques.

415 Brannan St. (at 3rd St.). © **415/369-0007.** www.kohsamuiandthemonkey.com. Highchairs, boosters. Reservations accepted. Main courses $8–$13. MC, V. Mon–Sat 11am–3pm; Sun–Thurs 5–10pm; Fri–Sat 5–10:30pm. Muni: No. 30-Stockton or no. 45-Union to Brannan St.

'wichcraft ✿ *Value* SANDWICHES New Yorkers know Tom Colicchio for his lauded restaurants Gramercy Tavern and Craft. You may know the award-winning chef for his role as head judge on the TV show "Top Chef." Now it's time to get to know him for his . . . um, sandwiches. Yes, Colicchio's West Coast debut is based on slices of bread with stuff inside. The "'wich" in "'wichcraft" is short for sandwich, get it? No matter. When you bite into his juicy BBQ flank steak sandwich with roasted shitake mushrooms and grilled red onions on a pressed ciabatta roll, you'll get it. Vegetarians may like the grilled gruyere and caramelized onions on rye, or even a tasty vegan option with chickpeas and roasted peppers. For kids, simply turn to the breakfast menu, which is served all day (and is cheaper). My older daughter ate her entire toasted ham, avocado, and butter sandwich, and loved it. The younger one had a hard time getting her mouth around an impressive triple-decker peanut butter and jelly sandwich, but she almost managed to finish it. Although 'wichcraft is located in the new Westfield San Francisco Centre, it's got the best location of any restaurant there:

Value **Bargain Alert!**

For a measly $7 and a one-drink minimum each, you can feed the kids at t
Fairmont Hotel's Tonga Room during happy hour from 5 to 7pm on weekdays.
Polynesian appetizers, including pot stickers, chicken drummettes, Shanghai
noodles, fruit, and crudités will fill 'em up, and the tropical storm cued to thun-
der on the half-hour will provide entertainment. There's nothing else like it.

---

outside. While the other dining spots are in the throes of the mall crowd, 'wichcraft
enjoys a corner spot with two 20-foot-high glass walls looking out onto the street.
OK, so the view is just of a parking structure, but the light and airy space—furnished
with many small tables and a few long, communal tables—is sleek and welcoming.
Word has it Colicchio will expand his offerings and open later into the evening. We'll
definitely be back for that.

868 Mission St. (between 4th and 5th sts.) ✆ **415/593-3895.** www.wichcraftnyc.com. Highchairs, boosters. No
reservations. Sandwiches $5–$10. AE, DC, DISC, MC, V. Mon–Fri 8am–9pm; Sat 10am–9pm; Sun 10am–6pm. Muni:
No. 30-Stockton or no. 45-Union-Stockton bus to Mission St.

4 Nob Hill

EXPENSIVE

Laurel Court AFTERNOON TEA   The Fairmont Hotel's lovely Laurel Court
restaurant, with ivory pillars surrounding lighted domes and a low ceiling that makes
the space feel quite intimate, is open for meals almost all day long. Taking the California Street cable car from the foot of Market up to Nob Hill for breakfast sounds
like fun to me, but you'll spend a small fortune on your waffles or eggs. Afternoon tea
is dear as well, but seems more fitting given the surroundings, and will be especially
appreciated by any girls in the family. The kid's tea menu isn't exactly to code: the
crustless sandwiches include peanut butter and jelly and tuna salad, and hot cider and
cocoa are non-tea alternatives.

Fairmont Hotel, 950 Mason St. (at California St.). ✆ **415/772-5259.** www.fairmont.com. Kids' menu, highchairs,
boosters. Reservations recommended. Tea service $34–$46, children's tea $30. AE, DC, DISC, MC, V. Daily 6–11am,
noon–2:30pm, and 6–10pm; afternoon tea daily 2:30–4:30pm. Muni: No. 1-California bus or California St. cable car
to the Fairmont Hotel.

5 Chinatown

MODERATE

Great Eastern Restaurant CHINESE   The specialty here is seafood, which you
can observe swimming around in tanks against the back wall. Dinner doesn't come
fresher than this, so if you're in the mood for steamed whole rockfish, crab served in
a dozen ways, shrimp, lobster, or whatever's in season, Great Eastern is the best choice
in the 'hood. Just don't let the waiter steer you away from the fish tanks towards more
"typical" Chinese-American fare; you'll get the same food you could have gotten for
less at a corner Chinese take-out joint. That's what happened to us some years back
when we were tourists in San Francisco—now we know better. Like the vast majority
of Chinatown restaurants, this one has big tables for extended families. The basement
dining room is comfortable, but we prefer the upstairs. One of the nice things about
eating in Chinatown is that you're almost expected to have kids in tow.

t and Kearny sts.). ✆ 415/986-2500. Highchairs, boosters. Reservations recom-
AE, MC, V. Daily 10am–1am. Muni: No. 15-3rd St. bus to Jackson St.

aurant CHINESE   I was struck by a recent newspaper article
.S. kids aged 10 to 13 surveyed said Chinese was their favorite
ess is these kids were thinking about well-known American-
cashew chicken and sweet and sour pork when they answered
the pollster. Well, Hunan Home's is made for them. I'm sure your kids will enjoy their
meal as much as mine did at this place, which offers all the old favorites in abundance.
Tired of Kung Pao chicken? Try Kung Pao squid. Even if you've seen it all before, rest
assured that the quality will be high and the portions generous. The family dinner
option includes egg rolls and wonton soup for $13 per person. There's also a fish tank
the kids will enjoy—just don't tell them it's dinner.

622 Jackson St. (at Kearny St.). ✆ 415/982-2844. http://hunanhome.citysearch.com. Highchairs, boosters. Reservations recommended. Main courses $6–$28. AE, DC, DISC, MC, V. Sun–Thurs 11:30am–9:30pm; Fri–Sat
11:30am–10pm. Muni: No. 15-3rd St. bus to Jackson St.

Lichee Garden   CHINESE   This longtime, consistently good Cantonese restaurant
is even a favorite among Chinatown residents. Lichee Garden's lengthy menu is filled
with familiar items like egg foo young, sweet-and-sour pork, delicious wonton soup,
and every other dish you remember from your childhood, assuming you weren't raised
in China. The kitchen caters to those who can't make the leap from American broccoli to Chinese broccoli by offering both, but the menu includes more adventurous
fare as well. The list of seafood showcases many scallop inventions, and live lobster and
crab in season—both highly recommended. The excellent dim sum makes a great
lunch option. Large and bright, the dining room has seen many families over the
25-plus years it's been open. Service is businesslike and you won't have to wait long
for your meal. Technically, it's not in Chinatown, but it's just 1 block west of it.

1416 Powell St. (between Broadway and Vallejo sts.). ✆ 415/397-2290. http://licheegarden.citysearch.com. Highchairs. Reservations recommended. Main courses $5.50–$14. MC, V. Daily 7am–9:15pm. Muni: No. 30-Stockton or
no. 45-Union-Stockton bus to Broadway.

R&G Lounge (Finds CHINESE   When you walk into this favored joint at the edge
of Chinatown, you've got two options: proceeding upstairs to the fancier dining room,
or descending into the basement. If you have little ones with you, it's likely the host
will send you downstairs. This troubled my husband greatly; the linoleum flooring,
fluorescent lighting, and omnipresent mirrors of the downstairs dining room offended
his aesthetic sensibilities. But the decor doesn't seem to bother most diners, who
return time and again to R&G for authentically prepared Cantonese fare featuring lots
of fresh seafood and plenty of meat dishes as well. Salt and pepper crab is a big hit, as
is the smoky barbequed pork. Something about putting all the dishes on a big lazy
Susan seems to encourage adventuresome dining, at least with my kids, who happily
munched on all kinds of crab, pork, and noodle dishes. For a real conversation-stop-
per, call 24 hours in advance and order the sweet-rice-stuffed chicken.

631 Kearny St. (at Commercial St.). ✆ 415/982-7877. www.rnglounge.com. Highchairs, boosters. Reservations
recommended. Main courses $7–$25 lunch, $10–$50 dinner. AE, DC, DISC, MC, V. Daily 11am–9:30pm. Muni: No. 30-
Stockton bus.

Dining Near Chinatown & North Beach

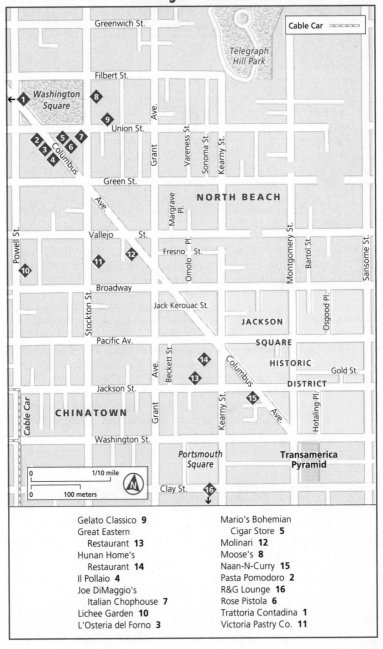

Gelato Classico **9**
Great Eastern
  Restaurant **13**
Hunan Home's
  Restaurant **14**
Il Pollaio **4**
Joe DiMaggio's
  Italian Chophouse **7**
Lichee Garden **10**
L'Osteria del Forno **3**

Mario's Bohemian
  Cigar Store **5**
Molinari **12**
Moose's **8**
Naan-N-Curry **15**
Pasta Pomodoro **2**
R&G Lounge **16**
Rose Pistola **6**
Trattoria Contadina **1**
Victoria Pastry Co. **11**

Finds **How to Tell Your Hakka from Your Hunan**

Chinese cuisine comes in many guises. If the menu doesn't state what province the recipes hail from, can you tell your Shanghai from your Szechuan? Here's a little cheat sheet you can use to impress your kids.

- **Cantonese:** Most of the Chinese restaurants in this chapter fall into this category. In the wet, coastal province of Canton, seafood and vegetables grew in abundance. Cantonese food thus relies on fresh ingredients, which are mildly seasoned with flavors like ginger, soy sauce, and spring onions. Specialties include dim sum, noodles, seafood, and vegetable dishes.
- **Hakka:** Hakka peoples' ancestors settled in the less fertile, hilly regions of southern China. Their cuisine uses dried and preserved ingredients and little seafood. Specialties include salt-baked chicken, stuffed bean curd, and crispy meatballs.
- **Hunan:** Hot weather in the mountainous Hunan region called for strong spices to help preserve food and mask spoilage. Today refrigeration keeps food fresh, but Hunan's fondness for chili peppers, shallots, garlic, and other piquant flavors remains. Familiar dishes include stir-fries, sweet and sour chicken, and Hunan beef.
- **Mandarin:** Mandarin, or Northern Chinese, cuisine stems from the nation's capital, Beijing, and neighboring provinces. Specialties include Peking duck and hot and sour soup.
- **Shanghai:** Hailing from the eastern coast of China, Shanghai cuisine is noted for using a lot of alcohol and sugar, in addition to soy sauce. Specialties include drunken chicken and crispy shrimp balls.
- **Szechuan:** This western Chinese fare is well known for its spicy, flavorful seasonings. Chile pepper pastes and oils are liberally used as cooks strive to combine hot, sour, sweet, and salty tastes in dishes. Specialties include twice-cooked pork and tea leaf duck.

---

6 The Embarcadero/South Beach

EXPENSIVE

Kokkari Estiatorio ★★★ GREEK This modern Greek restaurant provides a memorable and upscale dining experience that you can comfortably enjoy with kids. Although the subtle lighting, crowded bar, and roaring fire in the first room suggest a more adult establishment, don't be concerned. The expansive back room, made to feel warmer with the inclusion of heavy wood furniture and richly-hued tapestries, is an ideal place for families and large parties. The cozy booths along the hall connecting the two rooms are also very suitable for diners with kids. The delectable menu is based on traditional Greek cuisine, but is inspired by the Bay Area's bounty of fresh, local ingredients and, as such, changes seasonally. At any time of the year, however, look for such house specialties as moussaka (eggplant and lamb casserole) and delectable lamb chops made with naturally raised Niman Ranch meat. The plate of traditional Greek spreads and pita bread is great for sharing, but is less inspired than some of the more exotic appetizers, such as fried zucchini cakes with yogurt-mint dressing, or crispy smelts with lemon and parsley. For finicky eaters, the kitchen can fix up a plate of buttered orzo pasta. The staff insists the traditional spinach and cheese pastry spanakopita is a hit with kids—sounds like a sneaky way to get them to eat spinach!

200 Jackson St. (at Front St.). © **415/981-0983**. www.kokkari.com. Highchairs, boosters. Reservations recommended. Main courses $14–$21 lunch, $16–$35 dinner. AE, DC, DISC, MC, V. Mon–Fri 11:30am–2:30pm; Mon–Thurs 5:30–10pm; Fri 5:30–11pm; Sat 5–11pm. Muni: No. 10-Townsend to Jackson St., and then walk 2 blocks east.

Slanted Door 🍴🍴🍴 VIETNAMESE   This may well be the most popular restaurant in San Francisco. No matter that it has twice relocated to bigger spaces, moving from its original site in the Mission to a larger space in the Embarcadero to its current location in an enormous corner of the Ferry Building. The huge space, overlooking the water and framed by walls of glass, is still nearly impossible to get into without reservations. Even the expansive bar area has an hour-long wait on weekend evenings. But fame has not made Charles Phan, the owner behind this success story, rest on his laurels. The restaurant continues to produce mouth-watering delicacies based on traditional Vietnamese dishes such as shaking beef and lemongrass tofu, and the rave reviews keep pouring in. Although Bill Clinton did once eat at the Valencia Street location with Chelsea, this isn't necessarily a child-centered restaurant. Although chances are the kids will like the spring rolls with peanut sauce or chicken claypot with caramel sauce as much as you will, you now have an alternative to the crowds and the scene at the Slanted Door. Just head to the food court at the Westfield San Francisco Centre and try the scaled-down food at Phan's latest enterprise, called **Out the Door.**

1 Ferry Bldg. (at Embarcadero). © **415/861-8032**. www.slanteddoor.com. Highchairs, boosters. Reservations recommended. Main courses $10–$19 lunch, $16–$30 dinner. AE, MC, V. Daily 11:30am–2:30pm; Sun–Thurs 5:30–10pm; Fri–Sat 5:30–10:30pm. Muni: F-Market streetcar.

MODERATE

Bocadillos 🍴 SPANISH/TAPAS   Like many top cooks in San Francisco, lauded chef Gerald Hirigoyen was not content to have only high-end restaurants, like his Piperade, that only serves some of the people some of the time. At Bocadillos, the Basque-born Hirigoyen serves delectable bite-size tid-bits (*bocadillos* means just that in Spanish: bite-size snacks) in a cozy, low-key dining room with a long, communal table serving as its centerpiece. Essentially, what you get here are tapas, and each is delightful, from the roasted peppers to the Catalan sausage to the lamb chops with mango and peach chutney. While Bocadillos is casual and well priced, it may have too much of a boisterous after-work crowd for kids. Best to try it for lunch.

710 Montgomery St. (at Washington St.). © **415/982-2622**. www.bocasf.com. Reservations not accepted. Tapas $3–$12. AE, DC, MC, V. Mon–Fri 7am–11pm; Sat 5–11pm. Muni: No. 12-Folsom to Pacific, and then walk 2 blocks south, or no. 15-3rd St. to Jackson St., and then walk 1 block south.

Fog City Diner AMERICAN   A San Francisco institution immortalized in a Visa commercial, the Fog City Diner has quite a few things going for it: terrific location, fun metallic exterior, sleek wood interior, festive atmosphere, and great outdoor area. Because it's located near Levi's Plaza, kids can climb around the fountain on the opposite side of Battery Street or run around in the minipark next door. In fair weather, the outdoor seating lets you enjoy the bay views and green space. As for the food, the children are sure to be satisfied. The kids' menu features all the usual fare (hot dogs, grilled cheese, buttered noodles, kids' sundaes) and comes complete with a pack of crayons. The grown-up menu, on the other hand, tries a little too hard. Although it's nice that they've branched out from more common diner fare, some of the more inventive creations—such as mu shu pork burritos filled with stir-fried veggies—are not always as tasty as appear. You're best off sticking to the more basic items such as burgers or a "Cobb" sandwich. The cayenne-peppered onion rings are good, too.

1300 Battery St. (at Embarcadero). © 415/982-2000. www.fogcitydiner.com. Kids' menu, highchairs, boosters. Reservations recommended. Main courses $11–$20; kids' menu all items $6.50. DC, DISC, MC, V. Mon–Thurs 11am–10pm; Fri 11:30am–11pm; Sat 10:30am–11pm; Sun 10:30am–10pm. Muni: No. 10-Townsend bus or F-Market streetcar to Battery St., or no. 15-3rd St. to Jackson St., and then walk 1 block south.

Town's End ✿ CALIFORNIA/BRUNCH   Named after the street it's on, this low-key spot is in a part of town that really was once the "town's end," with little beyond it except warehouses and other industrial buildings. Now the little neighborhood of South Beach has a lot going for it, including the cleaned-up waterfront, AT&T Park, new condominiums, and wonderful restaurants like this one. In addition to tasty, reasonably priced food, Town's End has one of the best outdoor dining areas in the city. The kids can run around on the grass while you await your meal, but they may just want to stay put because the first thing that comes to the table is a basket full of house-baked goodies: muffins and scones at brunch, fresh breads and rolls at dinnertime. After that, feast on thick blueberry pancakes, creative omelets and frittatas, or organic salads. If you come for dinner, consider the prix fixe meal, which includes an appetizer, main course, and dessert. (On Tues, the prix fixe price is reduced, but beware the crowd.) Depending on the season, dinner offerings may include a New Mexico Caesar salad; ravioli with spinach, ricotta, and caramelized onions; or a naturally raised beef hamburger, served on a homemade roll, of course.

2 Townsend St. (at Embarcadero). © 415/512-0749. Highchairs, boosters. Reservations recommended. Main courses $6.50–$11 brunch, $9–$17 dinner; prix fixe $18 ($16 on Tues). AE, DC, MC, V. Tues–Thurs 7:30–11am, 11:30am–2pm, and 5:30–9pm; Fri 7:30–11am and 5:30–10pm; Sat 8am–2:30pm and 5:30–10pm; Sun 8am–2:30pm. Muni: N-Judah streetcar to Brannan Station, and then walk south towards Townsend St.

Yank Sing ✿✿ Finds DIM SUM   For many San Francisco families, gathering with friends on a weekend morning over dim sum is a frequent occurrence. Families come together in groups of 6, 8, or 10 and seat themselves at a table, while servers carrying trays or pushing trolleys offer an assortment of bite-size Chinese delicacies, usually served three or four to a plate, for everyone to share. For years, we headed out to the Sunset to brunch at Ton Kiang, which I still recommend. But more recently we've made our way to Yank Sing, which gets my vote for best dim sum in the city. Yank Sing makes more than 100 varieties of dim sum, and serves at least 60 of them on any given day. Scallion prawns, stuffed crab claws, and snow pea shoot dumplings are among the possibilities—and the quality is always top notch. While the price is higher than at Ton Kiang, if you eat at the Rincon Center location, you get the added bonus of dining inside a lovely atrium housing an 80-foot-high waterfall. The other good news is, since Yank Sing has two convenient downtown locations, you can always pop in during the week for lunch, a popular alternative for locals who work in the area.

One Rincon Center, 101 Spear St., (at Mission St.). © 415/957-9300. 49 Stevenson St. (alley between Market and Mission sts. and 1st and 2nd sts.). © 415/541-4949. www.yanksing.com. Highchairs. Reservations recommended. Dim sum $3.65–$10. AE, DC, MC, V. Rincon Center hours: Mon–Fri 11am–3pm; Sat, Sun, and holidays 10am–4pm. Stevenson St. hours: Daily 11am–3pm. Muni: F-Market streetcar. BART to Embarcadero St. (for Rincon Center) or Montgomery St. (for Stevenson St.).

INEXPENSIVE

Amici's East Coast Pizzeria PIZZA   Located across the street from AT&T Park, this is the second San Francisco location (the other is in Cow Hollow) of this regional pizza joint specializing in East Coast–style pizzas baked in wood-fired brick ovens. Although it's not my very favorite pizza in the city, it is pretty good, and there aren't too many other reasonably priced options near the ballpark. The menu features several other items as well, including an assortment of pastas, hearty sandwiches such as Italian sausage or eggplant parmigiana, and salads (the Caesar salad is quite tasty). With friendly waiters, crayons, and speedy service, what more could you need? Kids can get a mini cheese pizza for $6.35, or a small plate of plain noodles for just $1.95.

216 King St. (at 3rd St.). (C) 415/546-6666. Cow Hollow: 2200 Lombard St, (at Steiner St.) (C) 415/885-4500. www.amicis.com. Highchairs, boosters. Reservations not accepted. Main courses $8–$13. AE, DC, DISC, MC, V. Mon–Thurs 11am–10pm; Fri 11am–11pm; Sat 11:30am–11pm; Sun 11:30am–10pm. Muni: N-Judah streetcar to the 4th and King Station, and then walk ½ block east on King St.

Crossroads Café CALIFORNIA/BREAKFAST   Just a block off the Embarcadero, this cafe/bookshop with a fenced-in outdoor patio is a comfy haven for a snack, lunch, and a rest. Order turkey sandwiches, salads, smoked salmon plates, fountain treats, coffee drinks, and hot chocolate from the counter, and find a seat while you wait for your name to be called. The shop stocks a nice selection of children's books and gifts, and there are a few couches and overstuffed chairs to enjoy them in.

699 Delancey St. (½ block south of Embarcadero). (C) 415/836-5624. Reservations not accepted. Main courses $5–$8. AE, MC, V. Mon–Fri 7am–10pm; Sat 8am–10pm; Sun 8am–5pm. Muni: N-Judah streetcar to the Brannan Station, and then walk south towards Townsend St.

Long Life Noodle Company & Jook Joint ASIAN   If you want good, cheap noodles, this is the place. Although nothing here will wow you, you will get a better-than-average meal for little money. The theme is noodles from all over Asia prepared in a variety of ways. Egg, rice, and wheat noodles are served with soup, stir-fried, cold, or over salad in dishes with names like Buddha's Bliss (ramen noodles in miso broth with smoked trout, tofu, and enoki mushrooms) or Dragon's Breath (garlicky lo mein noodles wok-tossed with button mushrooms and parsley). You'll also find dishes made with rice or jook (rice porridge) and other pan-Asian favorites such as pot stickers, spring rolls, and fried wontons. The decor at this location of the small, regional chain is hyper-modern with too much neon. But with all entrees under $9, who's complaining? (You can also slurp Long Life noodles at their Sony Metreon food court branch.)

139 Steuart St. (at Mission St.). (C) 415/281-3818. Reservations not accepted. Main courses $6.25–$8.75. MC, V. Mon–Fri 11:30am–9pm. Muni: F-Market streetcar to Steuart St., and then walk 1½ blocks south.

Mijita Value MEXICAN   Tracy des Jardins, the talent behind this gem, is best known for her hyper-elegant establishment Jardiniere, which serves dinner to the black-tie set en route to the opera, symphony, or ballet. But when you've got kids to feed, not money to burn, this unpretentious joint serving simply prepared Mexican "street food" is a great way to enjoy des Jardins' culinary talents. Not only will you get hearty morsels like a freshly grilled fish taco with cilantro-avocado cream or a carnitas taco with crisped braised pork at amazing prices (under $5), but you'll enjoy a terrific view to boot. Located on the backside of the Ferry Building, Mijita looks out to the San Francisco Bay. Watch commuters catching ferries back home while you enjoy "queso fundido," melted Mexican cheeses and chorizo sausage served with soft tortillas. If it's warm enough to sit outside, let the kids run around while you take your time sipping a cold beer and munching spiced pumpkin seeds. The two kids' items on the short menu, a bean and cheese burrito or a crispy cheese quesadilla, are sure to draw the *chicos* back when the food has arrived. The amazing part is the tiny bill. Des Jardins is dedicated to supporting local farmers, fisherman, and ranchers who produce food sustainably. How she manages to do that and still serve $2 kids' burritos beats me . . . but who cares? Head back to the counter and order, "*Otra cerveza, por favor!*"

One Ferry Building, Number 44 (at the Embarcadero). ⒞ 415/399-0814. www.mijitasf.com. Highchairs. Reservations not accepted. Brunch main courses $6.50–$7. Lunch/dinner main courses $4–$5. Kids' menu $2. AE, MC, V. Mon–Wed 11am–7pm; Thurs–Fri 11am–8pm; Sat 9am–8pm; Sun 10am–4pm. Muni: F-Market streetcar.

Myth Café ⒜ CALIFORNIA   My husband and I are big fans of the place next door to Myth Café. That would be Myth Restaurant, opened in 2004 by acclaimed chef Sean O'Brien. While we like that Myth's prices aren't as high as other restaurants of its caliber, it's a far cry from family-friendly. In fact, by the time we're ready to take our kids to Myth, we'll be too old for its hip scene. So what's a good solution for an out-of-town family? Head to Myth Café for lunch. On a sunny day, it's an airy, light-filled space that contrasts sharply with the dark, wooded decor next door. The food at the cafe is still a little grown-up (the mac & cheese comes with sharp Vermont white cheddar and a parmesan brioche, for example), but no item is over $10 and, frankly, the chilled corn soup with avocado mousse is divine. The Cuban pulled pork panini will satisfy even the hungriest appetite and everyone, including the kids, will love the deviled eggs and the homemade truffle potato chips. The best value is the "brown bag lunch" including a sandwich, side salad, and sweet treat such as a cookie for $6.95.

490 Pacific Ave. (at Montgomery St.). ⒞ 415/677-4289. Highchairs. Reservations not accepted. Lunch main courses $7–$9. AE, MC, V. Mon–Fri 8am–4pm. Muni: No. 12-Folsom to Pacific, and then walk 2 blocks south.

Taylor's Refresher ⒜ *Finds* AMERICAN/HAMBURGERS   This must be what diner food tasted like 50 years ago, when cows still roamed pastures and a tomato still tasted like a tomato. Eating here made me understand how diners got to be so popular in the first place. The hamburgers, made with local, naturally raised beef, are mouth-watering, and the sweet potato fries were a hit with my kids (I ordered them without the chile powder). Even the cherry tomatoes on the garden salad were sweet and delicate, not the tasteless, hard-skinned variety one expects at a typical diner. Then again, this diner isn't exactly typical. The first, and still existing, Taylor's Refresher was established in 1949 in the heart of the Napa Valley, with plenty of nearby family farms to draw on for fresh, local ingredients. This site, housed in the Ferry Building, takes advantage of the neighboring Farmer's Market for its raw materials. Despite the gourmet touch, the food still comes on trays, the music is loud, and the price is right. On a sunny day, choose an outdoor table and order one of the awesome milk shakes or a root beer float—all made with San Francisco's luscious Double Rainbow ice cream.

1 Ferry Bldg. (at Embarcadero). ⒞ 866/328-3663. www.taylorsrefresher.com. Highchairs. Reservations not accepted. Main courses $4–$14. AE, DC, DISC, MC, V. Daily 10:30am–8:30pm. Muni: F-Market streetcar.

7 North Beach

EXPENSIVE

Joe DiMaggio's Italian Chophouse ✿ ITALIAN   For a taste of old San Francisco, head to this new joint on the corner of Washington Park. Although it opened its doors in June 2006, DiMaggio's will transport you back a half-century. The polished decor includes deep rich mahogany walls, generously sized plush leather booths, stunning Art Deco chandeliers, and, best of all, hundreds of black-and-white photographs of old San Francisco. You'll see photos of Joe and Marilyn (circa 1954) here, snapshots of besuited locals in fedora hats there, pictures of old baseball games around the corner. The dim lighting and stately bar make DiMaggio's feel quite adult, but the space accommodates all sorts of diners; the booths can easily fit a family of four and then some. I've seen other kids here who clearly enjoyed the experience.

In keeping with the old-time theme, portion sizes are definitely not nouvelle. While the menu contains enough new influences to keep it interesting, the servings are so generous I recommend sharing. The pork chop is large enough to feed two, and the potato gratin accompanying it measured a good 5 inches across. Salads like the tomato salad with shaved fennel and fried goat cheese are well executed, but not exactly a "light" start to a meal. The gnocci and smoked chicken in cream sauce is as rich as you'd expect it to be, and twice as big. Nonetheless, desserts like the dreamy Frangelico cheesecake with a rich hazelnut cream are good enough to make room for.

601 Union St. (at Stockton St.). ✆ 415/421-5633. www.joedimaggiosrestaurant.com. Highchairs, boosters. Reservations recommended. Main courses $16–$38. AE, DISC, MC, V. Daily 5–11pm. Muni: Powell-Mason cable car to Union St., and then walk 2 blocks east, or no. 30-Stockton bus to Union St.

Moose's ✿✿ CALIFORNIA   Although the name evokes thoughts of a dark and smoky joint with heavy, unimaginative food, Moose's is just the opposite. The appellation actually derives from its owner, longtime restaurateur Ed Moose. Overlooking Washington Park, Moose's serves innovative California cuisine using local, organic ingredients in a light and spacious setting. Despite the lack of real antlers (you'll see drawings of them everywhere), the restaurant does maintain a classic, old-fashioned feel—with a live pianist, professional waiters, and well-dressed clientele of all ages. It's easy to see how it has become a veritable San Francisco institution since its creation in 1992. The ever-changing menu may include such inventive offerings as a strawberry salad with locally grown cress and herb-infused Sonoma goat cheese, or wild king salmon with grilled Japanese eggplant and Thai basil puree. Dishes based on more traditional fare include grilled pork porterhouse chop with cranberry beans and maple-glazed cipollini onions. The restaurant has a verbal kids' menu with burgers, chicken fingers, or pasta with veggies for $6 apiece. If you don't mind foregoing the Italian fare that abounds in North Beach, you will eat well here.

1652 Stockton St. (at Union St.). ✆ 415/989-7800. www.mooses.com. Kids' menu, highchairs, boosters. Reservations recommended. Main courses $8–$16 brunch, $8–$25 lunch, $15–$34 dinner; kids' menu $6. AE, DC, DISC, MC, V. Thurs–Sat 11:30am–2:30pm; Mon–Thurs 5:30–10:30pm, Fri–Sat 5:30–11pm, Sun 5–10pm; Sun brunch 10am–2:30pm. Muni: Powell-Mason cable car to Union St., and then walk 2 blocks east, or no. 30-Stockton bus to Union St., and then walk 1 block east.

Rose Pistola ITALIAN   Rose Pistola didn't start as a family-friendly restaurant, but perhaps its location in North Beach meant it had to get better at accommodating tourists who may have their kids in tow. That's good news for you, as it means you can

Sandwich Bars & Picnic Spots

An urban picnic could be an adventure, or at least a novelty. To start, hunt for sandwiches at **Specialty's Café and Bakery** (© 877/502-2837; 1 Post St. at Market St.) or **Lee's Deli** (© 415/421-0648; 648 Market St. between Kearny and Montgomery sts., among other Financial District locations). Specialty's bakes its own bread and offers deli-style sandwiches with some inventive options such as Thai chicken and turkey curry. Lee's is fast, inexpensive, and basic: tuna or thickly sliced real turkey. Once you've packed your bag, you're ready to head to 100 1st Street. There you'll find the award-winning second-floor garden in the **Delta Tower,** a lush respite from busy Mission Street. The black granite and green glass fountain sculpture provides a soothing counterpoint to the street traffic. If you're in SoMa, stop by **A G Ferrari Foods** on 688 Mission St. (© 415/344-0642) to pick up delectable Italian sandwiches on fresh focaccia bread. Then head to **Yerba Buena Gardens** (p. 178) for an urban retreat.

Picnicking by the water may be an even better idea. Go to the **Ferry Building** (p. 176) on the Embarcadero and purchase sandwiches from **Mastrelli's Delicatessen** (© 415/397-3354). Then go out behind the building, grab a bench, and enjoy your picnic as you watch the ferries head out across the bay. At Fort Mason, pick up delicious vegetarian sandwiches like egg salad at **Greens to Go** (Building A, Fort Mason Center, © 415/771-6330) and then

enjoy the delightful offerings at this upscale Northern Italian establishment without feeling stressed about how the staff will react to the little ones. Your bigger worry will be getting a table at this ever-crowded hot spot, so make reservations or arrive early. The hot and cold antipasti may be the best thing on the menu: zucchini chips, roasted chili and garlic shrimp, and shaved artichoke salad are among the choices. Main courses highlight fish, pastas, and pizzas, and rotisserie grilled meats are also on offer.

532 Columbus Ave. (between Union and Green sts.). © 415/399-0499. www.rosepistolasf.com. Highchairs, boosters. Reservations recommended. Main courses $17–$34. AE, MC, V. Mon–Thurs lunch 11:30am–3pm; Fri–Sun lunch 11:30am–4pm; Sun–Thurs dinner 5:30–11pm; Fri–Sat dinner 5:30–midnight. Muni: Powell-Mason cable car to Union St., and then walk 2 blocks east, or no. 30-Stockton bus to Union St., and then walk 1 block east.

MODERATE

L'Osteria del Forno ⌀⌀ ITALIAN   A perennial favorite among in-the-know locals, L'Osteria seems to have as many people lining up outside as are actually seated inside. Once you have gotten a table, you'll appreciate the authentic, rustic feel in the cozy dining room. The terrific Italian dishes, which rank among the best in North Beach, include such delightful dishes as crepes filled with sautéed porcini mushrooms, ham, and béchamel sauce; and succulent skewered lamb marinated in ginger, rosemary, and garlic. If the kids are apt to be noisy, this tiny place may not be the best choice.

519 Columbus Ave. (between Union and Green sts.). © 415/982-1124. www.losteriadelforno.com. Reservations not accepted. Highchairs. Main courses $5–$19. No credit cards. Mon, Wed, Thurs, Sun 11:30am–10pm; Fri–Sat 11:30am–10:30pm. Closed Tues. Muni: Powell-Mason cable car to Union St., and then walk 2 blocks east, or no. 30-Stockton bus to Union St., and then walk 1 block east .

sit yourselves under a palm tree on the expansive lawn. If you're at **Crissy Field** (p. 173), grab a soup or sandwich at the Warming Hut. You'll find plenty of picnic spots outside.

North Beach provides more sources for filling your hamper. **Molinari,** 373 Columbus Ave. at Vallejo Street (℃ **415/421-2337**), is an Italian delicatessen with a fantastic assortment of imported foodstuffs and friendly staff who will create delicious, everything-on-'em sandwiches to go. Also consider takeout from **Mario's Bohemian Cigar Store** (reviewed below). You can't pass on dessert if you're anywhere near **Victoria Pastry Co.,** 1362 Stockton St. at Vallejo (℃ **415/781-2015**). The chewy almond cookies are divine, as are the cakes, all sold by the slice or whole. You may be able to find a bench in Washington Square Park if you can't wait to dig into your lunch. Otherwise, head to **North Beach Playground** at Lombard and Mason streets, where you'll find picnic facilities and a playground.

If you're headed out to Lincoln Park in the Richmond District, a convenient stop is **Angelina's Bakery** at 6000 California St., at 22nd Avenue (℃ **415/ 221-7801**). Pick up sandwiches, salads, or quiches and hop back on the no. 1-California bus to 32nd Street. Then walk north 2 blocks to Eagle's Point at the end of the Land's End trail. Enjoy your picnic with a priceless view of the Marin Headlands and western side of the Golden Gate Bridge.

Trattoria Contadina 🖈 *Finds* ITALIAN   So you brought the kids to North Beach and you just want a nice Italian restaurant where you can have a tasty, reasonably priced meal? And each tiny restaurant is already full and the street is jammed with other hungry-looking tourists? Here's a hint: get away from the crowds and start heading up Union Street (and I do mean "up"—the hill is quite steep) 2 blocks to this quaint, family-owned eatery. Trattoria Contadina isn't exactly spacious and you may still wait if you don't have reservations, but the restaurant does have more tables and a more welcoming feel than many of its counterparts on Columbus Street. In keeping with the ma-and-pa atmosphere, the food is hearty and no nonsense. The linguini with co-owner Anna Maria's homemade Italian meatballs will take you back to your own childhood, and the spinach, meat- and cheese-filled ravioli, served in a porcini mushroom cream sauce, is rich and delicious. There's no kids' menu, but the kitchen will happily serve up half orders at this very family-friendly trattoria.

1800 Mason St. (at Union St.). ℃ **415/982-5728.** www.trattoriacontadina.com. Highchairs, boosters. Reservations recommended. Main courses $12–$24. AE, DC, DISC, MC, V. Sun–Thurs 5:30–9pm; Fri–Sat 5:30–10pm. Muni: Powell-Mason cable car to Union St., or no. 30-Stockton bus to Union St., and then walk west (up) 2 blocks.

INEXPENSIVE

In addition to the options below, you can find a Pasta Pomodoro in this neighborhood (p. 151).

Gelato Classico 🖈 ICE CREAM   These tiny stores make gelato that's nearly as delicious as what you might have in Rome. The gelato is so rich and creamy, it's best had neat. But if you can't resist going all out, how about the "Coppa Carmelita," dark chocolate and hazelnut gelato covered in a luscious caramel sauce?

576 Union St. (between Stockton and Grant sts.). ℂ 415/391-6667. No credit cards. Cups $3.25–$4.65. Sun–Thurs noon–10pm; Fri–Sat noon–11pm. Muni: Powell-Mason cable car to Union St., and then walk 2 blocks east, or no. 30-Stockton bus to Union St., and then walk 1 block east.

Il Pollaio ⚸ CHICKEN   At Il Pollaio, located across the street from Washington Square Park, a table by an open window, a fragrant roast chicken, and a mixed salad speak of a gentle end to a good day. In addition to the signature chicken, you'll also see steak, pork chops, lamb chops, rabbit, and sausages on the grill. Beyond that, Il Pollaio offers a few salads, soup, and just two sides: French fries and marinated eggplant. Daily specials, consisting of roasted meat with fries and a salad, are the way to go.

555 Columbus Ave. (between Union and Green sts.). ℂ 415/362-7727. Highchairs. Main courses $6–$17. MC, V. Mon–Sat 11:30am–9pm. Muni: Powell-Mason cable car or no. 30-Stockton bus to Union St.

Mario's Bohemian Cigar Store ITALIAN   This corner storefront could truthfully be called Mario's Bohemian Shoebox, it's so small. Gone are the days when you could find a cigar on the premises, much less smoke one; instead, Mario's has been serving big, warm focaccia sandwiches filled with meatballs or breaded chicken cutlets, pizzas, salad, and drinks for about 20 years. Grab a seat at the funky wooden counter and watch the waitress efficiently fill the drink orders while the cook prepares the food in a miniature oven. Kids will love the Torani Italian syrups used to make sodas. You can also get the sandwiches to go, to enjoy them in Washington Park across the street.

566 Columbus Ave. (at Union St.). ℂ 415/362-0536. www.mariosbohemiancigarstore.com. Main courses $4.50–$8.50. MC, V. Mon–Sat 10am–midnight; Sun 10am–11pm. Muni: Powell-Mason cable car or no. 30-Stockton bus to Union St.

Naan-N-Curry *(Value)* INDIAN/PAKISTANI   When San Franciscans want good, inexpensive Indian/Pakistani food, they come to Naan-N-Curry. Flavorful tandoori-oven-baked meats, delightful curries, a great selection of vegetarian options, and plenty of naan breads are on offer here. Although some dishes can be too spicy for younger kids, we've found a few items that even our young daughters love, including chicken tikka masala, which is cooked in a mild yogurt sauce, and vegetable biryani, or vegetables with rice. With a casual atmosphere and hearty portions for just pennies, it's worth branching out from pizza, noodles, and the other usual suspects.

533 Jackson St. (at Columbus Ave.). ℂ 415/693-0499. Main courses $4–$10. MC, V. Mon–Fri 11am–11:30pm; Sat–Sun noon–11:30pm. Muni: No. 15 bus to Jackson St.

8 Fisherman's Wharf

VERY EXPENSIVE

Gary Danko ⚸⚸⚸ CALIFORNIA   Opened in 1999 by an award-winning chef of the same name, Gary Danko quickly earned the reputation as one of the best restaurants in the world. Although I would be remiss to omit it in a guidebook about the city, it is best visited without the little ones, unless they are older kids well accustomed to eating at exclusive restaurants. Novelist and San Francisco local Danielle Steele brings her children to dine here but reserves the private dining room at the back on such occasions. Richly decorated in blond oak and black granite, the atmosphere at Gary Danko is elegant and subdued. Diners can choose three, four, or five courses for

$61, $77, or $92 respectively. The ~~~ delicacies as lobster salad with melon ~~~ with wild mushrooms and roasted ap~~~ berries with vanilla crepes and lemon~~~ tions are advised 4 weeks in advanc~~~ the bar.

800 North Point St. (at Hyde St.). ℂ **415/749-20**~~~
Prix-fixe menu $61–$92. DC, DISC, MC, V. Daily 5:30–1~~~

EXPENSIVE

Ana Mandara ⟮ VIETNAMESE The momen~~~ serene restaurant, you are transported to Vietnam—~~~ interior includes facades of a Vietnamese-style home an~~~ palm trees, and other Indochinese artifacts. Yet the 18-foot~~~ ted with spotlights, as if to remind you that this is not Vietna~~~ The food seems to follow suit. Appetizers such as crispy rolls with crab, shrimp, and shiitake mushrooms and entrees such as tournedos of beef tenderloin with onions and peppercress are very tasty, but seem firmly grounded on this continent—which may be just as well for the little ones among you. Although there is no children's menu, kids do enjoy the beef tournedos, as well as the side of garlic noodles. There are a few truly exotic options, like the luscious mango soup with durian sorbet, which is a must-have for dessert. The dinner menu edges this restaurant into the expensive category, but lunch prices are more moderate, with main courses starting at $11.

891 Beach St. (at Polk St.). ℂ **415/771-6800.** www.anamandara.com. High chairs, boosters. Reservations recommended on weekends. Main courses lunch $11–$20, dinner $21–$38. AE, DC, DISC, MC, V. Mon–Fri 11:30am–2pm; Sun–Thurs 5:30–9:30pm; Fri–Sat 5:30–10:30pm. Muni: No. 30-Stockton bus to Polk St., and then walk 1 block north, or Powell-Hyde cable car to Beach St., and then walk 2 blocks west.

Franciscan AMERICAN/SEAFOOD It's all about the view here, which explains the upside-down nature of this oddly shaped, peach-colored structure. Stairs lead you from the crowded wharf below into a welcoming dining room, which offers bay views from practically every table. Given its location in the most heavily touristed part of town, you'll pay more than you should for a crab cake appetizer ($14) or slice of halibut ($24), but you do get a fabulous vista, friendly service, and better fare than at most restaurants in the vicinity. The pasta and sandwiches come in at under $15, and all kids' menu items are $5. The kids' fish and chips is big enough for adults and comes with crayons and drawing materials. I wouldn't go out of my way to eat here, but if you want a nice lunch without having to leave the neighborhood, the Franciscan may be worth the higher prices.

Pier 43½ (at Embarcadero). ℂ **415/362-7733.** www.franciscanrestaurant.com. Highchairs, boosters. Reservations accepted. Main courses $10–$50; kids' menu $5. AE, DC, DISC, MC, V. Daily 11:30am–10pm. Muni: F-Market streetcar to Mason St.

McCormick & Kuleto's ⟮ AMERICAN/SEAFOOD I'm not usually into extra-large restaurants with massive menus smack dab in the most touristy parts of town. But this establishment, which brings well-known local restaurateur Pat Kuleto together with the nationally renowned McCormick & Schmick's seafood restaurant chain, keeps high standards. Overlooking the lovely Hyde Street Pier, with Alcatraz in the background, it has one of the best views in all of San Francisco and is a good stand-by for visiting grandparents. The options are not especially inventive—cedar

...griddled parmesan-coated petrale sole are typical
...well prepared. Although the menu is dominated by
...are still plenty of choices for the fish-averse. The kids'
...and chips plate that you'll want to polish off if your little
...be sure to come in daylight to enjoy the view, but don't expect
...e can be slow.

...tween Larkin and Polk sts.). ✆ **415/929-1730**. www.mccormickandschmicks.com. Kids'
...eservations recommended. Main courses $13–$40; kids' menu $5.35–$7.75. AE, DC, DISC, MC, V.
...30am–10pm; Fri–Sat 11:30am–11pm; Sun 10:30am–10pm. Muni: No. 30-Stockton bus to Larkin St.,
...alk 1 block north, or Powell-Hyde cable car to Beach St., and then walk 1 block west.

...inforest Cafe *(Overrated)* AMERICAN   The phony flowers and plastic rain forest
complete with waterfall, aquarium, and African music in the background just cry out
for a B ticket (for those of you old enough to remember how things once worked at
Disneyland). The food at this merchandised-to-the-hilt restaurant is strictly pedestrian: a little fish, a little chicken, a hamburger, a steak—something for everyone.
With 500 seats, however, you're going to get production-line quality. My suggestion
is if you want the fun of a tropical storm, head for the Tonga Room at the Fairmont
Hotel. For a lot less money, in civilized surroundings, treat the kids to snacks and an
umbrella-bedecked drink with benign rainstorms on the half-hour.

145 Jefferson St. (next to the Wax Museum). ✆ **415/440-5610**. www.rainforestcafe.com. Kids' menu, highchairs,
boosters. Reservations not accepted. Main courses $11–$29; kids' menu $6–7. AE, DC, DISC, MC, V. Mon–Wed
11:30am–9pm; Thurs 11:30am–10pm; Fri–Sat 11:30am–11pm. Muni: F-Market streetcar to Mason St.

MODERATE

Blue Mermaid Chowder House AMERICAN/SEAFOOD   Blue Mermaid offers
a no-nonsense menu of chowders, sandwiches, salads, and a few bigger main course
options at pretty reasonable prices. The decor plays on the restaurant's location in The
Cannery, with boats suspended from the ceiling, heavy wood columns wrapped in
shipping rope, and hand-painted posters depicting advertisements of long-gone
canned fish and produce exporters. Outdoor seating in the lovely Cannery courtyard
is also available. Kids' meals, like fish sticks or hot dogs, are served up with French fries
in blue beach buckets. *Tip:* Stick to the traditional chowders, like the Manhattan or
New England, which are tastier than the restaurant's much touted Dungeness corn
and crab chowder.

471 Jefferson St. (at Hyde St.). ✆ **415/771-2222**. www.bluemermaidsf.com. Kids' menu, highchairs, boosters. Reservations not accepted. Main courses $9–$22; kids' menu $6.95. AE, DC, DISC, MC, V. Sun–Thurs 7am–9pm; Fri–Sat
7am–10pm. Muni: Powell-Hyde cable car to Beach St., and then walk 1 block north.

Cafe Pescatore ITALIAN   You could probably pay less for Italian fare a few blocks
away in North Beach, but this is the wharf, after all. Given the alternatives, this trattoria located on one corner of the Tuscan Inn hotel looks downright appealing. Floor
to ceiling windows open onto heated sidewalk seating, but there's no ocean view here
(the waterfront is 2 blocks away). Menu highlights include Caesar salad, wood-fired
pizza, and plenty of pasta options. Order simply, and you'll do fine. The kids' menu
includes pasta or pizza, which kids can have plain, with sausage, or with another top-
ping of their choice.

2455 Mason St. (at North Point St.). ✆ **415/561-1111**. www.cafepescatore.com. Kids' menu, highchairs, boosters.
Reservations not accepted. Main courses $8–$17 lunch, $9–$22 dinner; kids' menu $3.25–$6.95. AE, DC, DISC, MC,
V. Daily 7am–10pm. Muni: F-Market streetcar to Mason St., and then walk 1 block south.

INEXPENSIVE

In addition to the options below, you can find a Frjtz in this neighborhood (p. 149).

Ghirardelli Ice Cream and Chocolate Shop ICE CREAM   There's a reason for the ever-present line here: Ghirardelli makes a good product. If you haven't ever had a Ghirardelli brownie, order one under a scoop of ice cream.

Ghirardelli Sq., 900 North Point St. © 415/474-3938. www.ghirardelli.com. Desserts $5–$9. Sun–Thurs 9am–11pm; Fri–Sat 9am–midnight; Ice Cream shop opens at 10am. Muni: No. 30-Stockton bus to Larkin St., and then walk 1 block north, or Powell-Hyde cable car to Beach St., and then walk 1 block west.

In-N-Out Burger HAMBURGERS   Having spent my teenage years in California, I can tell you that In-N-Out is a statewide phenomenon. Fans, who insist it's the best fast food anywhere, tell me what makes the burgers so good are the toasted buns, crisp lettuce, and fresh tomatoes. They also swoon over the extra-crisp, extra-thin fries, which are, in addition to a grilled cheese sandwich, the only vegetarian option on the very short menu.

333 Jefferson St. (between Jones and Leavenworth sts.). © 800/786-1000. www.in-n-out.com. Main courses $2–$3. No credit cards. Sun–Thurs 10:30am–1am, Fri–Sat 10:30am–1:30am. Muni: F-Market streetcar to Jefferson and Taylor sts.

Norman's Ice Cream & Freezes ✶ (Finds) ICE CREAM   Although I list the Ghirardelli above, it's not really our favorite ice creamery in the Wharf. So if you're at Ghirardelli Square and your kids espy the line of people waiting for chocolate sundaes, do not despair. Just point your kids downhill and start heading northeast. As you reach The Cannery, you'll see a Ben & Jerry's, but keep on walking. Turn into the peaceful courtyard of The Cannery and there you'll find Norman's, purveyor of delicious, locally made ice cream in an unhurried and friendly fashion. Norman serves Mitchell's ice cream, the best in San Francsico, and you don't need to trek out to the Mission to get it. While he doesn't carry as many flavors as the Mitchell's store itself, he does offer quite a few, including coconut, Kahlúa mocha cream, mango, and even green tea—all so rich and creamy they put other ice creams to shame. And, of course, Norman gladly makes sundaes as well. But if you're feeling adventurous, consider the Halo-Halo, a Philipino concoction made with sweet beans and shaved ice.

The Cannery (Jefferson St., between Hyde and Jones sts.). © 415/346-3046. 1 scoop $2.50; 2 scoops $4.50. No credit cards. Mon–Thurs 11am–8pm; Fri–Sun 11am–10pm; summers open daily 11am–11pm. Muni: Powell-Hyde cable car to Beach St., and then walk 1 block north.

Oakville Grocery ✶ CALIFORNIA   As the sign above the door proudly proclaims, the original Oakville Grocery in Napa Valley has been in business since 1881. What you'll find here, as in the Napa Valley location, are excellent handcrafted cheeses, freshly baked breads, locally harvested fruit jams, specialty items—all of which have been attracting hard-core foodies and chefs for years. You'll also encounter foods deliciously prepared with local and seasonal ingredients, including gourmet pizzas, sandwiches, inventive side salads, entree-sized salads, and soups. The chicken potpie is a favorite with our kids, but the many savory *empanada* pastries (ham and egg for the less adventurous; Thai chicken for the bold) are also a hit. You can eat lunch at the counter or have it packed up to enjoy out on the grass by Aquatic Park. (If you didn't have the kids in tow, I'd say grab a seat at the back for some wine and cheese tasting, but that may have to wait for another trip.)

2801 Leavenworth (at Jefferson St.). © 415/614-1600. www.oakvillegrocery.com. Reservations not accepted. Main courses $5–$8. AE, DC, MC, V. Sun–Mon 10am–7pm; Tues–Sat 10am–8pm. Muni: F-Market streetcar, no. 19 Polk.

San Francisco Crepe Cart ⋆ (Finds) CREPES   A few of these crepe carts are scattered about Fisherman's Wharf, but this one is my favorite due to its location in the charming, brick-lined courtyard of The Cannery, adjacent to a small outdoor stage. Order a ham and cheese or spinach and goat cheese crepe, grab a table under the shade of a tree, and enjoy a quick, inexpensive meal accompanied by live music. Our kids love to listen to the jazz or folk musicians who play there regularly. For dessert, share a chocolate and banana or simple powdered sugar crepe.

The Cannery (Jefferson St., between Hyde and Jones sts.). Crepes $4.50–$7.50. No credit cards. Daily 10am–6pm. Muni: Powell-Hyde cable car to Beach St., and then walk 1 block north.

9 Civic Center/Hayes Valley

EXPENSIVE

Hayes Street Grill ⋆ CALIFORNIA/SEAFOOD   Chef-owner Patricia Unterman, the author of the *Food Lover's Guide to San Francisco,* is pretty much the authority on the local culinary scene—so it's no surprise her restaurant serves delicious, uncomplicated dishes that showcase local, in-season ingredients. The specialty here is very fresh fish: whatever's been caught that morning will be prepared simply and with integrity and be accompanied with crisp, thin fries. All sauces are thoughtfully served on the side. The non-fish selections, such as the grass-fed steak with mustard butter and balsamic onions, are equally flavorful. The atmosphere balances between informal and businesslike, with a clientele of politicians and professionals at lunch and artists and audiences eating a pre-show dinner. At lunch, kids might enjoy eating at the bar; it's situated in the front and commands a view of many tables and the door, so they can keep tabs on what's going on.

320 Hayes St. (between Gough and Franklin sts.). ℂ 415/863-5545. www.hayesstreetgrill.com. Highchairs, boosters. Reservations recommended. Main courses $13–$23 lunch; $18–$25 dinner. AE, DC, MC, V. Mon–Fri 11:30am–2pm; Mon–Thurs 5–9:30pm; Fri 5–10:30pm; Sat 5:30–10:30pm; Sun 5–8:30pm Muni: No. 21-Hayes bus to Franklin St. or any streetcar to Franklin St., and then walk north 3 blocks.

Zuni Cafe ⋆ CALIFORNIA/MEDITERRANEAN   For more than 2 decades, Zuni Cafe has served Mediterranean-infused California cuisine in this spacious, sunny, location. The whitewashed walls and two-story-high south-facing windows combine with odd angles, heavy wood, and exposed brick to give a casual, airy feel to the place. The eclectic, inventive, and always delicious cuisine from famed chef-owner Judy Rodgers (which can also be found in her fabulous 500-plus page cookbook) changes regularly, but her signature roast chicken with bread salad is always on the menu. It's no wonder this place still draws a crowd after all these years. Although there is no children's menu, the kitchen is always happy to whip up a special concoction. Whatever you do get for the kids, make sure it comes with the shoestring potatoes.

1685 Market St. (between Gough and Franklin sts.). ℂ 415/552-2522. Highchairs and boosters. Reservations recommended. Main courses $10–$19 lunch, $14–$39 dinner. AE, MC, V. Tues–Sat 11:30am–midnight; Sun 11am–11pm. Muni: F-Market streetcar to Gough St.

MODERATE

Citizen Cake ⋆ BAKERY/CALIFORNIA   When you walk into this cafe, you are faced with such a fetching array of cakes, tarts, cookies, pastries, and ice creams that all thought of the food pyramid dissipates as you grapple with the mind-bending question: *What do I choose?* You can take time to figure that out while drooling at the counter or sitting at one of the tables in the austere room, where ample windows keep you in touch with the street action. Brunch is a good time to eat here, as it will give you an excuse to order their homemade donuts. But you're best off making it a teatime treat. Lunch and dinner menus may be too esoteric and pricey for a family meal.

399 Grove St. (at Gough St.). ✆ 415/861-2228. www.citizencake.com. Highchairs. Reservations for brunch recommended. Main courses $10–$13 lunch, $17–$27 dinner. AE, MC, V. Tues–Fri 8am–10pm; Sat 10am–10pm; Sun 10am–5pm. Muni: No. 21-Hayes bus to Gough St., and then walk 1 block north to Grove St., or any streetcar to Van Ness St. station, and then walk 3 blocks north to Grove St. and 2 blocks west to Gough St.

INEXPENSIVE

Frjtz BELGIAN FRIES/CREPES   Among the hip boutiques and antique shops of Hayes Valley is this very narrow, very funky teahouse specializing in fries. Thick and crispy, and wrapped in a paper cone just like you get on the streets of Brussels, the starchy wedges are best eaten when they're as hot as your fingers can handle. If you feel guilty just feeding your kids fries for lunch, you can order them salads, sandwiches, or crepes, all of which are named after artists. Another location is at Fisherman's Wharf.

579 Hayes St. (at Laguna St.). ✆ 415/864-7654. Fisherman's Wharf: Ghirardelli Sq., 900 North Point St. ✆ 415/928-3886. www.frjtzfries.com. Fries $3–$4.50. Main courses $7–$8. AE, DC, DISC, MC, V. Mon–Thurs 9am–10pm; Fri 9am–midnight; Sat 10am–midnight; Sun 9am–9pm. Muni: No. 21-Hayes bus to Laguna St., or any streetcar to Van Ness St. station, and then walk 2 blocks north to Hayes and 4 blocks east to Laguna St.

10 Marina/Cow Hollow

EXPENSIVE

Greens ✮✮✮ VEGETARIAN   The setting is so lovely and the food so good at this vegetarian spot, even dedicated carnivores will enjoy it. Built by the San Francisco Zen Center in a converted warehouse, the restaurant boasts very high ceilings and a wall of windows that frames a stunning view of a marina, the bay, and the Golden Gate Bridge. Come in the early evening, and you'll be rewarded with a glorious sunset as well.

One taste of the delectable offerings, and you may decide meat is overrated. Start with baked goat cheese with grilled bread and golden beets, and follow it with risotto with snap, snow, and English peas, or yellow vegetable curry with cashew jasmine rice. For dessert, how about a warm fruit cobbler with buttermilk ice cream? Vegan appetizers, entrees, and desserts—like egg-free, dairy-free chocolate mousse—are also available. Most nights are a la carte, but on Saturday night a $48 four-course prix fixe dinner is served. Some folks gripe that meatless fare should be less expensive, but I feel Greens' prices are in line with vegetarian options at any upscale restaurant. If you can't get a table at lunchtime, pick up sandwiches from the Greens to Go take-out counter and have a picnic overlooking the bay.

Building A, Fort Mason (at Bay St.). ✆ 415/771-6222. www.greensrestaurant.com. Highchairs, boosters. Reservations recommended. Main courses $8–$14 lunch, $16–$23 dinner; prix fixe (Sat night only) $48. AE, DISC, MC, V. Tues–Sat lunch noon–2:30pm; Sun brunch 10:30am–2pm; Mon–Sat dinner 5:30–9pm. Closed Sunday for dinner. Muni: No. 30-Stockton bus to Laguna St. and transfer to the no. 28 bus to Fort Mason.

MODERATE

A16 ✮✮✮ ITALIAN/PIZZA   It's just a few years old, but this hopping Chestnut Street locale is already well established in the Bay Area's dining scene. It's named after the motorway that transverses the Italian region of Campania, home to Naples. As one might expect, A16's most acclaimed specialty is its wood-oven-fired Neapolitan pizza, which could blow away your youngsters' preconceptions of what pizza is all about.

Order a "pizza marinara," with just tomato, oregano, garlic, and olive oil, and they'll be amazed that something without melted cheese could taste so good. Of course, there are mozzarella-topped pizzas as well. The rest of the menu is also impressive (and changes seasonally). Dishes like house-made fennel sausage with grilled bread or wild salmon with basil, almonds, and lemon are deliciously inspired by southern Italian cuisine. For dessert, your options might include ricotta almond mousse or warm chocolate hazelnut cake. Although the menu is more limited at lunch, it may be the best time to bring younger children. They'll enjoy watching the pizzas being made or drawing on the paper-covered tables. The dinner scene is usually too noisy and grown-up for all but the hippest teenagers.

2355 Chestnut St. (between Scott and Divisadero sts.). © **415/771-2216.** www.a16sf.com. Highchairs, boosters. Reservations recommended. Main courses $8–$13 lunch, $8–$20 dinner. AE, DC, MC, V. Wed–Fri lunch 11:30am–2:30pm; Sun–Thurs dinner 5–10pm; Fri–Sat 5–11pm. Muni: No. 30-Stockton bus to Scott St.

Betelnut ⊛ ASIAN   When you first approach Betelnut, you may ask yourself why you've brought kids. The entire front of the restaurant opens out onto the sidewalk, where you'll find trendy 20- and 30-somethings sipping cocktails and nibbling on pan-Asian appetizers. Behind them lies a long bar and, off to the right, steps leading back to a dimly lit restaurant. But despite the boisterous, bar-like atmosphere, the restaurant is actually a very welcoming, low-key hangout that's become a neighborhood institution. Many local families bring their kids here regularly. The kids don't seem to mind the dark exterior, and the vibrant atmosphere (this is definitely a place for groups, not couples) will drown out any child whining about having spent the entire day sightseeing. Kids all love the chicken satays, but ask for the peanut sauce on the side, as it's mildly spicy. The Cecilia's minced chicken in lettuce cups and the Shanghai steamed chicken dumplings are also a hit with the kids. If the adults want something with a little more zing, try the five-spiced firecracker shrimp.

2030 Union St. (between Buchanan & Webster sts.). © **415/929-8855.** www.betelnutrestaurant.com. Kids menu, boosters. Reservations accepted. Main courses $6.75–$20. DC, DISC, MC, V. Sun–Thurs 11:30am–11pm; Fri–Sat 11:30am–midnight. Muni: No. 41-Union or no. 45-Union-Stockton.

Mamacita ⊛ MEXICAN   Disregard any preconceived notions of Mexican cuisine that those Tex-Mex chain restaurants have impressed on your psyche. This hip addition to the Chestnut Street dining scene serves up inventive, intensely flavorful Latin dishes prepared with top-quality ingredients like ultra-fresh seafood, naturally raised beef, and handmade tortillas. The carnitas made with slow-cooked pulled pork and the Mexican gulf prawns sautéed with jalapenos, smoked bacon, and roasted tomato–coconut milk are luscious possibilities. The kids' menu quesadilla is big and tasty, and the freshly made chips and guacamole are so good you could make a meal of them—but it would be a shame to miss the better offerings to come. Be warned: You'll find plenty of families dining in the early hours, but Mamacita's impressive selection of tequilas draws its fair share of margarita-swilling revelers later in the evening.

2317 Chestnut St. (between Scott and Divisadero sts.). © **415/346-8494.** Kids menu, boosters. Reservations accepted. Main courses $10–$18; kids' menu $6–$8. AE, MC, V. Mon–Sat 11:30am–10pm; Sun 11:30am–9pm. Muni: No. 30-Stockton bus to Scott St.

INEXPENSIVE

In addition to the options below, you can find an Amici's East Coast Pizzeria in this neighborhood (p. 139).

Dragon Well ★ *Finds* CHINESE   Dragon Well was established with the idea of serving light, fresh, flavorful, and reliably good Chinese food. It has succeeded. Traditional favorites like pork-filled potstickers (a big hit with my kids) and cashew chicken do not disappoint, and the tea-smoked duck, served in a bun with plum sauce, is not to be missed. Even kids can enjoy it, provided you leave out the fresh cilantro. The spacious and airy decor matches the light and healthful food.

2142 Chestnut St. (between Steiner and Pierce sts.). ✆ **415/474-6888**. www.dragonwell.com. Highchairs, boosters. Main courses $7–$11. MC, V. Daily 11:30am–10pm. Muni: No. 30-Stockton bus to Steiner St.

The Grove ★ AMERICAN/BREAKFAST   On weekends, we regularly hit the Grove for lunch. With a wooded interior, an eclectic assortment of tables and chairs, windows that open up like terrace doors, lots of plants, and plenty of outdoor seating, it's simply one of the most agreeable places to hang out on a sunny day. The menu is equally pleasing, with breakfast options like hot oatmeal with brown sugar and fruit or a breakfast burrito with guacamole and sour cream. Lunch options include fresh salads and unique sandwiches, like the Cuban pork or the turkey with chipotle mayo. Kids will enjoy the cheese quesadilla or the homemade macaroni and cheese. Another location is in the Pacific Heights neighborhood.

2250 Chestnut St. (at Alma St., between Scott and Pierce sts.). ✆ **415/474-4843**. Pacific Heights: 2016 Fillmore St. (between California and Pine sts.) ✆ **415/474-1419**. Highchairs. Main courses $7–$10. AE, DC, DISC, MC, V. Mon–Thurs 7am–11pm; Fri 7am–11:30pm; Sat 8am–11:30pm; Sun 8am–11pm. Muni: No. 30-Stockton bus to Scott St.

Mel's Drive-in HAMBURGERS   The original Mel's was opened in 1947 on Van Ness Avenue by Mel Weiss. It was demolished 25 years later, but not before George Lucas filmed *American Graffiti* there. In 1985 Mel's son Steven opened a new Mel's on Lombard Street but kept the old 1950s theme, complete with booths, chrome, and tabletop jukeboxes. He eventually opened three more San Francisco locations and a smattering elsewhere in the state. The food is nothing to write home about, but under-10s love this place—uniformed waitresses deliver their meals in cardboard Cadillacs, they can select '50s tunes on the jukebox, and they get balloons just for stopping by. The menu includes all the typical diner options: blue-plate specials, chicken potpie, salads, humongous desserts, and all-day breakfast. Among other Mel's locations are those in the SoMa and Richmond neighborhoods.

2165 Lombard St. (at Steiner St.). ✆ **415/921-2867**. SoMa: 801 Mission St. (at 4th St.; 3 blocks south of Union Sq.). ✆ **415/227-0793**. Richmond: 3355 Geary Blvd. (between Parker Ave. and Stanyan St.). ✆ **415/387-2255**. www.melsdrive-in.com. Highchairs, boosters. Main courses $5–$15. MC, V. Sun–Wed 6am–1am; Thurs 6am–2am; Fri–Sat 24 hours. Muni: No. 30-Stockton bus to Steiner St., and then walk 1 block south on Steiner St.

Pasta Pomodoro ITALIAN   Families, and the good fresh food, are responsible for making this locally-owned chain so successful. The fare isn't going to have you phoning home in a rapture, but it's cheap, healthy, and you can make everyone happy here with a plate of lasagna for meat-eaters, a nice linguine primavera for the vegetarian, plain capellini for the refusnik, and some sautéed broccoli because you need your veggies. The best news is that Pasta Pomodoro also delivers. Should you be in a hotel without room service, don't stress about taking exhausted kids out once again: those buttered noodles are just a phone call away. You can find other locations in the North Beach, Presidio Heights, Castro, and Sunset neighborhoods.

1875 Union St. (between Hyde and Larkin sts.). ✆ 415/771-7900. North Beach: 655 Union St. (at Columbus Ave.). ✆ 415/399-0300. Presidio Heights: 3611 California St. (at Spruce St.). ✆ 415/831-0900. Castro: 2304 Market St. (at 16th St.). ✆ 415/558-8123. Sunset: 816 Irving St. (at 9th Ave.). www.pastapomodoro.com. Highchairs, boosters. Main courses $7.50–$11. AE, MC, V. Mon–Thurs 11am–10:30pm; Fri 11am–11:30pm; Sat noon–11:30pm; Sun noon–10:30pm. Muni: No. 41-Union or no. 45-Union-Stockton bus to Laguna St.

11 Japantown/Pacific Heights/Presidio Heights

EXPENSIVE

Café Kati 👶👶 ASIAN FUSION   It's been around for years, but Café Kati is still a favorite local restaurant. It somehow manages to marry a sophisticated, inventive menu with a relaxed, neighborhood atmosphere. The eclectic decor is cozy and home-made, and the already-small space is divided into two even smaller dining areas in front and back rooms. As in all the best spots, the menu changes depending on what's available locally. It always reflects the unique influence of chef Kirk Webber, who likes to include a little something Eastern and a little something Western. Thus, you might find seafood steamed in red Thai curry and a marinated skirt steak with Vidalia onion rings giving patrons great pleasure. If you're lucky, the towering Caesar salad with Cajun cornmeal catfish will be on the menu as well. Be prepared to wait on the weekends, unless you have an early reservation. The staff is very kid-friendly, but the dim lighting and exotic menu may be too much for younger diners.

1963 Sutter St. (between Fillmore and Webster sts.). ✆ 415/775-7313. www.cafekati.com. Reservations recommended. Main courses $21–$32. AE, MC, V. Mon–Sat 5:30–10pm. Muni: No. 2-Clement, no. 3-Jackson, no. 4-Sutter, no. 22-Fillmore, or no. 38-Geary bus to Fillmore St., and then walk ½ block east on Sutter St.

MODERATE

Isobune JAPANESE/SUSHI   If you want to introduce the kids to sushi, this could be a fun to place to start. The spicy tuna rolls, *maguro* tuna, and a few vegetarian options cruise by on little boats in front of diners. See something that looks enticing? Go ahead and take it. The chefs are constantly at work, refilling the little boats on their aquatic conveyer belt. You won't find the greatest selection here, but you're best off sticking to the mainstream stuff like California rolls anyway. **Warning:** This is one place that's actually better when it's crowded. If you come at odd hours, you'll see limp fish that's been around the loop a few too many times.

1737 Post St. (in the Japan Center). ✆ 415/563-1030. Highchairs. Reservations not accepted. 2 pieces of sushi $1.80–$6.95, gratuity not included. AE, MC, V. Daily 11:30am–10pm. Muni: No. 38-Geary bus to the Japan Center at Webster St.

Juban Yakiniku House JAPANESE   Although the grill-your-own concept may not have the dramatic appeal of a Benihana's, where the chef comes to your table and sautés while you watch, it's really more fun to take responsibility for your own dinner. At Juban, a gas grill embedded in the center of your table quickly cooks thin slices of tender beef, chicken, short ribs, shrimp, and other items while you and yours handle the cooking implements. The wait staff makes sure the temperature is just so, but in any event, it's pretty difficult to ruin your dinner. Smoke is relieved by special down-draft grills. Juban is big and modern, with wide tables to hold the various plates of raw and cooked food, and an accommodating staff. *Yakiniku,* or grilling, works well for children, who can pick and choose what they like and in reasonable quantities.

1581 Webster St. (in the Japan Center). ✆ 415/776-5822. www.jubanrestaurant.com. Highchairs. Reservations recommended. Main courses $7–$20. AE, MC, V. Fri lunch 11:30am–2pm; Sat–Sun lunch 11:30am–4:30pm; Mon, Wed, Thurs dinner 5:30–9:30pm; Fri–Sun dinner 5–9:30pm. Muni: No. 38-Geary bus to the Japan Center at Webster St.

⌐ *Tips* **Sushi for the Whole Family**

San Francisco kids have grown up with sushi, and it's not unusual to see sushi served at lunchtime in some of the city's middle and upper schools. Even very young children in the city are used to accompanying their parents on sushi outings. For a fun Japanese dining experience, arrive early when the restaurant is less busy and sit your family down at the sushi bar. Your kids will love watching the sushi chef expertly patting the rice into oblong shapes and placing raw fish on top, or making artistic rolls and slicing them ever so precisely with a very big knife. Finicky eaters may prefer leaving the *hamachi* (yellowtail) or spicy tuna rolls to their parents and sticking to cooked shrimp or vegetarian rolls. Many sushi restaurants also serve other Japanese dishes like tempura, teriyaki chicken, or *udon* noodles. Don't forget to order *edamame* (soybeans in the shell) to start. They're fun to eat and healthy.

INEXPENSIVE

In addition to the options below, both The Grove (p. 151) and Pasta Pomodoro (p. 151) have locations in this neighborhood.

Ella's ⌐ AMERICAN/BREAKFAST   This is one of the best places for brunch in San Francisco. Maybe that explains why the line at Ella's usually goes well out the door. The menu changes frequently, but expect fresh baked breads, exceptional pancakes, and omelets with appetizing fillings like sausage, mushroom, roasted red pepper, and Gruyère. To skip the weekend wait, come for a regular weekday breakfast. If you just can't come by in the morning, lunch (think cashew egg salad on cornmeal molasses bread) and dinner (curried lamb stew, perhaps) are also fine times to try Ella's neoclassical American cuisine.

500 Presidio Ave. (at California St.). ⓒ 415/441-5669. www.ellassanfrancisco.com. Highchairs, boosters. Reservations not accepted. Main courses $8–$12 brunch, $5–$16 lunch/dinner. MC, V. Mon–Fri 7am–5pm; Sat–Sun 8:30am–2pm; Wed–Thurs, Sun 5–9pm; Fri–Sat 5–10pm. Muni: No. 1-California bus to Presidio Ave.

Tango Gelato ⌐ *Finds* ICE CREAM   Like the U.S., Argentina has had its fair share of Italian immigrants and, as a result, has a delicious array of gelaterias. Fortunately for San Franciscans, one enterprising Argentine made his (very long) way up north and opened a gelateria in Pacific Heights. In addition to recognizable Italian flavors like *nocciolo* (hazelnut) and *amaretto,* you'll find luscious South American favorites like *dulce de leche,* an ultrasweet caramel concoction, and coconut. You'll also find other Argentine specialties, such as *alfajor* cookies filled with *dulce de leche.*

2015 Fillmore St. (between California and Pine sts.). ⓒ 415/346-3692. No credit cards. Small cup $3; large cup $5.15. Sun–Thurs 11:30am–10pm; Fri–Sat 11:30am–11pm. Muni: No. 1-California bus to Fillmore, and then walk ½ block south.

2001 Thai Stick ⌐ THAI   The name of this place is so bad that I passed by it for years before a friend who lives in the neighborhood assured me that the food is actually quite good, and perfect for a casual family meal. He was right. My daughters gobbled up their pad Thai and loved the spring rolls. My green curry with chicken was lightly spiced and had the rich creaminess of coconut milk without being too rich. It was perfect. My husband loved the pork in peanut sauce. Even better was the price.

2001 Fillmore St. (at Pine St.). ℂ **415/885-6100.** Highchairs, boosters. Reservations not accepted. Main courses $5.95–$11. Sun–Thurs 11am–10pm; Fri–Sat 11am–11pm. AE, DC, DISC, MC, V. Muni: No. 1-California bus to California St., and then walk 1 block south.

Zao Noodle Bar ASIAN   What kid doesn't love a good plate of noodles? This small chain of Asian-style restaurants is sure to satisfy even the pickiest eater. The kids' menu is basically a choice of noodles served four ways: with chicken, with chicken and veggies, with peanut sauce, or just plain. Grown-ups can order more interesting options such as coconut-lemongrass soup or yellow curry salmon and prawns. The food isn't going to win any awards for Asian cooking, but the inexpensive kids' menu—complemented by plastic kids' cups, special kids' "chop sticks," and a tolerant staff—makes this a popular option for local families with young children.

2406 California St. (at Fillmore St.). ℂ **415/345-8088.** www.zaonoodle.com. Reservations not accepted. Highchairs, boosters. Main courses $8–$13. AE, MC, V. Sun–Thurs 11am–10pm; Fri–Sat 11am–11pm. Muni: No. 1-California bus to Fillmore St.

12 Russian Hill

EXPENSIVE

Antica Trattoria ✦✦✦ *Finds* ITALIAN   This neighborhood favorite is no ordinary Italian restaurant. Considered one of the best trattorie in San Francisco, its homemade pasta dishes are deliciously uncomplicated, accentuating high-quality, fresh ingredients over busy, heavy sauces. The menu also varies with the time of year. Although you can't go wrong with any of the pasta dishes, including such possibilities as fettuccine with porcini mushrooms, oven-dried olives, and brown-butter sage, if you consider a fish or meat dish for a change you will not be disappointed. Options such as Alaskan halibut and clams in white wine and tomatoes, or thinly sliced sirloin steak with arugula and roasted potatoes, are delectable. If you have room for dessert, the rich chocolate cake and airy tiramisu are transcendent. The crisp white walls, warm wood furniture, and unpretentious decor match the elegant food perfectly. Antica has no kids' menu, but the kitchen is happy to serve a kids' portion of hot buttered penne with veggies, and Vicki, the charming hostess, keeps a supply of crayons on hand. Whenever we eat at Antica, which is frequently, we wonder why we don't come even more often.

2400 Polk St. (at Union St.). ℂ **415/928-5797.** www.anticasf.com. Highchairs, boosters. Reservations recommended. Main courses $10–$21. AE, DC, DISC, MC, V. Tues–Thurs, Sun 5:30–9:30pm; Fri–Sat 5:30–10:30pm. Muni: No. 19-Polk to Union St., no. 41-Union, or no. 45-Union-Stockton bus to Polk St.

INEXPENSIVE

Boulange de Polk ✦ BAKERY   If you can claim one of the outdoor tables here on a sunny day, consider yourself very lucky. These are prime people-watching spots and exactly where you'd want to eat absolutely anything from this always busy, very French

---

⸂ **Moments**   **Picnic with a View**

The Powell-Hyde cable car stops a half block from ZA Pizza. Grab some slices to go and re-board the cable car for the ride to Aquatic Park. Munching on tasty slices of crisp-crusted pizza with a view of both bridges sounds like a special moment to me.

bakery. In the mornings, cappuccino and an almond croissant, or a chewy baguette with sweet butter and jam, will transport you to the Marais in Paris. Lunch items include smoked salmon quiche and *tartines* (savory tarts) served with salad. Kids will enjoy the chocolate croissants for breakfast or the ham and cheese baguette for lunch. (The original Boulange was at 2325 Pine St. Now you can find the bakeries at 1000 Cole St., 1909 Union St., 2043 Fillmore St., and the newest location at 543 Columbus Ave. in North Beach.)

2310 Polk St. (at Green St.). ℂ 415/345-1107. www.baybread.com. Lunch items $3.25–$9. MC, V. Tues–Sat 7am–6:30pm; Sun 7am–6pm. Muni: No. 19-Polk to Green St., no. 41-Union, or no. 45-Union-Stockton bus to Van Ness Ave. and Union St., and then walk 1 block south and 1 block east.

Polker's Gourmet Burgers AMERICAN/BREAKFAST/HAMBURGERS

Despite the carnivorous name, Polker's is probably best known as a terrific place for brunch, featuring an array of delicious omelets, French toast, and the best buttermilk pancakes you may ever taste. Of course, several burger options, including turkey and garden burgers in addition to juicy red meat, also grace the menu, as do entree-sized salads. The booth seats are perfect for families of four, and the round tables by the window can seat up to six. Don't come if you're in a rush—service can be a slow. On weekends, arrive early and write your name on the list by the door.

2226 Polk St. (between Vallejo and Broadway sts.). ℂ 415/885-1000. Highchairs. Main courses $6–$13. MC, V. Daily 8am–11pm. Muni: No. 19-Polk to Broadway.

Swensen's Creamery ICE CREAM

As is proudly advertised on its sign at the corner of Union and Hyde Streets, this is the original Swensen's creamery, established in 1948. You won't find the exotic flavors you get at Mitchell's Ice Cream, but they do offer three kinds of vanilla, which may be your little one's favorite flavor anyway. The location along the Powell-Hyde cable car route is pretty convenient, too. Stop here for a scoop, perhaps after you've lunched at nearby ZA Pizza (see below), and before walking 2 blocks to crooked Lombard Street.

1999 Hyde St. (at Union St.). ℂ 415/775-6818. Cones $2.45–$3.95. No credit cards. Sun, Tues–Thurs noon–10pm; Fri–Sat noon–11pm. Muni: Powell-Hyde cable car to Union St.

ZA Pizza 🖈 *Finds* PIZZA

On a tree-lined section of Hyde Street along the cable car route, this is a favorite neighborhood gathering spot. Families can hang out at the counter of this tiny establishment and watch a game on TV or take a seat at one of the few indoor and outdoor tables. The thin-crust pizzas, named after luminary characters, include the Pesto Picasso, with roasted chicken, sun-dried tomatoes, and fresh pesto; and the Popeye the Greek, with spinach and feta cheese. Two salads are also on the menu, but the house salad wins out over the plain-tasting Caesar.

1919 Hyde St. (between Green and Union sts.). ℂ 415/771-3100. Highchairs. Slices $3.50–$4.50. AE, DISC, MC, V. Sun–Wed Noon–10pm; Thurs–Sat Noon–11pm. Muni: Powell-Hyde cable car to Green St.

13 The Haight

MODERATE

Indian Oven 🖈 INDIAN

This is the best Indian food we've found in the city. It took us a while, and a few meals where our girls ate little more than baked naan, puffy poori bread, and rice, to find some non-starch items on the menu that wouldn't be too spicy for them. The secret is to order creamy dishes like chicken kor*ma*, cooked in a mild yogurt sauce, and simply explaining to the waiter that you want no spice in it whatsoever at all. It usually works, and despite the absence of chili peppers, the dish is still so delicious that even we adults enjoy it. Other delectable dishes for grown-ups include the *saag gosht,* lamb with creamed spinach, and the wonderful meats baked in the tandoori oven. As it's located in the Haight, Indian Oven is a low-key spot, but it's refined enough to include white tablecloths and very attentive staff who will kindly help newcomers to Indian cooking navigate the menu. Located on a corner, Indian Oven has two full walls of windows, making it a light-filled, welcoming space. We like to show up early, before it starts to fill up, and we've always seen another family or two introducing their own kids to this varied and wonderful cuisine.

233 Fillmore Haight St. (at Waller St., ½ block south of Haight St.). ℂ **415/626-1628.** http://indianovensf.com. Highchairs. Reservations not accepted. Main courses $8–$16. AE, DC, DISC, MC, V. Daily 5–11pm. Muni: No. 6-Parnassus, no. 7-Haight, or no. 71-Haight-Noriega bus to Fillmore St.

INEXPENSIVE

Ben & Jerry's ICE CREAM   I can't think of a more appropriate place to indulge in this politically correct frozen delight. Ben & Jerry's is all about social responsibility, which is clear enough from the unbleached recycled paper napkins and the pictures of hormone-free cows grazing happily in Vermont. But it's also about a counter-culture that once had its epicenter right in the neighborhood. How great is it to enjoy a scoop of Cherry Garcia just around the corner from where Jerry Garcia and the Grateful Dead lived during the '67 Summer of Love? And, with all those pure, natural ingredients, it's delicious as well.

1480 Haight St. (between Masonic Ave. and Ashbury St.). ℂ **415/626-4143.** www.benjerry.com. Cones from $3.25. AE, DISC, MC, V. Sun–Thurs 11am–9pm; Fri–Sat 11am–10pm. Muni: No. 6-Parnassus, no. 7-Haight, or no. 71-Haight-Noriega bus to Ashbury St.

Blue Front Cafe AMERICAN/BREAKFAST/MEDITERRANEAN   The Blue Front's menu is as eclectic as the upbringing of its friendly owners, three Greek Orthodox Christian brothers who were raised in the Old City of Jerusalem. The specialties are Middle Eastern/Mediterranean—spit-roasted lamb gyros in pita bread and falafel wraps are among the choices—but you'll find all-American turkey, club, and Reuben sandwiches on the menu as well. The Blue Front is also a good breakfast spot, serving up three-egg omelets, toasted bagels, and breakfast wraps in Mediterranean *lavash* bread. The room is nothing fancy—wooden tables are close together with plenty of people reading their papers and nursing their coffees—but the huge Genie hanging out front blends in well with the colorful neighborhood.

1430 Haight St. (between Masonic Ave. and Ashbury St.). ℂ **415/252-5917.** www.bluefrontcafe.com. Highchairs. Reservations not accepted. Main courses $5.25–$9.75. MC, V. Sun–Thurs 7:30am–10pm; Fri–Sat 7:30am–11pm. Muni: No. 6-Parnassus, no. 7-Haight, or no. 71-Haight-Noriega bus to Masonic Ave.

Burger Joint ☀ HAMBURGERS   In a setting reminiscent of a '50s-era TV sitcom, with vinyl-covered chairs and vintage Formica patterns on the tables, you can enjoy a really good burger. They're made with naturally raised, hormone-free Niman Ranch beef and served on a bun that has enough personality to handle a juicy hand-formed patty. The only alternatives to a hamburger or cheeseburger are a hot dog, free-range chicken breast sandwich, or veggie burger, all served with crispy fries. Yummy milkshakes and root beer floats are made with San Francisco's Double Rainbow ice cream. Another location is in the Mission neighborhood.

700 Haight St. (at Pierce St.). ℂ **415/864-3833.** Mission: 807 Valencia St. (between 19th and 20th sts.). ℂ **415/ 824-3494.** www.burgerjointsf.com. Boosters, highchairs. Main courses $5.45–$7.95. MC, V. Daily 9am–11:30pm. Muni: No. 6-Parnassus, no. 7-Haight, or no. 71-Haight-Noriega bus to Pierce St.

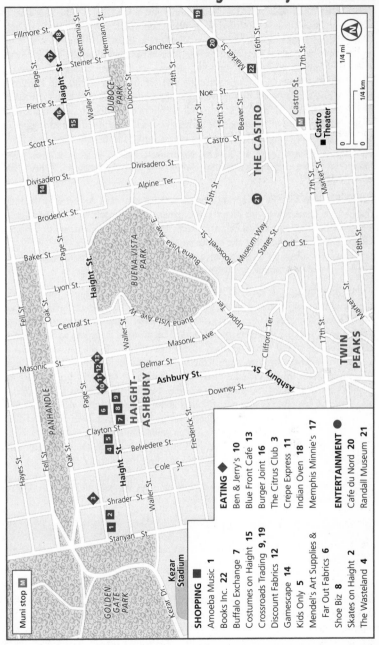

Haight-Ashbury & the Castro

Fillmore St.
Germania St.
Hermann St.
Steiner St.
Sanchez St.
19
20
Market St.
16th St.
17th St.

Page St.
Haight St.
Waller St.
DUBOCE PARK
Duboce St.
22
Henry St.
15th St.
Beaver St.
14th St.
Noe St.
Castro St.
Castro Theater

Pierce St.
16
15
Scott St.

Divisadero St.
14
Divisadero St.
Alpine Ter.
Castro St.
THE CASTRO

Broderick St.
Page St.
Haight St.
BUENA-VISTA PARK
15th St.
21
Museum Way
States St.
Ord St.
18th St.
17th St.
Market St.

Baker St.
Lyon St.
Buena Vista Ave. E.
Roosevelt St.
Buena Vista Ter.

Fell St.
Oak St.
Central St.
Waller St.
Masonic Ave.
Upper Ter.
Clifford Ter.
17th St.
TWIN PEAKS
Market St.

Masonic St.
Delmar St.
Ashbury St.
Downey St.
Ashbury St.

Page St.
10 11 12 13
6 9
8
7 5
4
Clayton St.
HAIGHT-ASHBURY
Belvedere St.
Frederick St.

Cole St.

Hayes St.
Fell St.
Oak St.
PANHANDLE
Haight St.
Shrader St.
Waller St.
Cole St.
3
1 2
Stanyan St.

GOLDEN GATE PARK
Kezar Dr.
Kezar Stadium

SHOPPING ■
Amoeba Music **1**
Books Inc. **22**
Buffalo Exchange **7**
Costumes on Haight **15**
Crossroads Trading **9, 19**
Discount Fabrics **12**
Gamescape **14**
Kids Only **5**
Mendel's Art Supplies &
Far Out Fabrics **6**
Shoe Biz **8**
Skates on Haight **2**
The Wasteland **4**

EATING ◆
Ben & Jerry's **10**
Blue Front Cafe **13**
Burger Joint **16**
The Citrus Club **3**
Crepe Express **11**
Indian Oven **18**
Memphis Minnie's **17**

ENTERTAINMENT ●
Cafe du Nord **20**
Randall Museum **21**

Muni stop Ⓜ

The Citrus Club *Value* ASIAN   You'll find tasty, nourishing noodle dishes in this extremely casual eatery furnished with plain laminated tables, a tile floor, and a counter lit by lamps cleverly covered in Vietnamese straw hats. Huge bowls of soup and Asian noodle salads are almost too big for one regular-size person and overwhelm those with smaller appetites, so consider sharing. Lunch here before a Golden Gate Park visit makes sense, as the restaurant isn't far from the Children's Playground entrance on Stanyan Street. In the evening, neighborhood folk queue up to order such delicacies as *pho-ga,* a Vietnamese soup full of thin rice noodles, chicken, cilantro, and chopped vegetables, or vegetarian offerings like buckwheat noodles and veggies in a spicy coconut-lime sauce. The surroundings are funky and suit the block just fine.

1790 Haight St. (at Shrader St.). © 415/387-6366. Boosters. Main courses $5–$8. MC, V. Mon–Thurs 11:30am–10pm; Fri–Sat 11:30am–11pm; Sun 11:30am–10pm. Muni: No. 6-Parnassus, no. 7-Haight, or no. 71-Haight-Noreiga bus to Shrader St.

Crepe Express CREPES   For an afternoon snack, you can't do better by the kidlets than a thin crepe filled with Nutella and bananas and topped with whipped cream. That's living. This very casual cafe also serves savory crepes, baguette sandwiches, and salads. The food is good, but the crepes are the reason to stop here.

1476 Haight St. (at Ashbury St.). © 415/865-0264. Main courses $3–$5. MC, V. Sun–Thurs 9:30am–8pm; Fri–Sat 9:30am–9pm. Muni: No. 6-Parnassus, no. 7-Haight, or no. 71-Haight-Noreiga bus to Ashbury St.

Memphis Minnie's *★* BARBECUE   If you've got a hankering for a tender piece of slow-cooked meat, head straight to Memphis Minnie's. The owner smokes his brisket for 12 hours and adds his own spice rub for kick and flavor. Other options are finger-licking-good ribs and succulent pulled pork. The protocol is simple: stand in line and choose your meat and two sides, such as sweet potato or corn muffin, and have a seat at one of the tables lined up against the bright yellow and red wall. Look around at the playful decor, which includes plastic pigs, black-and-white cow-print ceiling fans, pinned up trucker hats, and pithy sayings like "Never Trust a Skinny Cook." You can also read the favorable newspaper clippings about Minnie's under glass at each table. Once your meal is ready, choose from one of the three sauces at your table: red Texan, North Carolina vinegar, and South Carolina yellow mustard. Fortunately, each table has a full roll of paper towels on it as well. All the meat is delicious, and most of the sides, with the exception of the overly dry corn muffins, are tasty too.

576 Haight St. (at Steiner St.). © 415/864-7675. www.memphisminnies.com. Highchairs, boosters. Main courses $8–$15. AE, MC, V. Tues–Fri 11am–10pm; Sat 9am–10pm; Sun 9am–9pm. Muni: No. 6-Parnassus, no. 7-Haight, or no. 71-Haight-Noreiga bus to Steiner St.

14 The Mission District

If you're headed to or from any of these restaurants at night and you're not driving, I'd recommend taking a cab.

EXPENSIVE

Delfina *★★★* ITALIAN   This renowned Tuscan-Italian restaurant defines what's incredible about the city's neighborhood eats. Every day chef/co-owner Craig Stoll, who was one of *Food & Wine*'s Best New Chefs in 2001, whips up a new menu of delectable, ultra-fresh fare. Diners trek in from all over the city for it, even though there's absolutely nowhere to park. (Take a cab.) The Niman Ranch flat-iron steak with French fries is a standard, but a more seasonal option might be winter gnocchi

The Mission District

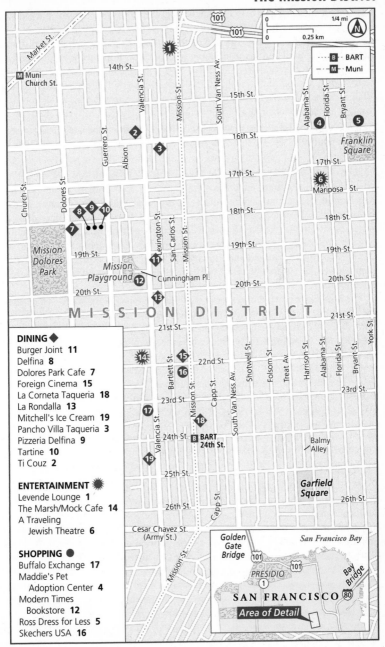

DINING ◆
Burger Joint **11**
Delfina **8**
Dolores Park Cafe **7**
Foreign Cinema **15**
La Corneta Taqueria **18**
La Rondalla **13**
Mitchell's Ice Cream **19**
Pancho Villa Taqueria **3**
Pizzeria Delfina **9**
Tartine **10**
Ti Couz **2**

ENTERTAINMENT ☀
Levende Lounge **1**
The Marsh/Mock Cafe **14**
A Traveling
    Jewish Theatre **6**

SHOPPING ●
Buffalo Exchange **17**
Maddie's Pet
    Adoption Center **4**
Modern Times
    Bookstore **12**
Ross Dress for Less **5**
Skechers USA **16**

with squash and chestnuts or lamb with polenta and sweet peas. Don't fail to order the buttermilk *panna cotta* for dessert. The yellow walls, close-together tables, and hip young clientele give this place an adult energy—but the staff is friendly and relaxed. Moreover, chef Stoll and his wife Annie, who works in front, are parents themselves and sure to be accommodating. But if you're in any way concerned that the place may be too much for your kids, just head next door to Pizzeria Delfina (see below). *Note*: While I've listed Delfina in the expensive category, the reasonable prices almost justify listing it in the moderate category, especially if the kids order the well-priced pastas.

3621 18th St. (between Dolores and Guerrero sts.). ℂ **415/552-4055**. www.delfinasf.com. Reservations recommended. Main courses $17–$21. MC, V. Sun–Thurs 5:30–10pm; Fri–Sat 5:30–11pm. Muni: J-Church streetcar to 18th, and then walk 2 blocks east.

Foreign Cinema ★★ *Finds* CALIFORNIA/MEDITERRANEAN   What sets this establishment apart from any other place in the city is its outdoor courtyard with a large exposed-cement wall onto which are projected foreign films, many of them Oscar winners. Heat lamps keep the place cozy, and, well, it's just an incredibly fun way to have a meal. The overall tone of the place is quite grown-up, with an adjoining, very hip bar next door. Fortunately, the chefs have a young boy of their own, who can be seen running around the courtyard in the early part of the evening. They've even added a kids' menu, so arrive early and bring the children. Or try the weekend brunch, which is the family-friendliest meal here.

The best part of the whole experience is that the food is very good—even though this place is so cool it doesn't need to be. Chefs/parents Gayle Pirie and John Clark are both veterans of two of the best kitchens in the Bay Area, Zuni Cafe and Berkeley's Chez Panisse. In addition to 20 different choices from the oyster bar, their seasonally changing menu may include such appetizers ("premieres") as beef carpaccio with fried herbs, Manchego cheese, and horseradish sauce. Main courses ("features") could include seared sea scallops with heirloom tomatoes, bacon aioli, and basil sauce. Their naturally raised beef hails from Montana and most of the produce is local and organic.

2534 Mission St. (between 21st and 22nd sts.). ℂ **415/648-7600**. www.foreigncinema.com. Kids' menu, high chairs, boosters. Reservations recommended. Main courses $22–$30; brunch $8.50–$18; kids' menu $7. AE, MC, V. Mon–Thurs 6–10pm; Fri–Sat 6–11pm; Sun 5–10pm (9pm during winter); Sat brunch 11am–6pm; Sun brunch 11am–5pm. Muni: BART to 24th St., and then walk 2 blocks north.

MODERATE

Pizzeria Delfina ★★ *Finds* PIZZA   You're in luck. The fact is you really want some excellent Italian food and you may even remember hearing about an amazing Tuscan restaurant in the Mission district called Delfina (see above). The trouble is your kids are tired (or loud), and you're afraid they just won't mix with a crowd of hip diners sipping wine and talking politics over dishes like local quail with polenta. Well, now you can have your cake and eat it too. Actually, make that pizza. Delfina's owners Craig and Anne Stoll have now opened an irresistible pizzeria next door to their original, and ever-popular, restaurant. At Pizzeria Delfina, your kids may not appreciate just how fresh the tomatoes and creamy the mozzarella are on their ultra-thin crust margherita pizza, but if it's a cheese pizza, they're also not likely to complain. You, meanwhile, are sure to savor the "Brocolli Raab," with rich ricotta and tangy oven-dried tomatoes, or the "Salsiccia" with homemade fennel sausage. The salads and antipasti are also impressive and, for dessert, the Bellwether ricotta cannoli is dreamy. The other great thing about Pizzeria Delfina is that, unlike at its fancy predecessor, you don't have to call weeks ahead to get a reservation . . . but you do need to show up early. Arrive before 7pm or you'll be waiting at least an hour.

3611 18th St. (between Dolores and Guerrero sts.). © 415/437-6800. www.pizzeriadelfina.com. Reservations not accepted. Pizzas $10–$16. MC, V. Mon 5:30–10pm; Tues–Thurs 11:30am–10pm; Fri 11:30am–11pm; Sat noon–11pm; Sun noon–10pm. Muni: J-Church streetcar to 18th, and then walk 2 blocks east.

INEXPENSIVE

In addition to the options below, you can find a Burger Joint in this neighborhood (p. 156).

Dolores Park Cafe *Finds* AMERICAN/BREAKFAST   The setting alone, across the street from Dolores Park with a spacious front deck, would probably be enough to guarantee this cafe's popularity. But it also happens to serve a terrific cafe latte, and plenty of other tasty items, like albacore tuna melts on whole grain bread and Niman Ranch honey glazed ham sandwiches. Breakfast items, soups, and salads are all worth stopping by for as well. Enjoy your meal in the sunshine, alongside other diners rocking strollers or perusing the newspaper. An all-ages music show Friday nights from 7:30 to 9:30pm is a big hit with kids, but it's also packed, so make sure to eat your dinner before the crowds stream in.

501 Dolores St. (at 18th St.). © 415/621-2936. www.doloresparkcafe.org. Highchairs. Reservations not accepted. Sandwiches/salads $5–$7.50. No credit cards. Daily 7am–8pm. Fri music nights until 9:30pm. Muni: J-Church streetcar to 18th, and then walk 1 block east.

La Corneta Taqueria MEXICAN   Taquerias abound in the Mission, so it may be useful to clarify what they actually sell, especially if you are not from the Southwest. They do not sell the crunchy, uniformly shaped "tacos" that break into a million pieces when you bite them, such as you find at the fast food chains Del Taco or Taco Bell. Mission taquerias sell flavorful tacos on soft corn or flour tortillas, in addition to tostadas, enchiladas, and even plated dinners. But the biggest reason most San Franciscans come to a taqueria is for the burritos. And at La Corneta, in addition to a more colorful, spacious, and clean-feeling dining room than you find at many neighborhood taquerias, you'll get a darn good burrito. Stand in line to choose beans (black, pinto, refried), a filling (beef, beef tongue, chicken, pork, shrimp, vegetarian), and your salsa preference (mild or hot). Make sure to ask for guacamole and sour cream as well. After that, you won't need to eat until tomorrow.

2731 Mission St. (between 23rd and 24th sts.). © 415/643-7001. www.lacorneta.com. Highchairs. Main courses $1.25–$13. MC, V. Daily 10am–10pm. BART to 24th and Mission.

La Rondalla MEXICAN   A Mexican friend of mine, who left Mexico for the woodsy hills of Marin County 2 decades ago, can't resist crossing the Golden Gate Bridge every few weeks to bring her kids here for a fiesta-like evening. The place is strung up in colorful Christmas lights all year-round, and mariachi music is sure to accompany every meal. Huge burritos, enchiladas, and tacos are served with the traditional rice and beans, and more interesting Mexican dishes like *carne asada* and chicken with mole sauce are also on the menu. The festive atmosphere is fueled by tasty, and potent, margaritas.

901–903 Valencia St. (at 20th St.). © 415/647-7474. Highchairs. Main courses $5–$15. No credit cards. Tues–Thurs 6–11:15pm; Fri–Sat 5pm–1:15am; Sun 2–9pm. Muni: BART to 24th St., and then walk west to Valencia St. and 3 blocks north.

Mitchell's Ice Cream ✿ *Finds* ICE CREAM   Getting to Mitchell's is going to require commitment on the part of anyone without a car because it's located in the outer Mission a few blocks from the nearest streetcar line. For true ice cream lovers, however, it's a schlep worth your time. Beyond the ice cream's incredible creaminess, Mitchell's is best loved for its lengthy menu featuring seasonal fresh fruit and such unusual ice cream flavors as *maíz/queso* (corn/cheese) and lychee fruit. I love the avocado, but *buko* (baby coconut) is hands-down the most popular flavor, with the cinnamony Mexican chocolate coming in second. Even plain old vanilla is delicious. Be sure to elbow your way inside this small store if you arrive after dinner or in the afternoon and take a number from the dispenser by the door. If you just can't make it out this way, a more limited selection of Mitchell's flavors can be found at the **Santa Barbara Ice Creamery** on 2240 Chestnut St. in the Marina (© **415/922-6417**) and at **Norman's Ice Cream & Freezes** (p. 147).

688 San Jose Ave. (at 29th St.). © 415/648-2300. www.mitchellsicecream.com. 1 scoop $2.10, 2 scoops $4.10. No credit cards. Daily 11am–11pm. Muni: J-Church streetcar to 28th St., and then walk east to Guerrero and turn right; Guerrero St. will become San Jose Ave.

Pancho Villa Taqueria ✿ MEXICAN   This is an old standby and one of the best *taquerias* in the city. The ever-present line testifies to the quality and consistency of the burritos, tacos, quesadillas, and enormous combination plates of prawns, *carne asada,* and chicken. The dining room isn't much to look at—utilitarian comes to mind—but who cares? With a choice of meats, beans, tortillas, salsas, and extras like sour cream or avocado, your eyes will be on your plate. Portions are substantial, and a late lunch will easily serve for dinner. Baby burritos are available for smaller appetites.

3071 16th St. (between Mission and Valencia sts.). © 415/864-8840. www.panchovillasf.com. Highchairs. Main courses $1.35–$10. AE, MC, V. Daily 10am–midnight. Muni: BART to 16th and Mission sts., and then walk 1 block west.

Tartine ✿ *Finds* BAKERY   Crowds from far and near are drawn by the smell of freshly baked bread at Tartine, considered by many to be the best bakery in San Francisco. You could be forgiven for forgoing dinner and simply dining on a loaf of oven-fresh walnut bread, which comes out of the oven after 4pm and sells out quickly. If the walnut bread is gone, all is not lost: Tartine also has some wonderful toasted sandwiches and plenty of other mouth-watering baked goods to choose from.

600 Guerrero St. (at 18th St.). © 415/487-2600. www.tartinebakery.com. No reservations. Sandwiches $7.50–$8.50. AE, MC, V. Mon 8am–7pm; Tues–Wed 7:30am–7pm; Thurs–Fri 7:30am–8pm; Sat 8am–8pm; Sun 9am–8pm. Muni: BART to 16th St., and then walk west to Guerrero Street and 2 blocks south.

Ti Couz ✿ *Finds* CREPES   This stylish stand-out started as a tiny creperie featuring Norman buckwheat crepes, which come served in folded squares. Combinations of fillings are suggested, but diners are also free to choose from such options as sausage, smoked salmon, mushrooms, or goat cheese. For dessert, fillings include fruit, chocolate, and ice cream. The soups and salads are also top-notch. The place got so popular that it soon expanded to include the neighboring storefront. On sunny days, put your name down and wait for an outside table.

3108 16th St. (between Guerrero and Valencia sts.). © 415/252-7373. Highchairs. Reservations not accepted. Crepes $2–$8. MC, V. Mon 11am–11pm; Tues–Thurs 5–11pm; Fri 11am–11pm; Sat–Sun 10am–11pm. Muni: BART to 16th and Mission sts., and then walk 1½ blocks west.

15 The Castro/Noe Valley

MODERATE

Firefly ★★ *Finds* AMERICAN   If you find yourself in this neck of the woods, I highly recommend this charming neighborhood alcove. Located at the residential end of 24th Street, Firefly is a bright and welcoming oasis of calm after a busy day of sightseeing. It's one of those places you sense is going to be good as soon as you walk in the door. The decor is subtle and welcoming; the space cozy but not crowded. The menu confirms that you will eat well here. It combines classic comfort foods—think fried chicken with mashed potatoes, Niman Ranch ribeye steak, and vegetarian lasagna—with more novel concoctions like grilled wild king salmon with lobster-mushroom sauce or roasted vegetable *tagine* (a Moroccon style of cooking). Make sure to start with a sharing plate of their signature shrimp and scallop potstickers, and end with the flourless chocolate cake if you have room. Everything is delicious. The dining room is teeny-tiny, so come early if you're toting young kids. A prix-fixe option Sunday to Thursday includes appetizer, main course, dessert, and coffee.

4288 24th St. (at Douglass St.). © **415/821-7652**. www.fireflyrestaurant.com. Highchairs. Reservations recommended. Main courses $17–$22; prix fixe $34. AE, MC, V. Daily 5:30–10pm. Muni: J-Church streetcar to 24th St. and transfer to the no. 48 bus west to Douglass St.

Lovejoy's Tea Room AFTERNOON TEA   Crowded with settees, chairs, lace-covered tables, and breakfronts holding teapots and china cups, Lovejoy's has successfully brought a bit of old England across the pond. Tea here is much less formal than hotel teas, and cheaper, so plenty of moms and children celebrate quality time over a cuppa without waiting for a special occasion. Crustless tea sandwiches come with cream cheese and apple, roast beef with horseradish, Stilton cheese with pear, and other very British combinations. Raisin scones are served with clotted cream and jam, and there's always a selection of sweets. The tea selection is bountiful, but children have the option of drinking cocoa, and jelly sandwiches are served with the Wee Tea. If you like the chair you're sitting on or the teacup from which you're sipping, go ahead and buy it. Lovejoy's doubles as an antiques store, and everything is for sale.

1351 Church St. (at Clipper St.). © **415/648-5895**. www.lovejoystearoom.com. Reservations recommended. Light tea $14; high tea $17; Queen's Tea $22; Wee Tea $13. MC, V. Wed–Sun 11am–6pm (kitchen closes at 5:30pm). Muni: J-Church streetcar to 26th St. to Clipper St.

INEXPENSIVE

In addition to the option below, you can find a Pasta Pomodoro in this neighborhood (p. 151).

Chow ★ AMERICAN   The raw ingredients in the kitchen include organic and local produce and naturally-raised meats. The end product on your table is flavorful, appealing comfort food. From chicken potpie to spaghetti and meatballs, the food here resembles something grandma might cook up . . . if she lived on an organic farm and had a high-tech kitchen. If you're in the mood for something a bit more exciting, wood-fired pizzas, delicious grilled meats, and a more inventive ethnic-inspired entrée or two are also on offer. With wooden floors and wainscoting, dark green walls, and close-together tables, the overall ambience is as comfortable as the food. With desserts like ginger cake with pumpkin ice cream and caramel sauce, and comfortable prices to boot, it's easy to see how this place stays so popular.

215 Church St. (at Market St.). ✆ 415/552-2469. Highchairs, boosters. Main courses $6–$11. DISC, MC, V. Sun–Thurs 11am–11pm; Fri–Sat 11am–midnight. Muni: F-Market or J-Church streetcar to Church St. Station, and then walk ½ block south on Church St.

16 The Richmond/Sunset

EXPENSIVE

Cliff House Bistro AMERICAN   This restaurant has a lot going for it, and our expectations were high. The building sits on a bluff overlooking the Pacific Ocean, with views to the north, west, and south. Moreover, it boasts a rich history. Three U.S. presidents visited the first 1863 Cliff House before it was destroyed by fire. In 1886 local millionaire Adolph Sutro built the second Cliff House, but 11 years later it, too, burned down. In 1909 Sutro's daughter built the third Cliff House, which was eventually acquired by the National Park Service.

In late 2004, the Cliff House reopened following a $19 million renovation. A stylish modern wing features an expensive new restaurant, Sutro's. I opted to take my family to the more casual Cliff House Bistro. The breathtaking view does not disappoint. The decor, with old-fashioned tile flooring and over 200 photographs of bygone movie stars, is charming. Unfortunately, the menu was a letdown. Perhaps people are expected to pay for the vistas, because in my book $26 is a lot for a crab Louie, especially when it's too salty. But in fact the view is so priceless, it may well be worth it. Just be sure to come during daylight hours and stick to simple dishes like fish and chips, which are pretty good but at $18 also pretty pricey. A smarter option may be to order a scramble, French toast, or even a salad off the breakfast menu, which is less expensive and available daily until 3:15pm.

1090 Point Lobos Ave. (Geary Blvd. turns into Point Lobos Ave. west of 48th Ave.). ✆ 415/386-3330. www. cliffhouse.com. Highchairs. Reservations not accepted. Main courses $7–$17 breakfast; $13–$26 lunch; $13–$27 dinner. AE, DC, DISC, MC, V. Daily 9am–9:30pm. Muni: No. 38-Geary bus to 48th Ave., and then walk 1 block or transfer to no. 18–46th Ave. bus.

MODERATE

Aziza 🍴🍴 MOROCCAN   Attention to detail is the watchword at this North African oasis nestled in the city's most multicultural neighborhood. The arched ceilings, Moroccan lamps, hand-painted Arabesque plateware, and traditional Moroccan dishes will transport you to a distant continent. The food is lovingly prepared using local, organic ingredients. The *bastilla,* saffron-braised chicken and almonds baked in phyllo dough and dusted with powdered sugar and cinnamon, is out of this world. It takes 25 minutes to prepare, though, which may be too much of a wait for tired, hungry kids. Everyone will be pleased with the classic "couscous Aziza": vegetables, grilled chicken, prawns, and spicy lamb sausage on a bed of steamed couscous. Grown-ups may opt for the Moroccan spiced prawn *tagine,* and kids will enjoy the chicken brochettes—made with naturally raised poultry, of course. The lighting is muted and the mood gets more adult as the evening wears on, so plan on arriving early if you have younger kids. That said, families dining on Friday, Saturday, or Sunday nights always stay past 7pm, when the belly dancer arrives.

5800 Geary Blvd. (at 22nd Ave.). ✆ 415/752-2222. www.aziza-sf.com. Reservations recommended. Main courses $16–$24. MC, V. Wed–Mon 5:30–10:30pm. Muni: No. 38-Geary bus to 22nd Ave.

Park Chalet 🍴 AMERICAN   Opened in April 2004, the Park Chalet has the best outdoor dining area in the city. Located on the ground floor behind the Golden Gate

Park Visitor's Center, it opens onto a lovely garden framed by the park's tall trees. With a glass ceiling, retractable glass walls, a stone fireplace, and upscale furnishings, it feels like a European countryside restaurant. The menu is essentially American, though, featuring classic salads, sandwiches, and meat dishes like barbeque pork ribs or shepherd's pie. The most inventive options are the individual pizzas, such as one with wild mushrooms, roasted garlic, goat cheese, truffle oil, and thyme. On weekends, you may even find a "brunch pizza," topped with artichoke, pancetta, mushrooms, and poached egg. If the Dungeness crab benedict is on offer, you're in luck. Kids get their own menus and crayons. Once your little ones have polished off their cheese pizzas or corndogs, let them run around on the well-tended lawn while you finish your meals in peace. There'll be lots of other kids out there as well.

1000 Great Hwy. (between Fulton St. and Lincoln Way). ✆ **415/386-8439.** www.beachchalet.com. Kids' menu, highchairs, boosters. Reservations recommended on weekends. Main courses $10–$17 lunch, $10–$24 dinner; kids' menu $5.25. AE, MC, V. Mon–Thurs noon–9pm; Fri noon–11pm; Sat 11am–11pm; Sun 11am–9pm. Muni: No. 5-Fulton, no. 31-Balboa, or no. 38-Geary buses, or N-Judah streetcar and transfer to no. 18–46th Ave. bus.

Pizzetta 211 ★ *Finds* PIZZA When you arrive at this miniscule storefront on an otherwise residential street far from downtown you'll feel like you've come upon a hidden gem. You have. The cozy pizzeria, with but a handful of indoor and outdoor tables, serves up thin-crust, wood-oven-fired *pizzette* from a weekly-changing menu. Whenever possible, organic produce, dairy, and grains are used to make delectable, crispy pizzas with inspired toppings like oven-dried San Marzano tomatoes, prosciutto, and local goat cheese, or roasted cauliflower, garlic, and bread crumbs. Salads and Italian desserts are also available. This is gourmet stuff, and the staff takes itself seriously, so at dinnertime remind the kids that normal pizzeria behavior does not apply—especially if you're seated indoors. A better option is to come for lunch after a morning hike at Land's End and sit outside.

211 23rd Ave. (at California St.). ✆ **415/379-9880.** Reservations not accepted. Individual pizzas $9–$14. No credit cards. Mon 5–9pm; Wed–Fri lunch noon–2:30pm, dinner 5–9pm; Sat–Sun noon–9pm. Muni: No. 1-California bus to 23rd Ave.

INEXPENSIVE

In addition to the options below, both Mel's Drive-in (p. 151) and Pasta Pomodoro (p. 151) have locations in this neighborhood.

The Canvas Cafe/Gallery BREAKFAST/ECLECTIC This loft-like space across the street from Golden Gate Park triples as an art gallery, lounge, and cafe. For local families, the operative word is cafe. Get there during daylight hours, and it's an optimal place to grab a bite before heading off to the Strybing Arboretum, the Japanese Tea Garden, or other park attractions within close walking distance. After munching on oatmeal or toasted bagels for breakfast, kids can run around the large area as you sip your coffee. For lunch, choose from an assortment of salads, several cold or grilled sandwiches, focaccia pizzas, and even a few pasta entrees like macaroni and cheese and meat or veggie lasagna. While you await your meal, look around at the paintings and sculptures for sale. Another bonus: This is one of the few San Francisco cafes with its own parking lot.

1200 9th Ave. (at Lincoln Way). ✆ **415/504-0060.** www.thecanvasgallery.com. Highchairs, boosters. Reservations not accepted. Main courses $7–$11. AE, MC, V. Mon–Thurs 10am–10pm; Fri 10am–7:30pm; Sat 9am–7:30pm; Sun 9am–10pm. Live music Thurs–Sun evenings. Muni: N-Judah streetcar to 9th Ave., and then walk 2 blocks north towards the park or no. 71 Haight-Noriega stops across the street at 9th & Lincoln.

de Young Cafe 🎈 *Finds* CALIFORNIA This is our new favorite lunch spot when visiting Golden Gate Park. Beyond inventively prepared soups, salads, and sandwiches—such as a Thai Beef sandwich with ginger roast beef, lemongrass, and sweet soy sauce—you can also enjoy tasty grilled options like fish tacos with cilantro-lime slaw and hot items such as pasta puttanesca or Dungeness crab cakes. The food is made with seasonal, local ingredients, most of which is produced, raised, or farmed within 150 miles of the cafe. The kids might enjoy the PB&J, pointedly made with organic peanut butter, or the Niman Ranch hot dogs. Although the offerings are appetizing, the cafe's best asset is its location within the de Young Museum, where it's open to all visitors. On sunny days, you can sit outside by the sculpture garden. A sesame chicken salad is always nice, but a sesame chicken salad next to a Henry Moore sculpture is terrific.

1200 9th Ave. (at Lincoln Way). ℂ 415/750-2614. www.thinker.org/deyoung/visiting. Highchairs. Salads/sandwiches $5.50–$14. AE, DC, DISC, MC, V. Tues–Sun 9:30am–4pm; Fri 9:30am–8:45pm. Muni: N-Judah streetcar to 9th Ave., and then walk north on 9th into the park or no. 44-O'Shaughnessy bus to Concourse Dr.

Giorgio's Pizzeria 🎈 *Finds* PIZZA If you were to ask San Francisco parents to name the most family-friendly restaurant in town, most would probably say Giorgio's. This festive, boisterous pizzeria serves consistently good thin-crust pizza with traditional toppings like pepperoni or mushrooms and sausage, as well as a few pastas. Every Wednesday from 4 to 6pm is "Kids' Happy Hour": kids can order any mini pizza and make it themselves. Giorgio's also has deals for lunchtime children's parties, and there always seems to be one taking place.

151 Clement St. (at 3rd Ave.). ℂ 415/668-1266. www.giorgiospizza.com. Highchairs, boosters. Reservations not accepted. Minipizza $7–$12, large pizza $13–$22. MC, V. Sun–Thurs 11:30am–10pm; Fri–Sat 11:30am–11pm. Muni: No. 2-Clement, no. 3-Jackson, or no. 4-Sutter bus to 3rd Ave.; or no. 1-California bus to 3rd Ave., and then walk 1 block south to Clement St.

Marnee Thai 🎈 *Finds* THAI Fortunately for out-of-town visitors, it's now no longer necessary to trek to the outer Sunset to try the best Thai food in San Francisco. Marnee Thai's new location is just steps away from Golden Gate Park, so you can easily come in for an early dinner after spending the afternoon visiting the Strybing Arboretum or Japanese Tea Garden. The spicy Angel wings (deep-fried chicken wings topped with chili, garlic, and sweet basil) are hugely popular and not too spicy for most kids. All the soups, curries, and noodle dishes are also fabulous. Be adventurous, skip the pad Thai, and try one of the many other wonderful dishes. If you're lucky, the owner's wife will pop by when you're there. In addition to being very opinionated about what you should order, she'll gladly tell you your fortune, free of charge.

1243 9th Ave. (between Irving St. and Lincoln Way). ℂ 415/731-9999. www.marneethaisf.com. Highchairs, boosters. Reservations recommended on weekends. Main courses $8–$14. AE, MC, V. Daily 11:30am–10pm. Muni: N-Judah streetcar to 9th Ave., and then walk 2 blocks north towards the park.

Park Chow 🎈 AMERICAN Just like Chow, its sister restaurant in the Castro, Park Chow balances good ingredients, a lively atmosphere, and amazing value to deliver a truly happy meal. Please see the Chow review on p. 163.

1238 9th Ave. (between Irving St. and Lincoln Way). ℂ 415/665-9912. Highchairs, boosters. Reservations not accepted. Main courses $6–$15. MC, V. Mon–Thurs 11am–10pm; Fri 11am–11pm; Sat 10am–11pm; Sun 10am–10pm. Muni: N-Judah streetcar to 9th Ave., and then walk 2 blocks north towards the park.

Ton Kiang *⋆ (Finds* CHINESE/DIM SUM   Perhaps the most popular place for dim sum in San Francisco, Ton Kiang starts getting crowded about half an hour after the doors open on weekend mornings. So come during the week, arrive early, or, better yet, try to round up enough people—eight or more—to make a reservation. We're always calling up friends at the last minute to join us because dim sum at Ton Kiang is best enjoyed with lots of people at a large, round table. Servers come by with freshly made batches of shrimp dumplings, pork buns, crisp-steamed vegetables, and other tiny treats, which they place on a big lazy Susan in the middle of the table. Save room for dessert—the walnut cookies, custard pancakes, and mango pudding are all divine. Something about the communal dining experience makes my kids more adventurous than usual, and there really isn't an item our normally choosy eaters don't like. That may explain why the upstairs dining room, where you'll probably end up, is always packed with families. If you can think of any reason to head out this way—perhaps you're off to the Legion of Honor or plan to walk on Ocean Beach—do so. *Tip:* They don't have booster seats, so try stacking one chair on top of another.

5821 Geary Blvd (between 22nd and 23rd aves.). ℂ **415/387-8273.** www.tonkiang.net. Highchairs. Reservations only for parties of 8 or more. Dim sum $2.50–$5.50. AE, DC, DISC, MC, V. Mon–Thurs 10am–10pm; Fri 10am–10:30pm; Sat 9:30am–10:30pm; Sun 9am–10pm. Muni: No. 38-Geary bus to 22nd Ave.

Toy Boat Dessert Cafe *⋆* ICE CREAM   This corner cafe is a treat for the eyes and tummy. High shelves are filled with the owner's own collectibles—among them tin wind-up toys, Pez dispensers, and the Pillsbury Doughboy—and some for-sale reproductions. Bagels and sandwiches are available to enjoy at one of the few booths and tables, but it's the ice cream sundaes with all the trimmings that'll rock your boat.

401 Clement St. (at 5th Ave.). ℂ **415/751-7505.** www.toyboatcafe.com. Highchairs. Main courses from $4–$8. MC, V. Mon–Thurs 7:30am–11pm; Fri–Sat 8:30am–midnight; Sun 8:30am–11pm. Muni: No. 2-Clement or no. 38-Geary to 5th Ave., and then walk 1 block north to Clement St.

7

Exploring San Francisco with Your Kids

San Francisco attractions fall into three categories. First are those that are specifically designed for kids, such as the Exploratorium and the Bay Area Discovery Museum. Most of the ones I've listed in this chapter are of such high quality, or in such a scenic setting, that parents will take pleasure in them as well. Second are attractions not specifically geared to kids, but that children would surely enjoy. Quite a few fall into this category, including riding the cable cars or strolling through bustling, colorful Chinatown.

Third are those attractions that may fascinate parents, but that younger kids will probably find a yawn. Fortunately, there aren't too many of these. Only a few indoor attractions will require a level of restraint beyond some kids' abilities. Fortunately, on weekend days many local museums offer drop-off art activities for kids. In other instances, you may be able to strike a deal with the little ones, where an hour (or less) of their patience can be

immediately rewarded with a kid-friendly activity. The California Palace of the Legion of Honor has nearby hiking trails, and the San Francisco Museum of Modern Art is adjacent to Yerba Buena Gardens and its children's activities.

In fact, the biggest challenge you may face on your San Francisco vacation is prioritizing amongst all the options. My best advice is to slow down and not try to do everything, particularly if you're traveling with very young children. Where possible, work in times for the kids to rest or play. Plan the big stuff in the morning, when everyone has more energy, and save afternoons for more leisurely pursuits. Above all, be flexible. If energy levels have suddenly dropped off, be ready to head back to the hotel—or to the nearest playground. As with much in life, less may be more. Fortunately, San Francisco is so lovely that just parking your family by a grassy knoll and having a picnic could be a worthy activity in itself.

1 The Top Attractions

Alcatraz Island ✰✰✰ **Ages 10 and up.** Spanish for "pelican," Alcatraz was so named in 1775 by Juan Manuel Ayala for the birds that nested there. From the 1850s to 1933, the military used Alcatraz as a fort to protect the bay's shoreline. In 1934, the government converted it into a maximum-security prison to house the country's most hardened criminals, including Al Capone, "Machine Gun" Kelly, and Robert Stroud (the Birdman). Given the sheer cliffs, frigid waters, and treacherous currents, the Alcatraz prison was considered inescapable.

I first toured Alcatraz when I was 12, and never forgot it. Stories of escape attempts and the harsh conditions on the island fascinated me. Families today will be no less moved by the audio tour, which features narration by former guards and prisoners. One story details how over several weeks three prisoners patiently enlarged the air vents in their cells with spoons and crafted dummy heads that appeared to be sleeping so they could escape overnight undetected. You even get to see the dummy heads, a detail my young girls enjoyed. Another story details a gruesome shoot-'em-up escape attempt, which may be the part teenage boys most enjoy. The audio tour gives a wonderfully rich and eerie sense of what it was like to be isolated in the middle of the bay—with unforgiving winds blustering through the barred windows and armed guards pacing the gun galley—yet so achingly close to the beautiful city of San Francisco.

With such a captivating history, it's no wonder Alcatraz has been the subject of so many Hollywood movies, including *Birdman of Alcatraz, Escape from Alcatraz,* and *The Rock.* My bet is that most young kids will enjoy the trip, which after all starts out with a fun ferry ride across the bay, although particularly sensitive children could get spooked by some of the audio tour's eerier details.

> **Tips Planning Ahead**
>
> You must reserve Alcatraz tour tickets at least 2 weeks in advance in the summer. Call ℂ **415/705-5555** to purchase them over the phone, or buy them online at **www.blueandgold fleet.com**.

Wear jackets (it's quite brisk out on the bay) and comfortable shoes—you'll be doing lots of walking. The ferry sells snacks, but you may want to bring some munchies along because the whole trip could take up to 2½ hours. Also, reserve for Alcatraz well in advance. I recommend booking the earliest ferry possible—the island will be less crowded and your kids more energetic.

In addition to doing the audio tour of the cell block, those visiting during fall and winter can view an orientation video about the island itself and tour the grounds outside the prison on a walking path. (The trail is closed during bird-nesting season from mid-Feb. to early Sept.) Older kids who don't frighten easily might enjoy the spooky "Alcatraz After Hours" tour. The ferry departs at 6:15 and 7pm during the summer; at 4:20 and 5:10pm in winter. Tours are Thursday through Sunday only. (Fares for the evening tour are $24 for adults, $21 for seniors 62-plus and kids 12–18, $14 for kids 5–11.)

Pier 41, at Fisherman's Wharf, the Embarcadero. ℂ **415/773-1188** for information. www.nps.gov/alcatraz. To reserve tickets call 415/705-5555 or visit www.alcatrazcruises.com. Admission (includes ferry and audio tour): $19 adults, $18 seniors 62 and older, $11 children 5–11. Without audio tour: $12 adults, $9.75 seniors, $8.25 children 5–11. Daily in winter 9:30am–2:15pm; summer daily 9:30am–4:15pm. Ferries run approximately every half-hour. Arrive 30 minutes before ferry departure in summer; 45 minutes before in winter. Muni: F-Market streetcar; Powell-Mason cable car; or no. 30-Stockton bus, which stops 1 block south.

Angel Island ✸✸   **All ages.** Just north of Alcatraz, Angel Island, the Bay's largest island, is a tranquil place for nature-loving families. It was originally a Miwok Indian hunting and fishing ground, then Spanish, British, and Mexican ships used the island as a port at various times beginning in 1775. Before the Civil War, the U.S. government turned the island into a military base, remnants of which are still visible. Between 1910 and 1940, Angel Island was used as a detention center mainly for Asian immigrants, which earned it the nickname "Ellis Island of the West." The immigration station at China Cove is open for tours and provides a poignant glimpse into an era when anti-Asian and anti-immigration policies placed hundreds of Chinese into

Major San Francisco Sights

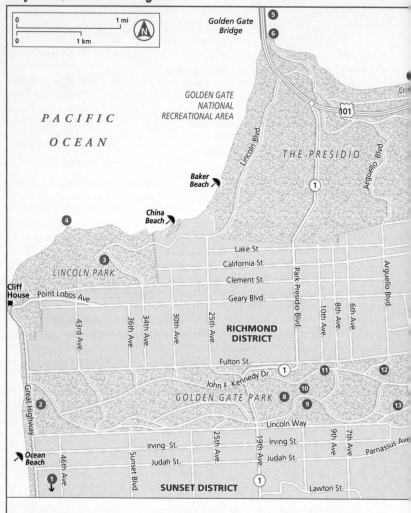

PACIFIC OCEAN

GOLDEN GATE NATIONAL RECREATIONAL AREA

Golden Gate Bridge

THE PRESIDIO

Baker Beach

China Beach

LINCOLN PARK

Cliff House

Point Lobos Ave.

Lake St.
California St.
Clement St.
Geary Blvd.

RICHMOND DISTRICT

43rd Ave.
36th Ave.
34th Ave.
30th Ave.
25th Ave.
Park Presidio Blvd.
10th Ave.
8th Ave.
6th Ave.
Arguello Blvd.

Lincoln Blvd.

Fulton St.

John F. Kennedy Dr.

GOLDEN GATE PARK

Great Highway

Lincoln Way

Irving St.
Judah St.
Lawton St.

SUNSET DISTRICT

Ocean Beach

46th Ave.
Sunset Blvd.
25th Ave.
19th Ave.
9th Ave.
7th Ave.
Parnassus Ave.

Cris

101

170

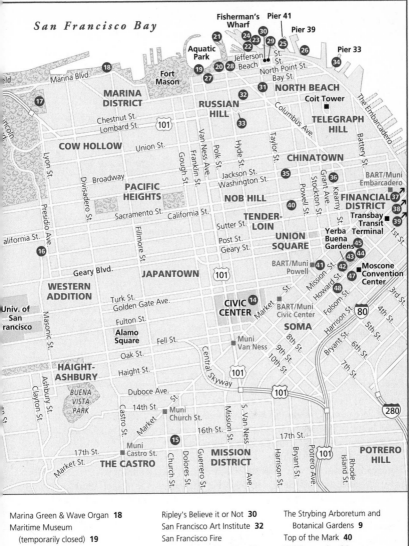

San Francisco Bay

Fisherman's Wharf **21** Pier 41

Aquatic Park

Fort Mason

Marina Blvd.

18

17

MARINA DISTRICT

Chestnut St.

Lombard St. **101**

COW HOLLOW Union St.

PACIFIC HEIGHTS

Broadway

Sacramento St. California St.

24 **30** **29** Pier 39 **23** **22** **25** **26** Pier 33 **34** **19** **20** **28** Jefferson St. Beach **27** North Point St. Bay St. **31** **NORTH BEACH**

RUSSIAN HILL **32**

33

Coit Tower

TELEGRAPH HILL

Columbus Ave.

CHINATOWN

Jackson St.
Washington St. **35** **36**

Grant Ave.
Stockton St.
Kearny St.
Powell St.

BART/Muni Embarcadero

FINANCIAL DISTRICT **37**

38

NOB HILL **40**

TENDER-LOIN

Sutter St.

Post St.

Geary St.

UNION SQUARE

Transbay Transit Terminal **39**

Yerba Buena Gardens **45**

43 **44**

16

Geary Blvd.

JAPANTOWN **101**

WESTERN ADDITION

Turk St.

Golden Gate Ave.

Fulton St.

Alamo Square Fell St.

Oak St.

HAIGHT-ASHBURY

Haight St.

BUENA VISTA PARK

Duboce Ave.

14th St. Muni Church St.

16th St.

17th St.

THE CASTRO

Muni Castro St.

Market St.

BART/Muni Powell **41** **42**

Mission St.

Howard St.

Moscone Convention Center **47**

48

Folsom St.

BART/Muni Civic Center

CIVIC CENTER **14**

Market St.

SOMA

80

Muni Van Ness

8th St.
9th St.
10th St.

Harrison St.

Bryant St.

7th St.

6th St.

5th St.

4th St.

3rd St.

101

Central Skyway

101

17th St.

15

MISSION DISTRICT

S. Van Ness Ave.

Harrison St.

Bryant St.

Potrero Ave.

101

Rhode Island St.

POTRERO HILL

280

Univ. of San Francisco

Masonic St.

Yerba Buena Gardens

map not to scale

Stevenson Street

City College Downtown Center

Marriott Hotel

St. Patrick's Church

Jessie Square (Future)

Parking

Mexican Museum

Argent Hotel

Mission Street

California Historical Society

Fifth & Mission Garage

Metreon (Sony Entertainment Center)

Butterfly Garden

Reflection

ESPLANADE

Stage

Ship Sculpture

Yerba Buena Center for the Arts Galleries & Forum

East Garden

Parking

San Francisco Museum of Modern Art

Fourth Street

Moscone West

Martin Luther King, Jr. Memorial

Shaking Man

Sister Cities Garden

Theater

Third Street

W Hotel

California Academy of Sciences

Howard Street

Moscone Convention Center

Carousel

Zeum

Children's Center

Moscone Garage

---

forced detention for weeks, months, and sometimes years. Poems carved into the walls of the barracks by lonely and isolated detainees were rediscovered in 1970 and inspired the preservation effort by the California legislature.

Ideal for hiking and biking—with a picnic, of course—a trip to Angel Island is so removed from city life that a day spent here is like a vacation from your vacation. Hiking trails crisscross the island's 740 acres, but the majority of trekkers head for the top of Mount Livermore. At 788 feet, the views of San Francisco and Marin County are stunning. Bicyclists ride along an easy 5-mile path that circles the island, and you can either rent bikes at Ayala Cove when you dock or rent in town and bring them on the ferry. One-hour motorized **tram tours,** offered between March and November (the schedule varies; phone ☏ **415/897-0715** or check the website for details), are another option for getting around. Cars are not allowed on the island.

Angel Island Association, P.O. Box 866. ☏ **415/435-1915** or 415/435-3972. www.angelisland.org. Access to Angel Island is by ferry from Pier 41. Daily Blue & Gold Fleet round-trip tickets, which include state park fees, are $14 adults, $8.50 children 6–12, free children 5 and under. Phone ☏ **415/773-1188** or visit www.blueandgoldfleet.com for tickets and schedules.

Cable Cars ☆☆ **All ages.** These beloved wooden icons, the only moving landmarks in the National Register of Historic Places, are not the most practical mode of

transportation in San Francisco, but they are certainly the most fu
part of any first-time visit to the city.

As the story goes, in 1869 British-born engineer Andrew Hallidie o.
of overworked horses pulling a heavily laden carriage up a steep, rain-sw
cisco hill. One horse slipped and the car rolled back, dragging the other
everything else down with it. Right then
Hallidie resolved to create a mechanical
device to replace these beasts of burden,
and by 1873 the first cable car traversed
Clay Street. The cars have no engines.
Instead, a steel cable is housed just under
the street in a rail, kind of like an inside-
out train rail. Powered by electricity, this
cable constantly moves, or runs, through
the rail—making a distinctive clickity-
clacking sound. Each cable car has a
lever that when pulled back, closes a pin-
cerlike grip on the cable. The person
who pulls the lever is thus called a "gripper," not a driver. The cable car is then attached
to the cable that runs through the rail under the pavement, and the car begins to move
at a constant 9½ mph—the speed at which the cable is set to travel.

As electric streetcars and buses became more economical, San Francisco's mayor
planned in 1947 to do away with the few cable cars still around. Alarmed, a group of
private citizens lobbied successfully to save the city's three remaining cable car lines.
Between 1982 and 1984, the city completely refurbished these lines and seismically
retrofitted the Cable Car Barn on Mason and Washington streets.

The Powell-Hyde line is the most scenic, passing crooked Lombard Street before
heading down Russian Hill towards Ghiradelli Square and offering a breathtaking vista
of Alcatraz and the San Francisco Bay. Unfortunately, the wait for this route, and the
Powell-Mason line, is seemingly interminable. Solutions are to catch the car early in the
morning or after dinner. Another option is to take the California Street line, which
runs through Chinatown and over Nob Hill, as lines to board the cars are a bit shorter.

Powell at Market or California at Market sts. Tickets $5 one-way; $1 each way before 7am and after 9pm. $1 one-way with a Muni weekly; free with a Muni monthly pass; free with a Muni Passport and for children under 5. Hours of operation are 6am–1:30am.

> **_Tips_ Fueling the Troops**
>
> Vacationing in a city is hard with small children. Keep them going with something healthy mid-morning and something more fun mid-afternoon. For dinner reservations after 7:30pm, bolster the kids around 5pm so that they don't collapse in a heap waiting for supper.

Crissy Field ☆☆☆ **All ages.** A 4-year effort converted this abandoned U.S. airfield into a lovely national park that is a wonderful retreat for the whole family. My husband and I take our girls here regularly, as well as any visitors who come into town. The kids can climb all over the grassy knolls or play at the beach while the adults savor the spectacular views of the Golden Gate Bridge to the west and the San Francisco skyline to the east. There's nothing specific to "do" here, so there's a chance teens will find it boring. For everyone else, the spot is so relaxing and beautiful, it's well worth a visit. The 100-acre site has a tidal marsh, sheltered picnic area, bike path, walking path, cafe, bookstore, and education center. You can pass through here on a hike to Fort Point, or just come for lunch at the Warming Hut. Located at the park's western end, the Warming Hut has a great gift shop and a tasty, organic cafe menu developed with input from renowned chef Alice Waters of Berkeley's Chez Panisse.

The What-to-Do-While-Waiting-for-the-Ferry-to-Alcatraz Quiz

1. **In what bay is Alcatraz Island located?**
   a. Marin Bay
   b. San Francisco Bay
   c. The Bay Area

2. **When was Alcatraz a federal maximum-security prison?**
   a. 1934 to 1963
   b. 1893 to 1964
   c. 1920 to 1973

3. **Which one of these people was a famous Alcatraz inmate?**
   a. Mack the Knife
   b. Fred Flintstone
   c. Al Capone

4. **How big was the average cell?**
   a. 5 by 9 feet
   b. 10 by 12 feet
   c. 4 by 6 feet

5. **How many prisoners were executed at Alcatraz?**
   a. 3
   b. 0
   c. 8

6. **Which three men managed to escape Alcatraz but were never seen again?**
   a. The Ringling Brothers and Marshall Pickford
   b. Bobby Carson, Al Capone, and Danny Marsh
   c. Frank Morris and the Anglin Brothers

Crissy Field Center, Bldg 603 on the corner of Mason and Halleck sts. ✆ 415/561-7690. www.crissyfield.org. Center and cafe Wed–Sun 9am–5pm; Crissy Field and the Warming Hut daily 9am–5pm. Muni: no. 28-19th Ave., no. 29-Sunset, or no. 43-Masonic bus.

Exploratorium ☆☆☆   **All ages.** *Scientific American* magazine described the Exploratorium as "the best science museum in the world," and most young visitors agree. The cavernous space, a former airplane hanger, is crammed with displays that encourage viewer participation. The exhibits are thematic, with matter examined near the entrance, examples of momentum and inertia by the cafe, light and optics at the rear, and biology and electricity on the mezzanine. Clearly written text describes each exhibit, and several teens volunteer as "explainers" to help out the most science-challenged among us.

Even with the explainers' help, kids younger than six may not grasp the science behind each of the 650-plus exhibits. But they'll still love fiddling with a machine that makes sand patterns with sound waves, a camera that photographs your shadow, or a massive soap-bubble maker. My 5- and 7-year-olds could easily spend a day here—more hours than I can handle. Given the dim lighting and ever-present crowds, this

7. How many cells were there?
  a. 455
  b. 336
  c. 90

8. What was the highest number of prisoners held at Alcatraz?
  a. 325
  b. 302
  c. 208

9. What was the lowest number of prisoners held at Alcatraz?
  a. 222
  b. 105
  c. 97

10. How long did the average prisoner stay?
  a. Life sentence
  b. 8 years
  c. 25 years

11. What was the nickname prisoners gave Alcatraz?
  a. "The Island"
  b. "The Cage"
  c. "The Rock"

12. Approximately how many tourists visit Alcatraz each year?
  a. Over 2 million
  b. Over 1 million
  c. About 750,000

Answers:
1) b 2) a 3) c 4) a 5) b 6) c 7) b 8) b 9) a 10) b 11) c 12) b

stimulating environment could overwhelm some, even as it enthralls others. Because most exhibits are hands-on, kids will be pushing, pulling, or doing whatever it takes to have a go at some nifty contraption. If your little ones can't fend for themselves, don't hesitate to tell big kids their turn is up. They usually politely step aside.

You can take your toddler to the under-4s play area for a break, but it seems a shame to spend too much time there, since it just has blocks and other items you'd find at any preschool. Better to step outside to the **Palace of Fine Arts** grounds that house the Exploratorium. The only remaining structure left of the 1915 Panama-Pacific Exposition, the lovely domed Palace and its adjacent grass and pond serve as the backdrop for many a wedding photo. Near the back of the museum is a cafe where you can pick up items for a picnic outside, including peanut butter sandwiches, free-range chicken salads, and hot dogs made from naturally raised beef. (An espresso stand at the entrance also sells coffee, ice cream, and cookies.) The **Tactile Dome,** inside the museum, is an experience older kids really enjoy. Participants crawl, slide, and slowly walk through the dome in complete darkness, feeling their way along a variety of surfaces.

Reservations are required in advance, and you must buy a separate, pricey $16 ticket. Phone © **415/561-0362** for times and tickets.

Palace of Fine Arts, 3601 Lyon St. at Marina Blvd. © **415/397-5673**. www.exploratorium.org. Admission $13 adults; $10 seniors, students with ID, and youth 13–17; $8 children 4–12, free for children under 4. Tactile Dome $16. Free first Wed of every month. Tues–Sun 10am–5pm. Closed on Mondays except Memorial, Labor, President's, and Martin Luther King, Jr. Days. Closed Thanksgiving and Dec. 25. Closed Dec. 24 at 3pm. Muni: no. 30-Stockton bus.

Ferry Building Marketplace 🎟️🎟️🎟️ All ages.

San Franciscans have a thing about food—especially local, organic, and naturally raised food—so it's no surprise that a building devoted to gourmet fare should be considered a major attraction in its own right. It helps, of course, that the historic 1898 building recently reopened after a 4-year, multi-million-dollar renovation, and that it is located on the picturesque Embarcadero, with lovely views of the Bay Bridge and East Bay hills.

The best time to visit is early on Saturday morning, before half of San Francisco arrives for its weekly shopping spree at the **Ferry Building Farmer's Market.** There you'll find booths featuring organic fruits and vegetables, artisan cheeses, naturally raised meats, fresh bread, and so on. You could make a meal out of the free samples doled out by proud farmers and cooks, but it's worth holding back so that you can buy breakfast from one of the restaurant trailer cars in back. Purchase your scrambled eggs with wild mushrooms, fresh tamales, and chorizo, or soft shell crab on sourdough, and enjoy it on a bayside bench with a view of the ferries going to and fro. Kids will also enjoy the musicians who come by on Saturday mornings to entertain shoppers and earn some change. A smaller version of the market occurs on Tuesdays and spring and fall Thursdays, and the Sunday Garden Market (in spring and fall) has more emphasis on flowers, seeds, and other items for folks with a green thumb.

Even on non–farmer's market days, the building's scenic location, historic architecture (including a 240-foot clock tower), and collection of upscale food shops make it well worth a visit.

One Ferry Building. © 415/291-3276 (Farmer's Market) or 415/693-0996 (Ferry Building). www.ferrybuilding marketplace.com. Free admission. Ferry Building open Mon–Fri 10am–6pm; Sat 9am–6pm; Sun 11am–5pm. Farmer's Market open Sat 8am–2pm (all year); Tues 10am–2pm (all year). Thurs 4–8pm (spring and fall); Sun 10am–2pm (spring and fall). Closed major holidays. Muni: F-Market streetcar.

Lombard Street 🎟️ All ages.

My family and I lived near the "crookedest street in the world" (actually a 1-block-long section of an otherwise unremarkable avenue) for over 5 years, and I still don't get why cars line up for blocks to drive down it. That said, I think Lombard Street is worth checking out on foot, and even worth driving down on weekday mornings when it's blissfully uncrowded. Not to disappoint the little ones, but Lombard Street isn't even the crookedest street in San Francisco (Vermont Street between 20th and 22nd streets in Portrero Hill is), but it is the most scenic. The zigzags were added in the 1920s, as the street's 27° pitch was too steep for cars. Cars are only permitted to descend, but pedestrians can take the stairs on either side. The street is loveliest in spring, when the hydrangeas are in bloom. At all times of year it offers views of Telegraph Hill and Coit Tower.

Lombard St. (between Hyde and Leavenworth sts.)

Metreon 🎟️🎟️ All ages.

A one-of-a-kind four-story, modern cement-and-glass entertainment center, Metreon houses restaurants, retail shops, an IMAX theater, 15 movie screens, an extensive arcade operated by Portal 1 Arcade, and temporary museum-style exhibits. In the center on the ground floor is an interactive floor display with colored lights that react to one's movements and steps; young kids can't seem to get enough of it. A theater on the second floor shows anime and action films on the weekends. Among the choices in the arcade, a favorite is Hyperbowl, a futuristic, big-screen virtual game where players "bowl" through the streets of San Francisco. Noisy and dark, the arcade is highly appealing to kids and young adults. (Children under 18 have to be accompanied by an adult in this area after 8pm.)

Metreon is also home to the "Walk of Game" (similar to the Hollywood Walk of Fame) meant to honor top video game achievements, with votes taken throughout the month of October. Each year, permanent stars are given to the top two game developers, games, and characters. The retail angle is as much fun as the attractions, since every store provides customers with a hands-on experience. The PlayStation shop is always crowded with kids of all ages trying the latest in video games, and gadget nuts can audition the latest and greatest in equipment at the Sony Style store. With a food court on the lower level and Yerba Buena Center out the back, this complex is popular with teenagers from all over town.

101 4th St. (at Mission). ✆ 415/369-6000. www.metreon.com. Free admission. Individual attraction prices range from $6–$20. Daily 10am–10pm. For Portal 1 Arcade, call ✆ 415/369-6013 or visit www.portal1arcade.com. Muni: Any streetcar to Powell St. station.

The San Francisco Zoo ★★★ **All ages.** Little kids will love this fun, educational menagerie. Established in 1929 in its current 125-acre oceanside location, the zoo is continuously adding to its impressive array of exhibits. Count on spending half a day here, although you could easily stay longer. If you've arrived in summer and found the zoo draped in fog, stop by the gift shop to pick up an overpriced logo fleece. Rest assured that proceeds from the purchase, or from any of the unusual gifts you might pick up there, go to a good cause.

At the 3-acre African Safari exhibit, giraffes, zebras, kudus, dik-diks, and other large mammals live together alongside colorful African bird species. At the Binnowee Landing exhibit, colorful Australian birds land on your hands and feed from the seed "lollipop" you get when you enter the enclosed aviary ($2 gets you into the aviary with one stick, but be sure not to come during the birds' afternoon naptime—no amount of prodding will get them to eat). Another great exhibit is the Lipman Family Lemur Forest, which houses five endangered lemur species. You can watch the lemurs leap among the trees and climb special activity towers into which visitors can hoist lemur-appropriate food provided by the zoo. The viewing platforms are also lined with signage describing the zoo's conservation efforts in Madagascar. Among the many other exhibits are an Australian walkabout featuring kangaroos and wallabies, a South American Tropical Forest Building housing a large anaconda and several colorful bird and reptile species, and the Lion House, with its rare Sumatran and Siberian tigers. The daily big cat feeding always draws a crowd.

The Children's Zoo is a destination in itself. Kids can crawl through tunnels underneath the exhibit of meerkats and prairie dogs, who pop up out of their own tunnels. At the Family Farm, kids may feed various rare and endangered breeds of goats and sheep, and visit horses and ponies. In the Hatchery, your children can observe incubated chick eggs in various stages of development and help feed newly born chicks. And the Insect House will fascinate them with giant walking sticks, tarantulas, and even a massive cockroach display. (Yech.)

Little ones will also enjoy the playground structure, the Dentzel carousel ($2/ride), and the cute little steam train (which requires a $3 ticket). The best place to lunch in

---

Tips **Zoo Events**

The zoo has special events throughout the year and daily activities for visitors. Most days you can meet the zookeepers during animal feedings. Penguins are fed at 2:30pm Thursday and 3pm Friday to Wednesday; lions and tigers are fed in the Lion House at 2pm Tuesday to Sunday. Also, daily in the summer and on weekends the rest of the year you can attend "Meet the Keeper" talks at these times: "Meerkats and Prairie Dogs" at 2pm; "Incredible Insects in Action" at 2:30pm; and "Native American Animals" at 3:15 and 3:45pm. For dates of events such as Family Overnights, phone or check the website.

---

the zoo is the Leaping Lemur cafe, which serves a mix of healthy and greasy choices including pizza, burgers, California rolls, salads, and sweets. The zoo is free the first Wednesday of the month; in summer, you're better off paying the entrance fee and coming on any other day to avoid the first-Wednesday crowds.

1 Zoo Rd., at the Great Highway. ✆ 415/753-7080. www.sfzoo.org. Admission $11 adults, $8 seniors 65-plus and youths 12–17, $3 children 3–11, free for children under 3. Disabled visitors receive 50% discount. Discounts for San Francisco residents. Free the first Wed of the month. Stroller rentals are available ($6/single stroller; $9/double stroller). Daily 10am–5pm. (Children's Zoo until 4:30pm). Muni: L-Taraval streetcar. Show your transfer for $1 discount on admission.

Yerba Buena Gardens and Center for the Arts 🌟🌟🌟 **All ages.** Opened in 1993, this 22-acre complex is an oasis of culture, fun, and greenery amidst an extremely urban slice of town. The center's two buildings, which include a 775-seat theater and three galleries, feature theatre, dance, and contemporary arts, often by local and emerging artists. Dance troupes, including ODC/San Francisco and Smuin Ballets/SF, call this space home. They perform periodic children's events as well.

Older kids will appreciate the art/technology center **Zeum,** which is detailed below. Younger kids will love the 1906 carousel; the playground with its two really, really tall slides; and the **Yerba Buena Ice-Skating Rink and Bowling Center.** Public skating times at the city's only year-round facility vary daily, so phone before making the trip over here. The tidy 12-lane bowling alley has bumpers available for novice bowlers, shoes, and a small menu of snacks.

Even if you don't have time for a round of bowling, take a moment to walk through the lovely grounds, which include a 5-acre garden dramatically framed by the city skyline. Among the many fountains is a particularly striking one designed in homage to Martin Luther King, Jr. In summer months, the Yerba Buena Gardens Festival features free classical and jazz concerts, an international music festival, dance and film series, and numerous events specifically for families and children.

701 Mission St. (at 3rd St.). ✆ 415/978-2700 or 415/978-ARTS (box office). www.ybca.org. Yerba Buena Ice Skating and Bowling Center: 750 Folsom St. (between 3rd and 4th). ✆ 415/777-3727. www.skatebowl.com. Skating admission $8 adults, $5.50 seniors, $6.50 children 12 and under. Skate rental $3. Bowling Center Sun–Thurs 10am–10pm; 10am–midnight Fri–Sat. Admission for adults starts at $3.50 per lane per game or $20 per lane per hour, although holiday rates increase to $6/game or $30/hour. Shoe rental $3. Advanced lane reservations are possible (rates increase to $25/hour). Muni: Any streetcar to Powell St. station.

Zeum 🌟 **All ages.** This wonderful art/technology center with hands-on labs lets kids create animated video shorts with clay figures; experiment with graphics, sound, and video in the production laboratory; and even create their own computer graphic

animation characters. Students from the American Conservatory Thea
stage dramas in Zeum's theater. Although the center was initially desig
kids and teens, I've seen plenty of young kids having a great time there.

221 4th St. (at Howard St.). ✆ 415/820-3320.
www.zeum.com. For information on ACT programs at
Zeum, call the Yerba Buena box office at ✆ 415/978-
ARTS or visit http://actactortraining.org. Admission $8
adults, $7 seniors and students, $6 kids 3–18, children
under 3 free. Wed–Sun 11am–5pm; mid-June–mid-Aug
Tues–Sun 11am–5pm. Muni: Any streetcar to Powell St.
station.

CHINATOWN ✰✰✰

The first Chinese arrived in California
in the 1800s to work as servants. Then
in 1848, gold was discovered at Sutter's
Mill, and thousands of Chinese immigrants left the Opium Wars and famine
in their own country to seek their for-

(Fun Fact **Stump the Tour
Guide**

Question: Where did Thomas Wat-
son answer the phone when Alexander Graham Bell made the first
transcontinental telephone call from
New York City? Answer: At the now
long-gone Pacific Telephone and
Telegraph Company on Grant
Avenue and Bush Street, San Francisco, January 25, 1915.

tunes in the California "Gold Mountain." Intending to send their riches home, they
found life in California didn't quite live up to their expectations. First employed in the
gold mines and later working on the railroads, Chinese laborers were essentially inden-
tured servants and faced constant prejudice.

The 1906 earthquake and fire destroyed much of Chinatown, and Chinese refugees
swamped relief camps in San Francisco and Oakland. A group of city officials tried to
permanently relocate them outside the city center, but the threat to political relations
with China and the potential loss of lucrative Asian trade to other western ports put
an end to this plan. So Chinatown continued to grow and thrive, in part because Chinese people were not allowed to buy homes outside of the area until 1950. Today Chinatown remains one of the most densely populated neighborhoods in the country and
has become a top tourist attraction in the area. To the local residents, Chinatown is a
complete community—where they shop, socialize, attend school, exercise, worship,
and play. The crowds of tourists don't seem to faze anyone—not the grandmas with
babies tied to their backs, the groups of schoolchildren, the senior citizens practicing
tai chi in the park, or the masses of determined Saturday shoppers.

Any cable car will drop you in or near Chinatown. Walking around Chinatown,
diving into the shops, sampling pork buns, and eyeing the sidewalk fruit and vegetable
displays can be more than enough entertainment for an afternoon. But, just in case,
here are some specific stops that will enhance your tour. If you want even more guid-
ance, check out the self-guided tour of Chinatown in chapter 8.

Chinese Culture Center   **Ages 10 and up.** Cross the pedestrian bridge on the east
side of Portsmouth Square that leads directly into the third floor of the Holiday Inn.
This is the home of the Chinese Culture Center. Within its small well-lit gallery, ever-
changing exhibits may feature photographs of pre-earthquake Chinatown, Chinese
brush paintings, or liu li (glasswork) by contemporary Chinese artists. Entrance is free
and the center is small. Kids won't have a chance to get bored and they'll likely see
something beautiful. The center also offers classes and walks. It's a good resource for
locals and visitors with an interest in Asian art and culture.

750 Kearny St., Third Floor. ✆ 415/986-1822. www.c-c-c.org. Free admission. Tues–Sat 10am–4pm.

Rainy-Day Activities

San Francisco is no Seattle, but rainy days can get in the way of enjoying our city. More often, the damp, misty fog is what really gets to folks, especially in July when the rest of the country is working on its suntan. But you don't have time to grouse about the weather. You have things to do, places to see . . . oh, you don't like getting wet? Okay. Here are a few rainy/foggy-day options.

- **Take high tea.** High tea at one of the many hotels that offers it is perhaps the most civilized way to keep dry. Try the **King George Hotel,** 334 Mason St. (© **415/781-5050**); the **Westin St. Francis,** 335 Powell St. (© **415/397-7000**); the **Sheraton Palace,** 2 New Montgomery St. (© **415/512-1111**); the **Fairmont Hotel,** 950 Mason St. (© **415/772-5000**); or the **Ritz-Carlton,** 600 Stockton St. (© **415/296-7465**). Neiman Marcus also has a lovely, reasonably priced tea service in the **Rotunda** restaurant, 150 Stockton St. (© **415/362-3900**), from 2:30 to 5pm daily.

- **Rock climb.** Rather than having the kids climb the walls of your hotel room, take everyone indoor rock climbing at **Mission Cliffs Rock Climbing Center** at 2295 Harrison St., at 19th Street (© **415/550-0515**). Open daily, the world-class facility caters to beginners and experts of all ages—teaching belay (rope handling) classes and renting whatever equipment is necessary, including shoes. Those who prefer to keep their feet on the ground will enjoy the on-site gym with locker rooms and sauna. (p 228).

- **Read a book.** The Fisherman's Wharf branch of **Barnes & Noble Booksellers** at 2552 Taylor St. (© **415/292-6762**) has a nice cafe downstairs and a spacious children's book section upstairs, complete with kid-sized tables, chairs, and a train set.

The Chinese Historical Society of America **Ages 10 and up.** This is a good place to develop an appreciation of the Chinese experience in California, and also worth a quick drop-in to add a little gravity to your day before digging into that dim sum. A museum and research center, the Historical Society documents the fascinating history of the Chinese in California through photographs, art, and changing exhibits. Its bookstore stocks children's titles as well as fiction and nonfiction on Chinese themes. The center also hosts occasional tours during the year, such as a "Ghosts of Chinatown" tour before Halloween, at additional cost.

965 Clay St. © 415/391-1188. www.chsa.org. Admission $3 adults, $2 seniors and college students, $1 children 6–17, free children under 6. Free first Thurs of month. Tues–Fri noon–5pm; Sat–Sun noon–4pm.

Golden Gate Fortune Cookie Company ⚑ **All ages.** You can't miss with a visit to this factory, where golden discs quickly become crispy cookies complete with a fortune. The place is small and you may have to wait your turn to watch the ladies handle the cookie-making machine. Bags of fortune cookies and yummy almond cookies to munch while you continue your excursion are available for a few dollars. The locals themselves prefer their cookies flat and round, without the little sayings tucked inside

- **Watch the weather.** Admire the storm from the confines of t House, 1090 Point Lobos Ave., on the Great Highway (© 415/386-3330), open daily. Reopened in October 2004 after a major renovation, the Cliff House Restaurant offers drinks, decent food, and amazing vistas. The nearest museum is the **Palace of the Legion of Honor** (p. 192), another great place to wait out the rain. The no. 18-46th Avenue bus will bring you to both locations.

- **Seek some cultural edification.** Now you have an excuse to spend more than 15 minutes in a museum. The **Asian Art Museum** (p. 190) and the **de Young Museum** are my picks for having the most kid-friendly exhibits.

- **Photograph your shadow.** Try that and other wacky science "experiments" at the **Exploratorium** (p. 174). You could spend a whole day at this incredible science museum; just bear in mind that on rainy days everyone else is here, too.

- **Head to SoMa.** The **Sony Metreon** and **Yerba Buena Gardens** make up a one-stop rainy-day haven. Teens can flex their independence at **Zeum,** and kids needing supervision will enjoy the Metreon play areas. Tour the spooky **Where the Wild Things Are,** take everyone bowling and ice-skating, or catch a movie. A block south of Yerba Buena is the **California Academy of Sciences.** Watch the penguin feeding and exotic sea life downstairs, or head upstairs to the educational area and tot spot.

- **Stay dry on the F-Market streetcar.** Grab an umbrella, then grab a seat for a ride to the Ferry Building. Have lunch, buy some sweets at Recchiuti Confections, and jump back on the F-Market towards **The Cannery.** There you can check out a few fun shops for the kids, including Lark In The Morning, with its wacky collection of musical instruments.

(they've read enough fortunes for a lifetime.) You can also buy cookies in their unfolded form—although they're not nearly as much fun. If you take pictures, it's polite to leave a tip.

56 Ross Alley (between Jackson and Washington sts.). No phone. Free admission. Daily 10am–7pm.

Portsmouth Square ⓐ **All ages.** In this spot, Yerba Buena officially became San Francisco when Captain John Montgomery claimed the settlement for the United States in 1846 on the eve of the Mexican-American War. Chinese immigrants ran businesses close to the square even then. Today, a handy parking garage is underneath, and a section of the park is devoted to a compact playground that entertains the local preschoolers. Benches invite contemplation of the glorious Financial District skyline featuring the Transamerica Pyramid.

Kearny St., between Washington and Clay sts. No phone.

Tien Hou Temple **Ages 8 and up.** Members of this temple, one of the oldest Chinese temples in the U.S., are used to elementary school students tiptoeing up the four narrow flights of stairs for a look. The sanctuary ceiling is covered in red paper

Fortune Cookies

Those crispy cookies with wise, prescient, or just plain confusing sayings slipped inside aren't Chinese at all. While the origin of fortune cookies isn't exactly known, they are believed to have been invented in San Francisco by Makoto Hagiwara, who managed the Japanese Tea Garden in Golden Gate Park from 1895 until 1925. You can visit a fortune cookie factory on Ross Alley in Chinatown (see above) and with this recipe you can make the cookies yourself at home, complete with your own fabulous fortunes.

Ingredients

¼ cup flour

2 tablespoons brown sugar

1 tablespoon cornstarch

2 tablespoons oil

1 egg white, beaten until stiff

¼ teaspoon vanilla

4 tablespoons water

Combine flour, sugar, cornstarch, and oil in a bowl. Fold in the beaten egg white. Add vanilla and water. The batter should have the thin consistency of crepe batter; if it's too thick, add more water. In a small nonstick or lightly oiled skillet over medium heat, pour one tablespoon of the batter, spreading it out into a 3-inch circle. Cook until browned, about 3 minutes. Turn the cookie and cook 1 minute more. Remove from the pan and place a paper fortune in the center. Fold in half, then bend the tips to form the fortune cookie shape. Be careful—the cookie will be hot. Place in an egg carton to hold the shape until cool. Makes about 12 cookies.

lanterns, and the smell of incense is pervasive. Altars are covered with offerings and one holds a statue of Tien Hou, also known as Tin How, the goddess of heaven and protector of fishermen. Remind the kids that this is a place for meditation and prayer—you'll likely see people doing just that—so they will need to keep the chatter down. Make a small donation or purchase some incense before heading back downstairs.

125 Waverly Place (off Clay St. between Stockton St. and Grant Ave.). No phone. Free admission. Daily 10am–4pm.

FISHERMAN'S WHARF 😄

The days when fishing boats hauled their catches back to the piers along Jefferson Street ended for the most part in the late 1960s. As warehouses were retooled into shopping centers and local waters became over-fished, tourism began to supplant maritime industries. Then PIER 39 opened in 1978, completing Fisherman's Wharf's metamorphosis into a major California tourist attraction, second only to Disneyland. Unless you get up very early in the morning and seek out what's left of the fishing fleet, you won't see any picturesque scenes of flapping flounders or salty sailors. Mostly what you see at Fisherman's Wharf are tourists gravely contemplating chocolate bars

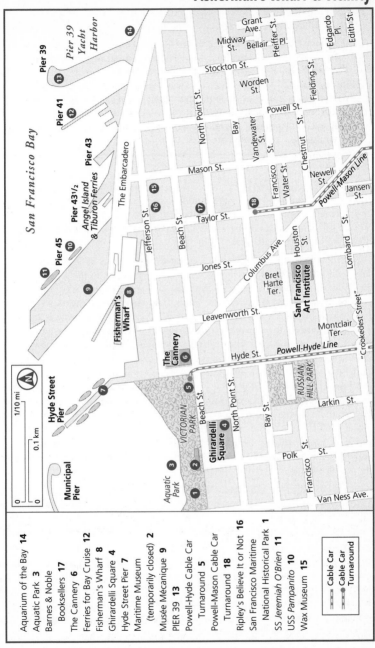

San Francisco Bay

Pier 39 Yacht Harbor

Pier 39
Pier 41
Pier 43
Pier 43½
Angel Island & Tiburon Ferries
Pier 45

Grant Ave.
Midway St.
Bellair
Pfeiffer Pl.
Edgardo Pl.
Edith St.
Stockton St.
Worden St.
Powell St.
Bay
Vandewater St.
Chestnut St.
Newell St.
Jansen St.
Francisco St.
Water St.
North Point St.
Mason St.
Beach St.
Taylor St.
Jefferson St.
Jones St.
Columbus Ave.
Houston St.
Bret Harte Ter.
Leavenworth St.
Hyde St.
Montclair Ter.
North Point St.
Beach St.
Bay St.
Larkin St.
Polk St.
Francisco St.
Van Ness Ave.
The Embarcadero
Fisherman's Wharf
The Cannery
Powell-Hyde Line
"Crookedest Street"
Powell-Mason Line
San Francisco Art Institute
RUSSIAN HILL PARK
VICTORIAN PARK
Ghirardelli Square
Aquatic Park
Municipal Pier
Hyde Street Pier

1/10 mi
0.1 km

Tips **Discount Coupons**

While many Fishermans' Wharf attractions are free or low-cost, others can dig into your pocketbook. Don't head to the Wharf without first checking the website at http://fishermanswharf.org. Click on "Discount Coupons" and print out coupons that will keep a few bills in your wallet, including $1 to $2 off on attractions such as Aquarium of the Bay, Ripley's Believe it or Not, and the Wax Museum. You may also get $3 off a Bay Cruise or $5 off a bike rental. Your hotel may help you print them out, or may even have some discount coupons available to give you.

---

and sportswear. Of course, there's more—some of it well worth your time, some not—so here's a rundown of what you'll find along the Embarcadero, and Jefferson and Beach streets, from PIER 39 to the Municipal Pier at the end of Van Ness Avenue. The Powell-Hyde cable car line will drop you off at the west end of this stretch, near The Cannery and Aquatic Park.

Aquarium of the Bay   All ages. Dedicated to the creatures that inhabit the San Francisco Bay ecosystem, this aquarium gives new meaning to the phrase "living life in a fishbowl." It's not entirely clear who's looking at whom in this attraction. After a brief introduction to the underwater world, facilitated by the Aquarium's loquacious band of naturalists, visitors descend to a moving walkway that slowly leads through two clear tunnels surrounded by 700,000 gallons of filtered bay water. The moving path cleverly keeps people from clustering around a particularly impressive Pacific electric stingray, so even the little ones get a chance to look in and spy an Angel shark burrowing in the sand. Thousands of fish swim on either side of the walkway and overhead as well; kids find it pretty cool. The last exhibit contains touch pools with starfish and such, always a hit with children. Should a trip to the Monterey Bay Aquarium be in your future, you can skip this smaller cousin altogether. But if you're already on PIER 39, it's a pleasant hour-long respite from the curios and candy shops.

PIER 39 at Fisherman's Wharf. © 800/SEA-DIVE. www.aquariumofthebay.com. Admission $14 adults, $7 seniors and kids 3–11, free children under 3, $30 family ticket for 2 adults and 2 children. Daily in summer 9am–8pm; otherwise Mon–Fri 10am–6pm, Sat–Sun 10am–7pm. Closed Dec. 25.

Ghirardelli Square   All ages. Named after the chocolate factory founded by Domingo Ghirardelli (pronounced Gear-a-*del*-ee), this series of brick buildings was built over 11 years beginning in 1893. When the chocolate factory was moved to a lower-rent location across the bay in the 1960s, prominent San Franciscans moved in to buy and restore the property. Granted landmark status in 1982, Ghirardelli Square is now home to a three-story mall with more than 50 shops. It hosts a roster of special events, including an annual chocolate-tasting benefit in September, and street performers entertain regularly in the **West Plaza.** From your kids' point of view, the Square's best feature may be the Ghirardelli Ice Cream and Chocolate Shop (p. 147).

900 North Point St. (between Beach and Larkin sts.) © 415/775-5500. www.ghirardellisq.com. Shops open Sun–Thurs 10am–6pm; Fri–Sat 10am–7pm. Restaurants are open later.

Hyde Street Pier ⭐⭐⭐   **All ages.** This noteworthy homage to San Francisco's seafaring past houses eight historic, refurbished ships, three of which you can tour. You may walk for free along the lovely pier, with its breathtaking views of the Golden Gate Bridge; however, there's a modest but worthwhile fee to tour the boats. At the far end of the pier is the most striking ship, and one of the few remaining square-riggers, the majestic *Balclutha*. She took her maiden voyage from Cardiff, Wales, on January 15, 1887, and over the course of her working life carried coal, wheat, lumber, and finally canned salmon from Alaska. In retirement she appeared in the movie *Mutiny on the Bounty*. Completely restored, the ship hosts events throughout the year, including some just for kids. But no event need be taking place for your kids to enjoy climbing into the crew's bunks, checking out the furnished captain's quarters, and visiting the galley. The 1890 steam ferryboat *Eureka* was the last of 50 paddle-wheel ferries that regularly plied the bay and made its final trip in 1957. Restored to its original splendor at the height of the ferryboat era, the 300-foot-long side-wheeler is loaded with deck cargo, including a sizable collection of antique cars and trucks. The third boat currently on display is a 1907 ocean-going tugboat *Hercules.*

The pier is part of the San Francisco Maritime National Historical Park. After visiting the pier, step into the park's **Visitor Center** across the street. Young kids will get a kick out of seeing tiny wooden models of the boats they've just toured. Or they may prefer the life-sized replica of a shipwrecked boat, complete with an eerie representation of a sailor being rescued. An hour and a half is enough time to enjoy this delightful outdoor museum and visitor's center.

Jefferson St. (at Hyde St.). ☏ 415/561-6662. www.maritime.org. Hyde St. Pier: Admission to the pier is free, but adults 17 and older must pay $5 to board ships; kids under 17 free. Family pass, with free admission to USS *Pampanito* is $20. Daily 9:30am–5pm (until 5:30pm late May–late Sept). Visitor Center: Free admission. Visitor center ☏ 415/447-5000. Daily 9:30am–5pm (until 7pm late May–late Sept). Pier and Visitor Center closed Thanksgiving, Dec. 25, and New Year's Day.

Maritime Museum   Ages 4 and up. Also part of the San Francisco Maritime National Historical Park, this white three-story structure shaped like an Art Deco ship is closed for a 3-year restoration project until 2009.

900 Beach St. (at Polk St.). Closed for restoration.

Musée Mécanique ⊛ **Ages 3 and up.** This may be the largest collection of antique mechanical and musical arcade games in private hands. The owner has been collecting these forerunners of pinball and video amusements since he was a kid back in the 1940s. Fortune-tellers, an intricate model of a fairground with working parts, an amazing baseball game, and the famous Laughing Sal, whose laugh really is infectious, are among dozens of machines from around the world in pristine condition.

⸌Tips Feeling Crabby?

If your blood sugar's low, head to the seafood counters at Fisherman's Wharf. Local **Dungeness crab** season begins in November and ends in May. If you don't see crates of live crabs ready for steaming, you are buying a once-frozen, precooked crab. With a loaf of sourdough and drinks (white wine for the grownups, perhaps?) you have the quintessential San Francisco meal. Take the food, some napkins, and your family and look for **Fish Alley,** just to the west of Jones Street and parallel to Jefferson Street. You'll find a peaceful shelter here where you can savor your snack sitting on the dock by the bay.

Bringing Culture to the Little Ones

Do your kids' eyes glaze over at the mere mention of the word "museum"? Here are some tips for making museum visits more fun for everyone:

- **Put the younger generation in charge.** Show kids the list of exhibits and ask them what they want to see.
- **Tantalize them.** Choose the exhibit you think kids will find most interesting and go there first. You're likely to hold their interest longer.
- **Go on a hunt.** Hand an exhibit catalog to each child. Give them one point for every piece of art they can find that's pictured in the catalog. (If desperate, make the points exchangeable for chocolate.)
- **Let kids surprise you.** Sometimes kids will actually enjoy a museum more than you think. Don't just assume the expedition will be a bust, or you'll have a self-fulfilling prophecy.
- **Prioritize.** Since chances are slim you'll actually get through an entire museum, decide what's most important to you and head there early on.
- **Follow the old rules.** As with any adult excursion you've dragged your kids to, remember to go early, move quickly, and keep snacks on hand.

The museum space itself has no charm, and the crowds are ceaseless, but kids will be highly entertained here—so bring a roll of quarters with you.

Pier 45 (at Taylor St.). ℂ 415/346-2000. http://museemecanique.org. Free admission. Weekdays 10am–7pm.

PIER 39   All ages. A two-level Venetian carousel beckons near the back of this ever-crowded wooden pier, its music competing with the footfalls of a herd of out-of-towners and the deafening noise of the video arcade hall on the left. On either side stretching back to the entryway are T-shirt shops, fried food counters, souvenirs vendors, candy stores . . . the commercialism goes on and on. Golden views of Alcatraz are clearly visible from the end of the pier, and huge sea lions loaf around on K dock to the west (follow the barking) from September through June. The ferries for Alcatraz and bay cruises leave from Pier 41 next door, but the Blue & Gold ticket office is part of this complex. Restaurants galore, including the **Hard Rock Cafe** (ℂ 415/956-2014; www.hardrock.com), fill in the cracks. If you arrive by car, park at a meter on adjacent streets or across from the wharf between Taylor and Jones streets. But be advised, the parking garage there is exorbitant. It's cheaper—and more fun—to take the F-Market streetcar down the Embarcadero.

Beach St. and The Embarcadero. ℂ 415/705-5500. www.pier39.com. Hours vary by season; between 10am–10pm for shops and attractions, closing as early as 7pm in mid-winter, and 11:30am–11pm for restaurants.

Ripley's Believe It or Not   Ages 8 and up. What this has to do with Fisherman's Wharf I'll never know, but if it's raining and you're desperate to fill an hour with the kids and you just happen to be out front, what the heck. If you're not familiar with the Ripley's franchise, it's all about weird people and things that are supposed to be too strange to be believed unless you "see" them with your own eyes. Exhibits cover stories such as the World's Tallest Man, the World's Shortest Man (featuring a wax

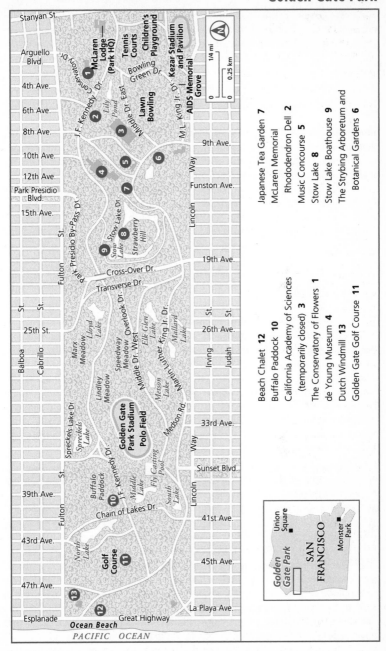

Stanyan St.

Arguello Blvd.

4th Ave.

6th Ave.

8th Ave.

10th Ave.

12th Ave.

Park Presidio Blvd.

15th Ave.

25th St.

Balboa

Cabrillo

39th Ave.

43rd Ave.

47th Ave.

Esplanade

Ocean Beach

PACIFIC OCEAN

McLaren Lodge — (Park HQ)

Tennis Courts

Children's Playground

Kezar Stadium and Pavilion

Bowling Green Dr.

AIDS Memorial Grove

Lawn Bowling

Lily Pond

Conservatory Dr.

J.F. Kennedy Dr.

Middle Dr. East

M.L. King Jr. Dr.

9th Ave.

Funston Ave.

Lincoln Way

19th Ave.

Stow Lake Dr.

Strawberry Hill

Stow Lake

Cross-Over Dr.

Park Presidio By-Pass Dr.

Transverse Dr.

St.

St.

Fulton

Lloyd Lake

Marx Meadow

Speedway Meadow Overlook Dr.

Middle Dr. West

Elk Glen Lake

Martin Luther King Jr. Dr.

Mallard Lake

26th Ave.

St.

St.

Irving

Judah

Lindley Meadow

Metson Lake

Golden Gate Park Stadium Polo Field

Medson Rd.

33rd Ave.

Way

Spreckels Lake Dr.

Spreckels Lake

J.F. Kennedy Dr.

Buffalo Paddock

Middle Lake

Fly Casting Pool

South Lake

Chain of Lakes Dr.

Sunset Blvd.

Lincoln

41st Ave.

Fulton

45th Ave.

North Lake

Golf Course

La Playa Ave.

Great Highway

Japanese Tea Garden **7**

McLaren Memorial Rhododendron Dell **2**

Music Concourse **5**

Stow Lake **8**

Stow Lake Boathouse **9**

The Strybing Arboretum and Botanical Gardens **6**

Beach Chalet **12**

Buffalo Paddock **10**

California Academy of Sciences (temporarily closed) **3**

The Conservatory of Flowers **1**

de Young Museum **4**

Dutch Windmill **13**

Golden Gate Golf Course **11**

1/4 mi

0.25 km

0

0

Golden Gate Park

Union Square

SAN FRANCISCO

Monster Park

and trees from five continents. Although the Conservatory has more than 17,000 (!) different species of plants, there's a good chance your children will be most fascinated by the carnivorous flora, with lidlike tops and some surprisingly large "pitchers" in which they digest their prey. In front of the conservatory is a colorful display of traditional flowers and, to the right, the captivating Dahlia Garden.

Just off John F. Kennedy Dr., near the Stanyan St. entrance. ✆ 415/666-7001. www.conservatoryofflowers.org. $5 adults; $3 for youths 12–17, seniors, and students w/ID; $1.50 children 5–11, free children under 5. Open Tues–Sun 9am–5pm (last visitor must enter by 4:30pm).

Japanese Tea Garden   All ages. Japanese landscape architect Makoto Hagiwara designed a small Japanese-style garden for the 1894 World's Fair, which later expanded to its current 5-acre size. Visitors walk along windy pathways, stepping stones, and bridges framed by koi ponds, Japanese maples, cedars, cherry trees, and bonsai. Highlights include a 1790 bronze Buddha, a Shinto wooden pagoda, and a Zen Garden. Young children find this small, intimate minipark particularly memorable, in part for the steeply arched Drum Bridge—which doubles as an excellent climbing structure. You'll need less than an hour to take it all in, but if you want to extend your experience, visit the teahouse for tea and snacks. Just steer clear of the junky gift shop, lest you lose the sense of serenity gained while strolling through these lovely grounds.

The garden entrance is to the left of the de Young Museum construction site. ✆ 415/752-4227. Admission $4 adults, $1.50 seniors and children 6–12, free children 5 and under; free entrance Mon, Wed, Fri between 9–10am. Open 9am–4:45pm; summer 9am–6pm.

The Strybing Arboretum and Botanical Gardens   All ages. With more than 6,000 species of well-tended plants, flowering trees, and theme gardens, you'll find this to be a splendid oasis. It is exceptionally lovely in late winter when the rhododendrons blossom and wild iris poke up in corners, and there is no more peaceful a place when the skies are drizzling. Docents give free tours daily at 1:30pm and weekends at 10:30am, departing from the bookstore. Children can run at will on the vast lawn not far past the entrance, and at the very end of the arboretum there's a children's teaching garden with vegetables, herbs, fruit, and sunflowers in season.

9th Ave. at Lincoln Way, left of the tour bus parking lot by the Music Concourse. ✆ 415/661-1316. www.strybing.org. Free admission. Mon–Fri 8am–4:30pm; Sat–Sun 10am–5pm.

2 Museums for Everyone

Asian Art Museum   All ages. After 35 years in Golden Gate Park, the Asian moved in 2003 to new quarters near City Hall. The museum owns one of the largest collections of Asian art in the Western world, covering 6,000 years and encompassing cultures throughout Asia. It's hard to say what kids might find interesting. The textiles are amazing examples of design and handiwork; the Chinese paintings are often more accessible than modern works and are achingly beautiful. My kids were enthralled with the intricate Indonesian puppets and the model Japanese home. The building itself is another reason to visit: Gae Aulenti, the Milanese architect who renovated the d'Orsay train station in Paris into the intriguing Musée d'Orsay, renovated the interior of the 1917 Beaux Arts former Main Library, creating 37,500 square feet of exhibition space.

The museum offers two "Family Festival" events per year, with specific activities geared towards families. Also, on the first Saturday of the month, kids and their families are invited to drop-in art classes. Also on those first Saturdays, as well as every

Sunday, the museum hosts a storytelling time for kids at 1pm. The first Tuesday of the month is "Target Tuesday" and usually features a demonstration and kids' activity. The museum has an elegant gift shop and an inviting cafe offering varied Asian specialties such as noodle soups, salmon misoyaki, or Tibetan lamb stew (simple salads and sandwiches can also be had).

200 Larkin St. (at Fulton St.). ⓒ 415/581-3500. www.asianart.org. Admission $12 adults, $8 seniors, $7 youths 13–17, free to children 12 and under, $5 all visitors (except kids 12 and under, who are free) Thurs after 5pm. Free first Tues of the month. Discount for same-day Muni riders. Tues–Sun 10am–5pm, Thurs until 9pm. Muni: Any streetcar to Civic Center.

Bay Area Discovery Museum ★★★ Kids up to 10. Ostensibly a museum for

children, this indoor/outdoor play and discovery space is fun for grown-ups as well. Tucked into a wooded national park at the foot of the Golden Gate Bridge, with lovely views of the San Francisco skyline, the location alone makes it an excellent place to hang out and have a picnic.

Out-of-towners will appreciate the Lookout Cove exhibit, a 2½-acre outdoor space dedicated to the Bay Area's history, geography, and ecology. Kids can don pint-sized construction helmets and "build" a smaller scale version of the Golden Gate Bridge, wade through tide pools into a sea cave (real tide pools and caves are found just north of San Francisco), search for treasure inside a sunken ship modeled after an actual 16th-century Manila galleon still at the bottom of nearby Drake's Bay, study artists' sculptures of local animals, and hike along the site's hillside perimeter. While kids play, parents can hang back and take in the view or read the detailed signs and photographs that provide rich detail about the San Francisco Bay's past and present.

In case the weather disappoints, the museum has several indoor play areas—including a tot spot, art area, and the San Francisco Bay Room featuring a life-sized fishing boat—although they're mostly geared to very young kids. You could easily spend a couple of hours here, so pick up lunch at the on-site cafe and grab a picnic table outside. Even though not strictly in San Francisco, the museum is too good to leave for a side trip. *Note:* If you take the bus, you'll have a 10- to 15-minute walk from the bus stop to the museum.

Fort Baker, 577 McReynolds Rd., Sausalito. ⓒ 415/339-3900. www.baykidsmuseum.org. Admission $8.50 adults, $7.50 children 1 and older; children under 1 free. $1 AAA discount. Tues–Fri 9am–4pm; Sat–Sun 10am–5pm. Closed Mon., except when noted. Muni: Weekends only 76 bus to Alexander Road/East Road exit; walk down East Road towards Fort Baker.

Cable Car Museum All ages. It won't take long to peer down at the machinery that

allows the cable cars to travel up and down the city's hills, but this seemingly simple piece of engineering is very cool. The car barn displays inventor Hallidie's original model from 1873, and there's a short video explaining how the cable cars work, plus a gift shop for those must-have mini cable cars.

1201 Mason St. (at Washington St.). ⓒ 415/474-1887. www.cablecarmuseum.com. Free admission. Daily 10am–5pm, until 6pm Apr 1–Sep 30. Closed New Year's Day, Easter Sunday, Thanksgiving, and Dec. 25. Muni: Powell-Mason or Powell-Hyde cable car.

California Academy of Sciences ★★ All ages. This wonderful natural history

museum—the country's fourth largest—has temporarily left its Golden Gate Park home to reside in a three-story, industrial SoMa building while a new seismically updated, eco-friendly facility is built for it in the park. (The new facility is slated to open in 2008.) Don't let the temporary site's unassuming concrete facade deter you.

Inside is a world-class institution dedicated to developing and disseminating knowledge about the natural world.

The first hall houses temporary exhibits, which have focused on such varied subjects as ants (this was more fascinating than you might imagine), chocolate, and dinosaurs. The Steinhart Aquarium, also on the ground floor, is home to unusual snakes, poison dart frogs, box turtles, and numerous exotic fish. Daily at 11am and 3:30pm, a biologist feeds a pod of penguins, offering surprising details about penguin life and taking questions from the audience.

Upstairs, the Astrobiology center focuses on the study of life in the universe, which includes researching life in extreme environments. The Naturalist Center offers story time for children ages 3 to 7 and classes for older kids. The Nature Nest features costumes, model animals, and puppets for infants and toddlers. Unfortunately, the Morrison Planetarium is closed during the Academy's restoration process. Although the museum's exhibits have been abbreviated to accommodate the smaller, temporary home, this is still an excursion nature- and science-loving kids will enjoy. Breakfast and lunch items, including bagels, fruit, sandwiches, salads, and soups, are available at the Academy's Grow Cafe.

875 Howard St. (at 5th St.). © 415/321-8000. www.calacademy.org. Admission $10 adults; $6.50 seniors, children 12–17, and students; $2 children 4–11; free children under 4; free for all the 1st Wed of the month. Admission is $5 after 5pm on the 3rd Thursday of the month. Daily 10am–5pm. Third Thurs of month until 9pm.

California Palace of the Legion of Honor   All ages.

Constructed as a memorial to California's soldiers lost in World War I and opened to the public on Armistice Day in 1924, this neoclassical structure is a replica of the Legion of Honor Palace in Paris. The exquisite setting inside Lincoln Park alone makes it worth a visit. Take in the expansive lawn, Monterey cypress trees, and breathtaking western vista of the Golden Gate Bridge. The museum's fine collection spans 4,000 years and includes European paintings (by Monet and Rembrandt, among others), drawings, decorative arts, and one of the world's best collections of Rodin's sculptures, including an original cast of *The Thinker.* International tapestries, print, and drawings are also on display.

On Saturday mornings from 10:30am to noon, the museum offers free (with paid admission) classes for kids 3½ to 12. Kids view art and then engage in their own creative projects, such as painting or printmaking. (Space is limited. Phone © 415/682-2483 for information.) The cafe, which offers healthy and flavorful snack and lunch items in a delightful indoor/outdoor setting, is only accessible through the museum. If you can, come on a weekend afternoon to catch the 4pm organ concert. The museum's impressive 1924 Skinner pipe organ has 4,500 pipes varying in size from a half-inch to 32 feet, all hidden behind canvas painted to look like marble.

Clement St. and 34th Ave. © 415/863-3330. www.thinker.org/legion. Admission $10 adults, $7 seniors, $6 youths 13–17, free children 12 and under; free to all 1st Tuesday of the month. Tues–Sun 9:30am–5pm. Organ concerts Sat and Sun at 4pm. Muni: no. 38-Geary to 33rd Ave., then transfer to the no. 18-46th Ave

Cartoon Art Museum   Ages 6 and up.

Cartoons are taken seriously in these parts. Exhibits in the museum's five galleries a half block from Yerba Buena Center trace the history of cartoon art from political jabs to underground comics. Temporary shows highlight individual artists, such as Bill Watterson and Edward Gorey, and specific forms, such as television cartoon animation. Most of the comic strips are geared to adults. Given the inviting name of the museum, kids may be disappointed. Certainly they'll appreciate the collection of Disney cels and backgrounds that were actually used to make classics such as *Fantasia* and *Snow White,* but you could be better off just renting a Disney movie. Contact the museum for information on cartooning classes and 1-day workshops for kids.

655 Mission St. © **415/227-8666.** www.cartoonart.org. Admission $6 adults, $4 students/seniors, $2 kids 6–12. Tues–Sun 11am–5pm. First Tues of the month is "pay what you wish" day. Closed on Mon and major holidays. Muni: Any streetcar to Montgomery St.

The Contemporary Jewish Museum   Ages 8 and up. This museum has been designed as an evolving space welcoming people of all backgrounds to come together to experience art, music, film literature, and other expressions of the Jewish spirit and imagination. Among recent exhibits was the thought-provoking "Jewish Identity Project: New American Photography," which featured the work of 13 artists, not all of them Jewish, who profiled different Jewish communities throughout the U.S.—and shattered some stereotypes along the way. The museum is scheduled to move in 2008 to a dynamic new space in SoMa designed by architect Daniel Libeskind.

121 Steuart St. (between Mission and Howard sts.). © **415/344-8800.** www.thecjm.org. Sun–Thurs noon–6pm. Admission $5 adults, $4 students and seniors, free for kids 12 and under. Admission free 3rd Monday of every month. Muni: F-Market streetcar.

de Young Museum ✸✸✸   All ages. Designed by the Swiss architecture firm Herzog & de Meuron, the de Young raised eyebrows when its gleaming copper facade, with a 144-foot-tall tower soaring well above the forest canopy, first became visible. Residents complained that the imposing building had no place in a park, despite assurances from the architects that the copper—perforated and textured to resemble light streaming through trees—would eventually turn green, blending more seamlessly into the surroundings. That the copper has indeed begun to take on a subtle green sheen now seems irrelevant. The museum has won locals over since its 2005 opening.

Among the museum's many assets is, in fact, its architecture. Once inside, elements of light and nature weave together compellingly with unexpected angles and modern materials such as exposed concrete and glass. And while the museum's tower does soar beyond the treetops, it also affords a terrific view all the way to the Marin Headlands. That view is accessible to any visitor, free of charge. That complimentary access is another feature that sets the de Young apart: while visitors must pay an entrance fee to visit the museum galleries, vast swaths of common space are open to everyone. On a stroll through the park, you can step into the de Young, take in the impressive painting by Gerhard Richter that watches over the main lobby, head to the tower room and contemplate ethereal wire creations by renowned local sculptor Ruth Asawa, pop up to the top floor to take in the priceless view, and then walk out to the sculpture garden to appreciate works by such well-known artists as Joan Miro and Henry Moore—all for free. (One must-see sculpture in the garden is the *Three Gems* structure by James Turrell. If your kids stand in the middle of the unusual orb and talk, they'll feel their voices vibrate.)

While you can enjoy so much for free, I encourage you to pay the entrance fee (which, since kids 12 and under are free, is very reasonable) as the de Young houses a first-rate collection of American art and one of the world's most formidable collections of art from Africa, Oceania, and the Americas. (In the Oceania area, my daughters especially liked the Indonesian prayer boards, which look a lot like surfboards.) Every Saturday, from 10:30am to noon, museum docents lead tours of current exhibitions, followed by studio workshops taught by professional artist-teachers, which are appropriate for children ages 3½ to 12, although children under age 8 must be accompanied by an adult. (This program is also available from 1:30–3pm for museum members.) The de Young also has a first-rate cafe and an irresistible gift shop.

75 Tea Garden Dr. © 415/750-3600. www.thinker.org/deyoung. Admission $10 adults, $7 seniors, $6 youths 13–17, free children 12 and under. Admission tickets to the de Young may be used on the same day for free admission to the California Palace of the Legion of Honor. Free to all the 1st Tuesday of the month. Tues–Sun 9:30am–5pm (Fri open until 8:45pm). Muni: N-Judah streetcar to 9th Ave, then walk north on 9th into the park; no. 44-O'Shaughnessy bus to Concourse Dr.

Mission Dolores   Ages 6 and up. Visitors from other parts of California, especially those with middle school kids about to study its history, should not miss touring this small, old mission, the sixth of 21 California missions built by Native Americans under the rule of Franciscan missionaries. Formerly known as Mission San Francisco de Asis, this 1795 structure has the honor of being the oldest building in San Francisco, having survived earthquakes, fires, and a stint in the 1840s as a gambling den. Of note is the graveyard where Hitchcock filmed scenes for *Vertigo.* The self-guided audio tour takes 40 minutes.

3371 16th St. (at Dolores St.). © 415/621-8203. www.missiondolores.org. Admission $5 adults, $3 seniors and children 7–17; free children 6 and under. Audio tour $5. Daily 9am–4pm. Good Friday 9am–noon. Closed Thanksgiving, Easter, Dec. 25. Muni: J-Church streetcar to 16th St.; walk 1 block east.

Museum of the African Diaspora ✲   **Ages 6 and up.** Opened in 2006, this colorfully and creatively arranged museum explores the art, culture, and history of the people of African descent across the globe. Before stepping inside, head across the street to appreciate the three-story-tall image of an intense, beautiful young girl taken by photographer Chester Higgins, Jr. As you head up the stairs inside the museum, you'll see that her image is actually composed of thousands of photographs of members of the African diaspora. While some of the museum's exhibits—such as the empty room filled only with the narration of former slaves—may be too esoteric for young kids, two exhibits will be sure to draw them in. One features a man, woman, and child composed of continuously changing faces and clothing. The other is an interactive area where kids can listen to different types of African-influenced music, from ragtime and jazz to salsa and samba, and listen to different instruments representing each musical style. The tiny gift shop includes interesting collectibles like tiny, beaded African dolls.

685 Mission St. (at Third St.). © 415/358-7200. www.moadsf.org. Admission $10 adults, $5 students w/ID and seniors, free for kids 12 and under. Mon, Wed–Sat 10am–6pm; Sun 10am–5pm. Muni: Any streetcar to Montgomery St.

San Francisco Fire Department Museum   Ages 4 and up. This one-room museum next to a firehouse features display cases filled with artifacts tracing the history of San Francisco's fire departments, from volunteer firefighters to the beginnings of the professional squads of today. The floor display of antique equipment, including two steam engines, shows how far we've come.

655 Presidio Ave. (between Bush and Pine sts.). © 415/558-3546 (recorded info) or 415/563-4630 (during open hours). www.sffiremuseum.org. Free admission. Thurs–Sun 1–4pm. Muni: no. 43-Masonic, no. 4-Sutter, or no. 2-Clement bus.

San Francisco Museum of Modern Art (SFMOMA) ✲✲✲   **All ages.** The first museum on the West Coast devoted solely to post-turn-of-the-20th-century art, the SFMOMA took up residence in 1995 in its current home designed by Swiss architect Mario Botta. The impressive brick facade, accentuated by a black and white tower, opens to a sleek atrium and a set of black and gray stone stairs leading up the museum's four stories. The permanent collection includes more than 26,000 works, including

I Spy with My Little Eyes—SFMOMA

This quiz begins as you arrive at the front of the museum. Keep score to see how much you see. (And, remember, don't touch any of the art!)

1. How many striped pillars are there in the front of the museum? (Score 1 point)
2. There are two rainbow-colored paintings in the atrium as you enter the museum. What is the main difference between them? (Score 1 point)
3. Can you find a painting of a woman with a colorful hat? (Hint: There are at least two. Score 2 points for each painting you find.)
4. Find a painting of a musical instrument. (Hint: There are at least two. Score 1 point for each one you find.)
5. Find paintings with two or more rectangles. (Hint: There are at least three. Score 1 point for each one you find.)
6. Find a shiny sculpture. (Score 3 points.)
7. Find a sculpture with rounded edges and one with rough edges. (Score 2 points for each.)
8. Find a painting with silver in it. (Score 3 points.)
9. Find a painting with circles in it. (Score 2 points.)
10. Go to the outdoor sculpture terrace with an adult. Look out into the city. How many flags can you see on the building tops? (Score 1 point.)
11. On the fifth floor, find the turret bridge and walk across it to the other side. Take an adult! (Score 2 points.)
12. Find a painting or sculpture you really like. Tell your mom or dad what you like about it. See if there's a postcard with it pictured in the gift shop. (Score 5 points if your parent buys you the postcard.)

Answers:

1) 4 2) The main difference is the curved versus the straight lines 10) 4.

Add up your points. If your score was:

> 20 points or more: Your powers of observation are very good.
>
> 15 to 20 points: You don't need glasses.
>
> Less than 15 points: Start over (just kidding).

5,000 paintings by the likes of Henri Matisse, Piet Mondrian, Jackson Pollock, and Robert Rauschenberg. Other artists represented include Diego Rivera, Georgia O'Keeffe, and Paul Klee. The first museum to recognize photography as a major art form, the SFMOMA also has more than 9,000 photographs from such notables as Ansel Adams and Henri Cartier-Bresson. Although not enough of these wonderful art pieces are on view at any one time, the museum also hosts excellent temporary displays. Perhaps because of the colorful and arresting nature of much contemporary art, we've always found something here to hold the attention of even our very young daughters.

On the third Sunday of the month from noon to 3pm, children up to 10 years old are invited to create some artwork of their own in the Family Studio of the **Koret Education Center.** This activity is free with museum admission, and prior registration isn't necessary. Also, for 1 day in June and October, Family Day offers reduced admission rates to the museum and a full day of activities and performances geared towards kids under 10. On other days of the week, the center offers educational art videos, activities for kids, and art books geared for children, (Koret Center, ℂ **415/538-4693;** closes 15 minutes before the rest of the museum.)

The **Caffè Museo,** offering grilled sandwiches, salads, and soups, is a great place to grab lunch, although it's packed on weekends. The **Museum Store** is one of the better gift shops in town, carrying unique educational toys for very young children. Museum admission is not required to enter the cafe or gift shop.

151 3rd St. (2 blocks south of Market St. between Mission and Howard sts.). ℂ 415/357-4000. www.sfmoma.org. Admission $13 adults, $8 seniors, $7 students w/ID, free for kids 12 and under. Half-price Thurs 6–8:45pm. Free to all 1st Tues of the month. Thurs 11am–8:45pm; Fri–Tues 11am–5:45pm. Closed Wed and major holidays. Muni: Take any streetcar to the Montgomery St. Station or the no. 15-3rd, no. 30-Stockton, or no. 45-Union/Stockton bus.

3 The Best Views

People like views. That much is clear from the wrangling that goes on to get a table with a view in restaurants or the extra tariff imposed on a room with a view, not to mention a home with a view. San Francisco is one major view, owing to all those hills. Following are some of the best.

Alamo Square 👁 From this vantage point you will see the famous restored Victorian residences of "Postcard Row," with the downtown skyline as a stunning backdrop. The most common house type in many San Francisco neighborhoods, Victorian homes dating from the late 1800s and early 1900s meshed a variety of styles but had in common wooden frames and decorative facades. The most elaborate and colorful of these earned the nickname "Painted Ladies." Since your kids will see these houses in calendars and postcards as long as they live, you may want to show them the real thing. Just note that Alamo Square Park is popular with dog owners, some of whom do not leash their canine companions.

Between Steiner, Scott, Hayes, and Fulton sts. Muni: no. 21-Hayes bus from Market St. drops passengers off at the crest of the park.

Beach Chalet Restaurant The waves along Ocean Beach, at the end of Golden Gate Park on the Great Highway, are at times soothing and at times violent enough to discourage beachcombing. In either case, you'll be as comfy as a babe in his crib if you get a table upstairs in the Beach Chalet restaurant, which overlooks the Pacific across the Great Highway. The building was designed by Willis Polk, and the first-floor visitor center is adorned by murals painted in the 1930s by the same artist who painted the frescoes at Coit Tower. The food is decent, but the beer is better, so you could make this a rest stop after visiting the zoo or Golden Gate Park. (Another option is having a drink here before heading downstairs for a meal at the Park Chalet, which has the same owners but serves better fare.) The waves crashing along the coast are mesmerizing any time of day, but come at sunset if you can.

1000 Great Hwy. (between Lincoln Way and Fulton St.). ℂ 415/386-8439. www.beachchalet.com. Sun–Thurs 9am–10pm; Fri–Sat 9am–11pm. Muni: No. 18-46th Ave. bus, N-Judah streetcar to the end; walk 3 blocks north toward the park.

Cliff House This historic building on a bluff overlooking the Pacific Ocean reopened in late 2004 after a $19 million restoration. Views are awe-inspiring. See the Cliff House Bistro write-up on p. 164 for a full review.

1090 Point Lobos (Geary St., west of 48th Ave.). ℂ **415/386-3330.** Daily 9am–10pm. Muni: No. 38-Geary bus to 48th Ave., then walk 1 block or transfer to 18 bus.

Coit Tower ⊛
Visible from almost any spot on the Embarcadero, this 210-foot landmark was erected in 1933 through the generosity of local character Lillie Hitchcock Coit—who bequeathed $125,000 to erect a monument that would add beauty to the city. In addition to the panoramic vista at the top of the tower, the inside also contains a collection of impressive murals. Commissioned in the New Deal era, their pro-worker stance caused quite a stir at the time. Reflecting the style of Diego Rivera, under whom many of the artists had studied, the murals' two-dimensional and cartoonlike qualities may be appealing to your kids. If not, move quickly to the elevator for a ride to the top, which will be sure to spark their interest.

Atop Telegraph Hill. ℂ **415/362-0808.** Free viewing of murals; ride $4.50 adults, $3.50 seniors, $2 children 6–12, under 6 free. Daily 10am–6:30pm. Muni: No. 39-Coit bus from Washington Sq. Park in North Beach, or walk from Lombard St. where it meets Telegraph Hill Blvd. (2 blocks east of Stockton St.).

de Young Museum Tower
From here you'll get one of the best free views in town. This 144-foot-tall tower is open to all visitors, even if they haven't paid to enter the museum. You'll see fabulous views of northwestern San Francisco, from where you can see Golden Gate Park, the impressively tall Presidio, Lincoln Park, even the Pacific Ocean and the Marin Headlands beyond. Plus, the tower houses a massive aerial map of San Francisco, so detailed that you can probably work out which building on it is your hotel. The map has proved so popular that the museum put a gift shop in the tower so visitors could take home their own poster-sized version of it.

75 Tea Garden Dr. ℂ **415/750-3600.** www.thinker.org/deyoung. Free admission. Tues–Sun 9:30am–5pm (open Fri until 8:45pm). Muni: N-Judah streetcar to 9th Ave, then walk north on 9th into the park; no. 44-O'Shaughnessy bus to Concourse Dr.

Dolores Park
The city and bay views over this stretch of green on a clear day are unforgettable. After soaking in the scenery and taking a stroll through the park, walk 2 blocks north on Dolores Street until you reach **Mission Dolores** (reviewed earlier in this chapter) at 16th and Dolores streets.

The park is bounded by 18th, 20th, Church, and Dolores sts. Muni: From any Muni Metro station (the Powell St. Station being the closest to Union Sq.) take the J-Church toward Daly City. Exit on 20th and Church sts., above Dolores Park.

Lincoln Park
One of the prettiest golf courses in creation, Lincoln Park is situated around the Palace of the Legion of Honor and above the entrance to the San Francisco Bay at Land's End. Standing in front of the museum, you can see in the distance

---

⸤ Fun Fact ⸥ Stump the Tour Guide

If you hear that Coit Tower was built as a memorial to the city's firemen, go ahead and set the record straight. Although the Tower was built with funds bequeathed by Lillie Hitchcock Coit, whose lifelong passion for firefighters helped to make her a legend in her own time, her will stipulated only that she wished to beautify the city she loved. The tower is not meant to resemble a fire hose nozzle, by the way. It's just a fluted column.

So, where is the memorial to volunteer firemen paid for by Lillie Hitchcock Coit? It's in Washington Square Park.

a snippet of downtown framed within the green branches of fir trees. From here, walk west down the street. You'll be stunned by a postcard-perfect view of the Golden Gate Bridge from a unique perspective, as if you're entering the bay. Take a seat on one of the benches thoughtfully placed along the street so you can survey the vista in comfort.

The park is located at the northwest corner of the city. Muni: No. 18-46th Ave. bus to the Palace of the Legion of Honor parking lot.

Top of the Mark   In 1939, the top floor of the Mark Hopkins InterContinental was converted into a glass-walled lounge with 360-degree city views. During World War II, wives and girlfriends of Pacific-bound servicemen watched their loved ones' ships sail eastward below the Golden Gate Bridge from the windows of the northwest corner— soon nicknamed "Weepers' Corner." Now a restaurant serving a pricey buffet breakfast and lunch Monday to Saturday, an extended champagne brunch on Sundays, and prix fixe dinners Friday and Saturday, as well cocktails and light snacks most evenings, the Top sees plenty of visitors just popping up for the panoramic view. Note that after 8pm the Top requests "smart casual" attire and does not permit minors.

1 Nob Hill (at California and Mason sts.). ⓒ 415/616-6916. www.topofthemark.com. Hours of operation vary, but you can probably pop up to espy the view anytime. Sun 10am–2pm; Mon 6:30am–2:30pm; Tues–Thurs 6:30am–11:30pm; Fri–Sat 6:30am–1am. Muni: Any cable car to Powell and California sts., then walk 1 block west to California and Mason sts.

Twin Peaks   On a clear day you really can see forever from what's nearly the tallest hill in pretty much the center of town. The trick is to go when the fog has lifted. Otherwise, it's cold, windy, and gray. Outside of the view, there isn't anything else up on Twin Peaks and it's not really near anything, so before you drive or take the bus up here, be sure it's something everyone wants to do. The bus stops near, but not at, the viewpoint, so some walking will be involved.

Crestline Blvd. Muni: 37-Corbett bus (connect to the bus from the Castro St. Muni station).

4 Outings on the Bay

For a more private outing, consider chartering one of the boats through **Saillola.com** (p. 231).

Blue & Gold Fleet   **All ages.** One-hour narrated cruises travel to the Golden Gate Bridge, around Alcatraz, and to the Bay Bridge; the soundtrack is prerecorded. The prerecorded soundtrack offers details into San Francisco's maritime past and the history of Alcatraz and other places you'll see along the way.

Pier 41, Fisherman's Wharf. ⓒ 415/773-1188. www.blueandgoldfleet.com. Tours run daily year-round. 1-hour rides $19 adults, $15 seniors and students 12–17, $11 children 5–11, under 5 free. Discounts available on the Internet.

Golden Gate Ferry   **All ages.** Part of the Golden Gate Transit District, these commuter ferries run back and forth from Larkspur and Sausalito in Marin County to the Ferry Building at the foot of Market Street. It takes about 30 minutes from start to finish and bikes are allowed on board. Although these boats don't pass under the Golden Gate Bridge, they do travel near Alcatraz and Angel Island. For a low-key, brief, and inexpensive way to get on the water, you can't beat it. If your gang is up to it, you can pedal across the bridge to Sausalito (a 9-mile ride) and then return by ferry.

San Francisco Ferry Building, Market St. at Embarcadero. ⓒ 415/923-2000. www.goldengateferry.org. Tickets one-way to Sausalito $6.75 adults, $3.35 seniors and children 6–12, children 5 and under free (limit 2 kids per paying adult).

5 Crossing the Golden Gate Bridge

As *the* San Francisco landmark, this glorious feat of engineering never fails to elicit admiration from the millions of people who come to gaze at or cross the bridge year after year. Spanning 1¾ miles and soaring hundreds of feet above the water, the Golden Gate Bridge opened in 1937, after 4 years of construction and 11 lives lost. To experience the bridge, you can walk its length, bike it, drive over it, cruise under it, or appreciate it from afar.

BY FOOT   Bundle up against the windy conditions, then set out from the **Roundhouse** on the east side of the bridge. It can get pretty noisy, but the views can't be beat. Keep in mind the walk is round-trip; once you get to the other side there's no way back but to walk. Know your family's limitations before you start out. Strollers are a good idea for anyone small enough to fit. Upon your return, take time to walk underneath the bridge to see the 5-acre garden (open to pedestrians 6am–6pm daily). The no. 28-19th Avenue or the no. 29-Sunset bus deposits you across from the viewing area, right by a parking lot. If you're driving, take 19th Avenue or Lombard Street and pay attention to the sign that indicates when to exit for the parking lot. Otherwise, enjoy your drive across the bridge: there's a $5 toll upon your return to the city.

BY BIKE   If your kids are old enough, this may be a better way to go than on foot. Just note the restrictions on which sidewalks are open to bikes—on the weekends from 6am to 6pm and weekdays from 3:30 to 6pm, use the west sidewalk. At all other times, you'll be sharing the east sidewalk with pedestrians, who always have the right-of-way. Walk your bike around the towers. For information on bike rentals, see chapter 9.

BY BUS   The **no. 76-Marin Headlands** Muni bus picks up from Market and Fremont streets or along Lombard and rumbles all the way to the beach at Fort Cronkite in Marin. This route only operates on Sundays and major holidays (© **415/673-6864;** www.sfmuni.com).

BY FIRE ENGINE   See the "Best Guided Tours for the Family" section below for a unique way to cross the bridge.

6 Taking a Hike

Fort Funston 🎯🎯   At this Golden Gate National Recreation Area park, trails lead down to the beach where, in good weather, you may see hang gliders. This is also an extremely popular spot for dogs—just about everyone in town with an ocean-loving pooch comes here for a run. The majority of the trails are suitable for kids, especially the Battery Davis and Sunset trails. The old gun emplacements you may see are left over from the era when this was a military site. There are portable toilets around, but no snack bar. The closest restaurants are by the zoo, and they aren't all that inviting.

Skyline Blvd. (off Great Hwy.). © 415/561-4323 (phone for Presidio Visitor's Center, which provides info regarding Fort Funston). www.nps.gov/goga/fofu/index.htm. Muni: No. 18-46th Ave. bus (which stops near the Battery Davis trail), or L-Taraval streetcar to the end of the line and walk ½-mile south on Ocean Beach.

Fort Point 🎯   Kids get a thrill poking around this fort (ca. 1861) that lies underneath the Golden Gate Bridge at the tip of the peninsula. It was armed with cannons over the course of the Civil War, and early era weapons are on display at the fort. Park rangers give interpretive talks. A 3½-mile walk to Fort Point, beginning at the Hyde

Street Pier, passes through the Marina Green and Crissy Field (you can decrease the mileage by starting at Crissy Field). Due to restoration, the top level of Fort Point is currently closed.

Long Ave. and Marine Dr. ℂ **415/556-1693** or 415/561-4395. www.nps.gov/fopo. Fri–Sun 10am–5pm. Muni: No. 28-19th Ave. or no. 29-Sunset bus to the Golden Gate Bridge; climb down from the viewing area to a short trail leading to the fort.

Land's End ☆☆☆   The poetic name of this piece of national park becomes easier to comprehend when you stand at the Eagle's Point trailhead and look back at the Golden Gate Bridge. It imposingly guards the entrance to the bay and the cities behind it, with nothing but open ocean and the barren hills of the Marin Headlands in front. There is indeed something end-of-the-earth-like about it. The spectacular views accompany you throughout the entire 1.5-mile walk along the northwestern edge of the San Francisco Peninsula. You'll end at Sutro Park, an 18-acre park atop a bluff overlooking Ocean Beach and Seal Rocks. The cliff-side path narrows at times, so tell your kids to walk, not run.

Eagle's Point (at El Camino del Mar near 32nd St.). ℂ **415/561-4323** (phone for Presidio Visitor's Center, which provides info regarding Land's End). Muni: No. 38-Geary to Point Lobos.

Muir Woods ☆☆☆   Named in honor of Sierra Club founder and conservationist John Muir, 553-acre Muir Woods is what's left locally of the redwood forests that once dominated the Northern California coastline. Although not as immense as Redwood National Forest farther north, this pocket of old-growth redwoods is magnificent, and a range of trails here will suit hikers of all abilities.

Mill Valley. ℂ **415/388-2595**. www.nps.gov/muwo. Daily 8am–sunset. To get there, drive over the Golden Gate Bridge and take the Stinson Beach/Hwy. 1 exit west and follow the signs. Parking is limited so set out early on weekends or go during the week.

The Presidio ☆☆   On the northern tip of San Francisco lies this former property of the U.S. Army, now part of the Golden Gate National Recreation Area. Numerous trails are contained in the 1,500-acre site, taking you through forests of eucalyptus and pine or along the dramatic coastline. The Ecology Trail starts at the Presidio Officer's Club, where you can pick up trail maps and other information. It takes you along an easy 2-mile hike by the park's largest redwood grove to Inspiration Point, where you'll find a stellar Alcatraz view. The Juan Bautista de Anza National Historic Trail can be reached at the Presidio Gate, at Funston and Lake streets. The moderate 3-mile trek passes Mountain Lake and ends at the Golden Gate Bridge. For a shorter route with the kids, head east from Mountain Lake towards Julius Kahn Park. It's an easier walk with a delightful playground at the end as a reward.

Presidio Visitor Center, Presidio Officers' Club, Building 50, Moraga Ave. ℂ **415/561-4323**. www.presidio.gov and www.nps.gov/prsf. Visitors' Center open daily 9am–5pm. Closed major holidays. Muni to Officer's Club: 76-Marin Headlands or 43-Masonic bus, transfer at Lombard and Broderick sts. to 29-Sunset. Muni to Presidio Gate: No. 1-California to Presidio Blvd, walk north on Funston St.

7 Best Guided Tours for the Family

All About Chinatown! Walking Tours ☆   **Ages 8 and up.** Owner Linda Lee has been giving tours in Chinatown for over 2 decades. Having grown up in Chinatown, she offers an insider's look at this fascinating section of the city. Tours depart from Old St. Mary's Cathedral and last 2 or 3 hours, depending on whether you stay for a dim sum meal at the end. Linda Lee's little company has grown up, and you may find someone else guiding you through Chinatown's crowded alleyways, but fortunately all the tours offered are low-key and flexible. If you have young kids with you, guides will be happy to linger longer at the fortune cookie factory and in the neighborhood playgrounds, while keeping stops at temples to a minimum.

P.O. Box 640145, San Francisco, CA 94164. © 415/982-8839. www.allaboutchinatown.com. Daily 10am. Walking tours take 2 hours; 3 hours w/lunch. Adults walk only $28, w/lunch $40; kids 6–17 walk only $15, w/lunch $27; under 6 free.

City Guides (ﾐ   **Ages 10 and up.** There's hardly a section of the city that isn't covered by a City Guides walking tour. Not all are going to be interesting to kids, but log onto their website and see if you and they can agree on one of the 1½- to 2-hour walks scheduled during your trip. This is a superb way to get to know a neighborhood and it's free (although donations are gladly accepted). Reservations aren't even necessary. Just show up at the designated meeting point.

Starting locations vary. © 415/557-4266. www.sfcityguides.org. Schedules vary.

Explorer's Club (ﾐ   **Ages 5 and up.** Susan Edwards, who spent over 20 years in child development and education before starting this business, provides two programs under the Explorer's Club name: individualized tours for children and families and a day camp for local kids that runs during the summers and over holiday breaks. Her avid interest in nature and the city's history, combined with gentle enthusiasm and energy, make her an ideal guide/child-care provider. She will plan a one-of-a kind, half- or full-day outing for a family, or you can choose a tour from her website, all of which include door-to-door pickup and delivery. Tours run the gamut from hiking in Muir Woods to taking an in-depth look at the most famous San Francisco sites. Edwards can also design a unique program just for children over 5—either during the day, if no camps are scheduled, or for a "Kids' Night Out," a nighttime tour that includes dinner and an activity such as seeing a play or toasting marshmallows over a campfire on the beach. If you will need child-care during your San Francisco trip, check the Explorer's Club Camp calendar online to see if Edwards will be out and about the day you need help. If she has room (she takes a maximum of 13 kids out, with another adult supervisor), you and your child will both be in luck.

Mailing address: 693 Dartmouth St., San Francisco, CA 94134. © 415/902-7014. www.eckidsclub.com. Kids' camp $65 per day. Individual tour prices vary.

Fire Engine Tours (ﾐ   **All ages.** Suspend your dignity to don a ratty woolen cap, fringed knit scarf, and heavy fireman's jacket, then check your seat belt and prepare to be amused on a bumpy 75-minute ride in a 1955 Mack Fire Engine. The big red shiny Mack truck drives over the Golden Gate Bridge into Sausalito and back, and it may just be the most delightful way to cross this bridge. Tour guide Marilyn Katzman only

---

(**Fun Fact** **Stump the Tour Guide**

Question: Where's the most crooked street in San Francisco? *Answer:* No, it's not Lombard Street, despite being nicknamed "the crookedest street in the world." Lombard may be the most attractive crooked street anywhere, but the most crooked street in San Francisco is in Potrero Hill. Vermont Street, between 20th and 22nd streets, boasts six turns in 270 feet. Lombard has eight turns in a relatively lengthy 412 feet.

Fun Fact **Stump the Tour Guide**

Nine out of 10—maybe 99 out of 100—locals wouldn't be able to tell you what the official flower of San Francisco is (the dahlia) or the city's official colors (black and gold). Most San Franciscans don't even know that we have official anything, but we even have an official musical instrument—it's the piano-accordion because the very first one produced in the U.S. was built in San Francisco by the Guerrini Company in 1907.

If you don't have a tour guide to quiz, go ask the hotel concierge.

---

quits talking, singing, and leading cheers when the truck passes through streets that require a modicum of quiet. As you move past various landmarks and sights, Marilyn tosses out historical facts and figures mostly relating to fires and the folks who put them out. The "captain," her husband, Robert, chimes in on cue but mostly keeps the truck heading forward, sometimes at speeds resembling a roller coaster. The fire engine is so much fun, it's regularly rented out for birthday parties as well; my kids still sing the "Big Red Shiny Mack Fire Engine" song they learned at one of those parties.

Outside The Cannery on Beach St. ☎ 415/333-7077. www.fireenginetours.com. Tickets $40 adults, $30 teens/seniors, $25 kids 12 and under. Tours Wed–Mon unless it rains. Daily tours depart at 1pm; tours added at 11am, 3pm, and 5pm on other days. Phone for a schedule.

Gray Line Tours   **All ages.** Orientation tours by bus can be tedious for kids, most of whom would rather be outside experiencing the city instead of stuck on a bus listening to recorded commentary. When you don't have a lot of time to visit and you want to hit the highlights, however, these tours come in handy. Gray Line is the big kahuna of the industry, with a number of tours around San Francisco and beyond in red double-decker buses, motorized cable cars, and smaller vans. The "Deluxe City Tour" takes you to Twin Peaks, Mission Dolores, the Cliff House, Golden Gate Park, and the Golden Gate Bridge, and there's also an Alcatraz Island option.

Departure points vary by tour. ☎ 415/558-9400. www.graylinesanfrancisco.com. Tours offered daily year-round. Tickets for the Deluxe City Tour #1 are $44 adults, $42 for seniors 60 and up, $22 kids 5–11, under 5 free.

Local Taste of the City Tours 🐾🐾   **Ages 6 and up.** For kids who have a gastronomic bent and an adventuresome palate, this could prove an interesting way to see the city. The brainchild of Tom Medin, a cookbook author and former national park tour guide with an interest in preserving local artisans, these neighborhood walking tours will have your family eating its way through the city. The 3-hour daytime or evening excursions focus on a specific SF neighborhood—North Beach, Fisherman's Wharf, Golden Gate Park, Chinatown, or Haight-Ashbury—taking guests into local bakeries, restaurants, and cafes to sample the food and meet the people who make it. Each tour is followed by the option of a full meal at a local restaurant. (Then again, after the North Beach tour, with its aromatic Italian bakeries and old-time coffee shops, you may not be able to eat a full meal for the rest of the day.)

Departure points vary by tour. ☎ 888/358-8687 or 415/665-0480. www.sffoodtour.com. Daily at 10am, 2pm, or 6pm. $59 adults, $39 youth 15–18; $15 ages 8–14; under 8 free.

Precita Eyes Mural Art Center 🐾   **Ages 6 and up.** The Mission is filled with exciting and politically charged murals, but why? And who painted them? For the answers to those questions and a tour of the paintings, sign up with this nonprofit arts center. The 6-block, 2-hour walk, which passes 75 murals, departs from the center Saturdays and Sundays at 1:30pm. A brief slide show on the history of mural art precedes the walk. On Saturdays at 11am, a slightly shorter walk showing 50 murals departs from Café Venice, 3325 24th St. (near the 24th St. BART station), and on Sundays at 11am the shorter tour departs from the Precita Eyes center.

2981 24th St. (near Harrison St.). ℭ 415/285-2287. www.precitaeyes.org. $12 adults (shorter 11am tour is $10 for adults), $8 students w/ID, $5 seniors, $2 children under 18. Reservations are not necessary unless you have a large group.

The Urban Safari   All ages. Your kids will be so excited to be riding in a zebra-striped Land Rover, donning their own personal pith helmets, while being driven by a guide in a full safari get-up—that they won't have time to get bored. You can choose from a variety of 4-hour morning tours, focusing on movies, plantlife, the bay, or whatever interests your family. You can also opt for 4-hour excursions at midday or in the early evening. The tours are pricey, but the Land Rover will come to pick you up at the location of your choice.

Departure points vary by tour. ℭ 866/MY-SAFARI (866/697-2324). www.theurbansafari.com. $100 for the first 4 guests, $75 for each additional person in the group.

8

Neighborhood Strolls

San Francisco is one of the few U.S. cities west of the Mississippi that came to fruition before the advent of the automobile. That pre-car development meant that neighborhoods grew up being pedestrian-friendly. Moreover, the city's quirky geography—at the tip of a peninsula with water on three sides—has prevented the sprawl seen elsewhere. San Francisco is in fact the second most densely populated city in the country.

What this implies for you and yours is that San Francisco is a wonderful place to take in the fresh sea air and savor the neighborhoods on foot. A leisurely stroll in most any quarter is sure to be full of visual treats, from shop windows to sidewalk cafes, from interesting architectural highlights to unexpected gardens, from enchanting views to the unique and colorful residents themselves.

The hills can be a challenge, of course, but the reward is often another jaw-dropping city vista. A more difficult task may be encouraging your kids to hoof it with you. Strollers will help, except on the staircases of Russian Hill and Telegraph Hill. Fortunately, I've noted playgrounds, coffee shops, and restaurants where you can take frequent rest stops. Just take your time and have fun!

WALKING TOUR 1	CHINATOWN

Start:	Dragon Gate.
Finish:	Portsmouth Square.
Time:	Two hours with shopping breaks; 3 hours with lunch.
Best Time:	Weekday mornings.
Worst Time:	Saturday when everyone is out.

Start your tour at the intersection of Bush Street and Grant Avenue, at:

❶ The Dragon's Gate

Chinatown's best-known entryway mirrors traditional gateway arches found in many Chinese villages. The stone lions on either side of the arch are meant to protect against evil spirits. The dragons and fishes on the pagoda atop the arch signify prosperity. It's tough to take a bad photo here.

Walk north up:

❷ Grant Avenue

This bustling street is lined with jewelry stores and tourist shops, whose overflowing array of eclectic wares will mesmerize your children. To keep the kids moving along, let them know that many more such shops lie ahead.

Continue up Grant Avenue to Pine Street. Turn right on Pine. Halfway down the block you'll find:

❸ St. Mary's Square

Here you'll find an imposing 12-foot tall, metal statue of Sun Yat-Sen, the first president of the Republic of China. Younger kids can enjoy a playground with fun, colorful structures.

herb shops sell dried plants and animal parts, which are weighed out using old-fashioned balance scales, following pre-scriptions written by traditional Chinese healers. Other stores sell ceremonial "money" and paper goods to be burnt as offerings to ancestors. Even paper DVD players and washing machines are for sale, as no one knows for sure what's needed in the afterlife.

Walk down to Clay Street and turn right. Go to 965 Clay St., to the:

⑫ Chinese Historical Society of America

Founded in 1963, the purpose of the society is to record and disseminate infor-mation about the history and contribu-tions of Chinese immigrants in America. Here you'll find artifacts, documents, and photographs, such as clothing from the earliest immigrants, traditional herbs, and the original Chinatown telephone book. (For open hours and admission, see p. 180.)

Now walk east on Clay Street past Grant Avenue. On your left you'll find:

⑬ Portsmouth Square

Captain John B. Montgomery of the USS *Portsmouth* raised a flag here in 1846 to declare San Francisco part of the United States. A year later California's first public school was opened on the plaza, and just a year after that Sam Brannan announced the discovery of gold in the state. Today, the square is an important communal center for Chinatown residents, who practice tai chi, gamble over cards, or bring children to frolic here. Grab a seat on a bench and let the kids run around to work up an appetite.

Walk down Clay Street to Kearny Street and make a right. Go to 631 Kearney St., where you can:

> **TAKE A BREAK**
> If you're ready for a substantial meal, try **The R&G Lounge,** which features more authentic menu items than you find in many Chinese restau-rants. See p. 134.

WALKING TOUR 2	THE EMBARCADERO & FISHERMAN'S WHARF

Start:	AT&T Park.
Finish:	Aquatic Park.
Time:	Half a day.
Best Time:	Any warm weekday.
Worst Time:	Any summer Saturday when PIER 39 is packed with tourists.

This is an easy, flat 3-mile stroll that's meant to take a good half day with stops to play and eat.

To get to AT&T Park, take the closest Muni street-car. All the underground streetcars, except certain N-Judah trains, end at the Embarcadero Station. If you are not already on an N-Judah that goes to the Mission Bay/Cal Train Station, cross to the other side of the platform at the Embarcadero Station and board one. As you come out from below ground, look for the large brick Hills Plaza, at 345 Spear St., constructed in 1925. Just south of this national landmark building is:

❶ AT&T Park

This home of the San Francisco Giants baseball team, located at 2nd and King streets, was the first privately financed major league baseball park since Dodger Stadium in 1962. A fun playground behind the bleachers has an 80-foot wooden Coca-Cola bottle with some of the best slides in town. There's also an

The "Only in San Francisco" Checklist of Rare or Unusual Sights

As you wander around town, look for the people and objects listed below. Some are easier to find than others, but if you check off more than half, you've really gotten around.

- **Art cars:** Keep your eyes peeled for weird and wonderful autos. You'll know one when you see it. There's a GI Joe–covered station wagon and other cars painted in weird and wacky colors, traveling canvases of public art. The end of September brings the ArtCar Fest to the Bay Area (**www.artcarfest.com**), a gathering of these wildly decorated vehicles and the people who love them.

- **Critical mass:** On the last Friday of every month at 5:30pm, a huge group of gonzo bicyclists takes over the streets, much to the consternation of any drivers who get caught unawares. The launch pad is usually the Embarcadero BART Station. The path varies.

- **A Chinatown funeral procession:** Look for a fancy convertible decorated with pictures of the deceased followed by the Green Street Band playing Western pop tunes. Funeral corteges generally tour North Beach and Chinatown.

- **The doorman at the Sir Francis Drake:** For over 27 years, Tom Sweeney has greeted guests of the Sir Francis Drake dressed in a traditional beefeater outfit.

- **Lotta's Fountain:** The meeting place every April 18 at 5:13am for the few remaining survivors of the 1906 earthquake and fire. The fountain served as a community bulletin board where people left notes for missing friends and family after the disaster. Thousands met here on the quake's 100th anniversary. You'll spot it on the corner of Market and Kearny streets.

- **The rock balancer:** Bill Dan rides his bike to Crissy Field many afternoons and promptly draws huge crowds by balancing large rocks on top of each other in apparently gravity-defying ways. He uses no glue, yet his towers miraculously withstand the afternoon breezes.

- **The twins:** Nob Hill residents Vivian and Marian Brown, blond, coiffed, 70-something identical twin sisters, are local celebrities simply for dressing exactly alike (fabulously so) and never being seen without one another. Spotting them is said to be good luck!

- **The wild parrots of Telegraph Hill:** A famous flock of wild green parrots, descendents of escapee pets, roosts in the trees around the Filbert Steps. Listen for the noise of their cawing and then see if you can spot these cherry-headed birds.

- **Robin Williams:** The actor/comedian lives near Baker Beach and is said to jog along Crissy Field. Occasionally he shows up unannounced at local comedy clubs.

Walking Tour: The Embarcadero & Fisherman's Wharf

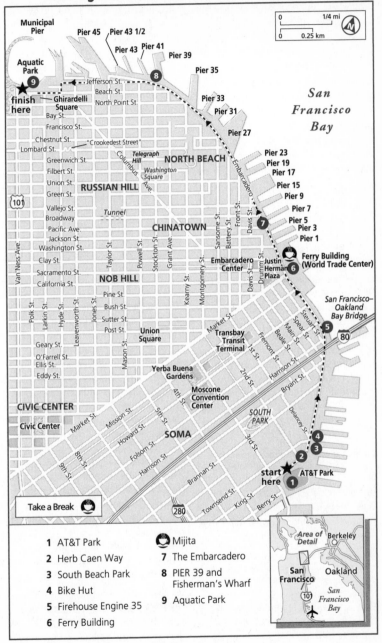

1 AT&T Park
2 Herb Caen Way
3 South Beach Park
4 Bike Hut
5 Firehouse Engine 35
6 Ferry Building

Mijita
7 The Embarcadero
8 PIER 39 and Fisherman's Wharf
9 Aquatic Park

area where kids can practice their own game of baseball and a parked cable car that's a hit with little ones. The play area is free and open to the public unless there's a game going on.

From the stadium, walk north on:
❷ Herb Caen Way

This section of the Embarcadero honors the departed newspaper columnist Herb Caen, who reported on the city's movers and shakers and wrote about San Francisco with humor and passion for 50 years.

On the right you'll come to:
❸ South Beach Park

This park contains a little playground suitable for preschoolers. The 70-foot-tall, 10-ton sculpture by Mark di Suvero is called "Sea Change."

Continuing along the Embarcadero, the next landmark you come to on Pier 40 is the:
❹ Bike Hut

The owner of this not-for-profit shop hires and trains at-risk youth to repair bikes, and he's a bit of a character in his own right. If you decide to abandon your walk in favor of a bike ride, you can rent a bike for $5 an hour or $20 per day. Fees include a lock and helmet. Open daily 10am to 6pm (© 415/543-4335; www.thebikehut.com).

Continue down the Embarcadero toward the Bay Bridge. On your right is Pier 24, the home of:
❺ Firehouse Engine 35

Peek through the fence to see Fireboat 1. If you've ever wondered what happens if a ship catches fire, now you know.

The view opens up as you pass the bridge. Sailboats ply the water, bicyclists and skaters zip by, and coming into view is the:
❻ Ferry Building

Built in 1898, this building was once the city's transportation hub. Today, the elegantly refurbished building houses some of the best gourmet food stores in the city. Before 2pm on Tuesdays, Saturdays, and spring and fall Sundays, you'll find a terrific farmer's market here (also on Thursday evenings in spring and fall). Saturdays are the big day, with musicians strumming in the back area while you enjoy free samples of ripe fruits, roasted nuts, and local cheeses.

TAKE A BREAK
On Saturdays, buy breakfast from one of the restaurant carts behind the Ferry Building. Grab a bench and enjoy a mouth-watering meal as you watch the ferries come and go. At other times, one of our favorite destinations in the Ferry Building is **Mijita** (p. 139), with its inexpensive, but top-quality, Mexican specialties such as fresh fish tacos and hearty burritos, all enjoyed with a view of the bay.

Continue northwest, along:
❼ The Embarcadero

The entire stretch of oceanfront walkway between the Ferry Building and Fisherman's Wharf is a magnet for pedestrians, cyclists, and runners. Pier 7 was a celebrated skateboarding destination for youths from diverse backgrounds until barriers were placed to prevent them from getting fresh air and exercise. Well, I'm not sure why the barriers were put there, but it's too bad. Anyway, what you will find along this stretch of city, in addition to views of the bay and urban skyline, are several 13-foot-tall metal pylons and bronze plaques embedded in the sidewalk. The pylons and plaques are imprinted with photographs, drawings, poetry, and historical facts about the waterfront.

Continue along the water until you get to:
❽ PIER 39 & Fisherman's Wharf

The distance from Pier 7 to PIER 39 is less than a mile, but as you approach Fisherman's Wharf the activity level rises

---

Tips Feet, Don't Fail Me Now

If little legs tire, there are alternatives. The F-Market streetcar makes several stops on its route down Market Street to the Ferry Building and just beyond PIER 39. You'll also see "pedicabs," pedal-powered minicabs, wheeling around the Embarcadero. Two or three people can fit on the single seat, and the driver will whisk you off to a nearby destination for $4 to $8 per person, depending on where you're headed.

---

dramatically. The number of families waiting for ferries to Alcatraz or Sausalito combined with tourists milling around the boardwalk gives a carnival-like feel to the atmosphere. It can overwhelm younger children, so keep an especially close watch on yours. There are plenty of things to see in this area (see the "Fisherman's Wharf" section under "The Top Attractions," in chapter 7, for details). You may want to end your tour here, but I'd suggest forging ahead, as the nicest part of the wharf lies just beyond.

Once you pass the masses on Jefferson Street, the crowd thins and the city begins to feel like it's yours again by the time you reach the end of this stroll at:

❾ Aquatic Park
You have reached the **Hyde Street Pier,** the Municipal Pier, a large grassy park, and a small strip of man-made beach. Every morning, hearty members of the Dolphin Club brave the beach's frigid waters, where temperatures usually linger in the low 50s (or low teens Celsius), rarely cresting 60°F (16°C). Kids will enjoy playing in the sand or running around on the grassy park. Walk out on the municipal pier for great views, or head up to **Ghirardelli Square** for views of the bay from on high.

WALKING TOUR 3   SOUTH OF MARKET

Start:	Palace Hotel.
Finish:	Westfield San Francisco Centre.
Time:	Two hours to a half day depending on how long you spend at Yerba Buena Gardens and the other attractions.
Best Time:	Weekends when there's entertainment at Yerba Buena Gardens.
Worst Time:	Anytime Zeum is closed.

This stroll doesn't cover much square footage, as the attractions south of Market Street are contained in the blocks between Market and Howard streets from 2nd to 5th streets. There are so many, however, that you could spend most of the day here.

Begin your walk at 2 New Montgomery St. at Market Street, at the:

❶ Palace Hotel
The stained-glass-domed Garden Court dining room at this historic landmark was formerly the carriage entrance. With its massive marble columns and ceiling made from 80,000 panes of glass, it is one of the most extraordinary public rooms in the city. Poke your heads into the **Pied Piper Bar** as well to regard the $2.5 million Maxfield Parrish painting of the same name.

Next, walk east on New Montgomery to Mission Street and turn right. Across the street, at 655 Mission St., is the:

❷ Cartoon Art Museum

This small gallery contains movie cels, political cartoons, and underground comics. Although younger kids may enjoy seeing scenes from Disney movies and teens may appreciate the more sophisticated political cartoons, I find this place somewhat limited, considering the entrance fee. If the weather is bad, step inside. Otherwise, give yourself more time at Yerba Buena Gardens.

Almost next door, at 685 Mission St., is the:

❸ Museum of the African Diaspora

This diminutive museum celebrates the contributions of peoples of African descent across the globe. Though a bit pricey for its size, it does have some worthwhile exhibits, starting with the 3-story-tall portrait of an African girl (made up of thousands of photos) visible from outside.

Now cross the street. At 678 Mission St., step into the:

❹ California Historical Society

The collection is aimed at researchers, but a quick look at the surveyor's maps, photographs, Native American artifacts, and exhibit on the California missions and Junipero Serra will take at most 20 minutes and could give your student a heads up in history class. Open Wednesday through Sunday. Call ☎ **415/357-1848** or visit www.californiahistoricalsociety.org for more information.

Continue heading down Mission Street. Make a left on 3rd Street. On your left will be the:

❺ San Francisco Museum of Modern Art (SFMOMA)

In addition to a spectacular permanent collection of 20th-century art and equally impressive temporary exhibits, the museum's Learning Lounge offers activities for kids.

> **TAKE A BREAK**
> The **Caffé Museo** at the SFMOMA has tasty soups, salads, and sandwiches, as well as indoor and outdoor seating.

A walk up 4th Street and a left onto Market Street brings you to the:

❻ Yerba Buena Gardens

After solemnly viewing modern art, your kids will be glad for the opportunity to run around and stretch their legs. Depending on ages and interests, they can enjoy the play area and slides, carousel, ice skating rink, bowling lanes, or Zeum. (The full list of options are described under "Yerba Buena Gardens" and "Zeum" in chapter 7.) Or you can just stroll around the gardens that border Mission Street. Here you'll find a waterfall memorial honoring Dr. Martin Luther King, Jr., which kids love to run behind, and a "Sister Cities" garden.

If your kids are ready for another educational experience, head southwest to Howard Street and turn right. Cross 4th Street to 875 Howard St., to the:

❼ California Academy of Sciences

In its temporary location until October 2008, this natural history museum and aquarium has an array of fascinating and instructive displays about the natural world.

From the front door, turn left on Howard Street and right on 5th Street. Walk up to the corner of Market Street. Here you'll find the:

❽ Westfield San Francisco Centre

If family members still have energy after the edifying excursion throughout SoMa, there's always the mall—and what a mall it is. The 1.5 million–square-foot complex, reportedly the largest shopping center in an urban area, features a 102-foot-wide skylit dome built in 1908. You'll find a massive Bloomingdale's and a sizable Nordstrom. Kids may like the Sanrio (makers of Hello Kitty) store below the

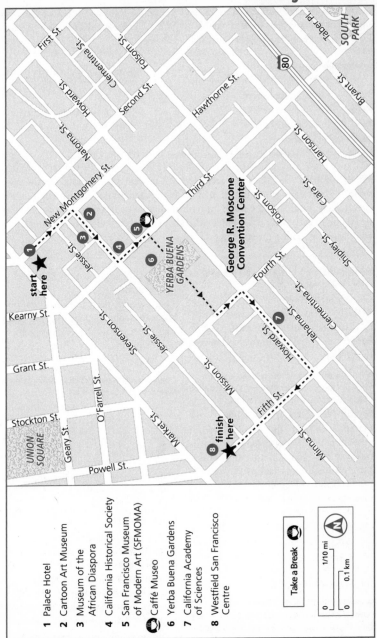

1 Palace Hotel

2 Cartoon Art Museum

3 Museum of the African Diaspora

4 California Historical Society

5 San Francisco Museum of Modern Art (SFMOMA)

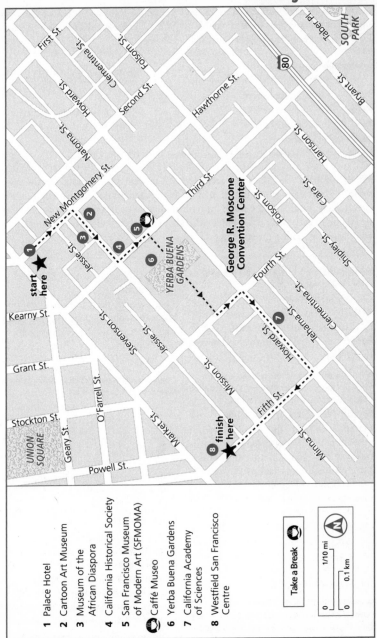 Caffé Museo

6 Yerba Buena Gardens

7 California Academy of Sciences

8 Westfield San Francisco Centre

Take a Break

start here

finish here

Kearny St.

Grant St.

Stockton St.

UNION SQUARE

Geary St.

Powell St.

O'Farrell St.

Stevenson St.

Jessie St.

Market St.

Mission St.

Fifth St.

Minna St.

Natoma St.

New Montgomery St.

Howard St.

National St.

Second St.

Folsom St.

Clementina St.

First St.

Hawthorne St.

Harrison St.

Third St.

Folsom St.

Fourth St.

Clementina St.

Tehama St.

Howard St.

Clara St.

Shipley St.

Bryant St.

Taber Pl.

SOUTH PARK

George R. Moscone Convention Center

YERBA BUENA GARDENS

Jessie St.

80

0   1/10 mi

0   0.1 km

Nordstrom or the Discovery Store in the mall's new wing. There are also plenty of kids' clothing options for ages 0 to 18. If everyone's ready to go home, the Powell Street Muni and BART stations are across the street.

WALKING TOUR 4   RUSSIAN HILL TO TELEGRAPH HILL

Start: Lombard Street.
Finish: Levi Strauss Plaza.
Time: Three hours.
Best Time: Mornings.
Worst Time: Weekend afternoons when Lombard Street fills with cars.

"Stroll" probably isn't the most accurate word to describe this walk. Encompassing some hills and stairways, you'll see many of San Francisco's best known sights, but this trek is really for kids who need to burn off some energy. If there's a chance you'll end up having to carry a child, I'd think twice about this tour. Hills are steep and strollers will make negotiating the stairways difficult.

Start anywhere you can pick up the Powell-Hyde cable car and exit at:

❶ Lombard Street

"The Crookedest Street in the World" isn't even the crookedest in San Francisco, but it is pretty. Walk down the staircases on either side of the car-clogged road.

At Leavenworth Street turn left and walk 1 block to Chestnut Street. Turn right and look for 800 Chestnut St., where you'll find the:

❷ San Francisco Art Institute

Founded in 1871, this is the oldest art school in the West. A fountain in the entrance courtyard has a handful of surprisingly small carp that tots may want to peer at before you enter the Diego Rivera Gallery (to your left) to admire a 1931 mural by the Mexican artist, as well a changing collection of student artwork. The **Art Institute Café** is a good place for an inexpensive lunch with a great view. Next to the cafe is a balcony offering an unobstructed bay view.

Walk downhill 1½ blocks east to Columbus Avenue, which cuts through North Beach. Head right to the junction of Columbus, Mason, and Lombard streets.

❸ Joe DiMaggio North Beach Playground

This 2½-acre park includes two pools, bocce ball courts, and a large playground (the entrance to the playground is on Greenwich St.). Take a break here before you head on your uphill trek.

From the park, walk ½ block south on Columbus Avenue to 754 Columbus Ave.

> **TAKE A BREAK**
> Fortify yourselves for the uphill trek. At **XOX Truffles,** sip an espresso and treat the kids to a chocolate truffle. Peanut butter and white chocolate are two flavors popular with the little ones. See p. 255.

Walk back to Greenwich Street. Walk east 2½ blocks. A half block past Grant Avenue are the Greenwich Steps, which lead to:

❹ Pioneer Park & Coit Tower

Listen for the wild parrots carrying on. Then get your camera ready to photograph both the birds and the stellar view from Coit Tower, a 210-foot landmark that boasts some of the greatest views in the city.

1 Lombard Street
2 San Francisco Art Institute
3 Joe DiMaggio North Beach Playground
XOX Truffles
4 Pioneer Park and Coit Tower
5 Filbert Steps
6 Levi Strauss Plaza

On either side of Pioneer Park are more stairs;
the wooden ones on the south side are the:

❺ Filbert Steps

Take the stairs down the hill, stopping to
exclaim over the Grace Marchant garden
and the Victorian cottages, some of the
oldest homes in the city. As you'll notice,
no cars can come this way . . . imagine
taking groceries home!

The steps will bring you to:

❻ Levi Strauss Plaza

Here are the headquarters of Levi Strauss &
Co, which was founded in San Francisco.

Legend has it that during the gold rush,
Levi Strauss had the idea of making
trousers out of tent fabric and he strength-
ened the pockets with rivets so that they
could withstand the work of mining and
the weight of gold. History is also found
under the plaza, below which lie some of
the hundreds of ships abandoned by
crews eager to head for the hills during the
height of the gold rush. The kids can
reward themselves for their walking efforts
with a frolic in the plaza's walk-through
fountain; they won't get wet unless it's on
purpose.

WALKING TOUR 5   **THE MARINA**

Start:	Palace of Fine Arts.
Finish:	Fort Mason.
Time:	At least 3 hours, depending how long you stay at the Exploratorium.
Best Time:	Mornings.
Worst Time:	Evenings.

This walk takes you through one of the more scenic residential neighborhoods of San
Francisco. Plan on spending all morning here, or longer, if you want more time for
the Exploratorium.

Starting from Union Square, take the no. 30-
Stockton bus to The Marina. Exit at the corner
of Broderick and Jefferson streets. Walk 1 block
east to Baker Street and continue across the
lawn. On your left you'll see the:

❶ Exploratorium

A terrific institution dedicated to interactive education, this science museum will
delight kids of all ages and their parents.
Plan to spend at least an hour here.

Adjacent to the Exploratorium is:

❷ The Palace of Fine Arts

This is the only structure left from the
Panama-Pacific Exhibition of 1915. Kids
can enjoy running around the lovely
grounds of this neoclassical dome and
gazing at the ducks, swans, geese, and
seagulls in the pond.

From here walk up Baker Street towards the
water. Cross Marina Boulevard and go straight

ahead to the Marina breakwater. Walk to the
end of the breakwater, where you'll find the:

❸ Wave Organ

Designed by scientists from the Exploratorium, this unusual structure is an amazing
piece of environmental art. Listening
tubes emerge from the water below the
concrete and rock structure, capturing
the ebb and flow of the ocean currents in
strange gurgling and humming sounds.

From here, walk back to the start of the jetty
and head east. You'll be walking along the:

❹ Marina Green

This stretch of lawn along the San Francisco Bay is a popular place to run, walk,
bike, or rollerblade. On weekends, it's full
with kids playing soccer and, especially
on windy afternoons, people flying myriad colorful and acrobatic kites.

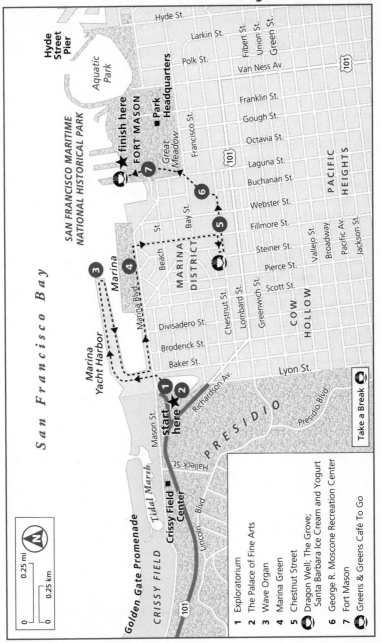

Walking Tour: The Marina

San Francisco Bay

Hyde Street Pier

Aquatic Park

SAN FRANCISCO MARITIME NATIONAL HISTORICAL PARK

Golden Gate Promenade

CRISSY FIELD

Tidal Marsh

Crissy Field Center

Marina Yacht Harbor

Marina

FORT MASON

Great Meadow

Park Headquarters

finish here

start here

PRESIDIO

COW HOLLOW

MARINA DISTRICT

PACIFIC HEIGHTS

Hyde St.
Larkin St.
Polk St.
Van Ness Av.
Filbert St.
Union St.
Green St.
Franklin St.
Gough St.
Octavia St.
Laguna St.
Buchanan St.
Webster St.
Fillmore St.
Steiner St.
Pierce St.
Scott St.
Divisadero St.
Broderick St.
Baker St.
Lyon St.
Richardson Av.
Presidio Blvd.
Lincoln Blvd.
Halleck St.
Mason St.
Marina Blvd.
Chestnut St.
Lombard St.
Greenwich St.
Vallejo St.
Broadway
Pacific Av.
Jackson St.
Beach St.
Bay St.
Francisco St.

101

Take a Break

0.25 mi
0.25 km

N

1 Exploratorium
2 The Palace of Fine Arts
3 Wave Organ
4 Marina Green
5 Chestnut Street
Dragon Well; The Grove; Santa Barbara Ice Cream and Yogurt
6 George R. Moscone Recreation Center
7 Fort Mason
Greens & Greens Café To Go

217

Walk until you reach Fillmore Street and then turn right. Walk down to Chestnut Street and turn right.

❺ Chestnut Street

Lined with shops and cafes, this popular street is in one of the most family-oriented neighborhoods of San Francisco. The plethora of strollers is a guarantee that you'll find plenty of family-friendly restaurants here. Your kids may want to stop at **Catnip and Bones** (2220 Chestnut St.) to pick up a gift for your pet back home. If another sibling is on the way, stop by **Dress Maternity** (2258 Chestnut St.) to shop for some of the most stylish maternity attire anywhere.

TAKE A BREAK
Among the many kid-friendly places to eat on this street is **Dragon Well** (p. 151), which serves fresh and healthy Chinese food. If it's sunny, snag an outdoor table at **The Grove** (p. 151), which has great salads and sandwiches. After lunch, buy a cone at **Santa Barbara Ice Cream and Yogurt** at 2240 Chestnut St., which carries **Mitchell's Ice Cream** (p. 162), the best in town.

Walk east on Chestnut Street, continuing across Fillmore Street. On your left you will see the:

❻ George R. Moscone Recreation Center

The soccer and baseball fields here fill up with boys and girls at team practice in the afternoons and weekends. Younger kids will love the enclosed playground, which has structures appropriate for toddlers and children up to 8 years old, as well as the only two seesaws I've seen in San Francisco. The Marina branch of the public library next to the playground has a nice children's section and will have a new teen zone when it reopens in early 2007.

From Chestnut Street you can catch the no. 30-Stockton bus back to downtown. If you are still raring to go, walk northeast across the park, towards the corner of Laguna and Bay streets. Cross Bay Street. On your right will be:

❼ Fort Mason

The collection of piers, buildings, and expansive lawn known as Fort Mason belonged to the U.S. military until 1972. During World War II and the Korean conflict, it was the point of embarkation for well over a million U.S. servicemen. Let kids run around on the grass while you enjoy the view or walk down to the **Fort Mason Center** to check out the many diverse museums there.

TAKE A BREAK
If you're ready to eat again, don't miss **Greens** (p. 149), a great vegetarian restaurant with one of the best views in town. Or stop at **Greens To Go**, where you can pick up a drink and pastry and then walk out to admire the view from the sailboat marina next to Fort Mason.

WALKING TOUR 6 **THE VERTICAL TOUR**

Start:	Union Square.
Finish:	Westin St. Francis Hotel.
Time:	Ninety minutes.
Best Time:	Sundays or any day at dusk.
Worst Time:	Check-in and checkout times at the hotels (9–11am and 3–4pm).

This tour takes you up, down, and around downtown as you hunt out the most exciting of the city's glass elevators.

From Union Square, walk east on Post Street toward Market Street. At Kearny Street, turn right and walk to Market Street. See who can find Lotta's Fountain, an important icon of the 1906 earthquake. (Painted gold, it's hard to miss.) Continue walking toward the bay down Market Street. Turn left on Drumm Street to the:

❶ Hyatt Regency Hotel

Inside the atrium lobby, look for the bank of five glass elevators. One was used in the Mel Brooks movie *High Anxiety*. There may be a line of people waiting to ride the 20 stories up to the Equinox Restaurant, which revolves and provides a fabulous panoramic view but only mediocre food. The mostly interior view from the elevators is grand; the lobby of the Hyatt, with its sculpture, greenery, and terraces, is a spectacular sight.

When you are finished with the Hyatt, stop by the Ferry Building across the Embarcadero to admire the restored atrium and glass skylights. Then board a California Street cable car (a ½ block from the Hyatt) and get off at Mason Street, which will put you right in front of the:

❷ Fairmont Hotel

You'll find the Fairmont's glass elevator at the east end of the hotel. Running at 500 feet per minute, it won't take long to ascend the 24 stories to the Fairmont Crown. You'll see Coit Tower to the left, Chinatown straight ahead, and SoMa and the South Bay to the right.

Back on the lobby level, walk down the hall on the California Street side of the hotel and out the back to the Fairmont's garden. When you are ready to resume, cross California Street and head downhill (south) on Mason Street. At Post Street, turn right and walk into the:

❸ JW Marriott Hotel

If it looks vaguely familiar, that's because its designer, John C. Portman, also designed the Hyatt Regency. The Pan Pacific's atrium is 17 stories and, again, the brass- and glass-enclosed elevator, moving at a dramatic 750 feet per minute, offers an interior view.

From the Pan Pacific, walk east 1 block to Powell Street and turn right. At the corner of Powell and Geary streets is our final stop, the:

❹ Westin St. Francis Hotel

Last but definitely not least, the five outside glass elevators at the Westin St. Francis are so awesome that school groups sometimes come by on field trips. The elevators are located at the 32-story Tower Building. Push "32" and prepare for a 30-second, 1,000-feet-per-minute rush to the top. The view of the bay and downtown is absolutely beautiful on a clear day. You may have to give this ride another go at night for comparison's sake.

Walking Tour: The Vertical Tour

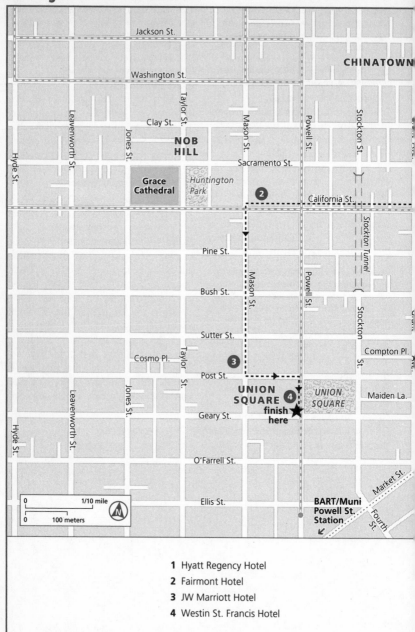

1 Hyatt Regency Hotel
2 Fairmont Hotel
3 JW Marriott Hotel
4 Westin St. Francis Hotel

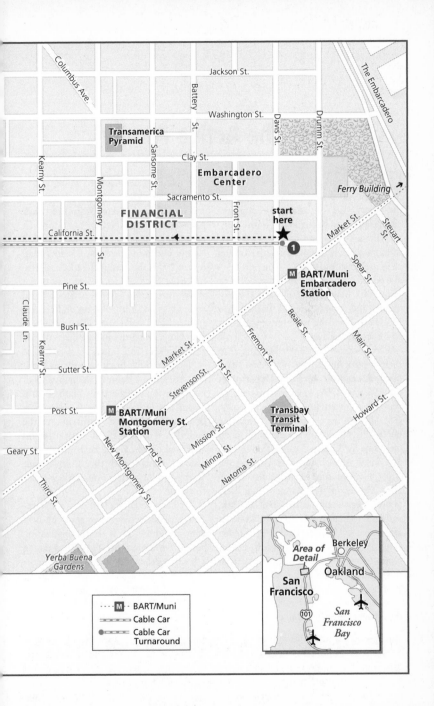

9

For the Active Family

Given its location in sunny California, San Francisco draws its fair share of outdoor and sports enthusiasts. Although the city proper may be fogbound in the summer, the temperate weather means staying indoors is rarely a more attractive option than getting outside. Green space is abundant—almost every neighborhood has a park or playground—and the bay, ocean, and woods are all immediately accessible. Even the mountains are just a few hours' drive away.

City residents have a terrific resource at their disposal in the form of the **San Francisco Recreation & Park Department** (© **415/831-2700;** www.parks.sfgov.org). Along with maintaining the parks, playgrounds, tennis courts, and swimming pools, this office runs all kinds of sports programs for kids and adults through the individual recreation centers found at the larger facilities such as Moscone Recreation Center in the Marina, Glen Park, Sunset Recreation Center, Balboa Park, and Potrero Hill. It even sponsors low-cost art classes at Sharon Studio in Golden Gate Park and a teen musical theater group that performs a few times a year. In the summer, basketball fans can attend exciting pro-am men's and women's basketball league games at Kezar Pavilion in the Haight for free. And did I mention

golf? San Francisco has five gemlike public courses within city limits.

The **Golden Gate National Park Association (GGNRA),** a nonprofit organization dedicated to the preservation of our local open space, works hand in hand with the National Park Service to make the 75,000 acres of parkland under their jurisdiction as user-friendly and enticing as possible. Docents and rangers regularly lead walks and talks on the flora and fauna, history, and geology of the area. Walkers and hikers have much to explore, from the brick and granite fortifications in Fort Point to the remnants of Fort Funston, to the trails in the Marin Headlands just across the Golden Gate Bridge. The newest addition to the GGNRA is **Crissy Field,** with a re-created tidal marsh, picnic facilities, an educational center, and the all-important Warming Hut, where you can get a hot chocolate.

For many kids, the best part of a vacation involves some active sport or outdoor adventure, be it ice skating, riding horses, swimming, fishing, or just taking a hike together. So although San Francisco's museums, shops, and restaurants may thrill parents, try to mix it up a little. There are plenty of wonderful, more active pursuits to consider as well.

1 Parks & Playgrounds

San Francisco supports many more parks in the city limits than those mentioned below. I've not listed playgrounds too far from the more touristed areas to be useful, unless there was a compelling reason to include them. For a more complete listing,

visit the **www.gokid.org** or **www.gocitykids.com** websites. (The Recrea
website doesn't really have any helpful information.)

Please note that some of San Francisco's parks are also popular with dog
owners. Some parks have designated off-leash areas, but—in keeping with
cisco's free-spirited attitude—a few owners don't want to constrain their pets freedom
by keeping them on a leash, even in areas where the law dictates they do so. When
dogs and kids find themselves occupying the same space, the result can be tension
between dog owners and parents. Most dogs are well-trained and accustomed to sharing green space with children, but some could get startled if a child runs at them. Likewise, your children may not be used to seeing dogs run around off leash. This is
usually only an issue at a handful of city parks, which I've noted here.

SOUTH OF MARKET

The San Francisco Giants baseball organization took a lot of flack when it allowed the
Coca-Cola Company to sponsor a play area behind the bleacher section at AT&T
Park. The source of the local indignation was an 80-foot wooden Coca-Cola bottle.
Despite the overt commercialism, it's still one nifty playground. The **Coca-Cola Fan
Lot** (© 415/972-2000; Willie Mays Plaza, 2nd and King streets; N-Judah toward Cal
Train Station) is open to the public June to August daily from 10am to 4pm and weekends September to May from 10am to 4pm. On game days, it's open only to ticket
holders. Entrance is free. That commotion-causing wooden bottle contains the most
exciting sets of slides in town: two 56-foot-long curving slides and two 20-foot-long
twisting slides. A 50-by-50-foot replica of the ballpark gives kids ages 3 to 7 an opportunity to play ball just like the big guys. Little sluggers can blast a homer off a batting
tee, use the pitching machine, or hit off a pint-sized pitcher if one's available, while
parents watch from the sidelines. Another section, a 45-foot base race from home to
first, lets kids show off how much faster they run than their parents. There's also a
speed pitch that times how fast your future MVPs can throw, a photo booth, and
plaques etched with the signatures of past Giants that can be used to make rubbings.
In addition to all this fun, the Fan Lot has some of the best views in town.

Just a bit down the Embarcadero heading toward the Ferry Building, look for **South
Beach Park.** This toddler playground is sunny, compact, and sweet, and on game days
you'll have the thrill of listening to the roar of the crowd. **Yerba Buena Gardens** (p. 178)
is an exceptional urban park and art center, and, along with its other attractions, there's a
rooftop playground in the vicinity of the bowling center/skating rink. This is no ordinary
playground. Besides some great slides, there's a bowl-shaped pit with a spongy surface and
sloped walls that is great for climbing around, musical pipes, and other unique play items.

CHINATOWN

Winner of a *San Francisco Bay Guardian* "Best of the Bay" award for the best multi-
generational park, the **Chinese Playground** on Sacramento Street (between Stockton
St. and Grant Ave.; © 415/274-0202) is a bi-level park built on the side of a hill.
Although it doesn't have a lawn, it does house two outdoor sandboxes, game and
sports fields, an indoor gym, and a recreation center.

Portsmouth Square, on top of Portsmouth Garage, is a regular stop on the Chinatown walking tour circuit. The sandy playground, suitable for kids under 7, is compact. There are plenty of benches, lots to look at—including locals practicing their tai
chi moves—and larger-than-life views of the Financial District. It's also historic: this
was the site of the city's first public school. Not far from there, at Grant Street,

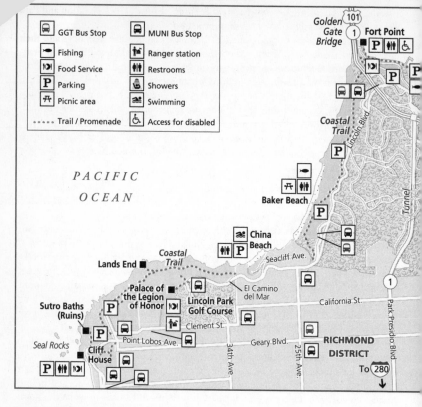

between Pine and California streets, **St. Mary's Square** is a pleasant spot with grass, benches, and a colorful play structure for toddlers.

NORTH BEACH

The **Joe DiMaggio North Beach Playground** (651 Lombard St., at Mason St.; ✆ 415/274-0200) reopened in spring 2005 after a $7.5 million renovation. One large pool was replaced with two pools—a lap pool and recreation pool—with different water temperatures to accommodate a range of aquatic programs. Swimming rates are $4 for adults, $1 for kids under 17, $3 for seniors. Drop-in swim lessons for kids are also available for an extra $2. With a new locker facility and clubhouse, it's a good place to cool off. The area also has a playground (which was not updated), picnic tables, tennis courts, a basketball court, and even bocce ball courts.

An old favorite of ours is **Michelangelo Park** (Greenwich St., between Leavenworth and Jones sts.). Well protected and almost hidden from view, it's actually very close to the crooked section of Lombard Street. Although it has a lovely lawn, I have never seen an off-leash dog here.

CIVIC CENTER & HAYES VALLEY

Famous for the Victorian row houses on Steiner Street known as the "Painted Ladies," **Alamo Square Park** (between Steiner, Scott, Hayes, and Fulton sts.) also features

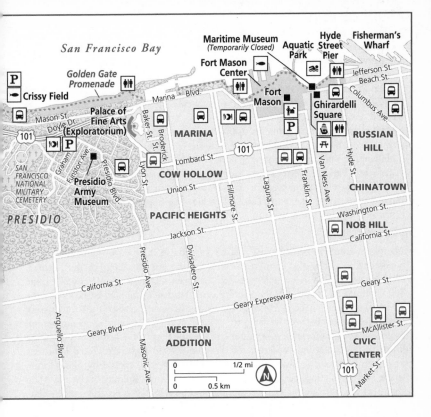

great views of downtown San Francisco. The park itself is small, only 4 square blocks, with a simple playground and a single tennis court. It's a meeting ground for neighborhood doggies.

After a trip to the Main Library, you could drop by the playground in **Civic Center Plaza** on McAllister Street and let the appropriate parties try out the new climbing structure. Unfortunately, you'll first want to check for vagrants.

THE MARINA & COW HOLLOW

For toddlers and younger children, the tiny **Cow Hollow Playground** on Baker Street, between Greenwich and Union streets, is a lovely protected and enclosed area. A kids' art studio is also open most weekdays, except from 1 to 2pm.

The spacious, enclosed playground at the **Moscone Recreation Center** ⟨⟨ (Chestnut and Laguna sts.; ℂ **415/292-2006**) was fully renovated in 2001, with creative climbing structures, slides, swings, and old-style seesaws. In addition, there are basketball and tennis courts, baseball diamonds, putting greens, soccer fields, and a gym. On school-year afternoons and weekends, the fields are busy with games. With all the kids here, dog owners do generally keep their furry companions leashed. If the weather turns sour, you can seek cover next door at the San Francisco Public Library's Marina Branch, which is scheduled to reopen in early 2007 after an extensive remodel.

PACIFIC HEIGHTS

In the heart of the city's most expensive neighborhood you'll find two lovely, well-tended parks with city views and expansive lawns. With so much grass, both parks are popular with dogs and their human companions. Fortunately, the play areas are fenced in, so everyone gets along.

Alta Plaza Park ⚐ (between Steiner, Scott, Clay, and Jackson sts.; ✆ 415/292-2002) is worth checking out for the city view alone, although the grass and trees are also delightful. Facilities include tennis and basketball courts. The entire playground reopened in the summer of 2006 after an extensive remodel, and now features every sort of climbing structure, swing, and slide a kid could want. When the breeze is blowing, this hilltop playground gets very windy.

Lafayette Park, between Gough, Sacramento, Laguna, and Washington streets, has walking paths, a fenced-in playground (with somewhat dated wooden structures), nice views, picnic tables, and tennis courts. It is also dog friendly, with an unfenced dog run available.

THE PRESIDIO

The oldest continuously operated military garrison in the nation—until its decommissioning in 1989—the Presidio of San Francisco was transferred to the National Park Service in 1994. Because it must become financially self-sustaining by 2013, the 800 buildings on the site, which include historic residences, military barracks, and the 23-acre Letterman General Hospital (no longer operating as such), are undergoing careful redevelopment. At the same time, the Presidio Trust, which is planning and overseeing the transformation, is mindful of the role these 1,491 acres may play in the future of the community at large. The Presidio is filled with recreational resources. Start with a stop at the **Visitor Center** (✆ 415/561-4323), open daily 9am to 5pm, which is currently located in the Presidio Officers' Club, Building 50, at the Main Post. You can obtain a map of the Presidio and browse the books and Golden Gate National Parks Association (GGNRA) souvenirs. Rangers are often on hand to answer questions and they regularly lead 1-hour walks. You can find a schedule of events on the Presidio Trust website, www.presidio.gov.

The grounds include 14 miles of bike paths, 11 miles of walking trails, a boardsailing and kite-surfing area at **Crissy Field,** beaches, picnicking facilities, a national cemetery, a pet cemetery, and a free shuttle service, PresidiGo, to help get you from here to there. **PresidiGo** operates weekdays from 6:30am to 8pm and weekends from 10am to 6pm, making 40 stops inside the Presidio. You can eat pretty well here during the day on weekdays: the **Acre Café** at the Thoreau Center (✆ 415/561-2273), open weekdays 7am to 3pm, uses organic produce and free-range meats in its soups, salads, sandwiches, quesadillas, and specials. Nearby, inside the Letterman Digital Arts Center opened in 2005 by George Lucas of *Star Wars* fame, you'll find the **Perk Presidio Cafe**

Fun Fact **A Little Park History**

The Presidio was established by Spanish soldiers in 1776, the same year the United States of America became an official independent entity on the other side of the continent. Mexico took over the area in 1822, and in 1846 the U.S. army assumed control of the post.

(ℂ **415/746-5456**), open weekdays 8am to 4pm, where you can pick up sandwiches to eat in or enjoy out front by the lovely pond that Lucas had added to the grounds. You can purchase organic, local, "made-from-scratch" breakfast and lunch goodies at **Dish** inside the San Francisco Film Centre near the Main Post (ℂ **415/561-2336**); open weekdays 8am to 4pm. **Crissy Field Center** (ℂ **415/561-7756**) has a cafe, open Wednesday to Sunday 9am to 5pm, and operates the **Warming Hut** (ℂ **415/561-3042**), open daily 9am to 5pm, on the west end of Crissy Field.

On the southern side of the Presidio, just 4 blocks from Sacramento Street, is the ever-popular **Julius Kahn Park.** The lovely playground sits next to the trees and features state-of-the-art playground equipment you probably haven't seen anywhere else: round swings, oddly shaped seesaws, and so on. There are picnic facilities, restrooms, tennis and basketball courts, playing fields, and hiking paths into the Presidio. The most convenient bus, the no. 43-Masonic, takes you close, but not to, this spot. The no. 1-California also gets you within a few blocks of it.

THE CASTRO & NOE VALLEY

Dolores Park, an easy commute on the J-Church streetcar, commands the sort of view that on a sunny day convinces out-of-towners that they ought to move to the city. Its grassy slopes lure sunbathers and picnicking couples, and the rolling lawn attracts children's birthday parties and local doggies. With a mediocre playground and many off-leash dogs, this isn't the best play area for toddlers—but it is a good place for kids to stretch their legs after visiting Mission Dolores (p. 194).

Duboce Park, between Scott and Steiner streets, has state-of-the-art equipment: a climbing wall, slides, the whole bit. The N-Judah streetcar passes right by. At the southwest corner is the **Harvey Milk Recreation Center** (ℂ **415/554-9523**), specializing in the arts. Classes in dance, music, photography, and drama are offered here at very low cost for adults and children as young as 6.

Douglass Playground, at Douglass and 27th streets in Noe Valley, has a large lawn, picnic tables, a sandy play structure, decent bathrooms, and a great big slide tucked into the hillside that borders the park. The hot new playground around here, the **Walter Haas Playground** (at Diamond Heights Blvd. and Addison St.), affords fabulous downtown views but is a bit out of the way for most tourists.

THE MISSION

Mission Playground, on 19th Street between Valencia and Linda streets (look for the mural), could be a handy park if you find yourself needing a play break while touring this neighborhood. The equipment is tops and an unlocked gate ensures that off-leash dogs are not a problem. Other facilities include a recreation center and tennis courts.

THE RICHMOND & SUNSET

Golden Gate Park, San Francisco's most famous public grounds, attracts more than 75,000 people on the weekends alone. The park is about 3 miles long (bigger

Tips Getting the Scoop on Special Events

The Golden Gate National Parks Association (GGNRA) partners with the National Park Service to help maintain much of the public land on San Francisco's coastline. The GGNRA sponsors educational programs at various sites—including Crissy Field, the Presidio, Fort Point, China Beach, and Fort Funston—on a quarterly basis. You can plan ahead to join ranger-led walks, talks, and other programs, some specifically for families, by logging onto **www.nps.gov/goga/parknews** and downloading the latest "ParkNews" newsletter.

than Manhattan's Central Park) and is best appreciated on foot or two wheels. If little legs are unable to travel the length of the park, don't worry: the deYoung Museum, Conservatory of Flowers, and Koret Children's Corner (formerly "Children's Playground"; scheduled to reopen in May 2007), some of the park's major highlights, are all within walking distance of each other. On weekends and holidays in the summer from 10am to 6pm, the free Golden Gate Park Shuttle runs at 15-minute intervals from McLaren Lodge on the eastern edge of Golden Gate Park to Ocean Beach, stopping at 15 locations in between. See p. 188 for more information on the park.

The lake in **Mountain Lake Park** was a 4-acre reservoir that provided San Francisco with water during the gold rush. Located on the edge of the Presidio Golf Course off Lake Street between 8th Avenue and Park Presidio Boulevard, this exceptional park is a great location for families with kids of all ages. There are two playgrounds, one more suitable for under-5s. Other facilities include basketball and tennis courts, playing fields, hiking trails, a small beach, and picnic tables. The no. 28L-19th Avenue bus drives by the park on its way into the Presidio.

In the inner Richmond, not far from Laurel Village, is **Rossi Pool and Playground** (Arguello Blvd. at Anza St.; ✆ **415/666-7014**). It's a nice pool at a bargain fee—$4 for adults, $1 for kids—with limited recreational swim hours, and the playground is big and well equipped. The park has tennis courts as well, making it a good destination for a variety of activities.

2 The Great Indoors

Gymboree   Ages infant to 4. You may know it for the frilly kids' clothes, but Gymboree actually started 30 years ago as a play and music group for young children. Its popular 45-minute playgroup sessions led by a Gymboree instructor led to its bigger success in retail. Gymboree's weekly music and movement classes for babies and parents to do together are designed to follow the appropriate developmental sequence. If you're here for a longer stay, Gymboree classes are a great way to meet other moms and babies. The first class is free, and subsequent drop-in sessions are $25 per class.

1525 Sloat Blvd., near the San Francisco Zoo. ✆ 415/242-5637. www.gymboreeclasses.com. Class times vary based on the age of your child; call for details.

Mission Cliffs ★★★ **Ages 6 and up.** This indoor climbing center provides 14,000 feet of wall to conquer for those days when just getting up in the morning doesn't cut it. If you sign up for the belay safety class (same-day registration at $28/person), you'll

get a day pass and equipment rental thrown in. Phone first to check
center is if you're arriving on a weekend. Kids love holding birthday

2295 Harrison St. (at 19th St.). ℂ 415/550-0515. www.touchstoneclimbing.com. Day pass $
$10 adults before 3pm on weekdays, $18 after 3pm and on weekends. Mon–Fri 6:30am–10pm

3 Beachcombing

Warm, sunny days along San Francisco's coastline are rarities because the outer Richmond and Sunset neighborhoods are often the last to escape the fog. But when the
sun does come out, the beaches are wonderful.

Be aware that the ocean is neither warm nor safe enough for swimming, and signs
note that waders and swimmers have died at San Francisco beaches. For one, unpre-
dictable "sneaker" waves, giant waves that form when two or three normal-sized
waves merge, can suddenly sweep onto the shore. Also, having surfed at Ocean
Beach a few times (and wondered what I've gotten myself into), I can attest to the
incredible strength of the rip current. In fact, the last thing you should do is enter
the water where you see surfers going in, since surfers usually look for a rip current
that can carry them out with minimal paddling. That current could sweep out even
a strong swimmer, who, without a wetsuit, would be quickly numbed by the
extremely cold water.

Most of San Francisco's beaches don't have the facilities you'd find further south in
the state, such as snack shacks, showers, or even restrooms. But the dramatic pound-
ing of the waves and the beauty of the jagged edges of the continent nonetheless lure
walkers, bicyclists, skaters, and families armed with buckets and shovels to the
beach—bundled up if necessary, but still managing to enjoy the sand and the scene.

The lengthiest stretch of sand is 4-mile-long **Ocean Beach** on the Great Highway.
At one end is **Fort Funston** (p. 199), a former U.S. military reserve where explorers
can still find the remains of a cannon. Fort Funston is also the premier hang glider
launch and landing site, and there's a viewing platform above the beach that provides
the perfect spot to watch the action. Around the end of Wawona Street, on the north
side of the zoo, a bike/skate path extends parallel to Ocean Beach to Golden Gate
Park. Ocean Beach ends near the Cliff House.

Heading north along the coastline, past Lincoln Park, is sheltered **China Beach.**
Again, this is no place to swim, but the small beach has an observation deck overlook-
ing the Pacific, grills for barbecuing, a grassy picnic area, and bathrooms. North of
China Beach, and part of the Presidio, is mile-long **Baker Beach,** probably the most
popular beach for families. Picnic tables are scattered among the cypress trees, the sand
is inviting, and the bridge and Marin Headland views are inspiring. Look for **Battery
Chamberlin,** built in 1904, which holds the last "disappearing gun" on the West
Coast. Demonstrations on how it operates are given on the first full Saturday and Sunday of each month between 11am and 3pm. Be aware that the northern tip of Baker
Beach is clothing optional—yes, there's a nude beach in San Francisco, which is surprising only because it gets so cold down there.

Inside the bay, the tiny beaches of **Crissy Field** are the best option for families with
younger children, since they have almost no waves, and wading is possible on warm
days. Just note that the bay currents are still fierce, and the water is very chilly. At the
eastern end of Crissy Field, you'll find bathrooms and showers, while the western end
has lovely picnic benches, restrooms, and the nearby Warming Hut, where you can
purchase a tasty lunch to enjoy at the beach.

Sports & Games

ARCHERY

Golden Gate Park has an archery field with nine hay bales off Fulton Street above the golf course. (Two of the bales are wheelchair accessible.) You can rent archery equipment at the nearby **San Francisco Archery Shop** (3795 Balboa St., at 39th Ave.; ℭ **415/751-2776**) for $25 for the day; this includes a lesson if you like. The bows are light-weight enough for kids 8 and up.

BASEBALL

In the spring, teams are organized and coached through the **Recreation & Park Department** (ℭ 415/831-6318; www.parks.sfgov.org), the **Police Activities League** (ℭ 415/401-4666; www.sfpal.org), the **Jewish Community Center** (ℭ 415/346-6040; www.jccsf.org), **SF Youth Sports** (ℭ 415/409-6884; www.sfyouthsports.com), and **Little League Baseball** (www.littleleague.org).

BASKETBALL

The **Nate Thurmond Courts** on the Panhandle, a narrow stretch of green between Oak and Fell streets on the eastern edge of Golden Gate Park, are the site of some regular and lively pickup games. If you want to shoot some hoops to keep your game up, check the park listings above for centers with basketball courts. You can also phone the **Embarcadero YMCA** (ℭ **415/957-9622**; www.ymcasf.org/embarcadero) about open-court play, or check with the **Presidio YMCA** (ℭ **415/447-9602**; www.ymcasf.org/presidio) about their Saturday night pickup games and youth programs. The **Recreation and Park Department, Police Activities League, Jewish Community Center,** and **SF Youth Sports** (see "Baseball" listing, above) field teams, and **City College of San Francisco** (ℭ 415/239-3401; www.ccsf.edu) offers summer basketball camps for kids aged 5 to 14.

BIKING

On Sundays, **Golden Gate Park** is closed to automobile traffic, as bikes and bicyclists of all sizes arrive in force, ready to pedal around the park's 7 miles of paved bike paths or take to the streets. On other days, two-wheelers need to pay some attention to the automobile traffic, but in general, drivers behave somewhat reasonably inside the park. Another popular route for bikes is the **Embarcadero,** which is flat and as scenic as can be. You can ride from AT&T Park all the way to the Golden Gate Bridge, with side trips in the Presidio. The bike paths at Crissy Field and Ocean Beach are also a pleasure. Helmets are recommended for adults and required by law for kids under 18. Bike maps are available from the San Francisco Visitor Information Center at 900 Market St. (at Powell St.) for $3 and at bike shops around town. Politically active bicyclists can join a Critical Mass ride (a group of cycling advocates) on the last Friday of the month at the Embarcadero BART station at 5:30pm.

BIKE RENTALS

Avenue Cyclery This place offers bike sales and rentals convenient to Golden Gate Park. Rental rates are $7 per hour or $28 per day and they do stock children's bikes and tandems. 756 Stanyan St. ℭ 415/387-3155. www.avenuecyclery.com.

Bike and Roll ⭐ In addition to renting cycles, Bike and Roll gives you the info you need to take self-guided tours to Muir Woods National Park, Mt. Tamalpais, or even the popular ride to Sausalito with a return by ferry. Less ambitious, but still scenic, options include cycling through a few of San Francisco's lovely in-city parks. 899 Columbus Ave. 🕻 **415/229-2000.** www.bikeandroll.com.

Bike Hut   The laid-back staff here are experts at bike and wheelchair repair and can discuss the best bike routes. Bike rentals are $5 per hour and $20 per day. Styles include basic mountain bikes and seven-speed cruisers. Child seats and trailers are available. The equipment is used and looks it, but everything is serviceable. A decent public bathroom is nearby. Pier 40 (end of Townsend St. at Embarcadero). 🕻 **415/543-4335.** www.thebikehut.com.

Blazing Saddles 🕻🕻   If you're wavering about a bike trip across the bay, the folks at any of five North Beach and Fisherman's Wharf locations of this experienced bike rental company will provide you with the information and encouragement—including ferry tickets for the return to San Francisco—that you'll need to tackle this route. (If you return late on the ferry, you can drop off bikes at the 24-hour Hyde St. location.) The bikes, for kids as young as age 5 to adults, are well maintained. Rental prices ($7/hour, $28/day) include helmets, locks, front packs, rear racks, maps, and advice. Tandem bikes, high-end road bikes, and full suspension mountain bikes rent for $11 per hour or $48 per day. Add-on tandems, kids' trailers, and baby seats are an additional $20 per day. 1095 Columbus Ave., 2715 Hyde St., 465 Jefferson St., Pier 431/2, and Pier 41. 🕻 **415/202-8888.** www.blazingsaddles.com.

BOATING

It's an absolute joy for kids to steer a boat on Stow Lake in Golden Gate Park. **Stow Lake Boat and Bike Rentals** (🕻 **415/752-0347**) provides the basics in watercraft. Rowboats are $14 per hour, pedal boats are $19 per hour, and those vintage electric motor boats are $29 per hour. It's cash only, on a first-come, first-served basis. Someone over 16 must be on the boat at all times. Prepare the kids to get a bit damp.

If you'd like to get out on the bay, bay tours—complete with audio guides—depart frequently from Fisherman's Wharf operated by the **Blue & Gold Fleet** (🕻 **415/ 773-1188;** www.blueandgoldfleet.com) and the **Red and White Fleet** (🕻 **415/ 673-2900;** www.redandwhite.com).

If sailing is your thing, be sure to check out **saillola.com** (🕻 **415/573-7030;** www.saillola.com). Parked at PIER 39 and captained by Chris Jordan, *Lola* is available for charters ranging from 1½ to 3 hours, with prices from $150 to $300. *Lola* fits six passengers, kids are welcome, and you can bring whatever food and drink you'd like. For larger groups, Captain Jordan can also take your group out on the *Adventure Cat* or *Adventure Cat II,* the largest sailing catamarans on San Francisco Bay.

Alternatively, **Cass Marina** at 1702 Bridgeway in Sausalito (🕻 **800/472-4595** or 415/332-6789; www.cassmarina.com) is a certified sailing school renting 22- to 35-foot sailboats, with prices ranging from $113 for a sunset cruise to $375 for an all-day excursion on the largest boat. Skippered charters are more expensive. Large sailing yachts also leave Sausalito on a regularly scheduled basis, so check the website.

BOWLING

Yerba Buena Bowling Center (🕻 **415/820-3532;** www.skatebowl.com), at Yerba Buena Gardens, is the most convenient location. It's open daily 10am to 10pm (until midnight Fri–Sat), and game rates range from $3.50 to $6. **Presidio Bowl** near the Main Post inside the Presidio (corner of Moraga Ave. and Montgomery St.; 🕻 **415/ 561-2695**) is an especially quaint bowling alley. The site of some memorable birthday parties, it's a little 12-alley pin palace with a snack bar selling pizza, beer, and sodas.

Bumper bowling, with frustration-proof guardrails to cover the gutters, is an option. Open daily from 9am until midnight weeknights and 9am to 2am on weekends, this is such a popular hangout, especially on weekends, so phone ahead. Rates are $4.25 per game for adults and $3.25 per game for kids before 5pm. After 5pm, rates are $5.50 per game on weeknights and $6.50 per game on weekends—for both adults and kids. Shoe rentals are $4. The no. 29-Sunset-Letterman bus will get you there.

DANCING

Although you'll find a variety of dance classes for little ones at places like the Presidio Dance Theater, Stardance, City Ballet, San Francisco Ballet, Shan-Yee Poon Ballet School, and the Jewish Community Center, these are all for multi-week sessions. Your best bet for drop-in classes is the **Metronome Dance Center,** 1830 17th St. (✆ 415/ 252-9000; www.metronomedancecenter.com), although the classes aren't strictly geared for kids. Wednesdays at 7pm you can take drop-in salsa classes, and Friday and Saturday nights the center offers a variety of drop-in dance classes, including East Coast swing, ballroom dancing, and salsa, which are followed by a dance party serving only snacks and nonalcoholic drinks.

FISHING

You'll find fly-casting pools at Golden Gate Park, on the western side of the Polo Fields, but you need to bring your own equipment unless you're content just to watch the regulars. **Hi's Tackle Box** at 3141 Clement St. (between 32nd and 33rd avenues; ✆ 415/221-3825) is considered the best store in the Bay Area for any equipment fresh- and salt-water fishing enthusiasts may need.

Sportfishing boats leave from Pier 41 (between Jones and Taylor sts.) every morning around 6am on half- and full-day trips for salmon, shark, or whatever happens to be running. Each boat captain works independently, but you can get pricing and an overview of the fleet at **www.sfsportfishing.com**. Of note is the *Lovely Martha* Sportfishing Charters (✆ 650/871-1691; www.lovelymartha.com), run by three generations of the same family. Boats can be chartered for deep-sea fishing, San Francisco Bay fishing, sightseeing, or parties.

GOLFING

San Francisco boasts several excellent public courses. **Golden Gate Park Municipal Golf Course,** built in 1950, is the best choice for beginners. It's a 9-hole course with a narrow, tree-lined fairway. The clubhouse is located between JFK Drive and Fulton Street near 47th Avenue (✆ 415/751-8987; www.goldengateparkgolf.com), and boasts a new restaurant serving Memphis-style barbecue. Greens fees are $14 for 9 holes ($4 for kids under 17) and $28 for 18 holes Monday to Thursday; Friday to Sunday, it's $18 for 9 holes ($6 for kids) and $36 for 18 holes. Club rentals and kids' classes are available. Advance tee times are not accepted.

Built in 1895 for the exclusive use of the military, **Presidio Golf Course,** off the Park Presidio Boulevard entrance at 300 Finley Rd. (✆ 415/561-4663; www.presidio golf.com), is currently the most popular public course in the city. Golfers were ecstatic when the army turned over that part of the Presidio to civilian use. Lined by eucalyptus and Monterey pine trees, its challenging 18 holes are played much of the year in foggy and windy conditions. Tee times may be reserved 30 days in advance, either online or by phone (✆ 415/561-4653). Greens fees vary widely—from $40 to $100 depending on time and day of the week—and are cheaper for Bay Area residents. Club rental is available, and there's a driving range and restaurant.

The Zoo & Lake Merced Area

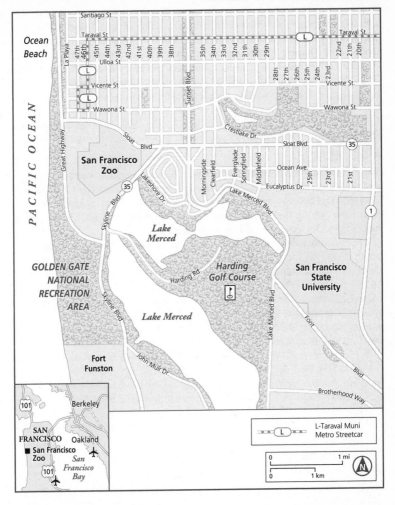

Farther west is the most beautiful of the public courses, **Lincoln Park** (300 34th Ave.; ✆ **415/221-9911**), which boasts exceptional views of the Golden Gate Bridge from its perch on the edge of the coast. Built in 1908, this hilly, par-68 course has 18 holes that sit amidst Monterey cypress and pine trees. Facilities include club rental and a restaurant. Arrange tee times by calling ✆ **415/750-4653** 6 days in advance. Greens fees, which were recently $31 to $35, were being revised at press time.

Just minutes from the San Francisco Zoo are Lake Merced and the **Harding Park Golf Course** (99 Harding Rd., on Lake Merced Blvd. behind San Francisco State University; ✆ **415/664-4690;** http://harding-park.com). Opened in 1930, the course has a regulation 18-hole course of flat, tree-lined fairways, plus a 9-hole executive course, a driving range, and a restaurant. The course underwent a $16 million restoration in 2003—including the construction of a new clubhouse—and hosted the 2005 PGA

World Golf Championships. Greens fees are $135 to $155 (less for Bay Area residents) and may be booked up to 30 days in advance by calling © **415/750-4653.** A $10 per player fee applies to reservations made more than a week ahead. You can also walk on to the 9-hole **Fleming Course** next door, which charges $25 to $30 greens fees.

South of downtown is John McLaren Park, home of **Gleneagles Golf Course** (2100 Sunnydale Ave.; © **415/587-2425;** www.gleneaglesgolfsf.com). The well-maintained, challenging 9-hole course features hilly fairways and has a reputation for being windy. Weekend tee times may be reserved 7 days in advance. Greens fees are $14 to $18 for 9 holes and $22 to $30 for 18 holes. McLaren Park is on the border of San Francisco and San Mateo counties, in a less-than-stellar neighborhood.

GYMNASTICS

There are three gymnastics studios in town, all with classes for young kids and a rigorous training program. Out in the Sunset, **American Gymnastics** (2520 Judah St.; © **415/731-1400;** www.americangymnasticsclub.com) offers an open gym night, *Kids Night Out,* on the last Saturday of the month from 6 to 9pm. The cost for non-members is $20; kids age 5 and up are welcome.

The staff at **AcroSports** (639 Frederick St.; © **415/665-2276;** www.acrosports.org), which is near the southeast corner of Golden Gate Park, teaches classes in circus arts, dance, physical performance skills, and gymnastics, with programs for kids as young as 18 months. Former and current visiting gymnasts with an urge to swing on the uneven parallel bars can attend classes as drop-ins. You must call in advance to attend a class within the appropriate age group and skill level. Fees are $13 for a 1-hour class, $20 for a 90-minute class, and $25 for a 2-hour class. Adult classes are also available; in any event, parents must accompany kids in order to sign the waiver form.

If you know locals who are members at **San Francisco Gymnastics** (920 Mason St.; © **415/561-6260;** www.sanfranciscogymnastics.com), you can be guests at their monthly *Parents Night Out* program. Parents drop off their kids aged 4 to 12 at 6:30pm and return by 10:30pm. SF Gymnastics provides a pizza dinner, coloring, an obstacle course, gymnastics events, and an animated movie. Parent's Night Out is scheduled twice a month, usually the first and third Friday, and registration is required by the Wednesday prior to the event. The fee is $25 for the first child and $20 for each additional sibling.

HIKING

You'll find plenty of hikes perfect for little legs in the Presidio, Golden Gate Park, and, our personal favorite, at Land's End (just make sure your kids stay close, as the trail hugs a cliff). For more ambitious hikes, head to Marin, where you'll find excellent, scenic trails on Mount Tamalpais, the Marin Headlands, and in Muir Woods. Hiking on **Angel Island** (p. 169) is also a treat. San Francisco Bay Area Hiker offers a good website (www.bahiker.com) for planning hikes in the city.

HORSEBACK RIDING

With the closure of the stables in Golden Gate Park, horseback riding in the city became a memory. Determined riders must now leave the city. One option is to cross the bridge to **Miwok Livery Stables** (© **415/383-8048;** www.miwokstables.com) in Mill Valley. Trail ride lessons are available Monday through Saturday, starting at 1:30pm with a half-hour safety lesson, followed by an hour ride through the beautiful Tennessee Valley hills, all for $50 per person.

Another option is to head 1 mile south from San Francisco Zoo. The **Mar Vista Stable** (2152 Skyline Blvd., Daly City; © **650/991-4224**; http://marvistastable. tripod.com) offers guided rides on Ocean Beach. It is open from 9am to 5pm on weekdays and from 9am to 6pm on weekends, and no reservations are required. One-hour rides are $30, 1½-hour rides are $40, and 2-hour rides for $50 are available only until noon. A 10-minute pony ride on a carousel is $10.

ICE SKATING

Year-round ice skating is available at the 32,000-square-foot **Yerba Buena Ice Skating Rink** at Yerba Buena Gardens (© **415/820-3532**; www.skatebowl.com). Every year, from the second Wednesday in November until January 2nd, a portion of Justin Herman Plaza across from the Ferry Building turns into the **Holiday Ice Rink at the Embarcadero Center** (© **415/837-1931**; www.embarcaderocenter.com). Skating sessions are 90 minutes long and cost $7 for adults and $3.50 for kids before 5pm. After 5pm, prices increase to $7.50 for adults and $3.75 for kids. Skate rental is an additional $3, and small sizes are available. The rink opens at 10am daily and is open until 10pm Monday to Thursday and until 11pm Friday to Sunday. Bring extra socks and have some gloves if possible, as it can get chilly out there. Expect crowds as well, which makes skating on the smallish rink a little intense at times if you're unsteady on your blades. The outdoor setting is really lovely, especially in the evening when the tall Embarcadero Center buildings are lit.

IN-LINE SKATING/ROLLER SKATING

On Sundays in Golden Gate Park at 6th Avenue and Fulton Street, skaters congregate for a hugely entertaining dance party from around noon to 5pm. The music is hip-shaking and the participants amazing in their skill on wheels. If you and the kids want to skate in the park, **Golden Gate Park Skate & Bike** on Fulton Street between 6th and 7th avenues (© **415/668-1117**) rents skates as small as kids' size 10 for $5 an hour or $20 per day. In-line skates are $6 an hour or $24 per day. Safety equipment is included in the rental. **Bike and Roll** rents skates from its Fisherman's Wharf location at 353 Jefferson St. (see contact info under "Biking," above) for $5 for 2 hours, with a 2-hour minimum, or $25 per day. They carry a variety of sizes, including skates for the littlest rollers.

JUGGLING & FLYING TRAPEZE

San Francisco is home to the **Circus Center** (755 Frederick St.; © **415/759-8123**; www.circuscenter.org), the premier training ground for circus arts in the U.S. Classes in such disciplines as Chinese acrobatics, hand-balancing, clowning, and flying trapeze are available for students age 5 and up. The school offers drop-in classes for flying trapeze on Saturday and Sunday mornings; cost is $42 per class. Other classes may be available for drop-ins, but the center recommends calling ahead of time to check availability and rates. The center is across the street from Kezar Pavilion at the southeast corner of Golden Gate Park.

KAYAKING

A memorable way to get as close to the bay as possible without actually getting in is by skimming the surface in a kayak. At **City Kayak** (Embarcadero at Townsend; © **415/357-1010**), kayaks rent for $15 per person per hour (kids under 8 free; 15% discounts for students). If you plan to explore the bay on your own, every member of your party must be at least 5 feet tall. City Kayak will permit small kayakers in your group if you hire one of their professional guides at $80 per hour, for a minimum of 2 hours. Tours depart from South Beach or PIER 39.

Across the bridge, **Sea Trek,** on Schoonmaker Point near the Bay Model in Sausalito (© 415/488-1000 or 415/332-4465; www.seatrekkayak.com), kids as young as 6 can join their parents in a two- or three-person kayak and Sea Trek personnel will join you on Sunday family tours around Sausalito, Angel Island, or in Tomales Bay. The cost runs from $65 to $75 for adults and $30 to $45 for kids 12 and under. Phone for details.

KITE FLYING

The Marina Green is one of the best places to fly a kite anywhere. On most windy afternoons, you'll see an impressive array of multi-colored stunt kites, complemented by the breathtaking bay and bridge views. Unfortunately, there is no place to rent kites, but you should be able to find one to buy that will fit in your suitcase when it's time to head home. The Warming Hut in Crissy Field sells smallish kites, or you could pick one up at the Chinatown Kite Shop (p. 256). (Although the Safeway supermarket across the street from the Marina Green ought to sell kites, don't waste your time asking. They don't.)

SKATEBOARDING

San Francisco was once a renowned skateboarding destination. According to a skate-obsessed teen from Ireland, Pier 7 used to be a "very famous" spot. Sadly, the city has since decided that skateboarders are a menace and even created a skateboarding task force. Why they consider young teens getting exercise a problem is unclear. The city did create a 150-square-foot skate park in Crocker Amazon Park, but it's practically in San Mateo County: no self-respecting skateboarder uses it. Although my Irish acquaintance said Pier 7 had been thoroughly "skate-stopped" (filled in with bumps and ridges on the ledges, stairs, and any other slide-able surface), he did find plenty of skaters doing tricks in the plaza in front of the Ferry Building. Skaters can also be found, in the wee hours of the night, at Union Square and at 3rd and Army streets.

SKIING & SNOWBOARDING

With world-class skiing just a few hours' drive away, it's no wonder so many Bay Area residents are avid skiers. The biggest resorts are **Squaw Valley** (© 530/583-6985; www.squaw.com) on Lake Tahoe's north shore and **Heavenly** (© 775/586-7000; www.skiheavenly.com) on the south side. Other good, medium-sized ski resorts include **Northstar-at-Tahoe** (© 800/466-6784; www.skinorthstar.com), east of Tahoe City, and **Sugarbowl** (© 530/426-9000; www.sugarbowl.com), off Highway 80 a good half-hour closer to San Francisco than most Tahoe resorts.

If you are traveling with kids who don't need to ski double black-diamond slopes, consider some of the smaller, truly family-oriented ski areas. Lift tickets are cheaper, and the overall feel is more personal. **Tahoe Donner** (© 530/587-9400; www.tahoedonner.com) is a quaint, family-oriented resort northwest of Lake Tahoe, and, on the Nevada side, petite **Mt. Rose** (© 800/754-7673; www.mtrose.com) is one of our favorite mountains—combining a laid-back attitude and kid-friendly slopes with a few steep runs for mom and dad. Lastly, **Kirkwood Mountain Resort** (© 209/258-6000; www.kirkwood.com) usually has the most snow and can be reached (when the road is open) via an alternative route (Highway 88) to ever-jammed Highway 80.

Most of the resorts offer ski school for children 4 and up, as well as day care for kids 3 and up, and many will give baby-sitting referrals for under 3s. Just note that every Friday evening (even in the summer) Highway 80 is clogged with vacationers heading to the mountains. If at all possible, drive up mid-week.

SOCCER

Drive by the Marina Green or through Golden Gate Park on a weekday afternoon or Saturday morning: the number of kids running after soccer balls is dizzying. Soccer is hugely popular in San Francisco, with teams organized by the **Recreation and Park Department,** the **Jewish Community Center, SF Youth Sports,** and the **San Francisco Police Activities League** (see contact info listed under "Baseball," earlier in this chapter). Soccer classes for the preschool set are offered by **Soccer Kids Inc.** (© 415/ 608-2608; www.soccerkids.com), while older kids can contact the **Presidio YMCA** (© 415/447-9602; www.ymcasf.org/presidio). The **San Francisco Viking Soccer Club** (© 415/753-3111; www.sfvikingsoccer.org) is one of the country's oldest leagues for youth soccer and organizes many of the games you're likely to see on any given weekend.

SURFING

Fifteen minutes south of San Francisco on Highway 1 is the tiny burg of Pacifica, a popular spot for many Bay Area surfers. **Surf Camp Pacifica** (© 650/738-5757; www.surfpacifica.com) at Linda Mar Beach runs 3-hour surf camps for kids 6 to 18 that run from 2 to 5 days, with rates from $140 to $270, including wetsuit rentals for $10 to $20. Linda Mar Beach has clean restrooms and showers, but the grayish-sand beach doesn't rank among Northern California's loveliest. It's best left to surfers and dog-walkers.

On most days, you're likely to see several surfers at Ocean Beach as well. However, with its strong current; steep, powerful waves; and icy-cold waters, Ocean Beach is suitable only for advanced surfers. I've seen kids surfing there only on summer days (the swell is usually not as strong in summer) when the waves were very, very small—and even then they were over 12 years old. Exercise caution: an inexperienced surfer disappeared here in 2006.

SWIMMING

The city's Recreation & Park Department maintains swimming pools in a handful of recreation centers. The cost to swim is modest—$3 for adults and 50¢ for children, or $5 for a family of four. Public swim times vary from pool to pool and are limited; call or drop by the centers to note times and days. Two of the best swimming pools are at the **Joe DiMaggio North Beach Playground** at Lombard and Mason streets (© 415/274-0200) and **Rossi Pool and Playground** (Arguello Blvd. at Anza St.; © 415/666-7014). The **Embarcadero YMCA** (169 Steuart St.; © 415/957-9622; www.ymcasf.org/embarcadero) and the **Presidio YMCA** (Letterman Pool, 1151 Gorgas Ave.; © 415/447-9602; www.presidioymcaaquatics.org) both have large indoor pools, and if you are a Y member in your hometown, you can use their facilities for $3. Nonmembers are charged $12 per day at the Presidio pool and $15 at the Embarcadero location. Call in advance to check on community swim hours and to be sure swim lanes are available. Over at the University of San Francisco campus on Turk and Parker streets near Laurel Heights is the **Koret Health and Recreation Center** (© 415/422-6811). It's primarily for students and locals, but nonmembers may use the Olympic-size indoor swimming pool on a drop-in basis for $15 for adults and $10 for youth 17 and under. Swim teams regularly practice in the pool Monday to Thursday afternoons; weekends and mornings are the best times for casual use. As with most pools in town, kids must be accompanied by adults.

TENNIS

The San Francisco Recreation and Park Department operates 132 free tennis courts at parks and recreation centers spread throughout the city. Most are available to players on a first-come, first-served basis. Additionally, the 21 courts in **Golden Gate Park Tennis Complex** can be reserved in advance for a nominal fee. Reservations for weekends are taken on the previous Wednesday between 4 and 6pm by calling ✆ **415/831-6301,** or on Thursday and Friday by calling the center directly at ✆ **415/753-7001.** Hopefully you're planning on playing with a local, because proof of residency is a requirement to use the courts at these peak times. Otherwise, feel free to try the courts at the Moscone Recreation Center, Dolores Park, Alta Plaza Playground, the Presidio, Joe DiMaggio North Beach Playground, and so on. City residents (kids and grown-ups) have the pleasure of signing up for free tennis classes offered through the Recreation and Park Department at courts throughout San Francisco.

WINDSURFING/SAILBOARDING

Before Crissy Field was converted into a national park, windsurfers from around the Bay Area would descend on the abandoned military airstrip and begin setting up their equipment. Now that it's a lovely recreation area, the eastern end of Crissy Field is even more popular as an access point to some of the best windsurfing in northern California. Since then, kite-boarding has exploded in popularity and most afternoons you'll see at least a dozen windsurfers and kite-boarders in the water, and on the windiest days you'll see hundreds. Watching the boarders attain death-defying velocities while towering cargo ships loom in the background is a heart-stopping spectacle. This challenging spot is for experts only; no rentals or lessons are available.

5 Classes & Workshops

Perfect for a rainy day or a time when you want a low-key activity, hands-on craft shops provide space and equipment for customers to create something useful to take home or wrap up for Grandma. Finding half-day or full-day workshops, on the other hand, is more challenging. Most of the many music, dance, art, and sports classes in the city require time commitments from 4 weeks to the rest of your life. Below are a few options that are available on a one-time basis. For more information, visit **www.gocitykids.com** and **www.gokids.org**.

ART CLASSES

Over at Fort Mason Center in the Marina is the **Children's Art Center** (Bldg. C; ✆ **415/771-0292;** www.childrensartcenter.org), with a full schedule of classes for kids from 2 to 10 years old. The center is open every day and for $25 to $28 kids are allowed to join classes on a drop-in basis. Phone for a schedule or check the website. Another local art center for kids is **Purple Crayon** (301 Cornwall St., at California St. and 4th Ave.; ✆ **415/831-0693;** www.purplecrayon.com). Wednesdays from 10am to noon are open to all drop-ins for $25. At other times, kids may drop in on classes if there is availability. Call ahead to inquire.

Every Saturday afternoon between 1 and 4pm at the **Randall Museum** (p. 277), some sort of art project is on hand for kids. Past crafts have included mask making, decorating paper lanterns, creating a Zen rock garden, and making a snow globe. Cost is minimal; $3 for kids or $5 for an adult/child combo.

The **Palace of the Legion of Honor** (p. 192) also has activities for kids on Saturday mornings from 10:30am to noon, free with museum admission. Doing and Viewing Art is a gallery tour and art class for kids 7 to 12 years old. At the Big Kids/Little Kids program parents and their 3½- to 6-year-old children do a gallery tour and art class together. Pre-registration is not required but space is limited. Saturdays are also great at the **de Young Museum** (p. 193), where guides lead tours of current exhibitions, followed by studio workshops taught by professional artist-teachers. The program, free after paid admission, is from 10:30am to noon for all visitors and 1:30 to 3pm for museum members. It's appropriate for kids ages 3 to 12, although children under 8 must be accompanied by an adult.

Other San Francisco museums offering art classes are the **SFMOMA** (p. 194), which the third Sunday of every month offers a special family studio featuring hands-on projects for kids and docent-led tours, and the **Asian Art Museum** (p. 190), which offers a drop-in art class for kids from 1 to 4pm on the first Saturday of the month, except on the twice-yearly "Family Festival" months.

COOKING

Apron Strings   Ages 10 and up. Conceived and run by Roberta Des Bouillons, an alumna of the Culinary Institute of America in Hyde Park, Apron Strings offers weekly cooking sessions for children. You can also reserve a spot in the 3-hour Saturday morning workshops, which run from 9am to noon and cost $65. Classes cover everything from Italian cooking, cake baking, and pie making to seasonal soups and ethnic delights. The morning ends with students (and parents) sharing the fruits of their labors. 1187 Franklin St. (at Geary St.) in the First Universalist Unitarian Church. ✆ **415/550-7976.** www.apronstringssf.com.

DROP-IN CRAFTS

Basic Brown Bear Factory   Ages 3 and up. Here at the original make-your-own-bear store, drop-in tours are available on the hour unless you have a large party. Your child can choose a bear color and style, let the sewers put him together, and then watch while he takes shape at the stuffing machine. The next task is to groom the new addition and pick out a new wardrobe to finish him off. Tours are free but the bears cost $14 and up. The Cannery, 2801 Leavenworth St. ✆ **415/409-2806.** www.basicbrownbear.com.

Terra Mia   Ages 4 and up. One of the original pottery painting studios in Northern California, this store was so successful it moved from its original quarters on 24th Street in Noe Valley to a larger space around the corner. Now parties have their own room with a patio, and drop-in artists have no problem snagging a table. The concept is exactly the same as above. Pick your pottery, pick your paints, and see what comes of it. 1314 Castro St., near 24th Street. ✆ **415/642-9911.** www.terramia.net.

10

Shopping with Your Kids

Shopping and kids don't always go together. Some kids get hives at the mere mention of the word. In our family, the problem is reversed. My daughters love to explore all kinds of stores, but I can think of better things to do than chase giggling girls out from behind clothes racks while being glared at by a 20-year-old sales attendant.

But we all need to buy stuff and sometimes it's inevitable that we'll have the kids in tow when we do so. Successful shopping with children calls for teamwork, moderation, give-and-take, and a flexible attitude. If there's something you really need to buy—like a present for the neighbor who's watering your plants while you're away—let the kids in on it and have them help you with the project.

Also, keep shopping trips short and strike a bargain with the little ones. For my children, a trip to the boutiques on Fillmore or Union streets means they get to stop at Jamba Juice, and an excursion to the Westfield San Francisco Centre comes with a (quick) visit to the Sanrio Store. If there's something small you can buy for your children, they'll feel the shopping excursion was intended for them as well. Lastly, be prepared to take a break if the kids have run out of steam.

Fortunately, San Francisco has plenty of stores that kids will enjoy checking out as much as their parents. And for those moments when everyone's had enough, there are always nearby parks or cafes where you can have a rest or a snack.

1 The Shopping Scene

San Francisco is a terrific place to shop. Those who enjoy leisurely perusing boutiques to find unique treasures can enjoy the city's amazing collection of locally-owned stores selling everything from distinctive clothes, toys, and gifts, to one-of-a-kind books, art, and housewares. For others who prefer convenience and known brands, the Union Square area is a shopper's paradise.

Most independent stores in neighborhood shopping districts like Chestnut, Fillmore, and 24th streets are open from 10am to 6 or 7pm Monday through Saturday and from noon to 5 or 6pm on Sundays, although larger chain stores may stay open later. Downtown, department stores and major retailers are open longer hours, with Macy's, Nordstrom, and Bloomingdale's open until 9pm every night but Sunday. If you plan to visit a particular store in the evening or on a Sunday, call to make sure it will be open.

California has a **sales tax** of 8.5% that's added at the register. Purchases shipped out of state by the store are not taxable, but the shipping charges may come to more than the taxes unless you're buying a very expensive item.

THE NEIGHBORHOODS

Union Square/Financial District   Stand in the center of Union Square and take a slow 360° turn. You are surrounded by some big names in retailing: Neiman Marcus, Macy's, Saks Fifth Avenue, Levi's, Niketown, and high-end brands like Louis Vitton and Tiffany's. Fan out a little and you'll find the Gap, Banana Republic, Old Navy, and myriad designer boutiques on Post Street and Maiden Lane, which is off the Stockton Street side of Union Square. More recent additions to the Union Square scene are the hip, well-priced European chains H&M and Zara. If your interest lies in home products or art, you'll enjoy shopping at William Sonoma's flagship store on the square, a Crate & Barrel nearby, and numerous galleries on Post and Geary streets.

Children may enjoy the **Disney Store** on the northwest corner of Union Square. Beyond that, most other kid-oriented stores are only for attire. In addition to the above-mentioned stores, you'll also find kids' clothing in the newly expanded Westfield San Francisco Centre, reportedly now the largest urban mall in the U.S. Nordstrom's has good kids' and teens' sections, and the brand-new Bloomingdale's, second in size only to the original store in Manhattan, carries foolishly priced couture brands for kids.

SoMa   The new Bloomingdale's has elevated SoMa's rank as an SF shopping destination. That's because the store opens to Mission Street and provides access to the entire Westfield San Francisco Centre mall through a doorway that lies south of Market Street. Before Bloomie's opened, one didn't really equate SoMa with shopping, as the only other stores in the neighborhood are the tech-oriented stores of the **Sony Metreon** and a few museum shops, such as SFMOMA's terrific **Museum Store** and the gift shops at Zeum, the California Academy of Sciences, and now the Museum of the African Diaspora.

Chinatown   The stores on Grant Street are clearly geared towards tourists, and you'll see plenty of cheesy plastic cable cars and "I ♥ SF" T-shirts here. But odds are you'll also come across interesting trinkets that make fun gifts for friends back home. Lacquered chopsticks, sake glasses, satin slippers, and silk robes are just a few of the pan-Asian goods you can find. With shops like the **Chinatown Kite Shop** and a plethora of knick-knacks in a dizzying array of colors, this is likely to be your kids' favorite shopping ground. For more traditional Chinese goods, such as herbal medicines, exotic foods, or ceremonial funerary papers, head to Stockton Street.

Fisherman's Wharf   Most shops here are strictly tourist bait, some more tasteful than others. One exception is the **Barnes & Noble** bookstore, which has a great children's section that makes a good rainy day escape. Also, stores in **Ghirardelli Square** and **The Cannery,** such as **Lark in the Morning,** are mostly owned by locals and are worth your while. Artists sometimes display their wares on the pavement in front of Victorian Park. The Powell-Hyde cable car drops you off right next to these places; the F-Market streetcar is another possibility.

North Beach   Much North Beach shopping is food-related. Delis are packed with Italian imports—sausages, cheeses, pastas, wine, and so on—at reasonable prices. A couple of stores specialize in Italian pottery, with **Biordi Art Imports** the undisputed king of hand-painted Tuscan plates and bowls. You'll also find antiques dealers and the occasional bookstore, including the historic **City Lights Bookstore.** Don't miss **Grant Avenue** between Green and Greenwich streets if you have a fashion-conscious teen in tow. The stores along this row are inspired, and the entire neighborhood is filled with cafes for when you need to recharge. From Union Square, it's an enjoyable walk through Chinatown to get here, or you could take the Powell-Mason cable car line.

The Embarcadero   Most retailers in this neighborhood are on the first two levels of the four buildings that make up the Embarcadero Center. This office/entertainment/retail complex between Clay, Sacramento, Battery, and Market streets is like an open-air mall with name-brand chains and a Giants baseball store. The other shopping spot in these parts is inside the **Ferry Building,** located on the Embarcadero at the end of Market Street. There you'll find an assortment of gourmet food shops, including those dedicated to chocolate, sweets, and ice cream. Outside the Ferry Building, the **Farmer's Market** is a four-times-weekly treat. The F-Market streetcar will bring you here, as well as to the Embarcadero Center.

Civic Center/Hayes Valley   The cool shops along Hayes Street will appeal to grownups, but with the exception of **Lavish,** don't offer much for kids. If you're solo for a few hours, come here for trendy and expensive fashions for home and body. Take any streetcar to the Van Ness Station to get within walking distance, or hop on the no. 21-Hayes bus from Market Street to ride down Hayes.

Marina/Cow Hollow   The best-known neighborhood shopping streets are **Union Street** in Cow Hollow and its counterpart **Chestnut Street** in the Marina. Take the no. 41-Union/Stockton bus for Union Street and the no. 30-Stockton for Chestnut Street. Both streets host a variety of restaurants, cafes, and shops, including national chains and locally-owned stores, specializing in home decor, fashion, cosmetics, accessories, and more. You can't go wrong with a stroll on either of these lovely lanes, which are as packed with trendy, young urbanites as with families pushing strollers. There's going to be something of interest here to everyone in your group, including the baby.

Pacific Heights   The well-to-do living in this neck of the woods do their shopping on Fillmore Street, between Jackson and Sutter streets. One of the rare **Kiehl's** cosmetic and body products stores is located on the corner of Fillmore and Clay streets (© **415/359-9260**). You'll find plenty of clothing boutiques for women, but not as many for men and children. Unenthusiastic shoppers can park themselves in one of the many coffee houses or patisseries, or even head over with a parent to Alta Plaza park. The no. 22-Fillmore bus travels the entire length.

Presidio Heights   This family-oriented, high-income neighborhood has two main shopping areas. **Sacramento Street** between Spruce and Divisadero streets is leafy and intimate, with many of its exclusive stores tucked inside old Victorians. You'll find children's furniture, shoes, clothing, and accessories, as well as antiques, women's fashion, and housewares. At Spruce and California streets, 1 block south, you'll spot **Laurel Village,** a 3-block-long strip of markets and stores, a fair number of which cater to children. Add a prenatal center, several pediatricians, and a pediatric dentist to the kid-oriented stores, and the number of children in this stretch of real estate really adds up. Free 90-minute parking is located behind Laurel Village and is often easier to manage than on Sacramento Street. The no. 1-California and no. 4-Sutter buses stop directly across the street.

Russian Hill   The stores in this fairly small shopping area centered on Polk Street north of Pacific Street include fascinating antique vendors, furniture stores, and some Frenchified gift shops. There's not much for kids except for delectable chocolate croissants at the patisserie **Boulange de Polk** (p. 154). The California Street cable car stops at Polk Street.

The Haight This grungy, colorful piece of San Francisco real estate is a mecca for teens, who will love the rich selection of vintage clothing stores, alternative music stores like **Amoeba Music,** and fashion that can set them apart from the herd. The city's best costume shop, which has a line out the door in the days before Halloween, is also here. Prices are reasonable, and inexpensive cafes dot every block. It's simple to get to Haight Street on either the N-Judah streetcar or the no. 6-Parnassus, no. 7-Haight, or no. 71-Haight-Noreiga buses from Market Street.

The Castro/Noe Valley The Castro, with few exceptions, pampers male shoppers with excellent or interesting taste. The one store that's fun for kids is **Cliff's Variety.** Just over the hill is Noe Valley's retail corridor, 24th Street. The J-Church streetcar stops at Church and 24th streets, an easy trip from downtown. If you want to know where the city's kids are growing up, come on over for bagels and coffee and just try not to trip over a stroller. The children's stores take care of kids until they turn 10 or so, and then there's a dearth of product for preteens (perhaps because families have by then fled for the suburbs). You'll find cafes, restaurants, a juice bar, and stores galore.

The Mission The best Mission shopping for non-food items is on Valencia Street. The blocks from 16th to 22nd streets contain a mix of hipster shops, storefront churches, and used-appliance and furniture dens. If you have an adventurous streak or want to see what's up and coming, talk a walk here. BART is the fastest and easiest way to reach the Mission, but please don't linger at the unsavory 16th and Mission streets station. The 24th and Mission streets station is only slightly better. Valencia Street is 1 block to the west.

The Richmond/Sunset Much of the shopping in these largely residential enclaves is concentrated around 9th Avenue and Irving Street. The N-Judah streetcar travels right to this corner, which is also close to the 9th Avenue entrance of Golden Gate Park. For kids, check out the magic shop **Misdirections** and the terrifically silly **Tutti Frutti** for gifts. If you head to the San Francisco Zoo, you could follow your visit with a stop by some West Portal shops, which are listed in this chapter. The L-Taraval, M-Oceanview, or K-Ingleside streetcars all stop at the West Portal station, and the M or K cars continue on to the Stonestown Galleria mall. On the Richmond side of the park, Clement Street is the prime retail area, starting at Arguello Street and heading south. This area is similar to Chinatown, only less crowded and more eclectic. The mix of stores includes French designer children's fashions, a terrific used bookstore, and a baby furniture store. Parking is metered and easiest to find before 10:30am. The no. 38-Geary bus stops 1 block to the south.

2 Shopping A to Z

ART & CRAFT SUPPLIES

Angray Fantastico Lots of dried and silk flowers, florist supplies, ribbons, baskets, and decorations. 559 6th St. ✆ **415/982-0680.**

Artsake Fine art supplies and classes for all ages in the heart of Noe Valley. 3961 24th St. ✆ **415/695-0506.**

Cliff's Variety ℛ This store is loaded with amusing, useful, necessary, or just plain fun items, among them art supplies. The store is half a block from the Castro Street Muni Station. 479 Castro St. ✆ **415/431-5365.**

San Francisco Shopping

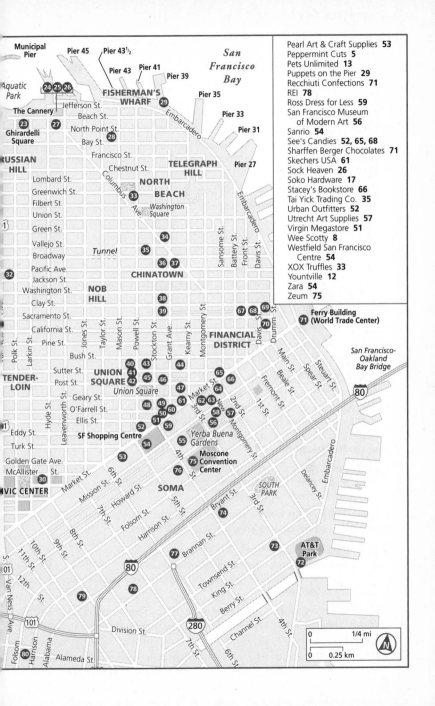

Municipal Pier

Pier 45 Pier 43½ Pier 43 Pier 41 Pier 39

San Francisco Bay

Aquatic Park

24 25 26

Pier 35

Jefferson St.

FISHERMAN'S WHARF **29**

The Cannery

Beach St.

Pier 33

23 **27**

North Point St. **28**

Pier 31

Ghirardelli Square

Bay St.

Francisco St.

Pier 27

RUSSIAN HILL

Chestnut St. **TELEGRAPH HILL**

Lombard St. Columbus Ave.

Greenwich St. **NORTH BEACH**

Filbert St. **33**

Union St. Washington Square

1 Green St.

Vallejo St. **34**

Broadway Tunnel **35**

Pacific Ave. **36 37**

32 Jackson St. **CHINATOWN**

Washington St. **NOB HILL** **38**

Clay St. **39**

Sacramento St. **67 68 69**

California St. **70**

Ferry Building (World Trade Center) **71**

Pine St.

Bush St. **FINANCIAL DISTRICT**

San Francisco-Oakland Bay Bridge

Polk St. Larkin St.

Sutter St. **UNION** **40 43 44**

TENDER-LOIN

Post St. **SQUARE** **41 45 46** **65 66**

80

Geary St. **42** **64**

48 49 61 62 63 58 57

O'Farrell St. **50 60** **56**

Ellis St. **51 59**

Eddy St. **52**

SF Shopping Centre **54** **55** Yerba Buena Gardens

Turk St.

Golden Gate Ave. **53** **75** **Moscone Convention Center**

McAllister St. **76**

30

CIVIC CENTER **SOMA**

SOUTH PARK

Mission St.

Howard St.

Folsom St.

Harrison St. Bryant St. **74**

Brannan St. **73**

77 **AT&T Park**

80 Townsend St. **72**

78 King St.

Berry St.

79 Division St. **280** Channel St.

0 ——— 1/4 mi

0 ——— 0.25 km

Pearl Art & Craft Supplies 53
Peppermint Cuts 5
Pets Unlimited 13
Puppets on the Pier 29
Recchiuti Confections 71
REI 78
Ross Dress for Less 59
San Francisco Museum of Modern Art 56
Sanrio 54
See's Candies 52, 65, 68
Sharffen Berger Chocolates 71
Skechers USA 61
Sock Heaven 26
Soko Hardware 17
Stacey's Bookstore 66
Tai Yick Trading Co. 35
Urban Outfitters 52
Utrecht Art Supplies 57
Virgin Megastore 51
Wee Scotty 8
Westfield San Francisco Centre 54
XOX Truffles 33
Yountville 12
Zara 54
Zeum 75

Discount Fabrics   In addition to pretty good deals on dressmaking and upholstery fabric, these stores stock notions and craft supplies. 525 4th St. ℂ 415/495-4201; 1432 Haight St. ℂ 415/621-5584; 2315 Irving St. ℂ 415/564-7333; 525 4th St. ℂ 415/495-4201.

Flax Art & Design ✰   Everything for the artist is available at Flax. You could lose yourself here just looking at all the pens, not to mention the papers, bound blank books, and ribbons. There's a special section just for kids and a sale basement. 1699 Market St. ℂ 415/552-2355.

Hobby Co. of San Francisco   Serious hobbyists find their way to the city's largest purveyor of model planes, jewelry-making supplies, art supplies, and kits. 5150 Geary Blvd. at 16th Ave. ℂ 415/386-2802.

Mendel's Art Supplies & Far Out Fabrics ✰   Providing exactly what the name says, this is a fun place to shop because it's packed with cool merchandise. 1556 Haight St. ℂ 415/621-1287.

Pearl Art & Craft Supplies   This store sells just about everything an artist needs except talent. 969 Market St. ℂ 415/357-1400.

SCRAP   A beloved resource for teachers, artists, and locals, SCRAP (Scroungers' Center for Reusable Art Parts) is a center for recycled fabric, wood, paper, and other bits and bobs usable for various creations. Prices are very low. Closed Monday, Friday, and Sunday. 801 Toland St.. ℂ 415/647-1746.

Utrecht Art Supplies   This comprehensive store frequented by art students from the Academy of Art is close to Union Square, SoMa, and the Financial District. 149 New Montgomery St. ℂ 415/777-6920.

BABY/NEWBORN SUPPLIES

DayOne ✰   When you reach the second floor of this corporate-style building across the street from bustling Laurel Village, you enter a peaceful environment where moms can relax, nurse their newborns, talk to a lactation consultant, and find everything they need—from top-of-the-line breast pumps to educational baby toys. 3490 California St., Suite 203. ℂ 415/440-3291.

Newborn Connections   Located in the hospital where many area moms have their babies, this shop stocks prenatal and newborn necessities. California Pacific Medical Center, 3698 California St., 1st Floor. ℂ 415/600-2229.

The Right Start   This store is part of a chain that sells high-quality baby gear, games, puzzles, and books. 3435 Sacramento St. ℂ 415/202-1901.

BABY & KIDS CLOTHING

Beleza   This store has its own independent line of beautiful hand-embroidered children's clothing made in Brazil. The rest of the precious items are European brands. 1947 Union St. ℂ 415/345-8900.

Citikids Baby News Store   This is primarily a baby furniture store, but you can stock up on sleepers, socks, newborn clothing, and baby toys, too. 152 Clement St. ℂ 415/752-3837.

Jacadi ✰   Go ahead and splurge on a special outfit at this purveyor of sophisticated, European kids' attire. Westfield San Francisco Centre, 865 Market St. ℂ 415/947-0088.

Jean et Marie   Here you'll find exquisite little French outfits that look remarkable and were probably designed for child models. 100 Clement St. ℂ 415/379-1111.

Kidiniki   Shop at Kidiniki for upscale designer togs for kids who don't get dirty. 2 Embarcadero Center. ℂ **415/986-5437.**

Kids Only   Here you'll find tie-dyed T-shirts, hats, and locally designed retro styles for your flower child. 1608 Haight St. ℂ **415/552-5445.**

Kindersport   This store stocks all kinds of serious high-quality sports clothing for toddlers to preteens. 3566 Sacramento St. ℂ **415/563-7778.**

Lavish   Baby clothing and gifts made by artists and designers based in the Bay Area or elsewhere in California. 540 Hayes St. ℂ **415/565-0540.**

Li's Trading Co.   We're going a little down-market here, but this funky Chinatown shop stocks flannel pajamas. 1111 Grant Ave. ℂ **415/986-9173.**

Mudpie   Expensive is the watchword at this refined store stocking elegant baby and kids' clothes, accessories, and children's furniture. Visit the basement for sale items. 1694 Union St. ℂ **415/771-9262.**

Oilily   This designer label carries very expensive, but oh-so-coveted, haute couture for kids up to age 12. Don't want to pay $145 for a toddler sweater? Then skip it. Westfield San Francisco Centre, 865 Market St. ℂ **415/593-4622.**

Pumpkin, Hip Clothes for Cool Babes ⚡   Contemporary, fashionable, and groovy children's clothing and accessories. 3366 Sacramento St. ℂ **415/567-6780.**

Small Frys   This is where Noe Valley parents pick up leggings, sweaters, and leopard-print coats for their little ones. 4066 24th St. ℂ **415/648-3954.**

Yountville ⚡   Yountville sells beautifully made clothing and knitwear better left for Grandma to buy. 2416 Fillmore St. ℂ **415/922-5050.**

BOOKS (INCLUDING COMICS & SPORTS CARDS)

Alexander Book Co.   Huge selection of books and a commitment to the community make this a fine resource. 50 2nd St. ℂ **415/495-2992.**

Barnes & Noble   This well-known chain has a children's department and seating. 2550 Taylor St. ℂ **415/292-6762.**

Book Passage ⚡   This new branch of the popular Marin County booksellers has a nice selection of hardbound kids' books and hosts bi-monthly readings by authors of children's literature. Marketplace Shop #42, One Ferry Building. ℂ **415/835-1020.**

Books Inc.   The oldest independent bookseller in town, Books Inc. has excellent children's and young adult sections and spot-on customer service. 3515 California St. ℂ **415/221-3666;** 2251 Chestnut St. ℂ **415/931-3633;** 2275 Market St. ℂ **415/864-6777.**

Booksmith   This terrific independent bookseller sponsors readings and book signings featuring contemporary authors. The kids' section is in the back. 1644 Haight St. ℂ **415/863-8688.**

Border's Books and Music   These three spacious branches of the national chain are conveniently located 1) on the corner of Union Square, 2) across the street from AT&T Park, and 3) somewhat near the zoo. 400 Post St. ℂ **415/399-1633;** 200 King St. ℂ **415/357-9931;** 233 Winston Dr. (Stonestown). ℂ **415/731-0665.**

Cartoon Art Museum   The small, specialized gift store in the museum has a sophisticated selection of comic books that aren't exclusively for kids. 655 Mission St. ℂ **415/227-8666.**

Christopher's Books   This fine neighborhood bookstore orders anything. It stocks children's books and displays photos of local dogs. 1400 18th St. ℭ **415/255-8802.**

Chronicle Books   San Francisco's best known publisher shows off its most interesting titles, many of which are for kids, at the Metreon. 101 4th St., Ground Floor. ℭ **415/369-6271.**

City Lights Bookstore ⬚   The most famous bookstore in the Bay Area, Lawrence Ferlinghetti's landmark shop dates back to 1953 and the birth of the Beat movement. Bring your kids in to get a feel for an authentic book-lover's den and to absorb a bit of history. 261 Columbus Ave. ℭ **415/362-8193.**

Cody's   Finally, the historic Berkeley bookstore opens shop in San Francisco. 2 Stockton St. ℭ **415/733-0444.**

Comic Outpost   Comic books, sports and fantasy cards, and models are the draw to get you out into this Sunset District shop. 2381 Ocean Ave. ℭ **415/337-6754.**

Cover to Cover Booksellers ⬚   This little bookstore sold so many copies of the first two Harry Potter books that J. K. Rowling did a book signing and reading here, much to the delight of every child in Noe Valley. 1307 Castro St. ℭ **415/282-8080.**

Educational Exchange   Mostly teachers shop here, but parents can also stop by to pick up workbooks, puzzles, and educational toys, many of which are great for car and airplane trips. 600 35th Ave. ℭ **415/752-3302.**

Green Apple Books and Music   Possibly the best used bookstore in town, with an especially enticing cookbook selection and lots of interesting picks for everyone in the family. 506 Clement St. ℭ **415/387-2272.**

Isotope Comics   Popular with collectors of Silver-Age comics, the store also carries Japanese Manga and animation video, action figures, and accessories. 326 Fell St. ℭ **415/621-6543.**

Modern Times Bookstore   This collectively owned progressive bookstore in the Mission stocks fiction and non-fiction for adults and children, plus an extensive collection of books in Spanish. 888 Valencia St. ℭ **415/282-9246.**

Natural Resources   This is a clearinghouse for classes and information on pregnancy, childbirth, and child-care, with books, toys, and other items for mothers and mothers-to-be. 816 Diamond St. ℭ **415/550-2611.**

Stacey's Bookstore   Founded as a medical bookstore and popular with the Financial District set, Stacey's also has a well-stocked children's section and is convenient to downtown hotels. 581 Market St. ℭ **415/421-4687.**

COSTUMES

Costumes on Haight ⬚   This is a must-stop for theatrical families or anyone caught short without a funny hat or fright wig. With more than 1,000 costumes and accessories galore, it's plain fun to look around. 735 Haight St. ℭ **415/621-1356.**

DEPARTMENT STORES

Bloomingdale's   The newest kid on the block carries ultra-chic, outrageously-priced brands like Juicy Couture, Diesel, Seven Jeans, and Quicksilver. Kids won't get bored as a few game kiosks have been installed across the children's department and a wide-screen TV is in the adjoining lounge. 845 Market St. ℭ **415/856-5300.**

Macy's   It can be tough to find what you're looking for at this densely stocked behemoth, but the kids' clothing department occasionally has good deals, though no kids' shoes. 170 O'Farrell St. ℰ **415/397-3333**; 3251 20th Ave. ℰ **415/753-4000**.

Neiman Marcus   The baby and children's department carries only the top American brands with prices that will make you laugh—or cry. This is one of the few places in the city you can find traditional winter wool coats. 150 Stockton St. ℰ **415/362-3900**.

Nordstrom   Teens tell me "BP," or the Brass Plum section of Nordstrom, is the go-to place for cool clothes. The children's clothing and shoe departments are also very good. Westfield San Francisco Centre, 865 Market St. ℰ **415/243-8500**; Stonestown Galleria, 285 Winston Dr. ℰ **415/753-1344**.

DISCOUNT SHOPPING

Arts & Craft Supplies Outlet   The place is so chaotically organized that little kids could get into a whole lotta mischief. Inveterate craftspeople, however, will find what they need among the shelves. 41 14th St. ℰ **415/431-7122**.

Christine Foley   Christine Foley has been making colorful, hand-loomed cotton sweaters for over 2 decades. Her little outlet south of Market sells seconds and discontinued styles at wholesale prices—*still* over $60 for child's sizes 2 to 12. 430 Ninth St. ℰ **415/621-5212**.

Mervyn's   Much of the kids' stuff here is chock-full of cartoon characters or other cross-marketing gimmicks, but for basics like jeans, socks, and underwear, the prices are right. 2675 Geary Blvd. ℰ **415/921-0888**.

Peek-a-Bootique   High-quality new and slightly-used clothes for infants and toddlers, in addition to used toys, strollers, and accessories. 1306 Castro St. ℰ **415/641-6192**.

Ross Dress for Less   The Market Street store is in constant disarray, but the branches outside downtown have tops and jeans that appeal to teenagers. 799 Market St. ℰ **415/957-9222**; 5200 Geary Blvd. ℰ **415/386-7677**; 2300 16th St. ℰ **415/554-1901**; 1545 Sloat Blvd. ℰ **415/661-0481**.

Skechers USA   The family can update their casual shoe wardrobe at this Mission District outlet and break them in looking for lunch on 24th Street. A regular store is downtown. 2600 Mission St. ℰ **415/401-6211**; 770 Market St. ℰ **415/781-8703**.

DOLLS & DOLLHOUSES

Angray Fantastico   A favorite with florists and craftspeople, Fantastico is one of the few places to carry a small stock of dollhouses. 559 6th St. ℰ **415/982-0680**.

FASHION & MATERNITY

Dottie Doolittle   Young socialites find plenty of dresses, sportswear, and accessories to make it through the season at this bastion of fashion. Sizes go from toddlers to 16 for girls and 12 for boys. 3680 Sacramento St. ℰ **415/563-3244**.

Due Maternity   You'll be the hottest pregnant mommy in your neighborhood with Due's stylish apparel. 3112 California St. ℰ **415/674-9854**.

H&M ⟲   You'll find hip duds, at irresistible prices, at this successful European chain. For H&M's popular, and very fashionable, kids' line, head to the Westfield location. 150 Post St. ℰ **415/986-0156**; 150 Powell St. ℰ **415/986-4215**; Westfield San Francisco Centre, 865 Market St. ℰ **415/543-1430**.

Japanese Weekend   Contemporary and comfortable maternity clothing made with quality fabrics. 500 Sutter St. ✆ 415/989-6667.

Minis-Kids and Maternity   This shop has you covered before and after the baby arrives. 2278 Union St. ✆ 415/567-9537.

Mom's the Word   Part of a national chain with stylish clothes for pregnancy, this shop also provides a play area for kids, stroller parking, and a restroom. 3385 Sacramento St. ✆ 415/441-8261.

Patagonia   This store is an excellent source for high-quality fleece and outerwear for children's sizes 3 to 14. 770 North Point St. ✆ 415/771-2050.

Pea in the Pod   A branch of the national maternity-wear chain. 290 Sutter St. ✆ 415/391-1400.

Sock Heaven   As you've already guessed, here you'll find novelty print socks for everyone. The store also sells sunglasses. The Cannery, at Leavenworth and Jefferson sts. ✆ 415/563-7327.

Wee Scotty   This funky children's clothing store offers sewing classes for children 7 and up, teens, and parents. 2266 Union St. ✆ 415/345-9200.

Zara 𝄞   It's hard enough to resist the grown-up designer knock-offs at this ultra cool retailer. But upstairs in the kids' section, you'll find super chic, and superbly priced, casual wear, coats, and even party clothes, and you're unlikely to leave empty-handed. The Westfield location does not carry the kids' line. 250 Post St. ✆ 415/399-6930; Westfield San Francisco Centre, 865 Market St. ✆ 415/ 817-5021.

GAMES

Gamescape 𝄞   This great store features specialty games and is run by folks who love their work and like to play. 333 Divisadero St. (at Fell St.). ✆ 415/621-4263.

GIFTS & SOUVENIRS

Biordi Art Imports   Beautiful examples of hand-painted Majolica dishes and serving pieces nearly too pretty to use. Think twice before letting young children come in to this store, which is jam-packed with fragile wares. 412 Columbus Ave. ✆ 415/392-8096.

Gump's   For tasteful, one-of-a-kind home accessories—including fine crystal, elegant tableware, and other artful items—and incredible service, head into this San Francisco institution. 135 Post St. ✆ 415/982-1616.

Just for Fun-Scribbledoodles   Stationary, cards, frames, board games, *Mad Lib* books, elegant journals, and other gift items are what you'll find at this popular Noe Valley store. 3982 24th St. ✆ 415/285-4068.

Kar'ikter   This fun Union Square store carries a huge line of merchandise based on licensed European characters—namely Tin Tin, Babar, Asterix, and The Little Prince. Items include books, T-shirts, posters, and miniature characters. 418 Sutter St. ✆ 415/434-1120.

Sanrio 𝄞   Little girls love this Japanese import with all kinds of *Hello Kitty* character-stamped items including stationary, art supplies, carrying cases, coin banks, you name it. Westfield San Francisco Centre, 865 Market St. ✆ 415/495-3056; Stonestown Galleria, 3251 20th Ave. ✆ 415/242-1870.

Mall, Rats!

While many San Franciscans enjoy checking out unique boutiques on cafe-lined shopping streets, some can't resist the benefits of an indoor mall: familiar names, nearby restrooms, and food courts. The Bay Area is loaded with malls, but the city itself didn't have much in the way of indoor shopping centers until the September 2006 opening of the expanded **Westfield San Francisco Centre** on the corner of 5th and Market streets. Reportedly the country's largest mall in an urban area, Westfield includes a Bloomingdale's, a Nordstrom, and a dizzying collection of trendy shops, such as H&M, Oilily, and Odysea. You'll find relatively high-end restaurants (for a mall) and even a 30,000-square-foot gourmet grocery. **Stonestown Galleria,** way out in the Sunset district, is a more typical, large indoor mall. Anchored by Nordstrom and Macy's, it has two long floors of stores broken up by a food court upstairs and a circular lobby downstairs. The Gap, Limited Too, Gymboree, The Children's Place, and Abercrombie & Fitch are among the brand names for kids and teens. Stonestown is located on 19th Avenue at Winston Drive, close to San Francisco State University, and the M-Oceanview runs right in front. Both Westfield and Stonestown are open daily.

Soko Hardware *(Finds* You'd never guess it from the name, but this Japantown store carries a great selection of Japanese housewares, including ceramic plates, tea sets, and sake cups—all of which make terrific gifts. 1698 Post St. © **415/931-5510.**

Sue Fisher King *(*★ This is where the San Francisco society set comes for precious home furnishings, including exquisite table linens, cashmere blankets, china, silver flatware, and more. 3067 Sacramento St. © **415/922-7276.**

Tai Yick Trading Company *(Finds* This is a real find for tiny china tea sets, miniature Chinese bowls, and all kinds of porcelain and pottery. It's a good Chinatown store for household goods. 1400 Powell St. at Broadway St. © **415/986-0961.**

Tutti Frutti *(*★ When you need a goofy gift for the child who has everything, come to this tiny shop. It's packed with oversized stuffed animals, lava lamps, eyeball candles, and other silly stuff for kids and infants. 718 Irving St. © **415/661-8504.**

HAIRCUTS
Peppermint Cuts Nervous kids calm down when they spy the pony that's used as a seat for the haircuts. 1772 Lombard St. © **415/292-6177.**

Snippety Crickets This place makes my girls feel special. With toys to keep them occupied and lollipops after it's all over, a trip to the hairdresser can actually be fun. Drop-ins are welcome, although you may have to wait. 3562 Sacramento St. © **415/441-9363.**

MAGIC SHOPS
House of Magic Plenty of gag gifts and sleight-of-hand tricks are on hand to wow your friends and impress Mom and Dad. Rubber masks and wigs are stocked as well. 2025 Chestnut St. © **415/346-2218.**

Misdirections ✿ Come here for all the rubber masks, tasteless jokes, novelties, and magic books your young magician needs. Closed Mondays. 1236 9th Ave. ✆ 415/566-2180.

MARKETS

Alemany Flea Market Get an early start on Sunday mornings for the one local, regularly scheduled flea market within city limits. Sellers take up position in a giant parking lot off I-280, at the southern edge of Bernal Heights (below the Mission District). There's a hodgepodge of junk including furniture and tools. The same site hosts the Alemany Farmer's Market, a smaller counterpart to the one at the Ferry Building, on Saturdays from 6am to 5pm. 100 Alemany Blvd., at the Hwy. 101/I-280 Interchange. ✆ 415/647-2043.

Ferry Plaza Farmers Market ✿ Saturday morning excursions to this big, beautiful outdoor market are a ritual for many families around the city. The mostly organic produce and fruit are the best quality anywhere, brought to market and sold by the growers. Vendors also sell olive oils, honey, flowers, and sausages; local restaurants, including the Hayes Street Grill, have booths set up to provide breakfast. The market also operates on Tuesdays until 2pm. In spring and fall, you can catch the evening Thursday market from 4 to 8pm and a garden market on Sundays until 2pm. One Ferry Building, The Embarcadero. ✆ 415/291-3276.

MUSEUM STORES

Asian Art Museum Store You'll find a small selection of stuff for kids here, from books and puppets to occasional origami kits or other exhibition-related items. 200 Larkin St. ✆ 415/581-3600.

de Young Museum Store ✿ Downstairs, this creative museum shop carries unique children's games and inspired art books designed just for kids, as well as exotic instruments from around the world (all certified as "fairly traded" to boot). Upstairs, sleek housewares like Scandinavian cutting boards or Japanese bowls tempt shoppers. Golden Gate Park, 50 Hagiwara Tea Garden Dr. ✆ 415/863-3330.

Legion of Honor Museum Store Unique merchandise for children is updated to reflect both current and permanent exhibitions. Legion of Honor, 34th Ave. and Clement St. ✆ 415/863-3330.

Museum of the African Diapora MoAD's gift shop is petite, but includes some interesting kids' books on Africa and African-Americans and a collection of adorable, beaded African dolls. 685 Mission St. ✆ 415/358-7200.

San Francisco Museum of Modern Art ✿ This is a great shop for gifts, with an intelligent selection of books and toys for children. Their satellite shop at SFO's International terminal is a great place to kill time. 151 3rd St. ✆ 415/357-4000.

Zeum This delightful shop is full of creative toys that may be as much for adults as for kids. Yerba Buena Center for the Arts, 221 Fourth St. ✆ 415/820-3348.

MUSIC

Amoeba Music ✿ You've found it: the holy grail of CDs, records, and cassettes, with in-store concerts and an intelligent staff. 1855 Haight St. ✆ 415/831-1200.

Clarion Music Center ✿ This fascinating Chinatown store stocks several unusual instruments, including drums, flutes, and shakers, from every culture. It's also great for CDs and gifts. 816 Sacramento St. ✆ 415/391-1317.

Guitar Center Come here for the best prices and service on guitars and amps for your child's garage band. 1645 Van Ness Ave. ✆ 415/409-0350.

Lark In The Morning Musique Shoppe ✿ Beyond an incredible selection of musical instruments, books, recordings, videos, and musical artwork from over 50 cultures, the Lark stocks plenty of charming instruments suitable for young children. The Cannery, 2801 Leavenworth St. ✆ 415/922-4277.

The Music Store This small CD, cassette, LP, video, and DVD shop in a residential neighborhood hosts Sunday afternoon American Roots music shows. 66 West Portal Ave. in the Sunset. ✆ 415/664-2044.

Virgin Megastore Park your adolescents here if you plan more boring shopping around Union Square. They'll know what to do. 2 Stockton St. ✆ 415/397-4525.

PARTY SUPPLIES

Angray Fantastico Lots of dried and silk flowers, florist supplies, ribbons, baskets, and decorations. 559 6th St. ✆ 415/982-0680.

One Stop Party Shop This small store at the southern end of Noe Valley has a thorough stock of themed accessories for your next fete. You can also order balloon bouquets here. 1600 Church St. ✆ 415/824-0414.

PET SHOPS & PET SUPPLIES

Catnip & Bones Dogs, cats, and their devoted owners will be delighted with the offerings at this cheery shop. From all-natural dog treats to catnip-infused playthings, everything is high quality and well priced. 2220 Chestnut St. ✆ 415/359-9100.

George The discerning pet owner will find hip dog and cat accessories like stylish bowls and decorative ID tags here. George carries cool clothing for pets' human companions as well. 2411 California St. ✆ 415/441-0564.

6th Avenue Aquarium Featuring 13,000 gallons of water in tanks around the store filled with a wide selection of fresh- and saltwater fish. 425 Clement St. ✆ 415/668-7190.

SCIENCE STORES

California Academy of Sciences The academy's temporary space in SoMa has a small store filled with educational materials, games, toys, and books. 875 Howard St. ✆ 415/321-8000.

Pet Heaven

Dog and cat lovers looking for a rainy-day activity, or parents wavering on the edge of giving into those pleas for a pet, should take a gander at **Maddie's Pet Adoption Center** (250 Florida St. at 16th St.; ✆ 415/554-3000; www.sfspca.org). An adjunct of the local SPCA, this clean and bright building is filled with doggie dorms and kitty condos furnished as if they were the guest quarters in a typical San Francisco Edwardian. Dogs loll around on beds and sofas watching TV or playing with toys, while cats perch on ledges watching the action in their aquariums. The idea is to resocialize the animals, so visitors are encouraged to tour the facilities.

Alternatively, **Pets Unlimited** (2343 Fillmore St. at Washington St.; ✆ 415/563-6700; www.petsunlimited.org) is a delightful multipurpose pet care center, animal hospital, and pet adoption center nestled amidst all the posh boutiques. Be warned that you may meet the dog or cat of your child's dreams.

Exploratorium 🏵 The shop inside this science center is well stocked and well maintained, with curb appeal for kids of all ages. You'll likely be as tempted by the offerings as your children. 3601 Lyon St., at Marina Blvd. ℭ **415/397-5673.**

SHOES

Brook's Shoes for Kids Stylish European and interesting American brands are on offer here, and the staff is knowledgeable and friendly. 3307 Sacramento St. ℭ **415/440-7599.**

The Junior Boot Shop An old-fashioned shoe store with patent leather Mary Janes, saddle shoes, and other styles you once owned. It also carries more contemporary designs and sneakers. 3555 California St. ℭ **415/751-5444.**

Niketown If it takes a village to shoe your children, this multilevel giant will fill the bill. 278 Post St. ℭ **415/392-6453.**

Shoe Biz Think tennis shoes, skate shoes, and bright red boots with thick rubber soles. This is where area teens find the latest footwear. 1440, 1446, and 1553 Haight St. ℭ **415/864-0990;** 3810 24th St. ℭ **415/821-2528;** 877 Valencia St. ℭ **415/550-8655.**

SPORTS STUFF

Aqua Surf Shop A cool surf shop with two locations in the city. 2830 Sloat Blvd. ℭ **415/242-9283;** 1742 Haight St. ℭ **415/876-2782.**

City Cycle Although mostly for adults, this shop at the corner of Union Street also stocks bikes for the younger set. 3001 Steiner St. ℭ **415/346-2242.**

Hi's Tackle Box *Finds* This all-purpose supplier of fishing gear draws enthusiasts from around the Bay Area. 3141 Clement St. ℭ **415/221-3825.**

Lombardi Sports This big store stocks clothing and equipment for teens and adults, with a few kids' items as well. The good news is validated parking underground. 1600 Jackson St. ℭ **415/771-0600.**

Odysea This brand new store in the Westfield mall has surf gear for both authentic wave riders and those who just want to evoke the beach lifestyle. 865 Market St. ℭ **415/882-SURF.**

Purple Skunk *The* hot spot for longboards, skateboards, and snowboards, with a helpful yet hip staff. 5820 Geary Blvd. ℭ **415/668-7905.**

REI Nature lovers will be delighted with the San Francisco branch of this preeminent sporting goods/outdoor adventure store. 840 Brannan St. ℭ **415/934-1938.**

Skates on Haight 🏵 A premier site for skates, skateboards, and skate rentals. 1818 Haight St. ℭ **415/752-8375.**

Sports Basement 🏵 Never mind that signs on the walls still read "Frozen Foods" and "Bakery" at this former military PX in the Presidio. This place now stocks the best-priced selection of sporting goods in town and has a huge parking lot to boot. A second location is near AT&T Park. 610 Mason St. ℭ **415/437-0100;** 1415 16th St. ℭ **415/437-0100.**

Wise Surfboards You'll find the biggest collection of surf stuff here: short boards, long boards, wet suits, and some cool clothes. 800 Great Hwy. ℭ **415/750-9473.**

STROLLERS, CRIBS & FURNITURE

Citikids Baby News Store This place is overflowing with cribs, strollers, changing tables, and other baby items you never knew you needed. 152 Clement St. ℭ **415/752-3837.**

Jonathan Kaye   The baby section has a sophisticated selection of unpainted and painted furniture to complete baby's room, including cribs, bedding, changing tables, and bureaus. For older children, they carry small tables and chairs, bunk beds, desks, toys, and accessories. The staff is knowledgeable and accommodating. 3548 Sacramento St. ✆ 415/563-0773.

SWEETS FOR THE SWEET

Cocoa Bella Chocolates   Sample artisan chocolates from around the world. Your kids will enjoy the hot chocolate and chocolate-covered gummy bears. 2102 Union St. ✆ 415/931-6213; Westfield San Francisco Centre, 865 Market St. ✆ 415/896-5222.

Ghirardelli Soda Fountain & Chocolate Shop   Order a sundae or enjoy a delicious chocolate confection at the former factory of Ghirardelli Chocolates. Or stop by the Union Square outlet, which just sells chocolate. 900 North Point St. ✆ 415/771-4903; 44 Stockton St. ✆ 415/397-3030.

Recchiuti Confections   A gourmet sweet shop in every sense, with sublime locally crafted chocolates, handmade marshmallows, and brownies. Ferry Building Marketplace Shop #30, One Ferry Building, The Embarcadero. ✆ 415/834-9494.

See's Candies   With locations all over town and kiosks in the airports, it would be difficult to miss out on a bag or box of the company's famous nuts and chews. The nice ladies behind the counter always have a sample for you of the sweet *du jour.* 350 Powell St. ✆ 415/434-2771; 542 Market St. (at Sansome St.). ✆ 415/362-1593; 3 Embarcadero Center. ✆ 415/391-1622; Stonestown Galleria, 3250 20th Ave. ✆ 415/731-1784.

Sharffen Berger Chocolates   In 1996 a former winemaker and his business partner decided to make the finest chocolates possible. Although Hershey bought Sharffen Berger in 1995, the shop's award-winning recipes have so far remained mercifully unchanged. Marketplace Shop #14, One Ferry Building, The Embarcadero. ✆ 415/981-9150.

XOX Truffles   The truffles, none much larger than a marble, are made on site and come in many luscious flavors. The white chocolate "Clarissa's favorite" may be your favorite, too. 754 Columbus Ave. ✆ 415/421-4814.

TEEN SHOPS

Abercrombie & Fitch   From the baggy jeans to the too-tight tank tops, teens love everything in this store. Westfield San Francisco Centre, 865 Market St. ✆ 415/284-9276; Stonestown Galleria, 3251 20th Ave. ✆ 415/664-3091.

Levi's   This flagship store contains some interesting pieces, like wildly decorated jean jackets and skirts, and a bathtub so that you can really shrink your jeans to fit. 300 Post St. ✆ 415/501-0100.

Urban Outfitters   Sells trendy attire that looks likes it's already been around the block a couple of times, but teens love it. 80 Powell St. ✆ 415/989-1515.

⌐ *Fun Fact* **Stump the Tour Guide**

Question: Why are Levi's jeans sewn with orange thread? *Answer:* In the 1800s, copper rivets were used to make the jeans stronger. The thread matches the color of the rivets.

THEME STORES

Disney Store   What can be said about these stores that you don't already know? The Union Square location is big and bright and will no doubt sing a siren song to your preschooler. 400 Post St. ℂ **415/391-6866**; 3251 20th Ave. (Stonestown Galleria). ℂ **415/564-8710**.

Giants Baseball Dugout Stores   If you're baseball fans, the official hats, jerseys, and jackets are terrific mementos of a San Francisco vacation. You'll also find cool souvenirs and possibly game tickets. The AT&T Park location is the best and is open daily. 24 Willie Mays Plaza. ℂ **415/972-2000**; 4 Embarcadero Center. ℂ **415/951-8888**; 3251 20th Ave. (Stonestown Galleria). ℂ **415/242-3222**.

TOYS

Ambassador Toys ⚸   Classic European dolls, wonderful wooden toys and puzzles, and clever games and books are among the great playthings at this delightful store. The clerks kindly gift wrap as well. 186 West Portal Ave. ℂ **415/759-8697**; 2 Embarcadero Center. ℂ **415/345-8697**.

The Ark Toys   This small shop is stocked with carefully selected wooden toys, Brio, puzzles, and wee costumes. 3845 24th St. ℂ **415/821-1257**.

Basic Brown Bear Store   You can find the exact teddy bear you want, or you can choose a style and stuff it yourself. 2801 Leavenworth St. ℂ **415/409-2806**.

Chinatown Kite Shop   From world-class stunt fliers to more modest models that could fit into your suitcase, an awesome array of kites is on display here. 717 Grant Ave. ℂ **415/989-5182**.

Cliff's Variety ⚸   You'll find classic games and toys here, plus that sparkly windup dinosaur that you've been looking for. 479 Castro St. ℂ **415/431-5365**.

Heroes Club   Japanese videos, action toys, and odd monsters fill this store. 840 Clement St. ℂ **415/387-4552**.

Jeffrey's Toys   This big crowded store between Union Square and SoMa carries brand-name toys. 685 Market St. ℂ **415/243-8697**.

Puppets on the Pier   I'd actually go to PIER 39 for this store. From kittens, bunnies, and puppies to whales, dragons, and even cockroaches, the collection of puppets is amazing. PIER 39, Beach at Embarcadero. ℂ **415/781-4435**.

Standard 5 & 10   This old-fashioned variety store contains an aisle of games, Barbies, and small toys, all at good prices. 3545 California St. ℂ **415/751-5767**.

VINTAGE CLOTHING

Buffalo Exchange   These stores are crammed with old and new attire from the 1960s, '70s, and '80s. It's a good place for your teens to see the latest street fashions. 1555 Haight St. ℂ **415/431-7733**; 1210 Valencia St. ℂ **415/647-8332**.

Crossroads Trading   Unlike other thrift stores, Crossroads gets some of its merchandise from wholesalers, so you'll also find new items in various sizes. 1519 Haight St. ℂ **415/355-0555**; 2123 Market St. ℂ **415/552-8740**; 1901 Fillmore St. ℂ **415/775-8885**; 555 Irving St. ℂ **415/681-0100**.

The Wasteland   The staff is choosy about what used clothes it'll take in, so clothing and accessories here are hip and retro at the same time. 1660 Haight St. ℂ **415/863-3150**.

Entertainment for the Whole Family

With the exception of movies, finding family entertainment can be a hit-or-miss proposition. On any given night, the offerings vary greatly. There may be something perfect for elementary school children or there may be nothing going on that would interest kids of any age. The small section of Union Square known as "The Theater District" usually has only a handful of productions on at any one time. If any of them are kid-friendly, you're in luck.

The **American Conservatory Theater (A.C.T.)**, one of the finest theatrical companies and schools in the nation, produces consistently excellent drama, but not every play is suitable family fare. Broadway road companies, on the other hand, drop into town for 2- to 6-week runs of musicals that have been playing New York for at least a year. Most shows appear to be chosen to please the widest audience. When *The Lion King* came to the Orpheum Theatre a couple of years back, you can be sure every child in town saw it at least once.

Vacation periods are the best times for entertainment. During the winter holidays, a wealth of music, dance, and theater productions for kids is available—from the ODC Dance Company's annual production of *The Velveteen Rabbit* to the San Francisco Ballet's *Nutcracker* performances. In the summer, concerts and circus performances take place in various parks nearly every weekend.

For teens, a few music clubs are open to under-21s. If you want to take your kids to a rock concert, stay abreast of who's coming to town and work the phone or the Internet for tickets.

Getting the fledglings motivated to attend any kind of performance after a full day of sightseeing can be a challenge. If it's possible to return to your hotel for an afternoon rest before an event, do so. Preplanning will also make a difference. Before you arrive, make a list of what's playing in town and talk it over with the family. With everyone's involvement, an evening of theater, a concert, or even a movie can become one of the highlights of your vacation. Also consider giving something new a try. If your family doesn't generally attend dance recitals, for example, consider seeing one of San Francisco's modern dance ensembles just to shake things up a little.

Use the Internet to find out what's playing in town during your visit. For entertainment directed at families with kids under 12, sign up for the **GoCityKids.com** weekly e-newsletter. For comprehensive listings, you can't beat the *San Francisco Chronicle's* website, www.sfgate.com. If you want more detailed information about specific performances, check out **www.SFArts.org**. While in town, the "Sunday Datebook" section of the *Chronicle* is the bible for entertainment listings. Otherwise, most hotels will have the monthly tourist magazine *Where San Francisco*, which has good coverage of events, in the rooms or at the concierge desk. You can also pick up *SF Arts Monthly* and *Theatre Bay Area* magazine at the TIX kiosk at Union Square. The free *San Francisco Bay Guardian,* available in street racks and in cafes, has a massive selection of listings, but it may be tough to discern what's good for kids. Look instead for a copy of *Bay Area Parent,* a monthly freebie covering San Francisco and the Bay Area. It's available in many children's stores.

TIX Bay Area (**www.theatrebayarea. org/tix**) is a one-stop resource for purchasing tickets online, by mail, or in person at Union Square, Tuesday to Thursday from 11am to 6pm, Friday 11am to 7pm, Saturday 10am to 7pm, and Sunday from 11am to 3pm. (closed Thanksgiving, December 25, and January 1). TIX also sells a limited roster of half-price tickets and is a Ticketmaster outlet. Half-price tickets, which go on sale at 11am, may be purchased from the office, cash only, for same-day performances. You can check the offerings in person or online. Ticket Web (www.ticket web.com) is a popular online box office with an easy-to-use interface and relationships with most clubs and entertainment venues. You can also ask your hotel's concierge to help obtain tickets to hot shows. Other resources include **City Box Office** (180 Redwood St., Suite 100, San Francisco, CA 94102; ✆ **415/392-4400;** www.cityboxoffice.com) and box offices at individual theaters and concert halls.

1 The Big Venues

The Cow Palace   Completed in 1941 and intended for use as a permanent livestock pavilion, the Cow Palace is a catchall for events requiring a whole lot of space. Regular customers include the Grand National Rodeo, Disney on Ice, Golden Gate Kennel Club, World Wrestling, The Great Dickens Christmas Fair, and Ringling Brothers, Barnum & Bailey Circus. Located near the Brisbane/San Francisco border, it's not the easiest place to find. If you have tickets to an event here, you'll be better off driving. Tickets are sold through Ticketmaster. Geneva Ave. (at Santos St.). ✆ **415/404-4111.** www. cowpalace.com.

Curran Theatre   The Curran opened in 1922 with the goal of hosting New York and European productions in San Francisco. Its "Best of Broadway" series has featured popular hits like *Les Miserables,* and 2007 will see *Jersey Boys* and *Edward Scissorhands* in town. Its partner theatres, the Orpheum and Golden Gate (see below) also hold big name shows such as *Jesus Christ Superstar* and occasional kid-friendly fare like Disney's *The Lion King.* Shows run anywhere from 2 to 6 weeks. Your best bet for advance tickets is through Ticketmaster. 445 Geary St. (between Mason and Taylor sts.). ✆ **415/551-2000.** www.shnsf.com. Tickets $30–$85.

Davies Symphony Hall   This stunning auditorium was built in 1980 to house the San Francisco Symphony. The hall's excellent acoustics and modern interior set this hall apart from many of San Francisco's more classic venues. See "Concerts," later in this chapter, for information on the Symphony's offerings. 201 Van Ness Ave. (at Grove St.). ✆ **415/864-6000.** www.sfsymphony.org.

The Fillmore Auditorium   Anyone who was listening to rock 'n' roll in the 1960s undoubtedly knows of the Fillmore. The late Bill Graham made his reputation here as a concert producer and promoter, and iconic musicians from Janis Joplin to Frank Zappa to Jerry Garcia played the former dance hall. Today, the Fillmore continues to rock with acts such as Los Lobos, Tom Jones, and Wilco. With the exception of babes in arms, you can bring your kids here. Seating is limited, so either prepare to stand in

---

Tips Comings & Goings

Cable cars will get you to Union Square theaters if you're coming from North Beach. From the Marina or Union Street, take a no. 30-Stockton or no. 45-Union/Stockton bus. If you prefer to take a cab to your lodgings afterward, walk to a big hotel to catch one. You can find a number of parking garages near Union Square with fees beginning at $10 for the evening.

You can reach the Civic Center, where the opera, ballet, and symphony are located, by any Muni Metro streetcar or any bus along Van Ness Avenue. Don't walk around this area unescorted after dark to get back to the Muni station. If a taxi isn't immediately available, walk to one of the many nearby restaurants and ask the host to call one for you. If you're driving, you can park in the garage on Grove Street between Franklin and Gough streets. The garage is well used by people attending performances, so you won't be alone walking back to your car after a show.

Venues located in SoMa or the Mission have troubles similar to the Civic Center. You can usually get to the performance by public transportation, but returning late at night by bus is less interesting (or perhaps more interesting, depending on your perspective). Again, if you're attending a show in this area, don't expect to automatically hail a cab afterwards. Instead, use your cellphone or walk to a nearby restaurant or bar and call one of these local cab companies:

Desoto Cab: ✆ 415/970-1300
Luxor Cabs: ✆ 415/282-4141
Metro Cab: ✆ 415/920-0715
Veteran's Cab: ✆ 415/552-1300
Yellow Cab: ✆ 415/626-2345

---

a crowded room (and be grateful for California's no-smoking laws) or head up to the balcony, where you'll also need to stand to see the show, but which is usually not too crowded. Tickets can be purchased through the website's Ticketmaster link or at the box office. 1805 Geary Blvd. (at Fillmore St.). ✆ **415/346-6000**. www.livenation.com. Tickets $17–$55.

Fort Mason Center   At first glance, this complex, a former military base between Aquatic Park and the Marina Green, looks like a large group of abandoned warehouse buildings. In fact, on any given day the activity level inside is impressive. Besides its collection of museums, galleries, and nonprofit organizations, Fort Mason supports the Cowell Theater, the Herbst Pavilion, the Magic Theater, and the Bayfront Theater. The 437-seat Cowell Theater is the site of performances by local artistic companies such as the Smuin Ballet/SF and the New Pickle Circus. The Magic Theater produces new works by playwrights such as Sam Shepard, and the Bayfront Theater is the site of Bay Area Theatresports, an improvisational group. The Herbst Pavilion is often used for craft fairs, garden shows, and other such events. You can find out what's happening at Fort Mason on its website, or by calling the information line at ✆ **415/345-7544**. Tickets may be purchased through its box office. Marina Blvd., at Buchanan St. ✆ **415/345-7575** (box office). www.fortmason.org.

San Francisco Entertainment

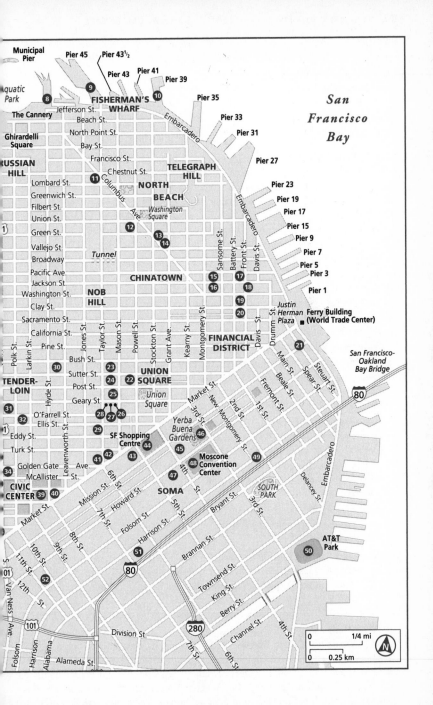

Municipal
Pier

Pier 45

Pier 43½

Pier 43

Pier 41

Pier 39

9

aquatic
Park

8

10

**FISHERMAN'S
WHARF**

Jefferson St.

Pier 35

Pier 33

Pier 31

Pier 27

The Cannery

Beach St.

North Point St.

Bay St.

Embarcadero

Ghirardelli
Square

Francisco St.

Chestnut St.

**TELEGRAPH
HILL**

Pier 23

Pier 19

Pier 17

Pier 15

Pier 9

Pier 7

Pier 5

Pier 3

Pier 1

**RUSSIAN
HILL**

Lombard St.

Greenwich St.

Filbert St.

Union St.

11

Columbus Ave.

**NORTH
BEACH**

Washington
Square

*San
Francisco
Bay*

1

Green St.

Vallejo St.

Broadway

Pacific Ave.

Jackson St.

Washington St.

Clay St.

12

Tunnel

13
14

Sansome St.

Battery St.

Front St.

Davis St.

Embarcadero

CHINATOWN

15
16

17

18

Sacramento St.

California St.

Pine St.

**NOB
HILL**

19
20

Justin
Herman
Plaza

Ferry Building
(World Trade Center)

Polk St.

Larkin St.

Jones St.

Taylor St.

Mason St.

Powell St.

Stockton St.

Grant Ave.

Kearny St.

Montgomery St.

**FINANCIAL
DISTRICT**

Davis St.

Drumm St.

21

San Francisco-
Oakland
Bay Bridge

Bush St.

23

30

Sutter St.

24

22

**UNION
SQUARE**

Post St.

25

Union
Square

Market St.

New Montgomery St.

Main St.

Beale St.

Fremont St.

1st St.

Spear St.

Steuart St.

80

**TENDER-
LOIN**

Geary St.

31

32

O'Farrell St.

Ellis St.

28 **27** **26**

29

Hyde St.

Leavenworth St.

**SF Shopping
Centre**

44

*Yerba
Buena
Gardens*

46

45

2nd St.

49

Embarcadero

1

Eddy St.

Turk St.

34

Golden Gate Ave.

McAllister St.

**CIVIC
CENTER**

39 **40**

41 **42**

43

47

48

**Moscone
Convention
Center**

*SOUTH
PARK*

Delancey St.

Market St.

6th St.

Mission St.

7th St.

Howard St.

SOMA

5th St.

3rd St.

4th St.

Folsom St.

Harrison St.

Bryant St.

8th St.

10th St.

9th St.

51

80

Brannan St.

50

**AT&T
Park**

52

11th St.

12th St.

Townsend St.

King St.

Berry St.

3rd St.

4th St.

Van Ness Ave.

101

S.
101

Division St.

280

Channel St.

6th St.

7th St.

Folsom

Harrison

Alabama

Alameda St.

| 0 | 1/4 mi |
| 0 | 0.25 km |

N

Golden Gate Theatre   See the Curran Theatre above for a description of the shows that play at the Golden Gate Theatre. 1 Taylor St. (at Market St.). ℂ 415/551-2000. www.shnsf.com. Tickets $40–$61.

Great American Music Hall (GAMH)   With the exception of dance shows, kids are welcome at most events here. GAMH's concerts feature local acts, singer/songwriters such as Jane Siberry, and bands such as Galactic. Built as an entertainment palace in 1907 (featuring gambling, dancing, and loose women), it's an impressive space with pillars, rococo touches, and a lovely wraparound balcony. The full kitchen serves throughout the shows. Tickets may be purchased through Tickets.com, www.virtuous.com, at the box office, or by downloading a ticket order form off the GAMH website and faxing the box office at ℂ 415/885-5075. GAMH is not in the best neighborhood. Its next-door neighbor is the Mitchell Bros. XXX Theater, so you might want to take a taxi here. If you're driving, there's parking 1 block toward Van Ness Ave. 859 O'Farrell St. (between Polk and Larkin sts.). ℂ 415/885-0750. www.gamh.com. Tickets start at $15 and vary according to the show.

Herbst Theatre   A historic 928-seat jewel inside the Veteran's Building, the Herbst Theatre was the setting for the birth of the United Nations, when Harry Truman signed the charter bringing the U.N. into existence in 1945. The stage is most often used by San Francisco Performances (see below) for classical music concerts and by City Arts and Lectures for conversations between authors and local pundits. Information and tickets to events are available from City Box Office (see the introduction to this chapter). 401 Van Ness Ave. (between Hayes and McAllister sts.). ℂ 415/392-4400. www.sfwmpac.org.

Lorraine Hansberry Theatre   Showcasing the work of African-American playwrights, this 300-seat theater near Union Square consistently offers a superb season of drama and musical revues between December and May. Get information on performance dates on the theater's website or by calling the box office. 620 Sutter St. (at Mason St., in the Sheehan Hotel). ℂ 415/474-8800 (box office). www.lorrainehansberrytheatre.com.

Marines Memorial Theatre   This 1927 building once featured national radio broadcasts with the likes of Bob Hope and Frank Sinatra and later became the first home of A.C.T. The small stage now hosts many top-quality local and touring productions, including monologues and plays. Tickets can be purchased by phone or through Ticketmaster. 609 Sutter St. (at Mason St.). ℂ 415/771-6900. www.marinesmemorialtheatre.com. Tickets $25–$40.

Orpheum Theater   See the Curran Theater, above, for a description of the shows that play at the Orpheum. 1192 Market St. (at Hyde and 8th sts.). ℂ 415/551-2000. www.shnsf.com. Tickets $26–$160.

The Warfield   If you find that a musician whom you or your teens really love is playing here, the Warfield is actually a manageable space in which to shepherd the kids. For those who are happier sitting down, the theater balcony has reserved seating. Bands who recently played at the Warfield include Cake and Alice in Chains. Tickets may be purchased through Ticketmaster. 982 Market St. (at 6th St.). ℂ 415/775-7722. www.livenation.com. Tickets $22–$35.

The War Memorial Opera House   Arthur Brown, Jr., the architect who designed two exceptional San Francisco landmarks, City Hall and Coit Tower, also designed the Beaux Arts–style War Memorial Opera House. Opened in 1932, it is now home to both the San Francisco Ballet and San Francisco Opera. The 3,200-seat theater was painstakingly retrofitted and updated after suffering damage from the Loma Prieta earthquake in 1989. The result was an intrinsically beautiful theater that is also one of

The Civic Center

the most technically modern in the world. 301 Van Ness Ave. (at Grove St.). ℂ **415/864-3330** (Opera tickets) and **415/865-2000** (Ballet tickets). www.sfwmpac.org. Tickets $22–$135.

Yerba Buena Center for the Arts and Yerba Buena Gardens   It's a rare weekend that you can't find something going on at this amazing city cultural center. Better yet, events in the gardens are free. From May through October in the Esplanade, the Yerba Buena Gardens Festival features outdoor classical, jazz, blues, and gospel music; dance recitals; children's festivals; and lunchtime concerts. 701 Mission St. (at 3rd St.). ℂ **415/978-2787** (box office). www.ybae.org.

OUTSIDE SAN FRANCISCO

Hearst Greek Theater   This Greek-styled outdoor amphitheatre is the loveliest place in the Bay Area to see a musical performance. The tiered concrete seating and immense stage has capacity for 8,000 fans under an open sky. Having once sat in the last row, I can attest that all seats are good, and the acoustics superb. It gets cold at night, though, so bring jackets. Paul Simon, Tom Petty and the Heartbreakers, Radiohead, and Train were among the performers in 2006. Off Gayley Road, UC Berkeley campus, Berkeley. ℂ **510/809-0100** (Greek Theater information line). For tickets, contact Cal Performances ℂ **510/642-9988**; www.calperfs.berkeley.edu, or Ticketmaster at **415/421-8497**, or check Another Planet Entertainment at www.apeconcerts.com.

Julia Morgan Center for the Arts The architect Julia Morgan, best known for the Hearst Castle, originally designed this ethereal redwood building in 1908 as a church. Now this community center, named in her honor, offers interactive and multicultural dance, music, theater, and educational events for families throughout the year. 2640 College Ave., Berkeley. ℭ 510/845-8542. www.juliamorgan.org.

Shoreline Amphitheater When the biggest names in music hit the Bay Area, they come to this massive outdoor amphitheater, 35 miles south of San Francisco. With room for more than 22,000 people, Shoreline also hosts daylong music festivals. Tickets are sold through Ticketmaster outlets. One Amphitheatre Pkwy., Mountain View. ℭ 650/967-3000. www.livenation.com.

Zellerbach Hall The major performance space on the UC Berkeley campus, Zellerbach plays host to an interesting array of world-class performers, including the Alvin Ailey American Dance Theater and the Bolshoi Ballet, in addition to touring solo artists and theater—all booked by Cal Performances. Shows that may interest kids include the Peking Acrobats or Japanese taiko drummers. Check out the Family Fare series on the website. Although season subscribers take the majority of tickets, you should be able to score seats if you plan in advance. Bancroft Way (at Telegraph Ave.). ℭ 510/642-9988. www.calperfs.berkeley.edu. Tickets $26–$72.

2 Seasonal Events

Black Nativity **Ages 10 and up.** This stirring annual gospel rendition of the Christmas story, as interpreted by Langston Hughes, is produced at the **Lorraine Hansberry Theatre.** 620 Sutter St. (at Mason St., in the Sheehan Hotel). ℭ 415/474-8800 (box office). www.lorrainehansberrytheatre.com. Tickets $25–$30.

A Christmas Carol **Ages 5 and up.** The **American Conservatory Theater** can be relied upon every December to stage this adaptation of the well-known tale of Ebenezer Scrooge and the people he hates to love. They always do a fine job of it, too. Geary Theater, 415 Geary St. (at Mason St.). ℭ 415/749-2228. www.act-sfbay.org. Tickets $25–$80.

Dance-Along Nutcracker **Ages 4 and up.** Sure, you've heard of the Sing-Along Messiah, but the Dance-Along Nutcracker? An idea whose time has come, this only-in-San Francisco annual event is the brainchild of the San Francisco Lesbian/Gay Freedom Band, and the 50-piece orchestra that provides the music and the tutu rentals. Audience members are cued when to twirl, but if you'd just rather watch, that's okay too. Two afternoon performances are scheduled in early December and take place at Yerba Buena Center for the Arts. 701 Mission St. (at 3rd St.). ℭ 415/978-2787. www.sflgfb.org. Tickets $16–$40.

Deck the Hall **Ages 3 to 10.** Members of the San Francisco Symphony present *'Twas the Night Before Christmas* with puppetry and narration, followed by post-show parties featuring arts and crafts activities and refreshments. The show only has two performances on a single December day. Book well in advance as this is a very popular event for locals. Davies Symphony Hall. 201 Van Ness Ave. (at Grove St.). ℭ 415/864-6000. www.sfsymphony.org. Tickets $32.

Music in Parks Series **All Ages.** The San Francisco Parks Trust is a nonprofit group that provides support for parks, open space, and city recreation centers. They hold free events at parks around the city to encourage residents to get out of the house. Concerts featuring local musicians are held Saturday afternoons throughout the summer and on Friday nights in September and October. The organization also sponsors the Multicultural Kite Festival in early August at Golden Gate Park, giving away kites for kids to decorate and fly and providing refreshments and entertainment. In April, the annual Song of the Earth Festival in honor of Earth Day brings youth music and dance groups together also in Golden Gate Park. All events are free. ℂ 415/750-5110. www.sfpt.org.

The Nutcracker **Ages 5 and up.** There's no shortage of Sugar Plum Fairies during Christmas, but the San Francisco Ballet's version of this classic is clearly the best-known and most-beloved in town. The company debuted the piece in 1944 and has been dancing it annually since 1949. It usually runs for about 2 to 3 weeks in December. On selected dates there's a party afterward with appearances by cast members. War Memorial Opera House, 301 Van Ness Ave. (at Grove St.). ℂ 415/865-2000. www.sfballet.org. Tickets $18–$188.

The Nutcracker by the City Ballet School **Ages 5 and up.** In case the San Francisco Ballet's Nutcracker doesn't fit into your calendar or your budget, a more modest, but delightful, alternative is the City Ballet School's version. The cast is composed almost entirely of students of the ballet school, many of whom are quite good. Cowell Theatre, Fort Mason (Marina Blvd. at Buchanan St.), Middle Pier. ℂ 415/626-8878. www.cityballetschool.org. Tickets $24.

Peter and the Wolf **Ages 3 to 11.** The San Francisco Youth Symphony Orchestra's annual holiday rendition of Prokofiev's famous piece features celebrity narrators who have included Robin Williams, Bobby McFerrin, and Rita Moreno. The December concert features Christmas carols and a sing-along to end the show. Davies Symphony Hall, 201 Van Ness Ave. (at Grove St.). ℂ 415/864-6000. www.sfsymphony.org. Tickets $15–$45.

Stern Grove Festival **All ages.** On summer Sundays, families laden with the newspaper, coolers, blankets, and low-rise lawn chairs shuffle into Stern Grove for free concerts in the park. The music begins at 2pm, but savvy locals know to show up early to claim the best spots on the lawn. It's a relaxing and carefree way to spend an afternoon. The lineup usually includes the San Francisco Symphony, San Francisco Ballet, jazz artists, and students from the San Francisco Opera's Merola Program. Stern Grove, Sloat Blvd. (at 19th Ave.). ℂ 415/252-6252. www.sterngrove.org.

The Velveteen Rabbit **Ages 5 and up.** Margery Williams's tale of a stuffed bunny that longs to be real is beautifully staged in this modern dance adaptation by **ODC/San Francisco** with music by Benjamin Britten and recorded narration by the actor/clown/comedian Geoff Hoyle. Young audience members have been known to bring along their own well-worn stuffies. Tickets are available through the Yerba Buena Center for the Arts box office. Performances take place in the Yerba Buena Center for the Arts Theater. 700 Howard St. (between 3rd and 4th sts.). ℂ 415/978-2787. www.odcdance.org.

3 Weekend Shows

California Palace of the Legion of Honor **Ages 8 and up.** This museum offers weekly organ concerts Saturdays and Sundays at 4pm. Professional organists talk to audience members about their music and about the museum's 1924 Skinner pipe organ, made with 4,500 hidden pipes. Listeners are invited to walk around the elegant marble space to hear how the organ sounds differently depending on where one stands. Lincoln Park, 34th Ave. and Clement St. ℂ 415/863-3330. www.thinker.org/legion. Museum admission: $10 adults, $7 seniors, $6 youths 12–17, free under 12.

Hyde Street Pier **All ages.** The pier holds music-oriented events on alternating Saturdays. The Sea Music Concert Series brings in internationally recognized performers to play instruments and sing historic sailor's songs amidst the antique vessels. Shows are at 8pm and tickets are $14. Best for kids are such no-fee programs like *Chantey Sing,* which invites families to sing traditional working songs aboard the historic ship *Balclutha* a select number of Saturdays in the fall. There's no fee for this event, but reservations are required. Daytime programs include *Music of the Sea for Kids,* which teaches children 6 and up about maritime history through music, and *Chanteying Aboard American Ships,* which explores the African American and Celtic roots of old sea songs. The daytime programs, 2pm on select Saturdays, don't require reservations, but vessel admission is charged. Jefferson St. at Hyde St. ℂ 415/561-6662 ext. 12. www.nps.gov/safr. Vessel admission: $5 adults, children under 17 free.

Noe Valley Ministry Music Series **All ages.** Everyone's favorite neighborhood concert hall is actually a treasured 110-year-old Victorian church. Saturday nights are given over to musicians playing a huge range of acoustic music, and the variety of performers is pretty amazing. Jazz, folk, bluegrass, roots, acoustic rock—the Ministry has hosted it all. Tickets go on sale 3 weeks before the performances, which are almost always at 8:15pm on Saturdays. Purchase tickets through **http://tickets.com** (ℂ **800/225-2277**) and at **Streetlight Records,** 3979 24th St. in Noe Valley (ℂ **415/282-3550**). 1021 Sanchez St. (at 23rd St.). ℂ 415/454-5238. www.noevalleymusicseries.com.

Randall Theater **Ages 4 and up.** Low-cost, high-quality family entertainment is the hallmark at this little theater inside the Randall Museum. At Buddy Club events, you might find magicians and jugglers, singer/songwriters, holiday cabaret, plays, or musicals on Sundays from 11am to noon. Cine Club is a program of classic film screenings for teenagers on Friday nights at 7pm. Tickets may be purchased at the museum on the day of the show. 199 Museum Way (off Roosevelt Way). ℂ 415/554-9600. www.randallmuseum.org. Tickets $7–$10 for most events.

West Coast Live ⁂ **Ages 10 and up.** The audience has a great time interacting with Sedge Thomson, the silken-toned host of this live radio show featuring Bay Area authors, artists, comedians, and musical groups. The show travels around these days but does broadcast 1 Saturday a month from 10am to noon at the Bayfront Theatre at Fort Mason. The shows are popular, so phone for reservations and a schedule. They take place in different San Francisco and Berkeley venues. ℂ 415/664-9500. www.wcl.org. Tickets $15 adults, $5 children under 18.

4 Theater

The shows at some of these theaters may or may not be appropriate for kids, depending on what happens to be playing when you're there. For theaters that offer one show or the same type of show consistently, I've suggested an age range. For the others, contact the theater to see what's on when you're in town.

American Conservatory Theater (A.C.T.) One of the finest theatrical companies and schools in the United States, the A.C.T. presents classic, new, and experimental work by playwrights from Shakespeare and Anton Chekhov to David Mamet and Tom Stoppard. Each season usually includes something you can bring the kids to see. The production values, not to mention the acting, are always superb. Tickets are available through the website and the box office, which is open daily noon to curtain time on performance days, and noon to 6pm on non-performance days. Geary Theater, 415 Geary St. (at Mason St.). © **415/749-2228**. www.act-sfbay.org. Tickets $11–$68.

Bay Area Theatresports (BATS) **Ages 13 and up.** Improvisational theater as sport is BATS's objective. In addition to offering classes, the group performs Friday through Sunday nights at 8pm. You never know exactly what you'll be seeing, which makes improvisational theater exciting and a little bit dangerous, at least for the performers. Fort Mason Center, Building B., Marina Blvd. at Buchanan St. © **415/474-8935**. www.improv.org. Tickets $5–$25.

Beach Blanket Babylon **Ages 10 and up.** For more than 10,000 performances since 1974, BBB has spoofed popular culture, politicians, the famous, and the infamous with actor/singers decked out in architecturally astounding hats and sparkly costumes. The story line—something about Snow White seeking true love—has altered little over the years, but the songs are updated regularly or at least after every election. Due to liquor licensing laws, minors are only allowed for Sunday matinees. Tickets go on sale 6 weeks ahead of time and may be purchased by phoning Club Fugazi at the number listed here. 678 Green St. (a.k.a. Beach Blanket Babylon Blvd.). © **415/421-4222**. www.beachblanketbabylon.com. Sunday matinee $25–$77.

42nd Street Moon **Ages 12 and up.** If you're fond of "lost" musicals and early-20th-century songwriters—Rogers and Hart, Cole Porter, the Gershwins, Oscar Hammerstein II—the staged concert versions of shows from the 1920s on up will delight you and, hopefully, the kids. 42nd Street Moon productions have no sets, minimal staging, and few costume changes, but the music shines brightly. Most shows take place at the Eureka Theater. 215 Jackson St. © **415/255-8207**. www.42ndstmoon.org. Tickets $20–$33.

Lamplighters Music Theatre **Ages 8 and up.** Since 1952, the Lamplighters have brought the works of Gilbert and Sullivan and other comic operas to stages around the Bay Area. The shows are great fun, and an excellent way to introduce light opera to the family. The season encompasses three productions scattered throughout the year, staged at the theater at Yerba Buena Gardens or Herbst Theatre. www.lamplighters.org. Tickets are sold through Yerba Buena Center for the Arts (© **415/978-2787**) and cost $30–$42 adults, $25–$37 ages 16–29 and seniors 65 and up, and $10–$17 kids under 16. Herbst Theatre tickets are sold through City Box Office, © **415/392-4400**.

New Conservatory Theatre Center **Ages 5 and up.** The YouthAware Educational Theatre at the New Conservatory offers theater aimed at educating young people about social issues and encouraging them to make healthier life choices. YouthAware programs cover topics such as HIV prevention, addiction, and acceptance of diverse communities and cultures. 25 Van Ness Ave. (at Oak St.). © **415/861-8972**. www.nctcsf.org. Performances are either free or low-cost.

Post Street Theatre (formerly Theatre on the Square) Tucked up next to the Kensington Park Hotel, this theater boasts high-caliber, smaller-scale off-Broadway and avant-garde theatrical attractions. This little theater may have something on the boards that you could happily bring your kids to, such as Marcel Marceau, or not. 450 Post St., 2nd floor (between Powell and Mason sts.). © **415/771-6900**. www.poststreettheatre.com. Tickets $25–$85.

Shakespeare in the Park **All ages.** On every weekend in September, the San Francisco Shakespeare Festival presents free performances of popular plays such as *The Tempest, Twelfth Night,* and *Much Ado About Nothing.* Bring your kids, blankets, and picnic

What to Do If You Have a Sitter

If you've been sightseeing with the kids all day and still have enough energy for a night on the town, I'm impressed. If you just want to dine somewhere special, consider **Gary Danko** (p. 144) or **Fleur de Lys** (p. 121). Dinner at either of these is an event in itself, and you'll have no time for any post-meal activities. If you want to eat with the kids and then hit the town, the options are bountiful. Be sure to check the listings in the *SF Weekly* or *Bay Guardian,* or on www.sfgate.com/eguide for details. Since most clubs don't get going until after 10pm, plan to take cabs anywhere not within walking distance of your hotel.

Finding some cool jazz   A 1930s supper club ambience and a sultry mood defines **Jazz at Pearl's,** 256 Columbus Ave. at Broadway Street (✆ **415/291-8255**; www.jazzatpearls.com), perhaps the best jazz venue in town. There's a two-drink minimum, but the $10 cocktail package for the 10:30pm show will get you better seating. For a swank evening of jazz and cabaret, check out the **Empire Plush Room,** 940 Sutter St. between Leavenworth and Hyde streets (✆ **415/885-6800**; www.plushroom.com), a former 1920s speakeasy in the York Hotel. Listen to jazz and cabaret singers of local and national renown. Tickets are $20 to $100.

Blues bars and other live music   The **Boom Boom Room,** 1601 Fillmore St., at Geary Street (✆ **415/673-8000**; www.boomboomblues.com), is open every night for dancing, cocktails, and jiving. Lines form on the weekends, so it doesn't hurt to arrive early and sip your drink slowly. Cover charges vary. For an eclectic music selection, try **Cafe du Nord,** 2170 Market St., at Sanchez Street (✆ **415/861-5016**; www.cafedunord.com), a basement-level club and restaurant with Victorian period interiors. Covers for the experimental and swing bands that play nightly run from $7 to $25. Some shows are open to under-21s.

Dancing   After 30 years, **The Endup,** 401 6th St. at Harrison Street (✆ **415/646-0999**; www.theendup.com), remains San Francisco's most popular dance club. The all-day/all-night club is a non-stop party every weekend until the wee hours of Monday morning. It's in a sketchy part of town and may be too crazy for some people, but if you want to dance, there's no place better. The current dance hotspot is **Mezzanine,** 444 Jesse St. off Harriett Street between 5th and 6th streets (✆ **415/625-8880**; www.mezzaninesf.com), a sleek, upscale, industrial-chic nightclub and gallery in SoMa. Admission prices vary. **The Ramp,** 855 China Basin, off 3rd Street at Mariposa Street (✆ **415/621-2378**; www.ramprestaurant.com), is an indoor/outdoor bar/restaurant. Between May and October you can dance to live jazz, salsa, and world music on Friday, Saturday, and Sunday evenings at no cover charge—weather permitting.

Swing and ballroom dancers will adore the **Metronome Ballroom,** 1830 17th St. (✆ **415/252-9000**; www.metronomeballroom.com). You can swoop by at 7:30pm to take a class and then stay for a dance party on Friday, Saturday, and Sunday night or simply arrive at 9pm to trip the light fantastic. This is strictly a social dancing venue; only snacks and nonalcoholic beverages are available. There's an $8 cover charge for just the party, and a $15 charge for the lesson and party. One Saturday a month, classes are taught to a live tango band. Those classes are $16, or $12 for just the party.

Drinking in the atmosphere The best place for a summer evening cocktail is the **Sky Terrace at Medjool** (2522 Mission St. at 21st St.; ℂ **415/550-9055**; www.medjoolsf.com). Although just a few floors up from the excellent Mid-Eastern restaurant at street level, it affords 360 degree views. The crowd is hip but unpretentious, and the *mojitos* are tasty. Another popular outdoor venue is the **Americano** at Hotel Vitale, 8 Mission St. at Embarcadero (ℂ **415/278-3777**; www.hotelvitale.com/dining). Most nights the entire Americano's outdoor area is jammed with 20-somethings. Another hot place to have a drink is **Levende Lounge,** at 1710 Mission St., near Duboce Avenue (ℂ **415/864-5585**; www.levendesf.com). Enjoy small plates, fancy cocktails, and DJ-spun tunes with trendy young urbanites. The international chain **Supper Club** in SoMa (657 Harrison St. at 2nd St.; ℂ **415/348-0900**; www.supperclub.com), offers food, drinks, music, performance art, and general weirdness. You'll see white walls, white stages, and huge white beds in lieu of sofas. **Frisson,** at 244 Jackson St. at Battery Street (ℂ **415/956-3004**; www.frissonsf.com), has sleek modern decor, good music, and pricey drinks. A cool Art Deco supper club, **Bix,** 56 Gold St., off Montgomery Street between Pacific and Jackson streets in the Financial District (ℂ **415/433-6300**; www.bixrestaurant.com), has the best martini in town. Looking to sip a little bubbly instead? Stop by **The Bubble Lounge,** at 714 Montgomery St. at Washington Street (ℂ **415/434-4204**; www.bubble lounge.com), the San Francisco sister to the cool NYC club, and choose from more than 300 champagnes and sparkling wines. The **Redwood Room,** in the überhip Clift Hotel, 495 Geary St., at Jones Street (ℂ **415/929-2372**; www. clifthotel.com), is still a popular cocktail lounge. Looking for a mellower place to have a drink? Stop by the classic **Tosca Café,** 242 Columbus Ave. at Pacific Street (ℂ **415/986-9651**), in North Beach, an understated old-style bar with perhaps a local celebrity or two.

Comedy clubs **Cobb's Comedy Club,** 915 Columbus Ave. (ℂ **415/928-4320**; www.cobbscomedyclub.com), has two shows nightly Thursday through Sunday for $15 to $40 and a marathon of local comics on Wednesday nights for $10. No one under 16 admitted. Next door to Embarcadero 1 is the **Punchline Comedy Club,** 444 Battery St., between Washington and Clay streets (ℂ **415/397-7573**; www.punchlinecomedyclub.com). Locally and nationally known comics play here twice nightly most days of the week. Shows are only open to folks 18 and over, and ticket prices start at $8. **The Marsh,** 1062 Valencia St. near 22nd Street (ℂ **415/826-5750**; www.themarsh.org), is a complex of theaters devoted to developing performances. On Saturday nights at 10pm, the **Mock Cafe** features local comics for a cover charge of $7. You won't normally find the polished acts that show up at the other clubs, although Robin Williams makes the occasional appearance, but you'll certainly be closer to the cutting edge of comedy.

baskets, and just show up at the parade grounds in the Presidio at 7:30pm on Saturdays and 2:30pm on Sundays. Main Post, The Presidio. (415/558-0888. www.sfshakes.org.

A Traveling Jewish Theatre (ATJT)   Original works with Jewish themes have been the focus of this 26-year-old ensemble company. Plays in 2006 included *Death of a Salesman* and *Rose,* which seem geared for more sophisticated audiences. 470 Florida St. (between 17th and Mariposa sts.). (415/522-0786. www.atjt.com. Tickets $15–$27.

STUDENTS ON STAGE

ACT Young Conservatory   A.C.T. uses Zeum's 210-seat theater as a second stage for student and professional productions. Recent shows included *Charley's Aunt* and *Really Rosie.* If your kids are interested in acting, see if you can arrange a trip when second-year Conservatory students work on scenes from plays by Shakespeare. Zeum Theater, Yerba Buena Gardens, 221 4th St. (at Howard St.). (415/749-2228. www.actactortraining.org (ACT Young Conservatory) or www.zeum.org (Zeum). Tickets $20.

Young People's Teen Musical Theater Company (YPT)   Ages 8 and up. A project of the Recreation and Park Department, this company of high school students puts out an impressive product. YPT stages two shows a year, one in the fall and one in the spring. They take place around town, sometimes at the Randall Theater, sometimes at the theater at San Francisco State University. (415/554-9523. www.sinasohn.com/yptmtc. Tickets $7–$9.

CHILDREN'S THEATER COMPANIES

Young Performer's Theatre   Ages 3 to 8. A popular birthday party venue, this is a casual theater experience perfect for tots who wouldn't be expected to sit through a lengthy production. This is also a theater school, so the plays feature youthful actors. Shows are presented Saturday and Sunday afternoons. Fort Mason (Marina Blvd. at Buchanan St.), Landmark Building C, 3rd Floor. (415/346-5550. www.ypt.org. Tickets $6–$9.

OUTSIDE SAN FRANCISCO

Broadway by the Bay   Ages 5 and up. In case no family-friendly musical is showing in San Francisco during your visit, try your luck at this community theater about a 15-minute drive from San Francisco. Many of the Bay Area's very talented, semi-retired performers gravitate to this theater company, which produces three musicals with professional sets and costumes during its season from April to October. In 2007 the group will stage *Show Boat, Annie Get Your Gun,* and *Beauty and the Beast*—all excellent choices for kids and adults. San Mateo Performing Arts Center, 600 N. Delaware Ave., San Mateo. (650/579-5565. www.broadwaybythebay.org. Tickets $21–$42.

5 Concerts

Glide Memorial Church   Nationally recognized Reverend Cecil Williams leads Sunday services at this socially active church in the heart of the Tenderloin, featuring rousing gospel choir music. Services start at 9am and 11am, but arrive at least 30 minutes early to get seats. 330 Ellis St. at Taylor St. (415/674-6000. www.glide.org.

Pocket Opera   Impresario Donald Pippin has been bringing his own, true-to-the-intentions-of-the-composer versions of opera to appreciative audiences for 29 years. The majority is sung in English by professional opera singers accompanied by the Pocket Philharmonic with minimal costumes and virtually no sets, but Pippin gets the point across and makes opera alive and understandable to everyone. He's done more to nurture new audiences for opera than anyone else around. Productions in San Francisco are held Fridays to Sundays at the Florence Gould Theater, Palace of the Legion of Honor (p. 192). ℂ **415/972-8934** (box office). www.pocketopera.org. Tickets $32 adults, $18 children under 18.

San Francisco Conservatory of Music   An often overlooked resource for classical music and opera, the Conservatory has been preparing young musicians for professional careers as teachers and performers since 1917. Recitals by students and faculty are given regularly at the school, often with no admission charge. Tickets may be purchased over the phone. 50 Oak Street (at Franklin). ℂ **415/864-7326**. www.sfcm.edu. Tickets $10–$15; some performances are free.

San Francisco Opera   One of the world's finest opera companies, the San Francisco Opera's repertoire is generally adult in nature. Outside of bringing schoolchildren around for short programs, it doesn't target youth. Nevertheless, should you be bringing along a young opera enthusiast or a kid who is curious about opera, you could hedge your bets by purchasing standing-room tickets, 200 of which are available for each performance. They are $10 and sold through the box office from 10am on performance days; 50 of them aren't sold until 2 hours before the show starts. Student rush tickets, at $25 if available (phone to inquire), are sold through the box office from 11am until 30 minutes before showtime on performance days. (Rush tickets are also available for $30 apiece to seniors 65 and up and military personnel with valid ID.) The season runs September through July. 301 Van Ness Ave. (at Grove St.). ℂ **415/864-3330**. www.sanfranciscoopera.com. Tickets $35–$195.

San Francisco Performances   Along with an October-to-April season of classical music, dance, and ensemble groups like the San Francisco Klezmer Experience, San Francisco Performances offers monthly 2pm matinees specifically for families. They're 1 hour in length, kids of all ages are encouraged to attend, and fidgeting is politely ignored. Concerts are held in various venues around town including the Herbst Theatre and Yerba Buena Center for the Arts. ℂ **415/392-2545**. www.performances.org. Family matinee tickets $10–$20.

San Francisco Symphony   Currently headed by the distinguished conductor Michael Tilson Thomas, the world-class San Francisco Symphony played its first concert in December 1911. Located in Davies Symphony Hall, the orchestra performs from October to early May. Programming includes a "Music for Families" series, which consists of Saturday afternoon concerts for kids 7 and older held four times a season, annual holiday concerts, and a Chinese New Year's matinee concert featuring Asian instruments and music. On select Wednesdays at 10am you can view featured musicians in open rehearsals, but you must buy tickets for the privilege. Davies Symphony Hall, 201 Van Ness Ave. (at Grove St.). ℂ **415/864-6000**. www.sfsymphony.org and www.sfskids.org. Music for Families concert tickets $10–$51, half price for children under 13. Open rehearsal tickets $18 and $30.

San Francisco Youth Symphony Orchestra   If you've wondered where the kids who actually practice end up, make every attempt to see this award-winning ensemble of 12- to 21-year-old virtuosos. They play Saturday matinees in November, March, and May; present *Peter and the Wolf* in an annual winter holiday concert; and perform occasional special concerts. Tickets are available through the box office or website. Davies Symphony Hall, 201 Van Ness Ave. (at Grove St.). ℂ **415/864-6000**. www.sfsymphony.org. Tickets $10 and 25.

All-Ages Music Venues

Here's the lowdown on the handful of places where you can take older children to hear music. At rock clubs, ear plugs are always a good idea, and a good habit for teens to get into before they head off to clubs on their own. The **Great American Music Hall** (p. 262), among the larger clubs, is the most physically comfortable. It has tables and chairs and a full menu. As in every club, the type of crowd drawn depends on the act, but aged Dead-Heads and folkies are the norm here. Shows generally begin at 8pm, so you won't want to bring sleepyheads with you. The **Warfield** (p. 262) and the **Fillmore** (p. 258) are similar kinds of halls, both in dodgy sections of town. They draw youngish crowds that might intimidate some kids, so I'd think twice before bringing kids under 16 to either place. At least at the Fillmore, you can hang out and watch the show from the balcony, since almost everyone else will be on the main floor. A smaller club that's both comfortable and cool for kids is **Slim's** (333 11th St.; ✆ 415/255-0333; www.slims-sf.com). Bands tend to be small national acts, locals, and up-and-comers. The best way to enjoy an evening here with kids is to buy dinner tickets, which give your party seating on the upstairs balcony. The food is simple—quesadillas, burgers, potato skins—but it's better than standing (dinner tickets cost $20, plus the regular show ticket price). Tickets for shows start at only $12 and top out at under $30.

Two other all-ages clubs won't impress the kids with how hip you've become, but if you like jazz, they are worth checking out. Near Union Square in a basement is **Biscuits and Blues** (401 Mason St.; ✆ 415/292-2583; www.biscuitsandblues.com). Local jazz and blues musicians are often on tap. The Southern-style food is just okay, but there's a children's menu, and dinner patrons get the best seats. For classier premises and straight-ahead jazz, check

6 Movies

There's no shortage of multiscreen theaters in town, all playing the latest Hollywood blockbusters. You can find a complete listing of theaters and films with playing times online at www.sfgate.com. The movie theaters listed below are those that are particularly easy to reach by public transportation or on foot from Union Square.

AMC Loews Metreon 15   With nine restaurants, 15 state-of-the-art screens, and an IMAX theater, you've got dining and entertainment choices to suit everyone in the family. 101 4th St. (at Mission St.). ✆ 415/369-6201. www.amctheatres.com. Tickets $7.50 child, $10.50 adult.

AMC 1000 Van Ness   This 14-screen theater on Van Ness is convenient to downtown but has only a handful of nearby dining options. 1000 Van Ness Ave. at O'Farrell St. ✆ 800/231-3307. www.amctheatres.com. Tickets $7 child, $10 adult.

Century San Francisco Centre 9   This brand new theatre complex is inside the new Westfield San Francisco Centre above Bloomingdale's. 865 Market St. at 5th St. ✆ 415/538-3456. www.cinemark.com. Tickets $7 child, $10 adult.

into **Jazz at Pearl's** (see the "What to Do If You Have a Sitter" box, earlier in this chapter). If you're coming with kids (teens, I hope), view the earlier show.

Some of the most family-oriented clubs are across the Bay Bridge. In Berkeley, **Ashkenaz** (1317 San Pablo Ave.; ℭ 510/525-5054; www.ashkenaz.com) is *the* place for world music and dance. On some Sunday afternoons, 1-hour shows for kids are held. These may be live music and dancing, puppet shows, Klezmer, or music with an international flair. Tickets, $4 for kids and $6 for adults, may be purchased at the door. **The Freight & Salvage** (1111 Addison St., Berkeley; ℭ 510/548-1761; www.freightandsalvage.com) does not serve alcohol, so there's never any question about under-21s attending shows. A coffeehouse that will take you back to your pre-Starbucks college days, this intimate club is great for folk, Cajun, and blues musicians, some local and some touring. Tickets are $4.50 to $26; children under 12 years of age are admitted at half-price. In Oakland, **Yoshi's,** the seminal jazz club and Japanese restaurant, has Sunday family matinees featuring whoever is playing the club that weekend. This means your kids get to see and hear greats such as Gato Barbieri or Charlie Hunter. With tickets at $5 for kids 2 to 17 years old and $15 for adults, this is just a tremendous opportunity to introduce the children to jazz legends. Teens may prefer going to hear a regular concert at the club. Ticket prices vary, but on Sundays students with ID pay half price. Yoshi's is at Jack London Square, 510 Embarcadero West, Oakland (ℭ 510/238-9200; www.yoshis.com). The best way to reach the club for matinees is on the Alameda/Oakland ferry, which drops you off across the street. For ferry information and schedules, phone ℭ 510/522-3300 or check **www.eastbayferry.com**.

Kabuki Cinema   This eight-screen theater is located in Japantown, which makes dinner and a major release very simple. 1881 Post St. at Fillmore St. ℭ 415/346-3246. Tickets $6.50 child, $9.50 adult.

ART, FOREIGN & EXPERIMENTAL FILMS

Castro Theatre   This 1922 Art Deco structure designed by Timothy Pfleuger is a true movie palace, with its own "Mighty Wurlitzer Organ" that's played on special occasions. The theater shows classic motion pictures and hosts many film festivals, including "Godzillafest" and an independent cinema festival. The Children's Classic Film Festival may feature such films as the original *Willie Wonka and the Chocolate Factory* and includes live entertainment, a raffle, and goody bags. Check the website for upcoming special occasions. Tickets may be purchased in advance through Ticketweb. com. 429 Castro St. (between 17th and 18th sts.). ℭ 415/621-6120. www.castrotheatre.com. Tickets $6 child, $9 adult.

Embarcadero Center Cinema   This is a great spot for stellar foreign language films like Pedro Almodovar's *Volver,* first-rate indie films, and award-winning documentaries. 1 Embarcadero Center (at Battery and Sacramento sts.). ℭ 415/267-4893. www.landmarktheatres.com. Tickets $10 adults, $8 children.

Opera Plaza Cinema Belonging to the same theater group as the Embarcadero Center, this small cineplex offers an alternative to Hollywood fare, with excellent foreign and independent films. You'll want to take a cab here in the evenings, but at least it's close to Union Square. 601 Van Ness Ave. (between Golden Gate and Turk sts.). ℂ **415/267-4893**. www. landmarktheatres.com. Tickets $7.50 child, $9.50 adult.

MOVIES FOR KIDS

Randall Museum Cine Club **Ages 13 to 18.** Classic films like *Fanny & Alexander* and *Wings of Desire* are shown in the comfortable Randall Theater on Friday evenings at 7pm. 199 Museum Way (off Roosevelt Way). ℂ **415/864-2026**. www.afcurrent.org. Free admission.

San Francisco Public Library Along with story times, many branch libraries screen films for preschoolers. At the Main Library, films are shown on Saturdays at 11am and on Wednesdays and Thursdays at 10 and 10:45am. For other times, see "Story Hours," below, or check the library's website. All events are free. 100 Larkin St. (at Grove St.). ℂ **415/557-4554**. www.sfpl.org.

7 Dance

Alonzo King's LINES Ballet **Ages 5 and up.** Founded by ballet master Alonzo King, LINES blends classical and contemporary ballet accompanied by music from the world's greatest living composers. This is a touring ballet company based in San Francisco and performs at the Yerba Buena Center for the Arts. 700 Howard St. (between 3rd and 4th sts.) ℂ **415/978-2787**. www.linesballet.org.

San Francisco Ballet **Ages 10 and up.** One of the country's finest ballet companies, the San Francisco Ballet officially begins its season in February and ends in May. (See "Seasonal Events," earlier in this chapter, for the ballet's annual *Nutcracker* production.) Productions are geared toward grown-ups, although serious dance lovers of any age will thrill to see these graceful creatures on stage. Tickets may be purchased through the website, by telephone, and at the box office (open on performance days only). War Memorial Opera House, 301 Van Ness Ave. (at Grove St.). ℂ **415/865-2000**. www.sfballet.org. Tickets $9–$130.

Smuin Ballet/SF **Ages 10 and up.** Smuin Ballet performances draw less on classical movements and more on theatricality, using music by composers like Elton John and the Beatles that give the pieces a modern spin. Smuin Ballet appears at the Yerba Buena Center for the Arts. Tickets may be purchased through either the Yerba Buena box office or **http://tickets.com**. 700 Howard St. (between 3rd and 4th sts.) ℂ **415/978-2787**. www.smuinballet.org.

8 Circus Shows

Acrosports City Circus **All ages.** The performance troupe from Acrosports is comprised of highly skilled circus performers from 11 to 21 years old who are experts in tumbling, hand balancing, contortion, aerial ropes, juggling, and more. They perform 2-week stints twice a year at venues like the Brava Theatre in the Mission. ℂ **415/665-2276**. www.acrosports.org.

Pickle Circus and San Francisco Youth Circus **Ages 5 and up.** These two groups encompass the performance division of Circus Center San Francisco (p. 235), a professional training school for circus performers. The Pickle Circus started out in

San Francisco in 1974 as The Pickle Family Circus, pioneers in creating intimate, vaudeville-like shows that highlight juggling, trapeze, and clowning, but shun the expected, including animal acts. Not glitzy like Cirque du Soleil but certainly in the same vein, Pickle Circus shows tell stories set to original music. The company performs an annual holiday show at the Palace of Fine Arts Theater (3301 Lyon St.). The San Francisco Youth Circus performs at two yearly fundraisers and occasionally at venues around town. For dates, log onto the website or phone the Circus Center for information. ✆ 415/759-8123. www.circuscenter.org. Tickets $24–$45.

9 Spectator Sports

Giants Baseball   If you are at all interested in the boys of summer, you should get tickets for a game in AT&T Park. The stadium is lovely, with stunning views, good food, a walkway on the bay, a terrific play area for kids, and generally fine weather.

Fanatics and businesses snapped up season tickets before the opening of the stadium in 2000, but there are ways to procure seats. On game days, bleacher seats are available at the stadium box office. The club also facilitates ticket sales between season subscribers and ticketless fans through the Double Play Ticket Window on the Giants website. These tickets won't necessarily be sold at face value and you'll be charged an extra 10% of the ticket price for the privilege of using the service, but it's safer than buying from a scalper. Another excellent resource for tickets is www.craigslist.com (see "San Francisco 49ers," below). 24 Willie Mays Plaza, 2nd and King sts. ✆ 415/972-2000. http://sanfrancisco.giants.mlb.com. Tickets $6–$77.

Golden State Warriors   Real basketball fans shake their heads in dismay whenever the Warriors are mentioned. They are a pretty lousy team and they've been a bit of a mess for a long time. However, kids into basketball will probably be thrilled to see a professional game no matter how the home team plays. The season runs from October through April and tickets are available through Ticketmaster or at the box office. Family weekend packages, which offer considerable savings, are worth asking about. Oakland Coliseum, 7000 Coliseum Way, Oakland. ✆ 510/986-2200. www.nba.com/warriors. Tickets $10–$90. BART: Fremont/Richmond line to Coliseum/Airport exit.

Oakland Athletics   The Bay Area's American League team plays at the Network Associates Stadium, aka the Oakland Coliseum or Arena. Tickets should be easy to obtain directly through the box office, unless the team becomes a contender for a title. 7000 Coliseum Way, Oakland. ✆ 510/568-5600. http://oakland.athletics.mlb.com. Tickets $7–$34 available from http://tickets.com. ✆ 800/352-0212. BART: Fremont/Richmond line to Coliseum/Airport exit.

Oakland Raiders   You should be aware that Raiders football games aren't regarded as very family-friendly affairs. Non-Raiders fans have had their cars trashed, and excessive swearing and fighting in the stands is standard operating procedure. The team plays at the Oakland Coliseum. 7000 Coliseum Way, Oakland. ✆ 510/569-2121. www.raiders.com. Single tickets are $47–$91 and can be purchased through Ticketmaster by phone ✆ 510/625-8497 or at www.ticketmaster.com. BART: Fremont/Richmond line to Coliseum/Airport exit.

San Francisco Bay Area Pro-Am Summer Basketball   From June through early August, current and retired college, high school, and professional basketball players mix it up in this 28-year-old league at Kezar Pavilion, at Stanyan and Waller streets, near Golden Gate Park. The level of play on the men's and women's teams is

Take Me Out to the Ballpark

Baseball fanatics can take a "backstage" tour of the ballpark, a terrific 75-minute guided walk (covering about 2 miles, including stairs) that takes in the luxury skyboxes, the dugout, the arcade level, and the visiting team clubhouse (locker rooms). The guides are fun and knowledgeable about baseball in general and the Giants in particular. You'll see great vintage photos from the days when the San Francisco Seals were the hometown team, before the Giants moved to San Francisco from New York. If your kids aren't passionate about baseball, the tour could drag. Take them instead to play at the **Coca-Cola Fan Lot** (see "Parks & Playgrounds" in chapter 9) any non-game day. Enter from the Seals gate on the plaza facing the bay.

Kids are allowed to run the bases after every Sunday home game. You needn't have a ticket, but you must be under 13. The line forms to the right of the Giants Dugout store, which is also where tours start.

For more information, call ✆ **415/972-2400.** Tours are at 10:30am and 12:30pm everyday except day games scheduled at AT&T Park. Tickets $10 adults, $6 children under 13, $8 seniors and AAA members. Purchase tickets at any Giants Dugout Store or online at **http://tickets.com**.

mighty. It's also a bargain: games are free. The men's league plays at 8pm on game days; the women shoot at noon, 2, and 4pm. www.sanfranciscoproam.com.

San Francisco 49ers   It's a party whenever the 49ers are playing at Monster Park. The hard-core tailgate galas start as early as 9am with elaborate barbecues, tents, lots of beer, and camaraderie among fans who have been following the team for years. In fact, season tickets have been passed from parents to kids since this football team played at Kezar Stadium back in the '50s. You can't buy single tickets at the box office—all games are sold out. However, you can go to the stadium a few hours before game time and try your luck buying tickets from people in the parking lot who have extras. A better alternative may be to log onto the website www.craigslist.com. Craigslist is a San Francisco–based community bulletin board that's been hugely successful in connecting people with jobs, housing, and 49ers tickets. San Francisco 49ers, Monster Park. ✆ 415/656-4900. www.sf49ers.com. Single tickets (if available) are $73 and can be purchased through Ticketmaster by phone or www.ticketmaster.com.

San Jose Sharks   Hockey fans will be pleased to know that the "Shark Tank" is less than an hour away from San Francisco. The Sharks have a dedicated fan base and the team has been going up the ranks every season. HP Pavilion, 525 West Santa Clara St., San Jose. ✆ 408/287-7070. www.sjsharks.com. Ticket are $18–$125. CALTRAIN: San Francisco to San Jose Diridon station.

10 Story Hours

California Academy of Sciences   Ages 3 to 7. Story time is held every Saturday at 10:30am and is free with museum admission. 875 Howard St. (at 5th St.). ✆ 415/321-8000. www.calacademy.org.

The Randall Museum **Ages 3 to 7.** There's a lot going on at the Randall on a typical Saturday, including animal story hour at 11:30am. The Randall is a good place for families with kids in different age groups since projects and events for toddlers to 12-year-olds all take place under one roof. Drop in Tuesdays through Fridays at the brand new Tree House Toddler Exploration Zone where kids can do arts and crafts, science activities, and play in the climbing structure. 199 Museum Way (off Roosevelt Way). © 415/554-9600. www.randallmuseum.org. Free admission (donations accepted).

San Francisco Public Library **All ages.** The Main Library in the Civic Center includes the Fisher Children's Center, a spacious children's room with exhibits, a space for films and special events, computers, and books for kids up to 13 years old. Saturday mornings at 11am features family story time. The library's website publishes a list of events for all branches, including story hours, concerts, and films. All events are free. The Main Library is open Sunday from noon to 5pm, Monday from 10am to 6pm, Tuesday to Thursday from 9am to 8pm, Friday from noon to 6pm, and Saturday from 10am to 6pm. 100 Larkin St. (at Grove St.) © 415/557-4554. www.sfpl.org.

For visitors, the following branch libraries are easy to reach on foot or by Muni streetcars or buses:

- **Chinatown Branch** Preschool story time is on Saturdays at 10:30am. 1135 Powell St. (near Jackson St.) © 415/355-2888. Muni: 30-Stockton or Powell-Mason or Powell-Hyde cable cars to Jackson St.
- **Eureka Valley/Harvey Milk Memorial Branch** Lap-sit/story time for infants to 5-year-olds is on Tuesdays at 10:30am. Children's films and videos are shown Thursdays at 10:30am. 3555 16th St. (between Sanchez and Noe sts.). © 415/355-5616. Muni: F-Market streetcar to 16th St.
- **Marina Branch** The Marina branch was closed for remodeling at press time, so its story time schedule was not available. 1890 Chestnut St. (at Webster St.). © 415/355-2823. Muni: 30-Stockton to Webster St.
- **Noe Valley Branch** The Noe Valley branch was closed for remodeling at press time, so its story time schedule was not available. 451 Jersey St. (near Castro St.). © 415/355-5707. Muni: F-Market to Castro St. and transfer to 24-Divisadero. Or BART to 24th Street station and transfer to 48-Quintara; walk 1 block south to Jersey St. and 3½ blocks east.
- **North Beach Branch** Infant/toddler lap-sit is on Thursdays at 10:15am and story time for 3- to 5-year-olds is at 11am. Children's films and videos are shown on Tuesdays at 6:30pm and on Thursdays at various times from 10am through 3:45pm. 2000 Mason St. (at Columbus Ave.). © 415/355-5626. Muni: Powell-Mason cable car to Columbus. 30-Stockton to Mason St.
- **Parkside Branch** Musical lap-sit is on Saturdays 10 and 11am. Preschool story time and videos are on Tuesdays at 10 and 11am. 1200 Taraval St. (at 22nd Ave.). © 415/355-5770. Muni: L-Taraval streetcar to 22nd Ave.
- **Richmond Branch** Story time for 3- to 5-year-olds is on Tuesdays at 11am. Family lap-sit for infants to 3-year-olds is on Saturdays at 11am. Children's films and videos are shown 1 Tuesday each month at 10:15am. 350 10th Ave. (between Geary and Clement sts.). © 415/355-5600. Muni: 38-Geary to 9th Ave.

Strybing Arboretum **Ages 4 to 8.** Docents at this beautiful botanical garden combine a Sunday morning children's story with a guided walk. This is an ongoing program on the first and third Sundays of the month starting at 10:30am. 9th Ave. and Lincoln Way in Golden Gate Park. © 415/661-1316. www.sfbotanicalgarden.org. Free admission.

11 Arcades

Musée Mécanique All ages. Open daily, this fun arcade has penny arcade machines, fortune tellers, games of skill, and beautifully restored antique mechanical musical instruments. Pier 45 (at Taylor St.). 🕾 415/386-1170. www.museemechanique.org.

Portal One Arcade Ages 10 and up. Located on the second floor of Metreon, this arcade has a pub inside where you can relax while your teenagers play hyperbowl, retro, sports, and virtual-reality video games. This place might be too overwhelming for the preschool and younger set. 101 4th St. (at Mission St.). 🕾 415/369-6013. www.portal1arcade.com.

Riptide Arcade Ages 8 and up. With 100-plus video games, virtual-reality units, and even a shooting gallery on offer, you run the risk of losing your hearing and a lot of quarters in this loud, dark room. PIER 39. 🕾 415/981-6300. www.riptidearcade.com.

OUT OF TOWN

Malibu Grand Prix Ages 6 and up. About 25 minutes south of San Francisco, Malibu Grand Prix gets the blood moving for kids with Indy-style ¾-scale cars that they can race on a ½-mile track. When that gets old, there are batting cages, a game room, and miniature golf. 320–340 Blomquist St., Redwood City. 🕾 650/366-6463. www.malibu grandprix.com. Directions: 101 S. to Seaport Blvd./Woodside Rd., stay left and turn east on Seaport and left on Blomquist.

Side Trips from San Francisco

San Francisco offers so much to see and do that visiting families could easily spend several days within city limits. But the fact remains that San Francisco is nestled in one of the most scenic corners of the world—with stunning natural beauty, world-class vineyards, and lovely national parks just a stone's throw away. Add to that its proximity to the East Bay cities of Berkeley and Oakland, both rich in family-friendly attractions, and you have a good excuse to hop on the BART or rent a car to explore further afield.

The big decision may be which way to go. Berkeley is so easily accessible by BART, there is almost no reason not to go, but some other East Bay attractions are more easily reached by car. If it's the great outdoors you seek, look no further than the Point Reyes National Seashore—certain to be a highlight of your trip to the Bay Area. Or, like many San Francisco visitors, you may have your heart set on visiting the wine country. While this may not be an intrinsically child-centered outing, even in Napa Valley you can find activities that will appeal to youngsters.

1 Berkeley

In 25 minutes, the BART will take you from Market Street to downtown Berkeley. When you emerge, you'll be in a different world. Berkeley is warmer, sunnier, and more wooded than San Francisco. Its Bohemian character is also palpable. Berkeley's spirit of idealism, in full swing when the University of California Berkeley was a focal point of 1960s student protests, persists today, even as the city takes in more families fleeing real estate prices in San Francisco. On the university campus and in Tilden Park, you'll find some terrific activities for kids. Teens will enjoy strolling down Telegraph Avenue and may even be inspired by a campus tour to start thinking about college. For the whole family, Berkeley is also a delightful place to eat and shop.

EXPLORING BERKELEY

Adventure Park and Playground **Ages 4 and up.** A fenced outdoor workshop/playground, this unusual park is heaven for any child whose idea of a good time involves a hammer, some nails, and a pile of wood. It's located at the Berkeley Marina, which offers several great options for a day outdoors, including Cesar Chavez Park, where you can picnic or fly kites, and the Shorebird Park Nature Center (see below). At the Adventure Park, with the help of students from UC Berkeley, kids are encouraged to create and build whatever they want, sawing and painting as they see fit. They can climb on towers and ships and play in shacks and other structures designed and assembled by fellow builders. They can also zip down a cable with the help of a pulley slide and play on a jungle gym made out of automobile tires. The playground is designed for kids 7 and up, but younger kids are also welcome as long as they stay within arm's reach of their parents. The park is so popular that groups arriving with 5 or more children must reserve ahead of time and pay a fee, starting at $52 for 2 hours.

Berkeley Marina (south of University Ave.). ℂ 510/981-6720. www.ci.berkeley.ca.us/marina/marinaexp/adventplgd. html. Free for children supervised by a parent/guardian, $6 per unaccompanied child for 3-hr. session. Weekends and school holidays 11am–4pm; summer weekdays 9am–5pm. Closed when raining and also Dec 24–26 and Dec 31–Jan 1. Phone to confirm. **To get there:** By car: Take I-80 to Powell St. Make a left under the freeway and a right onto Frontage Rd. Follow Frontage Rd. to University Ave. Take a left onto University and follow the signs for the marina.

The Berkeley Hall of Health   Ages 3 to 12.   Located across the street from Habitot, The Berkeley Hall of Health is an interactive museum designed to teach children about the human body, nutrition, and health. The museum includes hands-on exhibits on the human heart, the inside of the body, and how to prevent diseases.

2230 Shattuck Ave., lower level. ℂ 510/549-1564. www.hallofhealth.org. Suggested donation $3 per person, children under 3 free. Tues–Sat 10am–4pm. **To get there:** By BART: Exit at the Berkeley station; walk 1 block south to the museum. By car: Take I-80 to the University Ave. exit. Drive east (toward the hills) until you reach Shattuck Ave. Take a right on Shattuck and another right on Kittredge St. There is parking in the garage across from the main entrance.

Habitot Children's Museum   Ages infant to 7.   A hands-on exhibition center, Habitot helps children develop and explore creative and interactive skills that they will use for life. This delightful museum provides opportunities to explore art, science, history, cultural heritage, architecture, and technology through six exhibits. Each gallery offers a specific, age-appropriate activity. At the **Rocketship,** aspiring astronauts can don astronaut costumes, manipulate the mission control panel, and contemplate their futures in outer space. At **Waterworks,** kids can experience different types of water activity: a flowing river ramp, a pumping station, and a water table. The **Little Town Grocery & Cafe** provides a miniature shopping experience with kid-size shopping carts and plastic fruits, vegetables, and breads that kids can also sort themselves into grocery bins. Cash registers with working buttons and play money help them practice counting and encourage interactive play. The **Infant-Toddler Garden,** designed for crawlers, has carpeted walls depicting a garden mural landscape and interactive activities including a carrot patch, a pretend pond, and shapes to Velcro to the wall—all surrounded by a white picket fence. At the **Drop-in Art Studio,** kids of all ages can paint or draw their own wall murals, participate in various organized art activities, or create their own masterpieces on paper. A **Wiggle Wall** allows children to feel their way through an "underground" labyrinth. Habitot has kiddy cars and toys available to play with, offers special outreach programs to neighborhood families with special needs, and works closely with the Head Start program.

2065 Kittredge St. (near Shattuck Ave.), Berkeley. ℂ 510/647-1111. www.habitot.org. Admission $6 children, $5 adults, under 12 months free. Tues and Fri 9:30am–5pm; Wed 9:30am–1pm; Thurs 9:30am–7pm; Sat 10am–5pm; Sun (Oct 1–Mar 31 only) 11am–5pm. Closed major holidays and Sundays Apr–Sept. **To get there:** See "Berkeley Hall of Health," above. The entrance to the museum is on the lower level of the parking garage.

Shorebird Park Nature Center   Ages 4 to 12.   Here families can learn about San Francisco Bay ecology. Exhibits include a 100-gallon aquarium featuring marine plants and animals found in the San Francisco Bay. There are several wildlife displays to see and explore as well as a touch table, where kids can gently handle different species of marine life.

Berkeley Marina (east of the Adventure playground). ℂ 510/981-6720. www.ci.berkeley.ca.us/marina/marinaexp/ naturecenter.html. Tues–Sat 9am–5pm. Free admission. **To get there:** By car: Take I-80 to Powell St. Make a left under the freeway and a right onto Frontage Rd. Follow Frontage Rd. to University Ave. Take a left onto University and follow the signs for the marina.

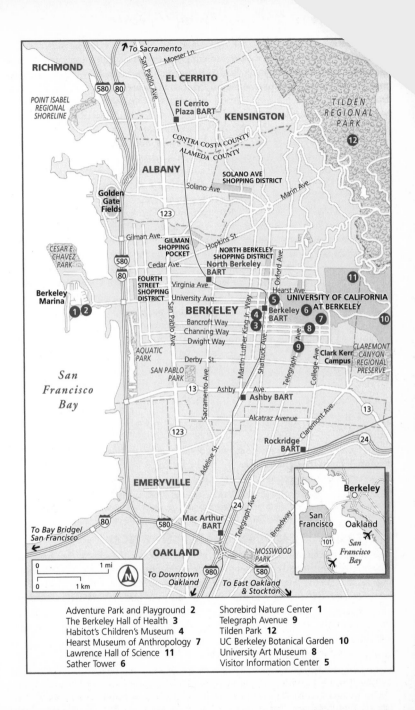

Adventure Park and Playground **2**
The Berkeley Hall of Health **3**
Habitot's Children's Museum **4**
Hearst Museum of Anthropology **7**
Lawrence Hall of Science **11**
Sather Tower **6**

Shorebird Nature Center **1**
Telegraph Avenue **9**
Tilden Park **12**
UC Berkeley Botanical Garden **10**
University Art Museum **8**
Visitor Information Center **5**

es. This 2,077-acre woodland park, which opened in the Berke-
...ome to numerous hiking and horseback riding trails, several pic-
...s for playing Frisbee or just running around. For those needing
..., the **Environmental Education Center,** open Tuesday to Sunday
...m, has a man-made canyon cavern that shows various species of
...be found around the park. Microscopes are available for getting a
close-up look at the life within the park's lakes and ponds.

Just beyond the education center is the **Little Farm,** open daily from 8:30am to 4pm, where kids can pet sheep, donkeys, cows, and other animals. Tilden Park is famous for the **Steam Train,** a scaled-down version of a real steam train that travels around the edge of the park through a miniature town, over bridges, and through tunnels (© **510/ 548-6100;** www.redwoodvalleyrailway.com; open 11am–6pm daily in summer and weekends and holidays during the school year, except Thanksgiving and Christmas; rides $2 each or five for $8, kids under 2 free). The **Herschell-Spillman Merry-Go-Round** is an antique carousel with features like hand-carved wooden frogs, lions, and giraffes (© **510/524-6773;** open 11am–5pm daily in summer and weekends and holidays during the school year; rides $1, $10 for a 13-ride book). The carousel closes for the month of November until the day after Thanksgiving, when it reopens for a "Christmas Fantasy" event nightly from 5:30 to 8:30pm through December 23. For more adventurous little ones, pony rides are available just beyond the carousel (© **510/527-0421;** open 11am–5pm weekends, 11am–4pm Tues–Fri in summer; rides $3).

Families visiting in the warm weather months can spend the afternoon swimming and sunning at **Lake Anza,** right in the center of the park. You can park nearby or hike to the lake area, where the facilities include changing rooms, showers, and, in the summer, lifeguards. There is a small snack bar open during the summer as well.

Another interesting area is **Jewel Lake,** a marshy wetland with lots of animals and birds, including ducks, squirrels, and turtles. Watch out for the poison oak. If you are around after a rain, you might see some California newts. Jewel Lake is not open for swimming.

For families interested in learning more about California's flowers and plant life, the **Regional Parks Botanic Garden** in Tilden Park is a lovely place to explore (visit www.nativeplants.org for more information).

© **510/562-7275.** www.ebparks.org/parks/tilden.htm. Daily 5am–10pm. **To get there:** By car: Take I-80 to the Buchanan St. exit. Go east and stay to the right; Buchanan turns into Marin Ave. Follow Marin to Grizzly Peak Blvd. and make a left. Turn right on Wildcat Canyon Rd., then left on Canon Dr. into the park.

UNIVERSITY OF CALIFORNIA AT BERKELEY (UCB)

The attractive campus tucked into the woodsy Berkeley hillside has produced 20 Nobel Prize winners and continues to be one of the finest institutions of higher learning in the United States. Its **Visitor Information Center** (© **510/642-5215;** www.berkeley.edu/visitors) is located at 101 University Hall, 220 University Ave., at Oxford Street. A free campus tour is available from the center at 10am Monday through Saturday and at 1pm on Sundays. Perhaps the best reason to visit the campus with kids is the Lawrence Hall of Science (see below).

Other notable UCB stops include the **Hearst Museum of Anthropology** at Kroeber Hall (© **510/642-3682;** http://hearstmuseum.berkeley.edu; Wed–Sat 10:30am–4pm, Sun noon–4pm; admission $4 adults, $3 seniors 55 and up, $1 students with ID, free children under 12, free every Thurs); the **Berkeley Art Museum** at 2621 Durant Ave. (© **510/642-0808;** www.bampfa.berkeley.edu; Wed–Sun 11am–5pm, Thurs 11am–7pm;

admission $8 adults, $5 seniors 65 and up, children 12–17, and non-UC Berkeley students, free children under 12); and the 307-foot-tall **Sather Tower,** also known as the Campanile, in the center of the campus. The Campanile houses 61 bells ranging in weight from 19 to 10,500 pounds and offers carillon concerts daily at 7:50am, noon, and 6pm, with longer concerts on Sundays at 2pm. Take the elevator to the top for the view (open Mon–Fri 10am–4pm; Sat 10am–5pm; Sun 10am–1:30pm and 3–5pm; admission $2 adults, $1 seniors and children 18 and under; free to UC Berkeley students and staff).

Above the campus at 200 Centennial Drive is the **UC Berkeley Botanical Garden** (✆ **510/643-2755;** http://botanicalgarden.berkeley.edu), boasting one of the most diverse collections of plants in the country, with more than 12,000 different species and subspecies. It's a wonderful place for an easy hike. (Open daily 9am–5pm; closed first Tues of the month, Thanksgiving, Dec 24, 25, and 31, Jan 1, and Martin Luther King, Jr. Day; admission $5 adults, $3 seniors, $1 children 3–17, free under 3.)

If you're driving to the campus, take I-80 to 580 and exit at University Avenue. Drive east on University for 2 miles until you reach the campus.

Lawrence Hall of Science (LHS)   Ages 2 and up. The Lawrence Hall of Science, which honors UC Berkeley's Nobel Prize winner Ernest O. Lawrence, is both a resource center for students and an exciting hands-on museum for the entire family. Sitting at the upper edges of the hillside campus, the entry plaza offers endless views of the bay and the cities beyond. On a clear day, take in the views as the kids climb all over a 60-foot-long DNA model.

LHS programs are renowned throughout the state for their imaginative interactive exhibits and multifaceted approach to teaching math and science to kids of all ages. Among the permanent exhibits is a biology lab where kids can pet snakes and befriend tarantulas, an insect zoo popular with young children, computer labs, and an earthquake exhibit with a working seismograph and tips on how to react during an earthquake (duck and cover). An area designated especially for toddlers is filled with blocks, books, and puppets.

Special weekend workshops are regularly scheduled. Participants must register a week in advance and workshop fees include museum admission. The museum's Holt Planetarium offers shows, films, and lectures on weekends and holidays and all summer for an additional $3 for adults and $2.50 children 18 and under. Most shows are for older kids, but some are geared for the younger set. The gift shop has fascinating books, toys, and kits. When you need a snack, a downstairs cafe offers hot dogs and sandwiches.

Centennial Dr., Berkeley. ✆ **510/624-5132.** www.lawrencehallofscience.org. Admission $9.50 adults, $7.50 students 5–18 and seniors 62 and over, $5.50 children 3–4, free 2 and under. Daily 10am–5pm. Closed Labor Day, Thanksgiving, and Dec 25. Planetarium shows Sat, Sun, and holidays 1, 2:15, and 3:30pm. Closed Dec 24. **To get there:** By BART: Exit at the Downtown Berkeley Station. Take the University of California local shuttle on the corner of Center St. and Shattuck Ave. to the campus. Once there, transfer to the Hill Service Shuttle at the Hearst Mining Circle (✆ **510/642-4834** for details on fares and times). By car: Take I-80 to 580. Exit at University Ave. Drive east on University 2 miles until you reach the campus. Turn left on Oxford St. Turn right on Hearst St., pass through 2 stoplights to the east side of campus. Make a right on Gayley Rd. Take your 1st left past the Greek Theatre, Stadium Rimway. Make a left at the stop sign, Centennial Dr., and continue 1 mile to the top of the hill.

WHERE TO DINE IN BERKELEY

Not far from the University on Shattuck Avenue is an area known as the Gourmet Ghetto, so named for its principal occupant **Chez Panisse** and the myriad imitators it has spawned. Chez Panisse is the creation of Alice Waters, who in the 1970s revolutionized California, indeed American, cuisine with her emphasis on using seasonal and local ingredients of the highest quality. If you can fit it in, a visit to Chez Panisse is well worth it. The light and airy upstairs cafe is suitable for kids at lunchtime (1517 Shattuck Ave.; ✆ 510/548-5049; www.chezpanisse.com).

The latest addition to the Gourmet Ghetto is **Epicurious Garden** (1509, 1511, and 1513 Shattuck Ave.; www.epicuriousgarden.com), featuring restaurants that offer gourmet take-out fare, a cooking school, and other specialty stores. Another casual dining option just next door is the **Cheeseboard Collective** (1504 Shattuck Ave.; ✆ 510/549-3183; http://cheeseboardcollective.com), serving good pizzas, fabulous cheeses, and fresh-basked breads. For a terrific brunch spot a few blocks off of Shattuck Avenue, try **Fat Apple's Restaurant and Bakery** (1346 Martin Luther King, Jr. Way; ✆ 510/526-2260).

In downtown Berkeley, **Caffe Venezia** (1799 University Ave.; ✆ 510/849-4681; www.caffevenezia.com) is a casual place for tasty Italian food, and **La Note** is a kid-friendly French bistro (2377 Shattuck Ave.; ✆ 510/843-1535; http://lanote restaurant.com). For the best pizza in town, head to **Zachary's Chicago Pizza** (1853 Solano Ave.; ✆ 510/525-5950; www.zacharys.com).

If chocolate is your meal of choice, Berkeley is home to a boutique producer of high-octane cooking and eating chocolate. **Scharffen Berger Chocolate Maker** (914 Heinz Ave., near 7th St.; ✆ 510/981-4050; www.scharffenberger.com) gives free 1-hour tours of its factory daily. Times vary, so check the website for hours and to sign up. Private tours are also available for a $35 fee; they occur at 11am and 4:30pm daily and include a $1 gift certificate for each participant with a limit of 40 guests. Tour guests must be at least 10 years old and wear closed-toe shoes for safety reasons. The factory is off the Ashby Avenue exit on I-80.

2 Oakland

Oakland has always been regarded as San Francisco's poor relation. The heavy crime rate and proximity to higher profile Berkeley and San Francisco have often kept this bayside city from getting its just due. But the city has one of the state's best museums right downtown and an excellent space science center in the hills. Moreover, Bay Area families have been visiting Children's Fairyland and the Paramount Theater for generations. Jack London Square is touristy, but it's a fine starting point for a bike ride and exactly where you want to be for hot Bay Area jazz.

Chabot Space and Science Center   **Ages 4 and up.** This 86,000-square-foot facility high in the East Bay hills will thrill youngsters with an interest in space—and is a must-visit for any kid studying the solar system. The center focuses on educating students, teachers, and the general public about astronomy and related sciences and has a number of delightful exhibits to do just that. The **Observatory** houses 3 powerful telescopes, among them one of the largest open to the public in the U.S. (Free access to the refractor telescope is available from 7–10pm Nov–Mar, and from dusk–10:30pm Apr–Oct.) The Ask Jeeves **Planetarium** offers dazzling shows using the most advanced digital technology to project stunning images across a 70-foot-diameter screen. The **Challenger Learning Center** boasts a full-size space station, and the **Discovery Room** offers activities for children under age 7. Every Friday night from 7 to 10pm (except holidays and Memorial Day weekend), the **Telescope Maker's Workshop** lets kids of any age make their own telescope. You'll find the drive up here well worth it, as the center is housed on 13 wooded acres full of lovely walking trails with wonderful bay views.

10000 Skyline Blvd., Oakland. ✆ 510/336-7300. www.chabotspace.org. General admission (required except when visiting evening shows or when exhibits are closed) $13 adults, $9 seniors, children 4–12, and students w/valid ID, free for kids 3 and under. Wed–Thurs 10am–5pm; Fri–Sat 10am–10pm; Sun 11am–5pm. Closed Mon–Tues except certain holidays; check website or call for details. **To get there:** Head east on I-580 to Highway 24 (towards Walnut Creek). From 24, go south on Highway 13 (Warren Freeway) towards Hayward. Take the Joaquin Miller/Lincoln Ave. exit. Turn left and proceed up the hill on Joaquin Miller to the crest, then turn left at the signal onto the two lane portion of Skyline Blvd. The center is 1.3 miles up Skyline on the right.

Children's Fairyland   Ages infant to 7. Fairy tales and nursery rhymes come alive at the delightfully low-tech and innocent Children's Fairyland. Purchase a magic key for $2 when entering, which lets the kids listen to nursery rhymes at each of 30 animated sets. The park has rides for the little ones including Jolly Trolly, a train that rounds the park, and a miniature Ferris wheel. Fairyland also offers daily puppet shows, arts and craft events, and special presentations throughout the year. For families with preschoolers, it is a magical place.

There's a picnic area, or you can pick something up (PB&J, burgers, hot dogs) at the Johnny Appleseed Cafe. Fairyland is located on the shores of **Lake Merritt**, a fine place for boating, lawn bowling, or a scenic stroll. From the **Municipal Boathouse** (✆ **510/238-2196**) you can rent sailboats, rowboats, pedal boats, and canoes for $8 to $15 per hour. The boathouse is open daily, with longest hours in summer. Another option is a Venetian-style gondola ride from **Gondola Servizio** (✆ **510/663-6603;** www.gondolaservizio.com), which operates from June to October.

Grand Ave. at Bellevue Ave. ✆ 510/452-2259. www.fairyland.org. Tickets $6 per person, children under 1 free. Adults must be accompanied by a child. Open Fri–Sun and holidays 10am–4pm in winter (Nov to mid-Apr); Wed–Sun and holidays 10am–4pm in spring and fall (mid-Apr to mid-June and Sept–Oct); Mon–Fri 10am–4pm and Sat–Sun 10am–5pm in summer (mid-June to Aug). **To get there:** By BART: Exit at the 19th St. Station. Take the 20th St. stairway and exit at street level. Walk down 20th St., make a left on Harrison St. Turn right on Grand Ave. Fairyland is 1 block over on the right-hand side at the intersection of Grand and Bellevue aves. By car: From the Bay Bridge, take I-580 East to Harrison St. exit. Turn right on Harrison and continue for approximately ½ mile. Turn left on Grand Ave. Fairyland is at the corner of Grand and Bellevue aves. There is parking available at the park.

Museum of Children's Art   Ages 18 months and up. This diminutive museum located in downtown Oakland near Chinatown features artwork created by children. On weekdays the museum offers drop-in classes for kids 18 months and up, covering fun themes like "Food Fantasies" or "Monsters and Magic," while weekend drop-in classes welcome the whole family.

538 9th St., Oakland. ✆ 510/465-8770. www.mocha.org. Free admission, Drop-in art studio $5 per child. Tues–Fri 10am–5pm; Sat–Sun noon–5pm. **To get there:** By BART: Exit at the 12th St. BART station; exit at the 11th St. gate and walk up Broadway 2 blocks to 9th St. and turn right. Museum is inside Swan's Marketplace at 9th and Washington sts. By car: Cross bridge and get on I-880 South towards San Jose. Exit at Broadway/Alameda and turn right at the bottom of the exit ramp onto 5th St. Turn left on Washington St. and continue 3 blocks; turn left on 8th St. Continue 1 block and turn right onto Clay St., head 1 block and turn left onto 9th St.

Oakland Museum   Ages 5 and up. The Oakland Museum is unique because of its emphasis on re-created "environments" rather than separate exhibits. Each floor of the museum presents the nature, art, and history of California. Life-size dioramas reflect California's vast environment and give children and adults a chance to experience California's natural wildlife on a simulated walk across the state. The aquatic gallery takes visitors along California's coastline and rivers to see the fresh water and marine animals living within. The Cowell Hall of California History takes kids back in time from the first missions to the gold rush and up to the present day. Touch-screen computers and

Oakland

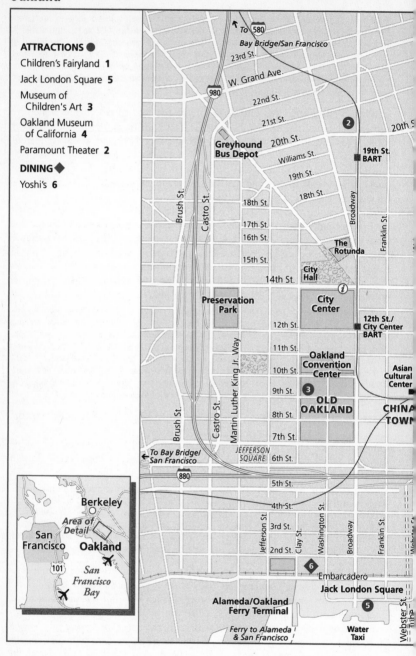

ATTRACTIONS ●

Children's Fairyland **1**

Jack London Square **5**

Museum of
Children's Art **3**

Oakland Museum
of California **4**

Paramount Theater **2**

DINING ◆

Yoshi's **6**

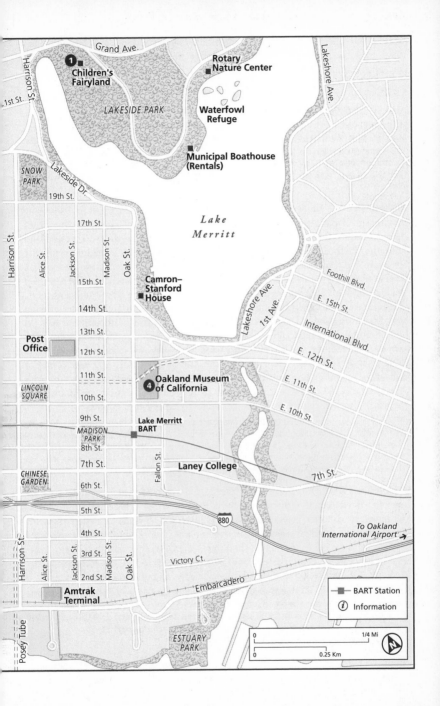

Grand Ave.

1 Children's
Fairyland

Rotary
Nature Center

LAKESIDE PARK

Waterfowl
Refuge

1st St.

Harrison St.

Municipal Boathouse
(Rentals)

SNOW
PARK

Lakeside Dr.

19th St.

*Lake
Merritt*

17th St.

Harrison St.

Alice St.

Jackson St.

Madison St.

Oak St.

15th St.

Camron–
Stanford
House

14th St.

Lakeshore Ave.

1st Ave.

Foothill Blvd.

E. 15th St.

13th St.

**Post
Office**

12th St.

International Blvd.

E. 12th St.

11th St.

*LINCOLN
SQUARE*

4 Oakland Museum
of California

10th St.

E. 11th St.

E. 10th St.

9th St.

Lake Merritt
BART

*MADISON
PARK*

8th St.

Fallon St.

7th St.

Laney College

7th St.

*CHINESE
GARDEN*

6th St.

5th St.

880

4th St.

To Oakland
International Airport

Harrison St.

Alice St.

Jackson St.

Madison St.

Oak St.

3rd St.

2nd St.

Victory Ct.

Embarcadero

**Amtrak
Terminal**

Posey Tube

*ESTUARY
PARK*

| ■ | BART Station |
| *i* | Information |

0   1/4 Mi

0   0.25 Km

video presentations make the trip through time fun and exciting for kids who are less than enthusiastic about history lessons. The museum's temporary exhibits have included cultural and ecological topics, and the California Art Gallery houses paintings, sculptures, and photographs all created by California artists.

If you get hungry, you can have lunch at the museum restaurant, which offers sandwiches, salads, and daily specials. Live jazz is played during the week.

1000 Oak St., Oakland. ✆ 510/238-2200. www.museumca.org. Admission $8 adults, $5 seniors, children, and students w/valid ID, free for kids under 6, free for everyone the 2nd Sun of each month. Wed–Sat 10am–5pm; Sun noon–5pm; open until 9pm the 1st Fri of each month. Closed Jan 1, July 4, Thanksgiving, and Dec 25. **To get there:** By BART: Exit at the Lake Merritt station. The museum is located 1 block north of the station. By car: Take I-880 to the Jackson St. off-ramp, follow signs south toward San Jose. Make a left on Oak St. and you'll see it on the right, between 10th and 12th sts.

Oakland Zoo   While we're big fans of the San Francisco Zoo, you'll find a healthy contingent of Bay Area residents who'll tell you the Oakland Zoo tops their list of local menageries. Located in the 525-acre Knowland Park in the wooded Oakland hills, the Oakland Zoo has long focused on housing the animals in environments that are more like where they would live in the wild. (The SF Zoo has made great strides in that direction, but still has a few enclosures that should be updated.) The extensive Valley Children's Zoo within the zoo offers kids a chance to learn more about tortoises, snakes, and other reptiles; to watch alligators swim from underwater viewing portals; to pet goats and sheep; to check out lemurs, bunnies, and even fruit bats (in a 50-foot-tall enclosure); and to inspect the creepy, crawly Bug House, among other activities. In addition to a zoo train that takes passengers on a scenic ride through the hills, offering lovely bay views, the Oakland Zoo houses a rides area with plenty of kids' rides similar to those you'd find at an old-time fair or boardwalk. The rides are a great way to wind up a day at the zoo. So far the zoo's food options are limited, but hopefully that will change as the zoo continues to expand and improve.

9777 Golf Links Rd., Oakland. ✆ 510/632-9525. http://oaklandzoo.org. Admission $9.50 adults 15–54, $6 seniors 55+ and children 2–14, free children under 2. Car parking is $6. Daily 10am–4pm. (Children's area and rides open at 11am.) Closed Thanksgiving and Dec 25. **To get there:** By BART: Exit at the Coliseum/Oakland Airport; take the AC Transit Bus #56 (90th Ave./Seminary) to Mountain Blvd. and Golf Links Rd. By car: Take I-80 East, merge onto I-580 E toward CA-24/Downtown Oakland/Hayward-Stockton. Exit at Golf Links Rd/98th Ave; turn left onto Golf Links Rd.

Paramount Theatre   A trip to this theater, built in 1931, will take you back to the age of Cary Grant and Katharine Hepburn. Built in Art Deco style, the restored theater is used for concerts, plays, old Hollywood films, and often the Oakland symphony. It still has an original Wurlitzer organ that is played before all films and some other events. Tours are offered on the first and third Saturdays of the month at 10am. Tickets for tours are $1 each; children must be at least 10 years old and accompanied by an adult. Call or check the website for specific dates and prices of other events.

2025 Broadway (at 21st St.). ✆ 510/465-6400 (24-hr. recorded hot line), or 510/893-2300 (office). www.paramount theatre.com. Tickets available at the box office (open Tues–Fri noon–5:30pm, Sat noon–5pm) or through Ticketmaster. **To get there:** By BART: Exit at the 19th St. station. The theater is about ½ block north of the station. By car: Take I-880 to the Broadway exit. Turn left on Broadway. The theater will be on the left, around 20th St.

JACK LONDON SQUARE

Built as a rival port to San Francisco, Jack London Square has an enviable location on the waterfront, steps from the pier where the Alameda/Oakland Ferry lands. Filled with lots of chain restaurants, souvenir shops, and a multiplex cinema, the square could be put to better use, but it is a convenient place from which to explore the immediate surroundings and get a great view of the Bay Bridge on a clear day.

You could drive, but the best way to get to Jack London Square is by a 40-minute ferry ride. Board the **Alameda/Oakland ferry** at PIER 39 or the Ferry Building. For a schedule and fares, contact Blue & Gold Fleet (© **415/773-1188;** www.blueand goldfleet.com).

By car, take I-880 from the Bay Bridge. Exit at the Broadway/Alameda off ramp. Make a right on Adelaide Street, a left on 3rd, and continue 12 blocks to Broadway and turn right. Lot parking is available.

By BART, exit at 12th Street/Downtown Oakland. Take a bus from the station or try the free downtown shuttle that runs weekdays between 11am and 2pm between Broadway and Jack London Square.

WHAT TO SEE At the **USS *Potomac's* Floating Museum** (© **510/627-1318;** www.usspotomac.org), Franklin Delano Roosevelt's restored presidential yacht is open year-round for dockside tours. Tours run on Wednesday and Friday between 10:30am and 2:30pm, Sunday noon to 3pm. Reservations are required for groups of 10 or more, and appreciated even for smaller groups. Tour admission is $7 for ages 13 to 59, $5 seniors 60 and over, free for kids 12 and under. Two-hour history cruises around the bay are offered on alternating weeks Thursday and Saturday at 11am, from May to mid-November. Tickets are $40 adults, $35 seniors 60 and over, $20 children 6 to 12, free for kids under 6. A 15-minute video accompanies the tour. Advanced ticket purchase is recommended and can be done through the website or by calling © **866/468-3399.** In addition, tours to Angel Island are available on an occasional basis in June through November.

Active families should check out the **Embarcadero Bay Bicycle Trail.** The 3-mile trail along the waterfront from Jack London Square to Alameda's Park Street Bridge is part of the 400-mile San Francisco Bay trail, which connects all nine Bay Area counties, 47 cities, and major bridges crossing the bay.

WHERE TO DINE You'll find several family-friendly restaurants and cafes at Jack London Square such as SFO Pizzeria, Kincaid's Bayhouse, and Hahn's Hibachi (Korean BBQ), as well as chains like Subway and Tony Roma's. The best place to dine at Jack London Square is **Yoshi's** (510 Embarcadero West; © **510/238-9200;** www.yoshis.com), a Japanese restaurant and jazz club. Yoshi's Sunday matinee jazz concerts are tailor-made to introduce young audiences to jazz, and matinee brunches offer special-priced options for families. Doors open at noon for the 2pm concerts.

A short walk from Jack London Square takes you to Broadway, Oakland's Chinatown, renowned for some of the best dim sum in the Bay Area. A couple of blocks off Broadway, at 1007 Clay St., you'll find **Le Cheval,** serving terrific Vietnamese food at large round tables in a very family-friendly atmosphere (© **510/763-8957**). Off Broadway between 40th Street and MacArthur Boulevard lies **Bay Wolf** (3853 Piedmont; © **510/763-8957;** www.baywolf.com), one of Oakland's most enduringly popular restaurants, offering flavorful California fare made with top-quality, seasonal ingredients. The dining room may be too small for some families, but the front deck has heat lamps and a radiant heat floor, allowing for year-round *al fresco* dining. Near the shores of Lake Merritt, **Zza's Trattoria** offers great pizza and other Italian fare (552 Grand Ave.; © **510/839-9124**).

3 Point Reyes National Seashore

Once you traverse the Golden Gate Bridge, a pleasant 1-hour drive through Marin County and Samuel P. Taylor State Park leads you to Point Reyes National Seashore, a mix of wild coastline and forest of unequivocal appeal to hikers, nature lovers, and wildlife-watchers of all ages. The rocky shore along this part of the coast is a direct result of earthquake activity. The San Andreas Fault separates Point Reyes, the northernmost landmass on the Pacific Plate, from the rest of California, which rests on the North American Plate. Point Reyes is moving towards Alaska at the rate of 2 inches a year. During the 1906 earthquake, it jumped north 20 feet in an instant.

Point Reyes Station, the minuscule town nearby, is a tourist magnet on the weekends, so it supports a handful of good restaurants and craft shops within its 4-block radius. You can easily drive to Point Reyes, spend the day, and get back to San Francisco by dinner, but if you'd like to spend a night or two, the area is well served by B&Bs. For information on what's available, contact **Point Reyes Lodging** (© 800/ 539-1872 or 415/663-1872; www.ptreyes.com).

To reach Point Reyes, cross the Golden Gate Bridge and exit on San Anselmo/Sir Francis Drake Boulevard. Turn left, heading west on Sir Francis Drake and stay on this road as it passes through the pricey suburbs of San Anselmo, Ross, Woodacre, and Lagunitas. The drive to park headquarters takes an hour in light traffic.

WHAT TO SEE At the junction of Highway 1 and Sir Francis Drake Boulevard in Olema, follow the signs to the **Bear Valley Visitor Center** (© 415/464-5100) about a minute away. The center has maps, informative park rangers, a book/gift section, and some interesting exhibits on the ecology of the area. Many trails begin here, including an under-1-mile earthquake trail along the San Andreas Fault. Another park attraction is **Kule Loklo**, a Coast Miwok Native Indian village replica. If you're visiting during the school year, you may run into groups of kids.

Hiking is the prime activity in the park. **Abbott's Lagoon** is a flat, short hike that is perfect for children, ending at the edge of the lagoon—offering plenty of bird-watching and sightings of local flora along the way. A drive to **Limantour Beach** is also a terrific option. You get to the beach by turning left on Bear Valley Road and left again on Limantour Road. Although swimming is not recommended (and it's usually too cold), you can bird-watch and picnic here.

Point Reyes Lighthouse is a big attraction in these parts all year long, but especially from January through March when migrating gray whales pass by. From the Bear Valley Visitor Center, the lighthouse is a 21-mile drive along Sir Francis Drake Boulevard through dairy farms and pastures, where you can see many a cow lounging around. At the end of the road is a parking lot. The lighthouse is a half-mile walk away, and down 300 steps. The cliffs all around this area are not stable enough to climb on, and you'll see lots of warnings to that effect. **Sea Lion Overlook** near the lighthouse is the place to watch those creatures as well as harbor seals.

From this stop, it's a short drive to **Drake's Beach** (just follow the signs as you drive to or from the lighthouse). Another fine visitor center with friendly park rangers is on the beach parking lot, next to a cafe specializing in deep-fried foods. As is the case at all the area beaches, there is no lifeguard on duty and the undertow can be dangerous, so swimming is absolutely discouraged. At the end of Drake's Beach, past the Point Reyes Lifeboat Station, is **Chimney Rock**. The **Elephant Seal Overlook** nearby is a good vantage point for observing elephant seals in the winter months.

Point Reyes National Seashore

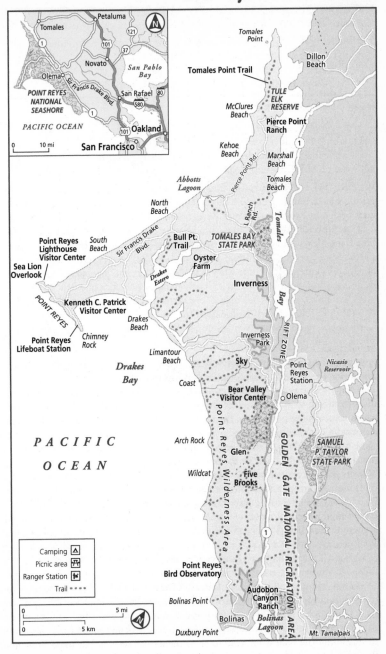

Petaluma

Tomales

121

101

37

Novato

Olema

San Pablo Bay

San Rafael

80

POINT REYES NATIONAL SEASHORE

580

PACIFIC OCEAN

1

101

Oakland

San Francisco

0   10 mi

N

Sir Francis Drake Blvd.

Tomales Point

Dillon Beach

Tomales Point Trail

TULE ELK RESERVE

McClures Beach

Pierce Point Ranch

Kehoe Beach

Marshall Beach

Abbotts Lagoon

Pierce Point Rd.

Tomales Beach

North Beach

L Ranch Rd.

TOMALES BAY STATE PARK

Point Reyes Lighthouse Visitor Center

South Beach

Sir Francis Drake Blvd.

Bull Pt. Trail

Oyster Farm

Sea Lion Overlook

Drakes Estero

Inverness

POINT REYES

Kenneth C. Patrick Visitor Center

Drakes Beach

Inverness Park

Point Reyes Lifeboat Station

Chimney Rock

Limantour Beach

RIFT ZONE

Point Reyes Station

Nicasio Reservoir

Drakes Bay

Coast

Sky

Bear Valley Visitor Center

Olema

PACIFIC

OCEAN

Arch Rock

Glen

SAMUEL P. TAYLOR STATE PARK

Wildcat

Five Brooks

Point Reyes Wilderness Area

GOLDEN GATE NATIONAL RECREATION AREA

1

Camping △

Picnic area ⊞

Ranger Station ▣

Trail • • • •

Point Reyes Bird Observatory

Bolinas Point

Audobon Canyon Ranch

0   5 mi

0   5 km

Bolinas

Bolinas Lagoon

Mt. Tamalpais

Duxbury Point

N

Tips **Taking a Dip**

If you're making this trip in August in warmer weather, some wonderful swimming beaches lie along Tomales Bay in Inverness. Look for signs on Sir Francis Drake Boulevard leading to **Chicken Ranch Beach** or **Shell Beach**. Other times of the year, dress warmly. Point Reyes gets foggy and cold.

At the northernmost tip of the seashore at **Tomales Point** is the **Tule Elk Reserve,** where over 500 of these once nearly extinct creatures live on 2,600 protected acres. The reserve is a 30-minute drive from Inverness. Stay on Sir Francis Drake Boulevard until you reach Pierce Point Road, which takes you directly into the reserve.

WHERE TO DINE   If you're hungry or want to gather a picnic, continue on Sir Francis Drake Boulevard until it meets Point Reyes–Petaluma Road. Drive across the little bridge and you'll be in Point Reyes Station. **Taqueria La Quinta,** 11285 Hwy. 1 (© **415/663-8868;** closed Tues), is a popular lunch and dinner spot serving traditional Tex-Mex fare, as well as rotisserie chicken and seafood. **The Station House,** 11180 State Rte. 1 (© **415/663-1515;** closed Wed), serves terrific breakfasts and lunch and dinner specials that draw on local and organic ingredients, such as fresh wild salmon or fresh local mussels. It's moderately priced, immensely popular, and hosts live music on weekend nights. For takeout, **Cow Girl Creamery,** 80 4th St. (© **415/663-9335**), open Wednesday through Sunday from 10am to 6pm, is well worth checking out for its award-winning cheeses. It's located next to a small grocer where you can pick up other goodies for a lovely picnic.

4 Calistoga & the Napa Valley

The Napa Valley is the country's most celebrated wine-growing region. Less than 30 miles from end to end, this fertile area is covered in vineyards and accessorized with world-class wine-tasting rooms, excellent restaurants, and marvelous resorts and inns. It's paradise for couples with time to relax. For families, it's welcoming but will require some flexibility. Many of the valley's copious bed and breakfasts are not open to children; room occupancy may be limited to two people, no interconnecting rooms may be available, or children may be expressly discouraged. Likewise, a number of restaurants may not be appropriate for young children.

That said, we have found ways to enjoy Napa with the kids. Romantic B&Bs aside, several family-friendly motels grace the area, and many have swimming pools. My suggestion is to head straight to Calistoga, at the northern edge of the Napa Valley. Well-preserved and historical, Calistoga offers the best of the Napa Valley in terms of relaxation. The restaurants are more casual than down valley, and with the great wine to be had with your meal, it's fortunate that most hotels are within walking distance.

The fastest route to Napa Valley is to cross the Bay Bridge (I-80) and continue east on I-80 until you see the Napa/Highway 29 exit near Vallejo. Highway 29 is the main road through the Napa Valley. Follow it past Yountville, Oakville, St. Helena, and drive another 8 miles until you reach Calistoga. An arrow on the right directs you into town. Once there, you won't need to face infamously crowded Highway 29 until it's time to head back to San Francisco.

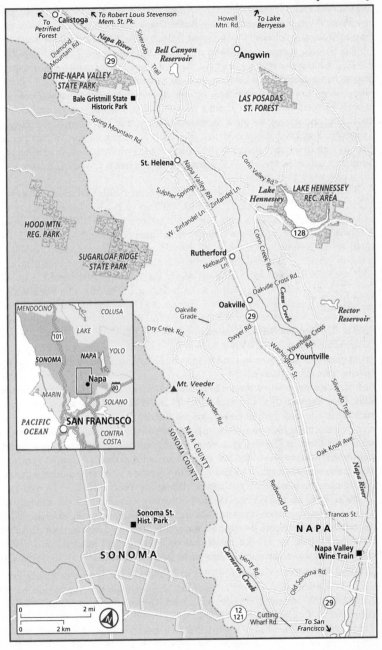

Napa Valley

WHAT TO DO If you gather the strength to drag the kids away from the pool, horseback riding past the redwoods in **Bothe–Napa Valley State Park** includes some history of the area delivered by the knowledgeable guide. **Old Faithful Geyser,** one of only three such geysers in the world, works full-time blowing off steam. The 350°F (177°C) water spews out to a height of about 60 feet every 30 to 40 minutes depending on barometric pressure, the moon, tides, and tectonic stresses. (The Exploratorium, on p. 174, in San Francisco, has an exhibit on geysers if you want to learn more.) The performance lasts about a minute, but you can stay as long as you like, picnicking and waiting for the next explosion. It's located just north of Calistoga off Highway 29 at 1299 Tubbs Lane. It's open daily from 9am to 6pm in summer and 9am to 5pm in winter; call ℭ 707/942-6463 for more information. Admission is $8 adults, $7 seniors 60 and up, $3 children 6 to 12, and free for children under 6. (AAA cards give you a $1 discount.)

Biking around the valley is another option. Rentals are available at **Calistoga Bikeshop** (1318 Lincoln Ave., Calistoga; ℭ 707/942-9687; www.calistogabikeshop.com), or you can reserve a guided bicycle winery tour with lunch or a mountain-biking tour through **Getaway Adventures and Wine Country Bike Tours** (ℭ 800/499-2453 or 707/568-3040; www.getawayadventures.com; office closed weekends). Soaring above the valley in a hot-air balloon is a coveted early morning adventure apparently, given the number of tour operators in Napa alone. **Balloons Above the Valley** (ℭ 800/464-6824 or 707/253-2222; www.balloonrides.com) provides pickup and drop-off within Napa Valley, a preflight snack, and post-flight brunch. The cost is $210 per person and $145 per child 12 and under, with an additional 8.6% service fee. Be sure to check the Web for discounts. **Bonaventura Balloon Company** (ℭ 800/FLY-NAPA or 707/944-2822; www.bonaventuraballoons.com) offers a balloon excursion and complementary champagne celebration for $220 per person and $145 to $172 for kids 12 and under; packages and discounts are often available.

If you do want to visit a winery, I recommend two in Calistoga when traveling with kids. **Clos Pegase** (1060 Dunweal Lane; ℭ 707/942-4981; www.clospegase.com), located close to Old Faithful Geyser, has a delightful picnic facility under an old oak tree. You can bring your own lunch or purchase one from the visitor's center, which is open daily from 10:30am to 5pm. After running around outside, the kids will probably be amenable to one of the free guided tours, offered daily at 11am or 2pm. Clos Pegase also offers tastings (for a fee) if you can get the kids to hang around while you contemplate the bouquet of your merlot. At **Sterling Vineyards** (1111 Duweal Lane; ℭ 800/726-6136 or 707/942-3345; www.sterlingvineyards.com) the children will appreciate the aerial tram that takes you from the parking lot to the dramatic hilltop winery. You'll have to pay for the ride, though. Fees to visit Sterling, open daily from 10am to 4:30pm, are $15 for adults ($20 on weekends and holidays), and $10 for anyone under 21 (under 3 free). Once there, however, wine tasting is complimentary.

WHERE TO STAY Calistoga has lots of hotels and motels with swimming pools and spa facilities, both of which are very important to make this retreat work for the entire family. If you plan far in advance, the ideal resort is **Indian Springs** (1712 Lincoln Ave., Calistoga; ℭ 707/942-4913; www.indianspringscalistoga.com; $185–$285 double weekdays; $235–$650 weekends and summer). The 24-unit property, consisting of charming wooden bungalows with furnished kitchens, was entirely renovated in 2006. Picnic tables and barbecues are placed on the lawn outside for guest use along with surreys (bikes with bench seats and awnings) and Ping-Pong tables. A fine 1913 bathhouse is now a spa with a full range of services including mud baths, facials, and massage. The topper is an Olympic-size heated mineral pool surrounded by lounge chairs and a mountain view that will mesmerize you. Pick up something to barbecue, a little fruit, and some drinks, and there will be no reason to leave the premises. If Indian Springs is completely booked (phone 48 hr. before you'd like to come to get in on cancellations), check availability at the **Best Western Stevenson Manor Inn** (1830 Lincoln Ave., Calistoga; ✆ **707/942-1112; $99–$244** double). It doesn't have the charm or amenities of Indian Springs, but the spacious motel rooms are nicely equipped, with fridges, coffeemakers, fireplaces, or whirlpool tubs available, and there's an enclosed pool with a hot tub, sauna, and steam room.

WHERE TO DINE   One benefit of staying in Calistoga is that the 4-block town and its restaurants and shops are walking distance from the lodgings. There are a lot of restaurants for a town this size, most somewhat expensive given that they cater to tourists. **All Season's Café** in the Mount View Hotel (1400 Lincoln Ave., Calistoga; ✆ **707/942-9111**) serves dinner Tuesday to Sunday (and lunch Fri–Sun), combining old-fashioned down-home dining charm with sophisticated, seasonally inspired dishes. There's no kids' menu, but the kitchen is always happy to whip up some buttered pasta for the little ones. An excellent place to pick up mouth-watering sandwiches for a picnic is **Palisades Market** (1506 Lincoln Ave., Calistoga; ✆ **707/ 942-9549**), where sandwich fixings include the usual turkey and provolone, as well as more refined options like Gruyere cheese or pesto.

Just south of Calistoga, in the town of St. Helena, you'll find **Taylor's Refresher** (933 Main St., St. Helena; ✆ **707/963-3486**). Open since 1949, this delightful diner is the older sibling of the terrific one in San Francisco (p. 140). Also in St. Helena is one of our favorite restaurants, **Tra Vigne** (1050 Charter Oak Ave., St. Helena; ✆ **707/ 963-4444;** www.travignerestaurant.com). The restaurant itself, a Napa institution, is always packed and may not be the best choice with kids. Instead, pick up sandwiches or salads at its adjacent Cantinetta delicatessen and eat in the lovely courtyard.

5 Amusement Parks

Paramount's Great America   **Ages 5 and up.** Since opening in 1978, this tawdry amusement park has undergone several incarnations and is currently owned by Paramount Studios, so many attractions feature a Nickelodeon theme. At Kidzville, the park area for younger children, you might run into characters from Blues Clues. SpongeBob SquarePants, Scooby Doo, Fred Flintstone, and other Hanna-Barbera characters can often be seen walking about as well. The park has the most coasters in Northern California; the newest addition, SURVIVOR The Ride, based on the TV series, is dubbed a "reality rollercoaster" (whatever that means). Daredevils will take pleasure in rides that take you free-falling, upside down, through loops, backward and forward at speeds up to 50 mph, or twisting and weaving on rides with names like Psycho Mouse, Invertigo, Vortex, and Demon. Some easygoing family rides include a white-water rafting expedition, the Columbia Carousel, and The Grizzly, a replica of an old-style wooden roller coaster. Crocodile Dundee's Boomerang Bay Beach Club is an 11-acre water park, complete with 13 water slides.

4701 Great America Pkwy., Santa Clara. ✆ 408/988-1776. www.pgathrills.com. Admission $52 ages 7–59; $35 seniors 60 and up and children 3–6; children 2 and under free. Weekends Apr–May, daily w/some few exceptions June–Aug, weekends Sep–Oct; open from 10am (closing times vary). Parking $10. **To get there:** Take 101 south to the Great America Pkwy. exit.

Safari West Wildlife Preserve **Ages 4 and up.** Get a little bit of Africa in the wine country. You and the kids will pile into real safari jeeps, amble over 400 acres of Savannah-like environment, and gaze upon giraffe, gazelle, ostrich, several species of African antelope, and even a scimitar-horned oryx (sounds exotic, doesn't it?). You'll also see zebras, lemurs, cheetahs, several species of exotic birds—over 400 mammals and birds in all at this wildlife preserve dedicated to the conservation of endangered animals. You can visit for the afternoon, but for the full African safari experience, your family can opt to overnight in a "safari tent" or cottage. On-site dining options include the Savannah Cafe, offering somewhat pricey safari ranch style BBQ meals, or the moderately priced Delilah's deli. Comfortable pants or jeans (shorts in summer), walking shoes, hats, and sunscreen are recommended.

3115 Porter Creek Rd., Santa Rosa. ⓒ 800/616-2695 or 707/579-2551. www.safariwest.com. Safari tour prices $62 adults, $28 children 3–12, free children under 3. Safari tour times daily 9am, 1pm, and 4pm (Apr–late Oct), 10am and 2pm (late Oct–Mar). Lodging tents $225 double-room and $25 each additional person requiring a futon; no charge to infants 2 and under not requiring a futon. Cottage $350 for 4 people; $25 for each additional guest. **To get there:** Take 101 North to River Road/Calistoga/Mark West Spring Rd. exit. Turn right off ramp and head east on Mark West Springs Rd. for 7 miles. Turn left into park entrance at Franz Valley Rd.

Six Flags Discovery Kingdom **Ages 4 and up.** Discovery Kingdom is America's only amusement park to combine thrills with a wildlife and marine park. A day here can have some family members free-falling at 70 mph on the 150-foot-tall V-2 Vertical Velocity or spinning floorless on Medusa, billed as the longest, tallest, most state-of-the-art roller coaster in the region. Calmer rides more suitable for families that like to keep their stomachs in one place include a submarine, a balloon Ferris wheel, and bumper cars. Giraffes, cougars, leopards, elephants, Bengal and Siberian tigers, and rare birds and reptiles have now joined the famous dolphins and sea lions.

Fairgrounds Dr. (off I-80), Vallejo. ⓒ 707/643-6722 (recording) or 707/644-4000 (voice). www.sixflags.com/parks/discoverykingdom. Season passes $70. Cal park for daily admission rates; also check website for discounts. Open daily 10am June–Aug, weekends and holidays Mar 15–May and Sept–Oct (closing times vary). **To get there:** From the end of May–end of Aug, the Blue & Gold Fleet provides ferry service from Pier 41 to the Vallejo dock with connecting shuttle bus transportation to the park. The ferry ticket price, which includes park admission, is $63 adults, $45 children 6–11, and $30 children 3–5. You can buy tickets online at www.blueandgoldfleet.com. By car: Take I-80 to the Hwy. 37 exit and exit at Fairgrounds Dr. Alternatively, you can drive over the Golden Gate Bridge on 101 North, to Hwy. 37 east to Fairgrounds Dr.

6 Another Family Outing by the Bay

Coyote Point Museum (CPM) **All ages.** Coyote Point Museum is an educational facility located at Coyote Point Park in San Mateo. The goal of the museum is nature education, thus kids are invited to observe daily otter and fox feedings, take a "nature" walk through a model of the Bay Area's different ecosystems, visit a variety of rescued animals, and bird-watch at the aviary. CPM assembles exhibits on different aspects of California's environment, most of which are hands-on, and children are encouraged to use the computers and interactive activities. Weekends feature animal talks (at 2pm), which are included with admission, and special events that may incur an additional fee.

Along with the museum, families can enjoy the walking trails, beaches, playgrounds, and marina at Coyote Point Park. Picnic facilities are available in the park and on the beaches are boat rentals. The park is open every day including holidays from 8am (closing time varies from 5–8pm depending on the season).

1651 Coyote Point Dr., San Mateo. ⓒ 650/342-7755; Coyote Point Recreation Area 650/573-2592. www.coyotept museum.org. Admission $6 adults, $4 seniors and children 13–17, $2 children 4–12, free children 3 and under. $5 car park entrance fee. Tues–Sat 10am–5pm; Sun noon–5pm; closed Mon except holidays; closed Dec 24, 25, and 31, and Jan 1. **To get there:** Take 101 south to the Poplar Ave. exit. Turn right on Humboldt St. to Peninsula Ave. Turn right on Peninsula. Drive over the freeway, then circle into the park. Parking is limited, so arrive early.

Index

See also Accommodations and Restaurant indexes, below.

The new way to get AROUND town.

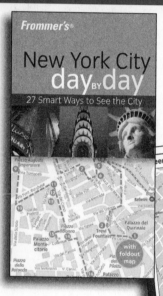
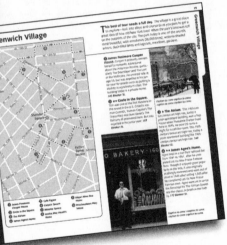

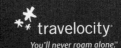

IF YOU BOOK IT, IT SHOULD BE THERE.

Only Travelocity guarantees it will be, or we'll work
with our travel partners to make it right, right away.
So if you're missing a balcony or anything else you
booked, just call us 24/7, 1-888-TRAVELOCITY.

travelocity